MGA & TWIN CAM

Gold Portfolio

1955~1962

Compiled by
R.M. Clarke

ISBN 1 85520 0783

Brooklands Books Ltd.
'Holmerise', Seven Hills Road,
Cobham, Surrey, England
Printed in Hong Kong

BROOKLANDS BOOKS

BROOKLANDS ROAD TEST SERIES
AC Ace & Aceca 1953-1983
Alfa Romeo Alfasud 1972-1984
Alfa Romeo Alfetta Coupes GT. GTV. GTV6 1974-1987
Alfa Romeo Giulia Berlinas 1962-1976
Alfa Romeo Giulia Coupes 1963-1976
Alfa Romeo Giulietta Gold Portfolio 1954-1965
Alfa Romeo Spider 1966-1990
Allard Gold Portfolio 1937-1958
Alvis Gold Portfolio 1919-1967
American Motors Muscle Cars 1966-1970
Armstrong Siddeley Gold Portfolio 1945-1960
Aston Martin Gold Portfolio 1972-1985
Austin Seven 1922-1982
Austin A30 & A35 1951-1962
Austin Healey 100 & 100/6 Gold Portfolio 1952-1959
Austin Healey 3000 Gold Portfolio 1959-1967
Austin Healey Sprite 1958-1971
Avanti 1962-1983
BMW Six Cylinder Coupes 1969-1975
BMW 1600 Col. 1 1966-1981
BMW 2002 1968-1976
Bristol Cars Gold Portfolio 1946-1985
Buick Automobiles 1947-1960
Buick Muscle Cars 1965-1970
Buick Riviera 1963-1978
Cadillac Automobiles 1949-1959
Cadillac Automobiles 1960-1969
Cadillac Eldorado 1967-1978
High Performance Capris Gold Portfolio 1969-1987
Chevrolet Camaro SS & Z28 1966-1973
Chevrolet Camaro & Z-28 1973-1981
High Performance Camaros 1982-1988
Camaro Muscle Cars 1966-1972
Chevrolet 1955-1957
Chevrolet Corvair 1959-1969
Chevrolet Impala & SS 1958-1971
Chevrolet Muscle Cars 1966-1971
Chevelle and SS 1964-1972
Chevy Blazer 1969-1981
Chevy EL Camino & SS 1959-1987
Chevy II Nova & SS 1962-1973
Chrysler 300 1955-1970
Citroen Traction Avant Gold Portfolio 1934-1957
Citroen DS & ID 1955-1975
Citroen SM 1970-1975
Citroen 2CV 1949-1988
Shelby Cobra Gold Portfolio 1962-1969
Cobras and Cobra Replicas Gold Portfolio 1962-1989
Cobras & Replicas 1962-1983
Chevrolet Corvette Gold Portfolio 1953 1962
Corvette Stingray Gold Portfolio 1963-1967
High Performance Corvettes 1983-1989
Daimler SP250 Sport & V-8250 Saloon Gold Portfolio 1959-1969
Datsun 240Z 1970-1973
Datsun 280Z & ZX 1975-1983
De Tomaso Collection No.1 1962-1981
Dodge Charger 1966-1974
Dodge Muscle Cars 1967-1970
Excalibur Collection No.1 1952-1981
Facel Vega 1954-1964
Ferrari Cars 1946-1956
Ferrari Dino 1965-1974
Ferrari Dino 308 1974-1979
Ferrari 308 & Mondial 1980-1984
Ferrari Collection No.1 1960-1970
Fiat-Bertone X1/9 1973-1988
Fiat Pininfarina 124 + 2000 Spider 1968-1985
Ford Automobiles 1949-1959
Ford Bronco 1966-1977
Ford Bronco 1978-1988
Ford Consul. Zephyr Zodiac MkI & II 1950-1962
Ford Cortina 1600E & GT 1967-1970
Ford Fairlane 1955-1970
Ford Falcon 1960-1970
Ford GT40 Gold Portfolio 1964-1987
Ford RS Escorts 1968-1980
Ford Zephyr Zodiac Executive MkIII & MkIV 1962-1971
High Performance Escorts Mk1 1968-1974
High Performance Escorts Mk II 1975-1980
High Performance Escorts 1980-1985
High Performance Escorts 1985-1990
High Performance Capris Gold Portfolio 1969-1987
High Performance Mustangs 1982-1988
Holden 1948-1962
Honda CRX 1983-1987
Hudson & Railton 1936-1940
Jaguar and SS Gold Portfolio 1931-1951
Jaguar XK120 XK140 XK150 Gold Portfolio 1948-1960
Jaguar MkVII VIII IX X 420 Gold Portfolio 1950-1970
Jaguar Cars 1961-1964
Jaguar Mk2 1959-1969
Jaguar E-Type Gold Portfolio 1961-1971
Jaguar E-Type 1966-1971
Jaguar E-Type V-12 1971-1975
Jaguar XJ12 XJ5.3 V12 Glold Portfolio 1972-1990
Jaguar XJ6 Series II 1973-1979
Jaguar XJ6 & Series III 1979-1986
Jaguar XJS Gold Portfolio 1975-1988
Jeep CJ5 & CJ6 1960-1976
Jeep CJ5 & CJ7 1976-1986
Jensen Cars 1946-1967
Jensen Cars 1967-1979
Jensen Interceptor Gold Portfolio 1966-1986
Jensen Healey 1972-1976
Lamborghini Cars 1964-1970
Lamborghini Cars 1970-1975
Lamborghini Countach Col No.1 1971-1982
Lamborghini Countach & Urraco 1974-1980
Lamborghini Countach & Jalpa 1980-1985
Lancia Stratos 1972-1985
Land Rover 1948-1973 - A Collection
Land Rover Series I 1948-1958
Land Rover Series II & IIa 1958-1971
Land Rover Series III 1971-1985
Land Rover 90 & 110 1983-1989
Lincoln Gold Portfolio 1949-1960
Lincoln Continental 1961-1969
Lotus and Caterham Seven Gold Portfolio 1957-1989
Lotus Cortina Gold Portfolio 1963-1970
Lotus Elan Gold Portfolio 1962-1974
Lotus Elan Collection No.2 1963-1972
Lotus Elite 1957-1964
Lotus Elite & Eclat 1974-1982
Lotus Turbo Esprit 1980-1986
Lotus Europa Collection No.1 1966-1974
Marcos Cars 1960-1988
Maserati 1965-1970
Maserati 1970-1975
Mazda RX-7 Collection No.1 1978-1981
Mercedes 190 & 300SL 1954-1963
Mercedes 230/250/280SL 1963-1971
Mercedes Benz SLs & SLCs Gold Portfolio 1971-1989
Mercedes Bens Cars 1949-1954
Mercedes Bens Cars 1954-1957
Mercedes Bens Cars 1957-1961
Mercedes Bens Competion Cars 1950-1957
Mercury Muscle Cars 1966-1971
Metropolitan 1954-1962
MG TC 1945-1949
MG TD 1949-1953
MG TF 1953-1955
MG Cars 1959-1962
MGA & Twin Cam Gold Portfolio 1955-1962
MGA Roadsters 1955-1962
MGA Collection No.1 1955-1982
MGB MGC & V8 Gold Portfolio 1962-1980
MGB Roadsters 1962-1980
MGB GT 1965-1980
MG Midget 1961-1980
Mini Cooper Gold Portfolio 1961-1971
Mini Moke 1964-1989
Mini Muscle Cars 1961-1979
Mopar Muscle Cars 1964-1967
Mopar Muscle Cars 1968-1971
Morgan Three-Wheeler Gold Portfolio 1910-1952
Morgan Cars 1960-1970
Morgan Cars Gold Portfolio 1968-1989
Morris Minor Collection No.1
Mustang Muscle Cars 1967-1971
Oldsmobile Automobiles 1955-1963
Old's Cutlass & 4-4-2 1964-1972
Oldsmobile Muscle Cars 1964-1971
Oldsmobile Toronado 1966-1978
Opel GT 1968-1973
Packard Gold Portfolio 1946-1958
Pantera Gold Portfolio 1970-1989
Plymouth Barracuda 1964-1974
Plymouth Muscle Cars 1966-1971
Pontiac Tempest & GTO 1961-1965
Pontiac GTO 1964-1970
Pontiac Firebird 1967-1973
Pontiac Firebird and Trans-Am 1973-1981
High Performance Firebirds 1982-1988
Pontiac Fiero 1984-1988
Pontiac Muscle Cars 1966-1972
Porsche 356 1952-1965
Porsche Cars in the 60's
Porsche Cars 1960-1964
Porsche Cars 1964-1968
Porsche Cars 1968-1972
Porsche Cars 1972-1975
Porsche Turbo Collection No.1 1975-1980
Porsche 911 1965-1969
Porsche 911 1970-1972
Porsche 911 1973-1977
Porsche 911 Carrera 1973-1977
Porsche 911 Turbo 1975-1984
Porsche 911 SC 1978-1983
Porsche 914 Gold Portfolio 1969-1976
Porsche 914 Collection No.1 1969-1983
Porsche 924 Gold Portfolio 1975-1988
Porsche 928 1977-1989
Porsche 944 1981-1985
Range Rover Gold Portfolio 1970-1988
Reliant Scimitar 1964-1986
Riley 11/2 & 21/2 Litre Gold Portfolio 1945-1955
Rolls Royce Silver Cloud 1955-1965
Rolls Royce Silver Shadow 1965-1981
Rover P4 1949-1959
Rover P4 1955-1964
Rover 3 & 3.5 Litre Gold Portfolio 1958-1973
Rover 2000 + 2200 1963-1977
Rover 3500 1968-1977
Rover 3500 & Vitesse 1976-1986
Saab Sonett Collection No.1 1966-1974
Saab Turbo 1976-1983
Shelby Mustang Muscle Cars 1965-1970
Stubebaker Gold Portfolio 1947-1966
Stubebaker Hawks & Larks 1956-1963
Sunbeam Tiger & Alpine Gold Portfolio 1959-1967
Thunderbird 1955-1957
Thunderbird 1958-1963
Thunderbird 1964-1976
Toyota Land Cruiser 1956-1984
Toyota MR2 1984-1988
Triumph 2000. 2.5. 2500 1963-1977
Triumph GT6 1966-1974
Triumph Spitfire 1962-1980
Triumph Spitfire Col No.1 1962-1982
Triumph Stag 1970-1980
Triumph Stag Collection No.1 1970-1984
Triumph TR2 & TR3 1952-60
Triumph TR4-TR5-TR250 1961-1968
Triumph TR6 1969-1976
Triumph TR6 Collection No.1 1969-1983
Triumph TR7 & TR8 1975-1982
Triumph Herald 1959-1971
Triumph Vitesse 1962-1971
TVR Gold Portfolio 1959-1990
Volkswagen Cars 1936-1956
VW Beetle Collection No.1 1970-1982
VW Golf GTi 1976-1986
VW Karmann Ghia 1955-1982
VW Kubelwagen 1940-1975
VW Scirocco 1974-1981
VW Bus. Camper. Van 1954-1967
VW Bus. Camper. Van 1968-1979
VW Bus. Camper. Van 1979-1989
Volvo 120 1956-1970
Volvo 1800 1960-1973

BROOKLANDS ROAD & TRACK SERIES
Road & Track on Alfa Romeo 1949-1963
Road & Track on Alfa Romeo 1964-1970
Road & Track on Alfa Romeo 1971-1976
Road & Track on Alfa Romeo 1977-1989
Road & Track on Aston Martin 1962-1990
Road & Track on Auburn Cord and Duesenburg 1952-1984
Road & Track on Audi & Auto Union 1952-1980
Road & Track on Audi 1980-1986
Road & Track on Austin Healey 1953-1970
Road & Track on BMW Cars 1966-1974
Road & Track on BMW Cars 1975-1978
Road & Track on BMW Cars 1979-1983
Road & Track on Cobra, Shelby & GT40 1962-1983
Road & Track on Corvette 1953-1967
Road & Track on Corvette 1968-1982
Road & Track on Corvette 1982-1986
Road & Track on Datsun Z 1970-1983
Road & Track on Ferrari 1950-1968
Road & Track on Ferrari 1968-1974
Road & Track on Ferrari 1975-1981
Road & Track on Ferrari 1981-1984
Road & Track on Fiat Sports Cars 1968-1987
Road & Track on Jaguar 1950-1960
Road & Track on Jaguar 1961-1968
Road & Track on Jaguar 1968-1974
Road & Track on Jaguar 1974-1982
Road & Track on Jaguar 1983-1989
Road & Track on Lamborghini 1964-1985
Road & Track on Lotus 1972-1981
Road & Track on Maserati 1952-1974
Road & Track on Maserati 1975-1983
Road & Track on Mazda RX7 1978-1986
Road & Track on Mercedes 1952-1962
Road & Track on Mercedes 1963-1970
Road & Track on Mercedes 1971-1979
Road & Track on Mercedes 1980-1987
Road & Track on MG Sports Cars 1949-1961
Road & Track on MG Sprots Cars 1962-1980
Road & Track on Mustang 1964-1977
Road & Track on Nissan 300-ZX & Turbo 1984-1989
Road & Track on Peugeot 1955-1986
Road & Track on Pontiac 1960-1983
Road & Track on Porsche 1961-1967
Road & Track on Porsche 1968-1971
Road & Track on Porsche 1972-1975
Road & Track on Porsche 1975-1978
Road & Track on Porsche 1979-1982
Road & Track on Porsche 1982-1985
Road & Track on Porsche 1985-1988
Road & Track on Rolls Royce & B'ley 1950-1965
Road & Track on Rolls Royce & B'ley 1966-1984
Road & Track on Saab 1955-1985
Road & Track on Toyota Sports & GT Cars 1966-1984
Road & Track on Triumph Sports Cars 1953-1967
Road & Track on Triumph Sports Cars 1967-1974
Road & Track on Triumph Sports Cars 1974-1982
Road & Track on Volkswagen 1951-1968
Road & Track on Volkswagen 1968-1978
Road & Track on Volkswagen 1978-1985
Road & Track on Volvo 1957-1974
Road & Track on Volvo 1975-1985
Road & Track - Henry Manney at Large and Abroad

BROOKLANDS CAR AND DRIVER SERIES
Car and Driver on BMW 1955-1977
Car and Driver on BMW 1977-1985
Car and Driver on Cobra, Shelby & Ford GT 40 1963-1984
Car and Driver on Corvette 1956-1967
Car and Driver on Corvette 1968-1977
Car and Driver on Corvette 1978-1982
Car and Driver on Corvette 1983-1988
Car and Driver on Datsun Z 1600 & 2000 1966-1984
Car and Driver on Ferrari 1955-1962
Car and Driver on Ferrari 1963-1975
Car and Driver on Ferrari 1976-1983
Car and Driver on Mopar 1956-1967
Car and Driver on Mopar 1968-1975
Car and Driver on Mustang 1964-1972
Car and Driver on Pontiac 1961-1975
Car and Driver on Porsche 1955-1962
Car and Driver on Porsche 1963-1970
Car and Driver on Porsche 1970-1976
Car and Driver on Porsche 1977-1981
Car and Driver on Porsche 1982-1986
Car and Driver on Saab 1956-1985
Car and Driver on Volvo 1955-1986

BROOKLANDS PRACTICAL CLASSICS SERIES
PC on Austin A40 Restoration
PC on Land Rover Restoration
PC on Metalworking in Restoration
PC on Midget/Sprite Restoration
PC on Mini Cooper Restoration
PC on MGB Restoration
PC on Morris Minor Restoration
PC on Sunbeam Rapier Restoration
PC on Triumph Herald/Vitesse
PC on Triumph Spitfire Restoration
PC on VW Beetle Restoration
PC on 1930s Car Restoration

BROOKLANDS MOTOR & THOROUGHBRED & CLASSIC CAR SERIES
Motor & T & CC on Ferrari 1966-1976
Motor & T & CC on Ferrari 1976-1984
Motor & T & CC on Lotus 1979-1983

BROOKLANDS MILITARY VEHICLES SERIES
Allied Mil. Vehicles No.1 1942-1945
Allied Mil. Vehicles No.2 1941-1946
Dodge Mil. Vehicles Col. 1 1940-1945
Military Jeeps 1941-1945
Off Road Jeeps 1944-1971
Hail to the Jeep
US Military Vehicles 1941-1945
US Army Military Vehicles WW2-TM9-2800

BROOKLANDS HOT ROD RESTORATION SERIES
Auto Restoration Tips & Techniques
Basic Bodywork Tips & Techniques
Basic Painting Tips & Techniques
Camaro Restoration Tips & Techniques
Custom Painting Tips & Techniques
Engine Swapping Tips & Techniques
How to Build a Street Rod
Mustang Restoration Tips & Techniques
Performance Tuning - Chevrolets of the '60s
Performance Tuning - Ford of the '60s
Performance Tuning - Mopars of the '60s
Performance Tuning - Pontiacs of the '60s

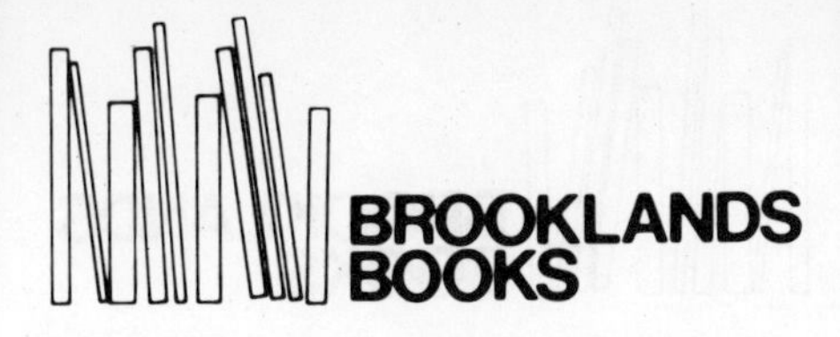

CONTENTS

ACKNOWLEDGEMENTS

It is many years now since we produced our first book on MGAs, but the cars' popularity continues unabated and we believe that enthusiasts would welcome this further collection of road tests and other articles. None of them appears in our earlier volume, MGA Roadsters, 1955-1962.

Our policy at Brooklands Books has always been to make available once again that valuable information which otherwise perishes as the magazines in which it is published cease to be current. In this endeavour we would be unsuccessful were it not for the understanding of the leading publishers, who kindly allow us to reprint their material. For the articles reproduced in this book, we are grateful to the managements of Auto Age, Autocar, Autosport, Car and Driver, Classic and Sportscars, Enjoying MG, Modern Motor, Motor, Motor Racing, Motorsport, Motor Sport, Motor Trend, Practical Classics, Road & Track, Safety Fast, Speed Age, Sports Car Graphic, Sports Cars Illustrated, Sports Car Reports, Sports Car World, Thoroughbred and Classic Cars, Top Gear and Wheels. Our thanks are also extended to Richard Monk of the MG Owners Club for supplying the splendid cover photographs and to motoring writer and historian James Taylor for his words of introduction.

R.M. Clarke

The MGA arrived in 1955 to replace the TF1500, the last of the "traditional" MGs. To a rigid new chassis-frame, it added the 1,489cc BMC B-series engine and a streamlined and curvaceous full-width body unlike that seen on any earlier production MG, though it did have links with a 1951 TD-based Le Mans "special'. Moreover, this was an MG with modern performance: in original, roadster-only, form, an MGA was good for 100mph. Even better, it handled well, it was fast and it felt (and was) safe to drive fast.

After only a year's production, the original Roadster was joined by a coupé version, which added a smart hardtop, wraparound windscreen and wind-up windows to make a very pretty closed two-seater. Sales – particularly in the USA – remained buoyant, and the car racked up a number of sporting successes, but there was no denying that a little more performance would be welcome in what was, after all, a relatively heavy sports car.

That extra performance came in 1958 with the introduction of the MGA Twin-Cam, which had a twin-overhead-camshaft, 1,588cc version of the B-series engine. There were also four-wheel disc brakes and centre-lock disc wheels, and performance was markedly improved over that of the standard cars. Unfortunately, the engine proved unreliable, and the car was dropped after only 18 months. Spare disc-braked Twin-Cam chassis were fitted with standard pushrod engines and used up in what was marketed as the De Luxe version of the standard car.

This, meanwhile, had benefitted from the experience of the Twin-Cam, being uprated in 1959 to an MGA 1600 with the 1,588cc block and disc brakes on the front wheels. Just two years later, the Mk.II 1600 appeared, this time with a further enlarged engine (to 1,622cc) and minor styling changes at front and rear. Performance improvements in each case were limited to acceleration rather than top speed, but the MGA remained competitive right up to the time of its demise in 1962, when it was replaced by the MGB. More than 100,000 of all derivatives had been built.

Today, the MGA remains among the most popular British sports cars of its time, and many specialists have sprung up to help enthusiasts keep their cars in tip-top condition. I believe the enjoyment of owning an MGA can only be enhanced by a book like this one, which recaptures so much of the atmosphere of the times in which the cars were produced.

James Taylor

The M.G. Series-M.G.A. Two-seater

An Uncommonly Roadworthy 1½-litre Sports Car of High Performance

Individual modern styling marks the new M.G.—and more than that. At 60 m.p.h. the M.G.A. requires 27% less power to maintain its speed than the TF Midget. Hood and sidescreens continue the smooth shape as far as is possible.

CARS, like people, are in their varying degrees martyrs to fashion, and whether the current dictates of fashion are a good or a bad thing sometimes makes little difference. Some are brought up to date almost year by year to embody the very latest in everything, others hold out until the very last before falling into line with the majority, and a few, after a period of resistance, change their fashion only for a new one entirely their own.

It is to the last group, oddly enough, that the M.G. "A" two-seater (described in *The Motor*, September 28, 1955) belongs. The new car has, to be sure, a smooth and good-looking body whose lines follow contemporary style, and a performance which puts it at least on a competitive footing with the smaller fast sports cars to which we have become accustomed. There, however, the resemblance virtually ends, for alongside the small machines with moderately stressed engines of 2 or more litres there is now a car of comparable size with an engine capacity of 1,489 c.c. The fact is, of course, of primary importance to the competitions driver as putting the car in the 1½-litre class; aside from competition, there are virtues in a small (and therefore light), engine which will be mentioned again later.

In its essence the M.G.A , although not in title a "Midget," is still small; it is compact, manoeuvrable and lively, regards the carriage of luggage as secondary to the sport of motoring, and responds to its driver's wishes in a way the larger car can seldom hope to do except at much greater expense.

However good its intangible qualities, it is by performance that a sports car will inevitably be judged in the first instance, and the figures recorded on the opposite page, which were established as usual on the Belgian motor road, provide all the assurance that may be needed that the car can hold its own in good company. On the noisy side mechanically in comparison with present-day touring designs, the M.G. engine was prone to run-on if switched off quickly after a fast drive, but was otherwise tolerant of all premium-grade fuels. The exhaust note will obviously please many buyers, its loudness increasing progressively with engine speed and throttle opening.

The special significance of a return to 1½ litres for a sports car lies in re-teaching an old lesson that the smaller the proportion of weight, and within limits the less the actual weight on the front wheels of a car, the more responsive will be its "handling"—a comprehensive term which needs no elucidation to the enthusiast. It will be seen that the M.G., without driver but ready for the road and with a small quantity of fuel in the tank, has some 53% of its weight carried by the front wheels, or only a few pounds more on the front than the back, while the position of seats and fuel tank ensures that the greater part of any additional load will bear on the back wheels. The total weight of the pre-production model supplied for test, which in contrast to subsequent production models had aluminium panelled doors and bonnet and boot lids, may raise a few eyebrows in a theoretical appraisal of power-weight ratios, but the majority verdict amongst

In Brief

Price: £595 plus purchase tax £249 0s. 10d. equals £844 0s. 10d.

Capacity	1,489 c.c.
Unladen kerb weight ...	18¼ cwt.
Fuel consumption	26.7 m.p.g.
Maximum speed	97.8 m.p.h.
Maximum speed on 1 in 20 gradient	80 m.p.h.
Maximum top gear gradient	1 in 13.7
Acceleration:	
10-30 m.p.h. in top ...	11.0 sec.
0-50 m.p.h. through gears	10.8 sec.

Gearing: 17.0 m.p.h. in top at 1,000 r.p.m.; 72.8 m.p.h. at 2,500 ft. per min. piston speed.

The Motor Road Test No. 23/55 (Continental)

Make: M.G. **Type:** M.G.A. Two-Seater

Makers: M.G. Car Co., Ltd., Abingdon-on-Thames.

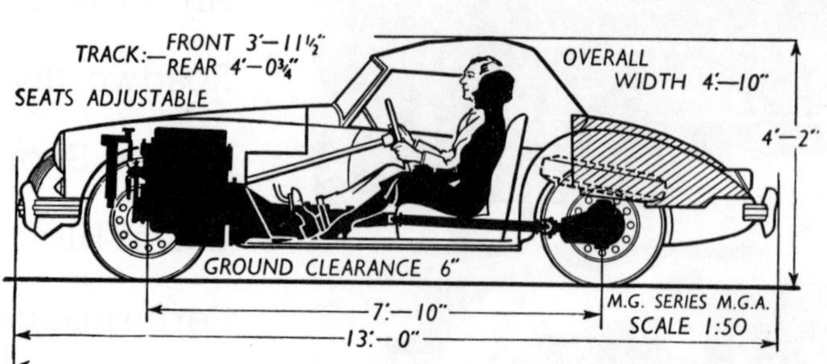

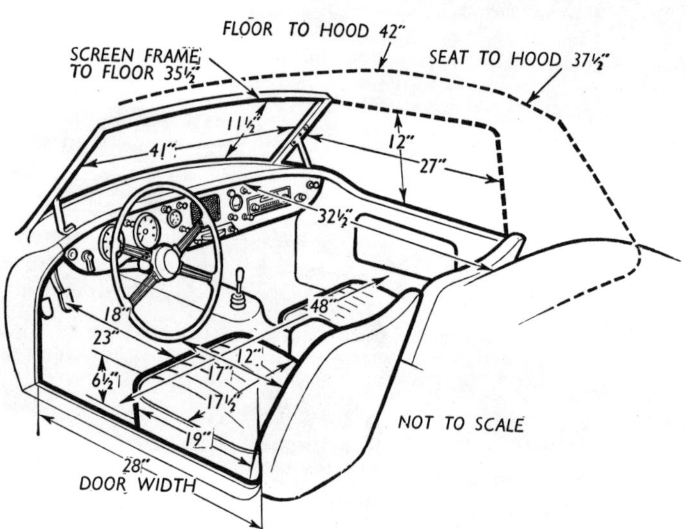

Test Data

CONDITIONS. *Weather: Hot with light wind (temperature 55°-75°F., barometer 29.9-30.0 in.) Surface: dry tarmac and concrete (Ostend-Ghent motor road). Fuel: British and Belgian premium petrol. Tested with hood and sidescreens erect.*

INSTRUMENTS

Speedometer at 30 m.p.h.	2% fast
Speedometer at 60 m.p.h.	7% fast
Speedometer at 90 m.p.h.	6% fast
Distance recorder	Accurate

MAXIMUM SPEEDS

Flying Quarter Mile

Mean of four opposite runs	97.8 m.p.h.
Best time equals	98.4 m.p.h.

Speed in gears (at recommended maximum 5,500 r.p.m.).

Max. speed in 3rd gear	68 m.p.h.
Max. speed in 2nd gear	42 m.p.h.
Max. speed in 1st gear	26 m.p.h.

FUEL CONSUMPTION

44 m.p.g. at constant 30 m.p.h.
44 m.p.g. at constant 40 m.p.h.
41 m.p.g. at constant 50 m.p.h.
38 m.p.g. at constant 60 m.p.h.
33 m.p.g. at constant 70 m.p.h.
26½ m.p.g. at constant 80 m.p.h.
21½ m.p.g. at constant 90 m.p.h.

Overall consumption for 941 miles 35.3 gallons =26.7 m.p.g. (10.6 litres/100 km.).
Fuel tank capacity 10 gallons.

ACCELERATION TIMES Through Gears

0-30 m.p.h.	4.9 sec.
0-40 m.p.h.	6.8 sec.
0-50 m.p.h.	10.8 sec.
0-60 m.p.h.	16.0 sec.
0-70 m.p.h.	21.9 sec.
0-80 m.p.h.	30.0 sec.
0-90 m.p.h.	44.6 sec.
Standing Quarter Mile	20.4 sec.

ACCELERATION TIMES on Two Upper Ratios

	Top	3rd
10-30 m.p.h.	11.0 sec.	8.6 sec.
20-40 m.p.h.	11.7 sec.	7.8 sec.
30-50 m.p.h.	11.4 sec.	7.8 sec.
40-60 m.p.h.	14.0 sec.	8.4 sec.
50-70 m.p.h.	14.9 sec.	9.6 sec.
60-80 m.p.h.	14.7 sec.	—
70-90 m.p.h.	21.4 sec.	—

WEIGHT

Unladen kerb weight	18¼ cwt.
Front/rear weight distribution	53/47
Weight laden as tested	21½ cwt.

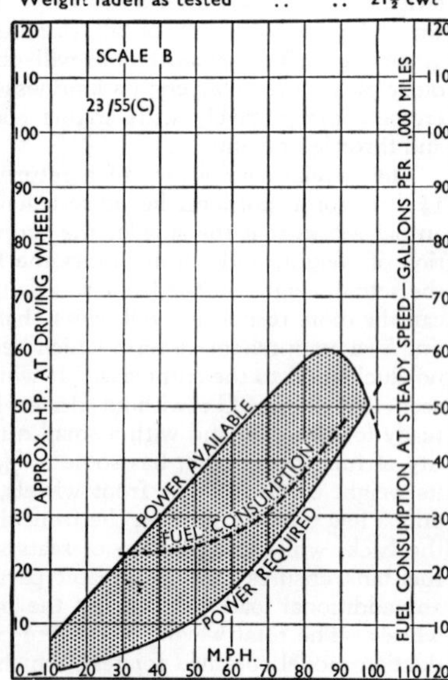

Drag at 10 m.p.h.	33 lb.
Drag at 60 m.p.h.	100 lb.

Specific Fuel Consumption when cruising at 80% of maximum speed (i.e. 78.2 m.p.h.) on level road, based on power delivered to rear wheels .. .. .. 0.74 pints/b.h.p./hr.

HILL CLIMBING (At steady speeds)

Max. top gear speed on 1 in 20	80 m.p.h.
Max. top gear speed on 1 in 15	67 m.p.h.
Max. gradient on top gear	1 in 11.1 (Tapley 200 lb./ton)
Max. gradient on 3rd gear	1 in 7.5 (Tapley 295 lb./ton)
Max. gradient on 2nd gear	1 in 4.8 (Tapley 465 lb./ton)

BRAKES at 30 m.p.h.

0.96g retardation	(=31¼ ft. stopping distance) with 95 lb. pedal pressure
0.83g retardation	(=36¼ ft. stopping distance) with 75 lb. pedal pressure
0.52g retardation	(= 58 ft. stopping distance) with 50 lb. pedal pressure
0.30g retardation	(=100 ft. stopping distance) with 25 lb. pedal pressure

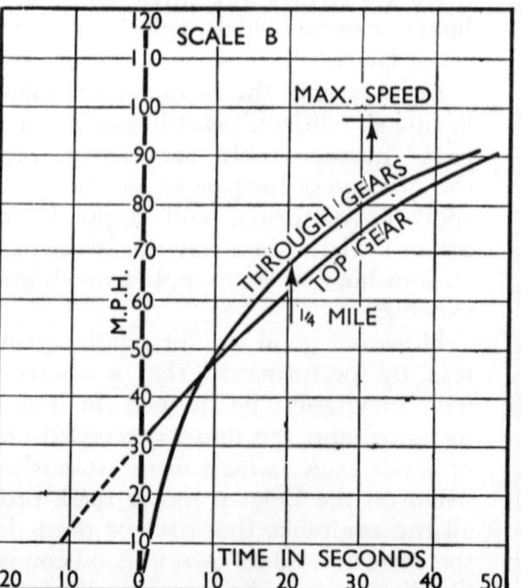

Maintenance

Sump: 6¼ pints, S.A.E. 30. **Gearbox:** 4 pints, S.A.E. 30. **Rear axle:** 2¾ pints, Hypoid 90. **Steering gear:** Hypoid 90. **Radiator:** 10 pints (2 drain taps). **Chassis Lubrication:** By grease gun every 1,000 miles to 9 points. **Ignition timing:** 7° B.T.D.C. **Spark plug gap:** .019-.021 in. **Contact breaker gap:** .014-.016 in. **Valve timing:** I.O. 16° B.T.D.C.; I.C. 56° A.B.D.C.; E.O. 51° B.B.D.C.; E.C. 21° A.T.D.C. **Tappet clearances:** (Hot) .017 in. **Front wheel toe-in:** Nil. **Camber angle:** 1°. **Castor angle:** 4°. **Tyre pressures:** Front, 17 lb., rear, 20 lb. (fast driving, 18 lb. and 23 lb.) (see text). **Brake fluid:** Lockheed. **Battery:** Lucas SG9E, 12-v. **Lamp bulbs:** Head, 42/36 w. Side/indicator, 21/6 w. rear/indicator/stop, 21/6 w.

pedal with too long a travel for heel-and-toe downward gear changes to be made.

There are, on the other hand, no half measures about the brakes. Ten-inch drums with a friction lining area of 134 sq. in. not only show excellent results on a Tapley meter with moderate pressure, but were almost unaffected by a series of deliberate hard applications in the rapid descent of a long French main road hill. If under extreme conditions further brake cooling were ever necessary, it should be provided by the wire wheels which are

High-sided, the cockpit is unusually draught-free even in its most open condition. Instruments are where they should be, and the horn button on the facia M.G.-fashion. Forethought is shown by wind-screen struts which do double-duty as grab handles.

the several members of our staff who drove the car was that the extra pounds put into a superlatively strong and rigid chassis were weight well spent.

To drive the M.G.A. on a winding open road is sheer enthusiast's delight. Rack and pinion steering and small cars have always gone well together, and the lightness of the steering with a small, four-spoked wheel is matched by a quickness and precision which might not be expected from the lock-to-lock figure (for a very compact lock) of 2$\frac{3}{4}$ turns. In this case the secret lies in an admirable example of useful and controllable oversteer. In point of fact an improvement in the handling was found possible by inflating the tyres from the recommended fast-driving pressures of 18 lb. front and 23 lb. for the rear wheels to approximately 26 lb. on all four. The effect of the oversteer then was merely that the driver, rather like a pilot in some types of aircraft, steered into a turn and then virtually centralized the wheel to keep the car on its course. It was notable that to some tastes at least the extra sponginess of the tyres at lower pressures did not make for a more comfortable ride, and had the further disadvantage of causing tyre squeal on corners, otherwise entirely absent.

Quite apart from steering characteristics, the cornering power of the car is extremely good, holding it down in a manner to give the driver complete confidence, and seeming almost indifferent to the type of road surface. As is often the case a wet road gives an earlier indication of the car's behaviour when pressed to the limit on a corner, sliding of the rear wheels beginning quite gradually and being easily transformed into a controlled drift. Wheelspin is very quickly provoked in starting from rest in the wet, due possibly to the combination of a small, high-revving engine and a throttle control which on the left-hand drive model under test was awkward in the extreme. It is an unfortunate thing that a sports car should have its throttle opened by an enclosed cable (which is the same on left- or right-hand drive models), and a small source of joy to the sporting driver is denied him by an accelerator

optional equipment for the M.G. An effective fly-off handbrake lever is placed horizontally on the right-hand side of the transmission tunnel, convenient with right-hand drive but on a left-hand drive car close to the passenger's legs.

Like the brakes, the clutch is hydraulically operated by a hanging pedal, and most surprisingly is smooth even to the point of slipping under really brutal treatment. It may be observed that the latter was very much a feature of our acceleration tests, since the gearbox synchromesh was good enough to allow full-throttle "snatch" changes upwards through all the gears. The M.G. Company have always had a good name for the handiness of their remote-control gear levers, and this model is no exception, although an almost universal complaint amongst drivers, admittedly unused to changing gear with their right hands, was a difficulty in moving quickly from third to second gear. If the choice of ratios can be criticized it is in a second gear equivalent to only 42 m.p.h. at the maxi-

Power beneath a low bonnet has been obtained with practically no sacrifice of accessibility, excepting only the batteries which are carried behind the seats. The distributor is just out of sight below the sparking plugs.

Shallow and very much occupied by spare wheel and tools, the boot can carry a couple of soft grips if need be. A grid for more awkward luggage is an available accessory.

Less noise but still quite good weather protection is obtained with hood up and side-screens stowed away. Visibility to the rear is reasonable through a wide plastics window.

mum recommended engine speed of 5,500 r.p.m., but the willingness of the engine to rev freely up to and even occasionally beyond this limit largely makes up for the restriction. In the light of modern practice it is often a surprise to cruise in top-gear comfort and then discover that the engine is turning over at 4,500 r.p.m., and some form of higher gear is a tantalizing consideration for the long distance motorist.

Driving Position

Although the ride itself is remarkably comfortable, low slung seats result in a driving position needing a straight and unbraced left leg and a right knee (this again in the left-hand drive car) which, owing to proximity of the steering wheel rim, would have been happier with a universal joint, while all the assorted shapes of *The Motor* staff found a lack of support for the small of the back. The seats nevertheless are well sprung and well covered in leather, and excellently shaped to prevent passengers being flung about in fast cornering. The central bulge over the transmission is covered with padded leather. The low build ensures that tall drivers do not find themselves in the slipstream above the curved windscreen, which throws the airstream well to the side of the cockpit, and sidescreens with spring-hinged lower sections can help to make the car yet more snug even when open. Some advantage is indeed to be gained by driving in this trim in anything less than rain or snow, particularly if the very powerful heater is fitted, as the level of noise in the cockpit rises a great deal with the hood in place.

Mundane matters of convenience must weigh to some extent with the most sporting of car owners, and the virtues which largely give the M.G. its personality have been bought to some extent at the expense of creature comfort. To raise or even to lower the hood single-handed is an exercise in skill and patience, so that the full-length tonneau cover proved a most valuable "extra" on the test car. The space left free behind the seats when the hood is erect will, however, take a fair number of parcels, which might otherwise have to be left at home. The sidescreens are normally carried in separate compartments of a bag in this space, and the spare wheel on the floor of the luggage locker. Tools in a large roll are strapped on top of the spare wheel, leaving enough luggage room for two canvas grips and smaller objects, but scarcely for hard suitcases. The list of extra items available for the car includes an external luggage carrier for the boot lid, one of which was fitted to the test car and proved rather frail. Maps, torches and the rest of the small oddments which go with travelling find a home in open door pockets.

Circular instrument dials, with markings which have suffered a little at the stylist's hands, are grouped where they may be easily seen by the driver; speedometer, rev counter, water thermometer and oil pressure and fuel gauges are included, but no ammeter. The distinctive M.G. feature of a convenient horn button on the centre of the facia is preserved. Lights, starter, choke, windscreen wipers and a map-reading light for the passenger are controlled by pull-out switches, and a manual windscreen washer is part of the optional equipment. The accessibility of the engine and chassis for maintenance or servicing, often a question of personal interest to the driver of this type of car, is uniformly good with the sole and outstanding exception of the batteries; placed on either side of the car behind the seats, they can only be inspected on removal of a plate which is itself obstructed until the spare wheel is unclamped from the boot.

Lest there be any risk, however, of a number of small notes of criticism leaving a false impression, the newest M.G. must be summed up as enthusiastically as it was everywhere received. That the modern styling is generally approved there can be no doubt, but far more important is the introduction of a small car with a degree of roadworthiness high by any standards. The famous slogan of the factory has indeed never been better applied.

Mechanical Specification

Engine	
Cylinders	4
Bore	73.025 mm.
Stroke	89 mm.
Cubic capacity	1,489 c.c.
Piston area	25.97 sq.in.
Valves	Pushrod o.h.v.
Compression ratio	8.3/1
Max. power	68 b.h.p.
at	5,500 r.p.m.
Piston speed at max. b.h.p.	3,210 ft. per min.
Carburetters	2 inclined S.U. 1½-in.
Ignition	12-volt coil
Sparking plugs	14 mm. Champion NA8
Fuel pump	S.U. electrical, rear-mounted
Oil filter	Full-flow Tecalemit
Transmission	
Clutch	Single dry plate
Top gear (s/m)	4.3
3rd gear (s/m)	5.908
2nd gear (s/m)	9.52
1st gear	15.652
Propeller shaft	Open
Final drive	Hypoid bevel
Top gear m.p.h. at 1,000 r.p.m.	17.0
Top gear m.p.h. at 1,000 ft./min. piston speed	29.1
Chassis	
Brakes	Lockheed hydraulic (2 l.s. front)
Brake drum diameter	10 in.
Friction lining area	134.4 sq. in.
Suspension:	
Front	Coil and wishbone, i.f.s.
Rear	Semi-elliptic
Shock absorbers:	
Front	Armstrong incorporated in upper wishbone pivots
Rear	Armstrong hydraulic
Tyres	Dunlop 5.60—15
Steering	
Steering gear	Rack and pinion
Turning circle (between kerbs):	
Left	30¾ ft.
Right	28¼ ft.
Turns of steering wheel, lock to lock	2¾
Performance factors (at laden weight as tested):	
Piston area, sq. in. per ton	24.1
Brake lining area, sq. in. per ton	125
Specific displacement, litres per ton mile	2,440

Fully described in *The Motor*. *September 28, 1955*

Coachwork and Equipment

Bumper height with car unladen:
Front (max.) 18 in., (min.) 9½ in.
Rear (max.) 21 in., (min.) 12½ in.

Starting handle	Yes
Battery mounting	Behind seats
Jack	Screw-type
Jacking points	Front wishbones and rear springs

Standard tool kit: Ring-type tappet spanner, wheelbrace (copper hammer with wire wheels), tappet gauge, sparking plug spanner, pliers, grease gun, adjustable spanner, 2 tyre levers, cylinder head nut spanner, tyre valve spanner, distributor screwdriver and gauge, tyre pump, 3 box spanners, 3 o/e spanners, screwdriver, recessed screwdriver, tommy bar, jack, brake bleeder tube, gearbox plug spanner, touch-up paintpencil, tool roll.

Exterior lights: 2 head, 2 side-indicator, 2 rear/brake/indicator.

Direction indicators: Flashing type, self-cancelling.

Windscreen wipers	Electric, self-parking
Sun vizors	No

Instruments: Speedometer with decimal trip distance recorder, rev. counter, oil pressure gauge, water thermometer.

Warning lights	Ignition, indicators, headlamp main beam
Locks:	
With ignition key	Ignition
With other keys	None
Glove lockers	None
Map pockets	2
Parcel shelves	None
Ashtrays	None
Cigar lighters	None
Interior lights	Instrument panel, map-reading light
Interior heater	Re-circulating or fresh-air type with de-mister
Car radio	Optional, H.M.V.

Extras available: Radio, heater, wire wheels, fog lamp, whitewall tyres, 4.55/1 axle gears, twin horns, external luggage carrier, overall tonneau cover, radiator blind, rim embellishers, telescopic steering column.

Upholstery material	Leather over foam rubber
Floor covering	Carpet

Exterior colours standardized: Black, Orient red, Tyrolite green, Glacier blue, Old English white.

Alternative body styles	None

The M.G. Series "A"

–New "1500" at Basic Price of £595!

Another Cutaway Drawing by "Autosport" Staff Artist Theo Page

Based on the prototype Ex 182, which did so well at Le Mans, the Series "A" M.G. is the type of car for which M.G. enthusiasts have been waiting for several years. As can be seen from Theo Page's cutaway drawing, it bears a close resemblance to the prototype machine, but is, of course, completely equipped for road work.

The power-unit is developed from the four-cylinder, push-rod operated Magnette engine. Of 1,496 c.c. (73.025 x 90.88 mm.), it develops 68 b.h.p. at 5,500 r.p.m. on a compression ratio of 7.3 to 1. Twin semi-d.d. SU carburetters with separate air-cleaners are employed, drawing fuel via an SU electric fuel pump from a 10-gallon rear tank with quick-release filler cap. Lucas coil ignition is employed.

A box-section chassis is specially braced for rigidity, and the side-members are carried over the rigid rear axle, which is supported by semi-elliptical springs. Front suspension is independent, by means of helical springs and wishbones; hydraulic dampers are used front and rear. Transmission is via a hydraulically controlled 8 ins. Borg and Beck clutch, a four-speed synchromesh gearbox, Hardy-Spicer open propeller shaft to a three-quarter floating hypoid-bevel rear axle. Gear ratios are : 15.652, 9.520, 5.908 and 4.3 to 1 (reverse, 20.468 to 1). A remote control gear lever is employed. Four-stud fixing disc wheels are fitted as standard with 5.60 x 15 ins. tyres, but wire wheels are available if specified when ordering. The Lockheed hydraulic brakes work in 10 ins. drums, and the hand-brake is of the racing "fly-off" type. Steering is by direct rack and pinion.

Coachwork is of light-section steel, the bonnet being hinged at the rear. The luggage compartment also carries the spare wheel. A full-width, curved windscreen is fitted and the all-weather equipment consists of a waterproof fabric hood and detachable side-screens. The bucket seats are fully adjustable. Instruments include speedometer, revolution counter, oil, petrol, water temperature and ammeter gauges.

At a price of £844 0*s.* 10*d.* (including P.T.), this new M.G. represents real value in the sports car field. Left-hand or right-hand drive can be obtained, and amongst the extra equipment available are H.M.V. radio, heater, fog lamps, tonneau cover, exterior luggage rack, telescopic steering wheel, "Rad-blind" and twin-horns. A 4.55 to 1 axle may also be marketed.

It is intended, also, to list certain competition equipment, including wire wheels with steel or alloy rims to carry 5.50 x 15 "Road-speed" tyres, racing windscreens, 20-gallon rear tank, alternative gear-ratios (3.7, 3.9 and 4.1 to 1), special valves and guides, competition camshaft, oil cooler, extra fuel pump, high-compression pistons and so on. The new "A" will be on view at next month's Earls Court Motor Show, and a road-test report by John Bolster will appear in a forthcoming issue.

A NEW M.G

SMOOTH in external shape, the new M.G. has lower wind resistance than its smaller-engined predecessors yet is more roomy internally.

Fast 1½-litre Model Based on the Prototypes Raced at Le Mans

AFTER an interval of some months during which only Magnette saloons have been built, the M.G. car company are once again making 2-seater models at a considerable and increasing rate. The title "M.G. Midget," which has been associated with a series of four-cylinder 2-seat models since 1929, from the original M-type of 847 c.c., through models of 939 c.c., 1,292 c.c. and 1,250 c.c., to the recent TF1500 of 1,466 c.c., is in abeyance; but the new 2-seater which will be known as the Series M.G.A., will undoubtedly be greeted as a worthy bearer of the famous octagonal radiator badge. The new production model is very closely related to the

THE M.G. SERIES – M.G.A.

Engine dimensions	
Cylinders	4
Bore	73.025 mm.
Stroke	89 mm.
Cubic capacity	1,489 c.c.
Piston area	25.97 sq. in.
Valves	Pushrod, o.h.v.
Compression ratio	8.3/1
Engine performance	
Max. power	68 b.h.p.
at	5,500 r.p.m.
Max. b.m.e.p.	129 lb./sq. in.
at	3,500 r.p.m.
B.H.P. per sq. in. piston area ...	2.62
Peak piston speed ft. per min. ...	3,210
Engine details	
Carburetters	Two 1½in. S.U. inclined
Ignition	12-volt coil
Plugs: make and type	Champion NA8, 14 mm.
Fuel pump	S.U. electrical, rear mounted
Fuel capacity	10 gallons
Oil filter	Full-flow
Oil capacity	6½ pints
Cooling system	Pump and fan
Water capacity	10 pints
Electrical system	12-volt c.v.c.
Battery	12 volt (2 x 6)
Transmission	
Clutch	Borg & Beck 8-in. s.d.p., hydraulically operated
Gear ratios:	
Top (s/m)	4.3
3rd (s/m)	5.908
2nd (s/m)	9.520
1st	15.652
Rev.	20.468
Prop. shaft...	Open
Final drive	¾ floating hypoid axle
Chassis details	
Brakes	Lockheed hydraulic, 2 l.s. front
Brake drum diameter	10 in.
Friction lining area	134.4 sq. in.
Suspension:	
Front	I.F.S. by coil springs and wishbone
Rear	Semi elliptic
Shock absorbers	Armstrong hydraulic
Wheel type	4-stud ventilated disc (Centre-lock wire wheels as optional extra)
Tyre size	5.60—15 Dunlop
Steering gear	Rack and pinion
Steering wheel	Spring-spoke
Dimensions	
Wheelbase	7 ft. 10 in.
Track:	
Front	3 ft. 11½ in. (with wire wheels 3 ft. 11⅞ in.)
Rear	4 ft. 0¾ in.
Overall length	13 ft. 0 in.
Overall width	4 ft. 10 in.
Overall height	4 ft. 2 in.
Ground clearance...	6 in.
Turning circle	28 ft.
Dry weight	17½ cwt.
Performance data (at dry weight)	
Piston area, sq. in. per ton ...	29.7
Brake lining area, sq. in. per ton	154
Top gear m.p.h. per 1,000 r.p.m.	17.0
Top gear m.p.h. at 2,500 ft./min. piston speed	72.8
Litres per ton-mile	3,000

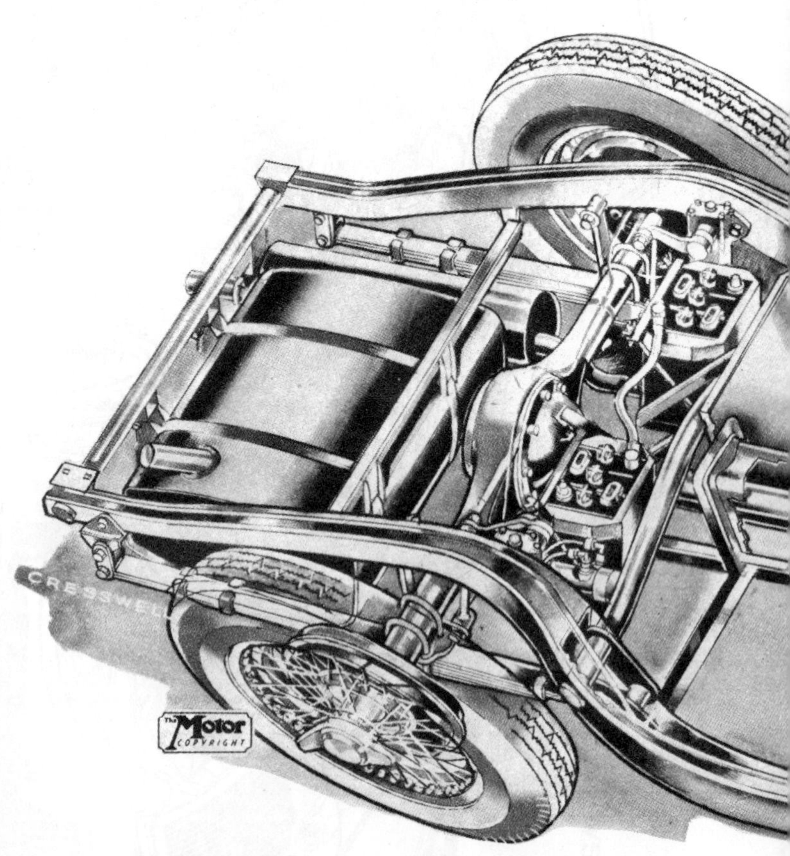

FOUNDATION of this lower and more shapely M.G. two-seater is this sturdy chassis, with box-section side members swept out to allow for seats between them, and with especially sturdy bracing to provide torsional rigidity from the scuttle forwards. Power unit is a 1,489 c.c. B-series B.M.C. engine, with high compression ratio, two large S.U. carburetters and a special camshaft. Centre-lock wire wheels are an optional extra.

TWO-SEATER

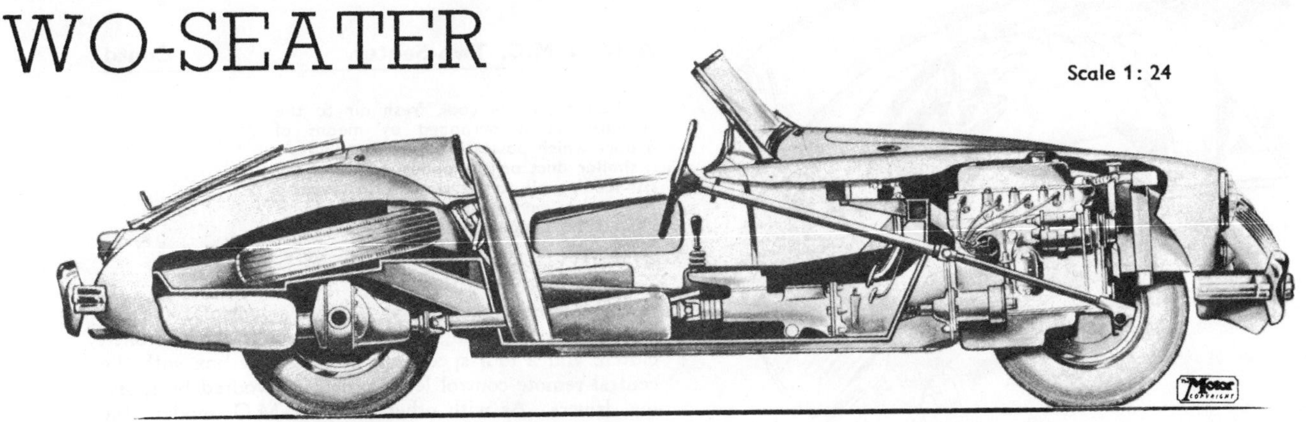

three cars which first ran in the 24-hour race at Le Mans in June, and whilst it is designed to maintain a high reputation for sturdiness established by other post-war M.G. 2-seaters it offers greatly enhanced performance—a Road Test Report published on pages 298-301 makes this abundantly clear.

Streamlining is fundamental to this new model, the external lines of which may be traced back to a special body built on a TD-series chassis for the 1951 Le Mans race. With bodywork improved from pre-war designs, the TF-series M.G. 2-seater was found by the M.G. engineers to need 97 b.h.p. if 100 m.p.h. was to be attained. In contrast, the new Series-M.G.A. should be able to attain that speed with an engine developing around 70 b.h.p. and production models are claimed to be 95-m.p.h. cars with truly safe chassis characteristics.

Designed and developed in the M.G. works at Abingdon-on-Thames, although incorporating standard or modified British Motor Corporation components wherever they are suitable, the series-M.G.A. is 2½ inches lower in overall height than was the TF Midget. The new chassis which allows this has been tested up to over 150 m.p.h. at Utah, and has its side members swept outwards to permit the floor of a wide cockpit to be set low down between them. Essentially it is a conventional chassis based upon two box-section side members, the "space frame" used to provide rigidity with less weight on some competition models having been rejected as incompatible with good doors. Ahead of the doors, however, this frame is truly three-dimensional, the scuttle structure having been braced into it in a manner which ensures extreme rigidity in the vital forward half of the chassis.

Fundamentally orthodox, the suspension has been very carefully worked out in detail, to give good riding

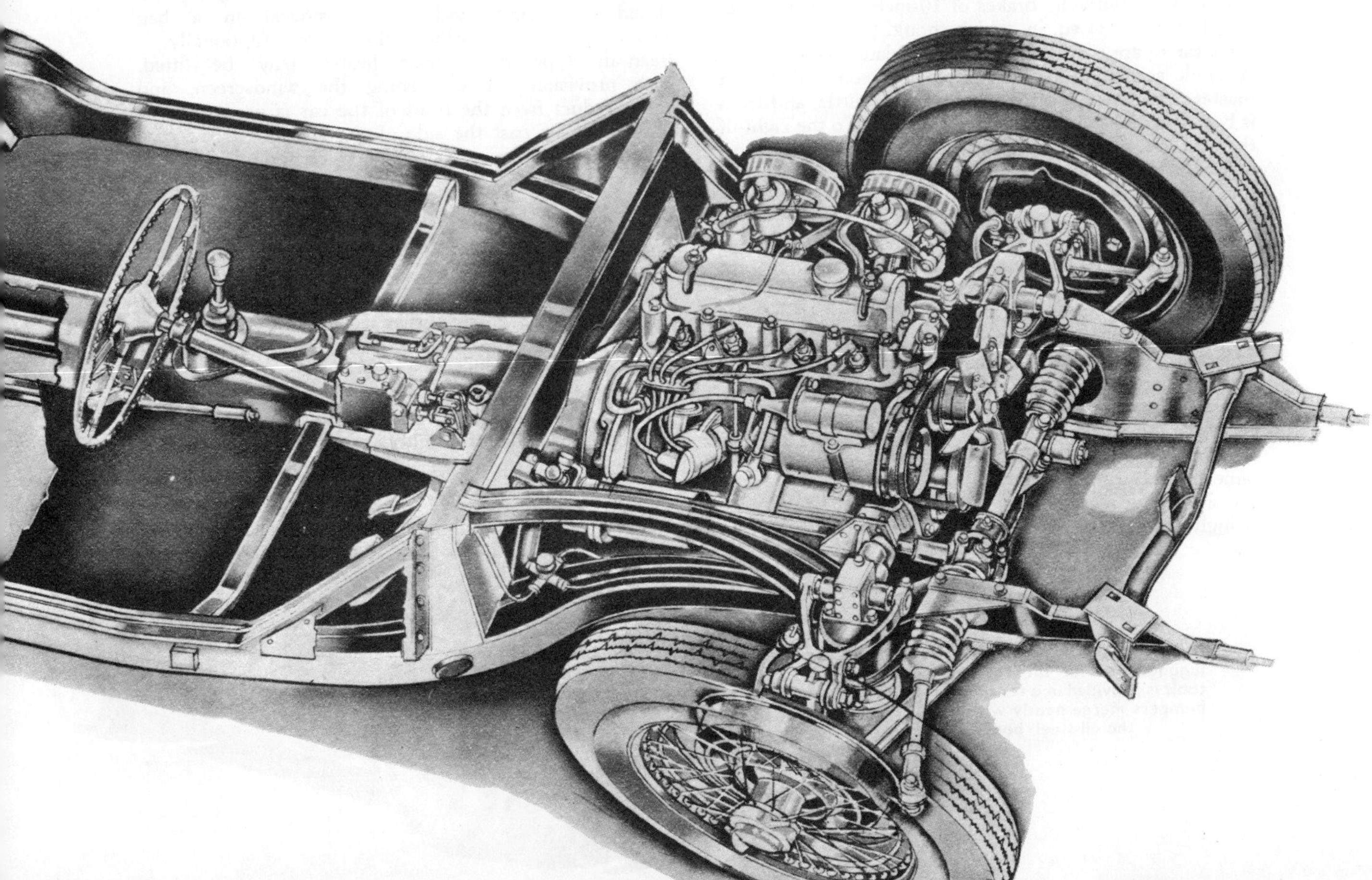

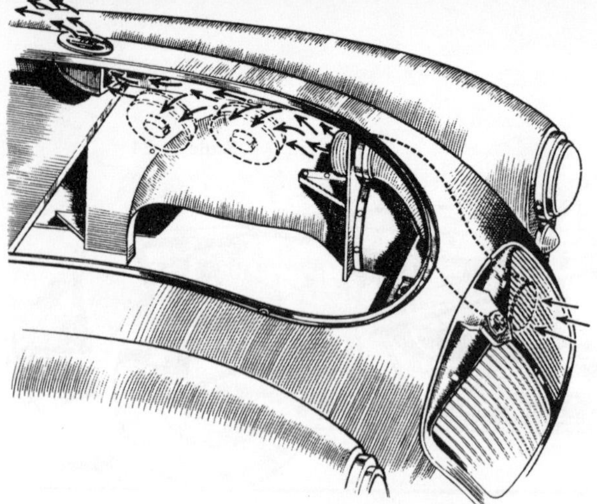

DIRECT supply of cool, fresh air to the carburetters is arranged by means of a duct which passes around the radiator, a similar duct on the opposite side of the car feeding air to the car interior heater. Air outlets on top of the scuttle help to keep under-bonnet temperatures moderate at all times.

comfort and also safe handling characteristics with adequate warning when the limit of tyre adhesion is being approached, without expensive mechanical complexity. A box-section front cross-member carries the independent front wheel suspension linkage, which is of the unequal-length wishbone type with Armstrong shock absorbers forming the pivots of the upper wishbones. Coil springs are interposed between the lower wishbones and the extremities of the front suspension cross-member. Ahead of the suspension, a rack and pinion steering gear is mounted, with a universal joint in the steering column to bring the wheel to the desired angle. Simplicity and the use of rubber bushes have kept the number of greasing points on the front suspension and steering down to six.

Rear Axle Location

Semi-elliptic rear springs are mounted below the chassis side members, which are upswept to pass over a ¾-floating rear axle incorporating 4.3/1 hypoid bevel gears. Control of the rear springs is by Armstrong shock absorbers of lever-arm type, and positive but cushioned limitation of the range of axle travel is provided by bump rubbers and rebound check straps.

Lockheed hydraulic brakes of 10-inch size give a frictional area of 134 sq. in. which should be very adequate for a car of approximately 18¼ cwt. unladen kerb weight. A single accessible hydraulic fluid reservoir and duplex master cylinder unit is mounted on the scuttle, and from it both the brake and clutch pedals hang. To the right of the gearbox, a fly-off handbrake is mounted on the floor, a flexible cable from this applying the left rear brake and the equal and opposite reaction on the flexible cable outer casing applying the right rear brake. Standard equipment on the series-M.G.A. will be steel disc wheels with four-stud fixing, but wire wheels with knock-off hubs can be supplied as an alternative at extra cost.

Powering the new car, the B-series engine of the British Motor Corporation is more highly tuned than when used in the M.G. Magnette saloon. Externally it features two inclined S.U. carburetters of 1½-inch size, mounted on a cast inlet manifold which incorporates a balance pipe, and drawing air from a pair of dry-element air filters. Internally, it differs from other versions of the same basic engine in such respects as having high-compression pistons, and a camshaft which emphasizes power at high r.p.m. rather than extreme mechanical silence. It may be recalled that this four-cylinder engine with its pushrod-operated o.h.v. has a displacement of 1,489 c.c.

In unit with the engine are the hydraulically controlled clutch, and a four-speed synchromesh gearbox with the central remote-control lever which is favoured by sporting drivers. As with other post-war M.G. models, the production cars are planned for the average buyer who may wish to combine some competition driving with large mileages of ordinary road motoring. Those especially interested in competitions will be able to obtain advice from the factory as to how extra performance can be obtained, and to buy special parts and equipment.

What the average buyer is most likely to appreciate, however, is the fact that the new low-drag body which permits speeds in excess of 90 m.p.h. is also good looking and much roomier than its predecessors. It is purely a 2-seater, with individually adjustable bucket seats separated by a central armrest over the propeller shaft. Accommodation is however provided for a certain amount of luggage inside the body, in a boot the external lid of which is released from inside the car. Also enclosed in the boot are a single spare wheel and the tools, whilst below it is a fuel tank of generous 10-gallon capacity—an external luggage grid is available for mounting on the boot lid.

Disappearing completely from view when folded, the hood is covered in durable plastics material and incorporates a large flexible rear window. When it is raised, some space for parcels becomes available inside the body. Rigid framed sidescreens have hinged flaps, held closed by springs and can be stowed in a bag which also hangs behind the seats. Optionally, a fresh-air type of interior heater may be fitted, with provision for de-misting the windscreen, and another duct from the front of the car is used to carry cool, fresh air past the side of the radiator to the carburetter air intakes—a provision which should help usefully to ensure that test-bed horse-power is truly available on the road. Extras for which provision has been made also include fog lamp, car radio, radiator blind, telescopic steering column, and full-length tonneau cover with central zipp-fastener division. Bumpers with overriders, and a map-reading lamp on the facia panel, are standard equipment. Instruments fitted are: speedometer, matching rev. counter, fuel contents gauge, oil pressure gauge, and water thermometer.

Described as "first of a new line," and planned with the M.G. slogan, "Safety Fast," clearly in mind, this new model is to be sold at the highly competitive price of £595.

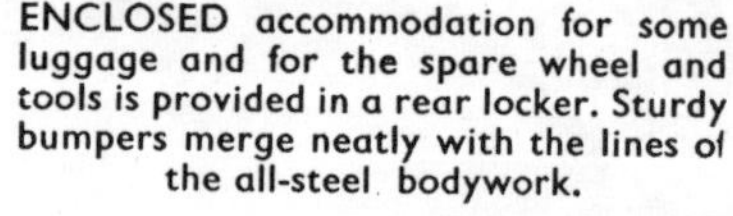

ENCLOSED accommodation for some luggage and for the spare wheel and tools is provided in a rear locker. Sturdy bumpers merge neatly with the lines of the all-steel bodywork.

★

SVELTE: Gone are the "square" lines of the traditional M.G. In its place is the new "A", the aerodynamic shape of which brings the Abingdon product completely up to date. It is shown in completely standard form, but knock-on wire wheels can be had if specified.

★

JOHN BOLSTER TESTS THE M.G.A.

Abingdon's new 1½-litre two-seater a fast, smooth performer —80 m.p.h. cruising speed, over 95 m.p.h. maximum

"THE racing car of today is the touring car of tomorrow". How true are those oft-quoted words when applied to the new M.G.! We first saw the prototype chassis in August, 1954, when George Eyston broke eight International Class F records in a car called Ex 179. The next appearance included the body as we now know it, and, under the number Ex 182, the team performed marvels at Le Mans. Now, fully fledged as the M.G.A., the new model is on the market, and I have recently done a week's hard motoring in one of the first production cars.

When I tested Ex 182 in July, I described the chassis briefly, and I had already given a more detailed account in the issue of 3rd June. Suffice it, therefore, to say that the frame is of box section, and wide enough for the driver and passenger to sit within its members. The independent front suspension is by helical springs and wishbones, while at the rear the semi-elliptic springs locate the hypoid axle on the Hotchkiss principle.

The engine is a well-known model of the B.M.C. range, but developed in this case to the point where it produces 68 b.h.p. at 5,500 r.p.m. This is a sturdy design, with twin carburetters and push-rod-operated overhead valves. It is assembled in unit with a four-speed gearbox, synchronized on the upper three ratios, and with a traditional M.G. central remote control. Also traditional is the fly-off hand brake—why don't all cars have them?

The body follows the lines of the Le Mans cars, but is more elaborately appointed. The grille preserves memories of the old M.G. radiator, but the octagon motif has, thank goodness, gone from the instrument panel, appearing only unobtrusively on the steering wheel boss. The instruments are indeed round, plain, and functional, and the test car's speedometer was completely accurate.

POWER-PLANT: The 1½-litre, push-rod engine is accessible enough for all normal maintenance. Large "trunk" on the left is the heater air-intake. The 1¼ ins. SU carburetters have separate air-cleaners.

There is none of that continuous up-and-down movement that mars so many modern cars. The stability is exceptional, and the M.G. corners fast under perfect control.

This is a car of very definite character. It is obviously a sports model, but it remains at all times practical. With the hood and sidescreens erect, the heater turned on, and the radio playing, it can serve very well as a town carriage. Milady's dress will not be soiled if she is going to a dance, and though the low build exacts a certain technique of entry and exit, that is soon acquired. This is as good a shopping car as any other, and the latent performance can temporarily be forgotten.

As befits a genuine sports car, it is better without the hood for long, fast journeys. With the top folded away, there is no wind noise, and the engine revs. willingly as the miles or kilometres pass quickly by. At the slightest check, the left hand has found a lower gear almost before the driver realizes it, and

RECOGNITION is made easy (above) by retaining the typical Abingdon shape for the "radiator" motif.

ANTI-CRASH arrangements (right) for the neat tail include a substantial bumper with over-riders.

The upholstery, trim, and finish are most attractive. At the rear, the luggage boot has a moderate capacity, because the spare wheel, in a soft cover, takes up a good deal of the space. The hood gives plenty of head room, good rearward vision, and folds neatly out of sight. The excellent sidescreens, with spring-loaded hinged bottom panels, have their own compartment in the flap which covers the hood. The backs of the seats fold forward, providing easy access to the all-weather equipment.

The driving position gives a good sense of control. I would perhaps prefer the steering wheel to be a little farther away, and my own preference is for a rather more reclining seat back with a cushion giving better support to the legs. However, these slight changes could easily be made by the owner if desired, and an adjustable wheel is available. The forward vision is excellent, thanks to a falling bonnet line.

On driving off, one is at once impressed with the gearbox. It is as nearly crash-proof as anything I have driven outside the automatic class. The changes go through beautifully, and third gear is high enough for frequent use on the open road. After being baulked by a slow vehicle, one takes a *coup de troisième* and the speedometer is soon climbing into the seventies again. The clutch is smooth in action, but can be made to slip if fast changes are attempted. As the hydraulic operation gives agreeably light control, it would be easy to fit stronger springs for competition work.

The makers suggest 80 m.p.h. as a cruising speed, which seems to suit the car admirably. I had the speedometer on the 100 mark a score of times, under favourable conditions on the road. One tends to drive fast because the riding comfort is so good. The first impression is that the suspension is fairly hard, but this soon disappears, and at the higher speeds the comfort is most marked.

FIRST sports two-seater M.G. ever to have a separate luggage compartment is the "A". The spare wheel is covered by a fabric envelope, and anchored by grips to the locker floor.

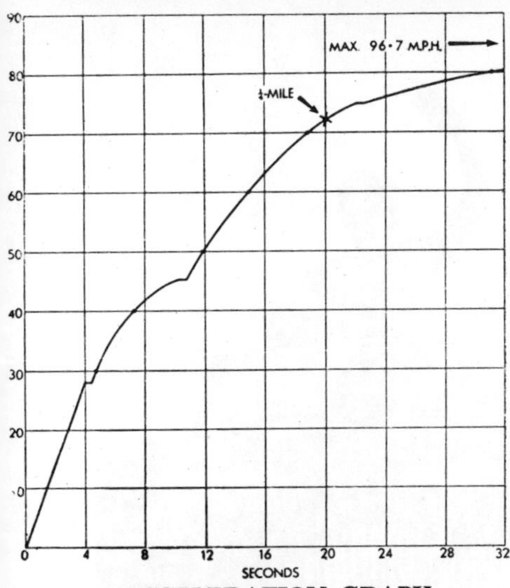

ACCELERATION GRAPH

FACIA PANEL is well thought out, and purists will note the provision of a tachometer. Provision is also made for H.M.V. radio (shown) and the shape of the spring-spoked steering wheel allows the instruments to be read easily.

the car is accelerating away without any excessive exhaust noise.

The acceleration is not of the kick-in-the-back variety, but the well-chosen gear ratios allow the best use to be made of the available performance. This is really quite a big, roomy car, and nobody would guess that it had only a 1½-litre engine. Large enough to be comfortable but small enough to be nippy in traffic, it is an ideal size of vehicle for many purposes. Thanks to its roadholding and brakes, it can put up a better average in safety than certain sports cars with considerably larger engines.

Very powerful brakes are a valuable safety feature. They can be used hard and often without the slightest sign of fading, and the usual increase in pedal travel does not manifest itself. In fact, the brakes are more than adequate to the speed and weight of the car. The lights are sufficiently effective for 60 m.p.h. cruising, but I would prefer to add a spotlamp before driving at maximum speed in the dark, except on roads I know particularly well.

For those requiring additional performance, perhaps with competition work in mind, the makers can supply all the necessary parts and information. Wire wheels with knock-off hub caps are another extra that will appeal to many. In its standard form as tested, however, the M.G. A is a most attractive car. It is fast and a delight to drive, but it is comfortable and practical as well. Its appearance excited universal admiration wherever I went, and the more discerning were quick to remark that it was beautifully made. Above all, at a basic price of £595 it represents remarkable value.

Having driven the competition model, Ex 182, from which this car was derived, I can say that little has been lost and a great deal gained in grooming the machine for production. The excellent roadholding and steering of the prototype are fully retained, and the loss in performance is less than I expected. The sound and heat insulation make a big difference, and the hot driving compartment of the "racer" has been eliminated. This is a jolly good little sports car; if you want one, hurry up and get in the queue!

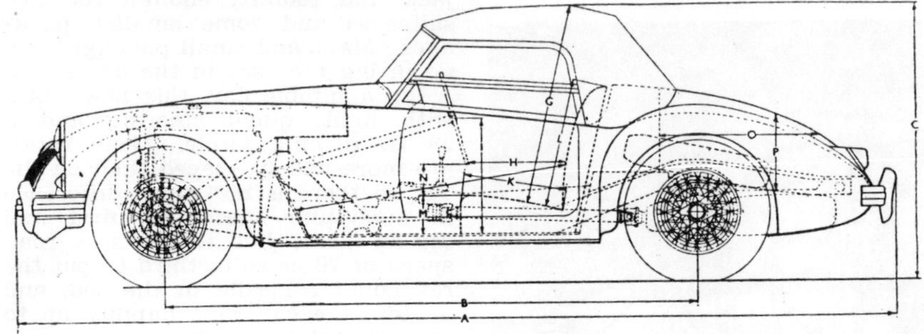

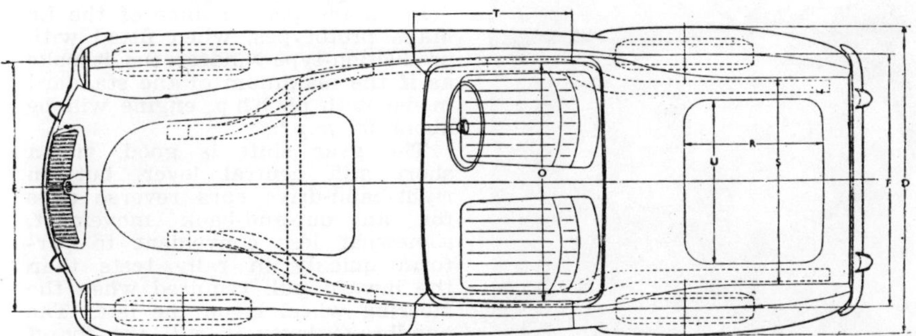

SPECIFICATION AND PERFORMANCE DATA

Car Tested: M.G. A Sports 2-seater. Price £595 (£844 0*s*. 10*d*. including P.T.).

Engine: Four cylinders 73.025 mm. x 89 mm. (1,489 c.c.). Pushrod-operated overhead valves. 8.15 to 1 compression ratio. 68 b.h.p. at 5,500 r.p.m. Twin S.U. carburetters. Lucas coil and distributor.

Transmission: Borg and Beck 8 ins. single dry plate clutch with hydraulic operation. Four-speed gearbox with short central remote control lever. Ratios, 4.3, 5.908, 9.520, and 15.625 to 1. Open propeller shaft. Hypoid rear axle.

Chassis: Box section frame swept out to full width of body and passing above rear axle. Independent front suspension by wishbones and helical springs with rack and pinion steering. Rear axle on underslung semi-elliptic springs. Twin-piston hydraulic dampers all round. Bolt-on pierced disc wheels, fitted 5.50 x 15 ins. tyres. Lockheed hydraulic brakes, 2 L.S. in front, in 10 ins. x 1¾ ins. drums.

Equipment: 12-volt lighting and starting, speedometer, rev.-counter, ammeter, water temperature, oil pressure and fuel gauges. Radiator blind, heater and demister, radio, flashing direction indicators, self-parking wipers.

Turning circle, 28 ft. **Weight,** 17 cwt. **Ground clearance,** 6 ins.

Performance: Maximum speed, 96.7 m.p.h. Speeds in gears: 3rd, 75 m.p.h.; 2nd, 45 m.p.h.; 1st, 28 m.p.h. Standing quarter-mile, 20 secs. Acceleration: 0-30 m.p.h., 4.8 secs.; 0-40 m.p.h., 7.2 secs.; 0-50 m.p.h., 11.8 secs.; 0-60 m.p.h., 15 secs.; 0-70 m.p.h., 18.8 secs.; 0-80 m.p.h., 31.2 secs.

Fuel Consumption: Driven hard, 29 m.p.g.

Dimensions

A *Overall length, 13 ft. 0 in.*
B *Wheelbase, 7 ft. 10 ins.*
C *Overall height, 4 ft. 2 ins.*
D *Overall width, 4 ft. 10 ins.*
E *Front track, 3 ft. 11½ ins.*
F *Rear track, 4 ft. 0¾ in.*
G *Seat to roof, 3 ft. 1 in.*
H *Steering wheel to seat back, 1 ft. 5 ins. max., 11 ins. min.*
I *Floor to centre of steering wheel, 1 ft. 9 ins.*
J *Seat back to front floor board, 3 ft. 11 ins. max., 3 ft. 5 ins. min.*
K *Length of seat, 1 ft. 6½ ins.*
L *Height of seat, 1 ft. 9 ins.*
M *Floor to edge of seat, 7 ins.*
O *Length of boot, 2 ft. 6 ins.*
P *Height of boot, 1 ft. 2 ins.*
Q *Width at elbows, 3 ft. 8½ ins.*
R *Length of boot door, 2 ft. 2 ins.*
S *Width of boot, 3 ft. 3½ ins.*
T *Width of door opening, 2 ft. 4½ ins.*
U *Width of boot door, 2 ft. 6 ins.*

Wheels takes you driving in the new M.G.

By Gordon Wilkins, our European Correspondent.

Better handling, better comfort, better wind protection, better speed — that's how the new M.G.A.-type stacks up against the old TF.

NO doubt the appearance of the new 1½-litre M.G. sports car will create a storm among the diehards.

Until they drive it, that is. For, having tried the new M.G. on behalf of "Wheels" readers, I find it hard to see how anyone could hanker after the old car.

The modern shape pays off in performance and passenger protection; in personal comfort and substantially more cover luggage space.

One steps down into separately adjustable leather-upholstered bucket seats, set low between the chassis side members. There is much more room; interior width is up to 48 in. across the seats, although external width overall is an inch less than on the TF.

There's more space for elbows and feet.

The four-spoke flexible wheel is new, and the instruments are now in circular dials (no more octagons) grouped in front of the driver. There is a 110 m.p.h. speedometer, a rev counter with a yellow segment starting at 5,500 r.p.m. and a red sector at 6,000 r.p.m., oil pressure gauge, water thermometer, and, at last, a fuel gauge. In front of the passenger is a hooded lamp for the reading of maps and route cards.

The view is unobstructed ahead, across both front wings and the sloping bonnet. The detachable curved screen has small supporting struts at the corners shaped to form hand grips and excellent protection is given by the easily erected hood. This has a leather-like finish.

There are rigid side screens, with spring-loaded flaps for signalling.

There is reasonable luggage space in the boot, above the spare wheel jack and toolkit; enough for two suitcases and some smaller packages. Maps and small packages can go in big recesses in the doors.

It's a nimble car, this new M.G., with light, quick steering and a 28 ft. turning circle. Gear ratios are more widely spaced than on the TF, so there is not much difference in maximum speeds on first and second gear, but it takes a road speed of 70 or so in third to put the rev counter needle in the red, and on top, the car runs happily up to over 90 quite quickly.

From the performance of the Le Mans prototypes, when fitted with production-type windscreens, it looks as if the maximum of the standard model with 68 b.h.p. engine will be about 95 m.p.h.

The gear shift is good, via a short stiff central lever, but on right-hand-drive cars reverse calls for an out-and-back movement, somewhat less convenient to perform quickly in rally tests than the inward pull required when the steering wheel is on the left. The handbrake lever is still the fly-off

There's much more room in the new A-type. Notice the new wheel, the instruments, the screen. There is an arm-rest between the seats.

racing type, but smaller and a little less convenient than the lever on the TF.

The reduction in engine revs permitted by a 4.3 to 1 axle and 5.60 inch tyres on 15 rims means pleasant cruising at 70 with much less sensation of mechanical effort.

Handling and roadability constitute a big step forward. The oversteer I noticed on the old car seems to have gone, and the back end is slower to break away. Roll is negligible, and the brakes, the same size as used at Le Mans, gave me a lot of confidence. Acceleration from 0 to 50 m.p.h. takes about 12 secs. and unofficial tests with an MGA at steady speeds have shown 38 miles per Imp. gal. at 50 m.p.h.

There is less wind buffeting and draughts in the new car; additionally, one can have a heater with adjustable blower.

So far, no tuning stages have been announced for the B-type engine. Presumably the most advanced stage might incorporate the Weslake cross flow cylinder head, with four carburettors; two on the hot side for part throttle running, and two more on the cold side to be brought in for full power.

However, no such equipment is available at present, but immediate competition requirements are met by sodium filled exhaust valves with over-bored guides, racing clutch, racing wire wheels with light alloy rims, a 24-gallon fuel tank, racing bonnet straps, and a choice of several axle ratios.

Other extras on the list are radio, screen washer, adjustable telescopic steering column, 5.90 section road speed tyres, radiator blind, external mirror and cockpit cover.

For high-speed tuning the standard two carburettors (above) could quite easily be supplemented by two more on the other side of the Weslake cross-flow cylinder head. This photograph by "The Motor", England.

SPECIFICATION

ENGINE

4-cylinder, pushrod o.h.v., 73.425 x 89 mm (2.875 x 3.5 in), 1,489 cc (90.88 cu.in.). Compression ratio 8.15 to 1. Max power 68 bhp at 5,500 rpm. Max torque 77.4 lb. ft. at 3,500 rpm. Two inclined S.U. carburetters.

TRANSMISSION

Single plate dry clutch, 8 in; hydraulically operated 4-speed gearbox with central lever. Synchromesh on second, third and top. Open propeller shaft, hypoid bevel rear axle. Overall gear ratios 4.3, 5,908, 9,520, 15.652 to 1. Reverse 20.468 to 1. 17 mph per 1,000 rpm on top gear.

SUSPENSION AND STEERING

I.F.S. by coil and wishbone. Half-elliptic springs at rear. Opposed piston hydraulic dampers. Rack and pinion steering.

BRAKES

Hydraulic, 21-s. at front. Drums 10 in x 1¾ in. Total friction lining area 134.4 sq. in. Fly off racing type handbrake.

WHEELS AND TYRES

Bolt-on perforated disc wheels with 5.60-15 in. tyres. Centre lock wire wheels optional at extra cost.

ELECTRICAL SYSTEM

12 volts constant voltage generator control. Coil ignition with centrifugal and vacuum spark control.

DIMENSIONS

Wheelbase 94 in. Track 47½ (front 48¾ in. (rear). Overall length 156 in. Width 58 in. Height 50 in. Curb weight, 1,990 lb. Fuel tank capacity, 10 imp. gallons. Ground clearance 6 in.

Smooth, speed-giving lines are handsome as well. The wheels can be discs or wires, according to customer preference. This photograph by "The Motor", England.

the new MG model a

WHEN a proud old family produces a new heir, there is understandable speculation on whether the new arrival will maintain the standards expected. Not to draw the analogy too fine, this is the situation with the famous MG marque. The characteristic family physiognomy has had a severe lifting . . . in this case, a concession to progress, and the laws of aerodynamics.

The classic appearance of the MG family: the flowing wings, square front, angular tail — in general, plane surfaces as opposed to the flowing line, had been retained from the introduction of the J2 Midget (see above) in 1932 through the TF, introduced to the public in 1954. The Nuffield people, however, felt that the traditional shape had become a limiting factor, performance-wise. Even the newer, 1½ liter TF was up against its own sound barrier at about 85 mph.

Hence, the long-awaited MG A, built in close accord with the lessons learned from the Le Mans entry, the prototype of the A. This development traces its source from George Eyston's MG Special which smashed 8 International and 29 American Class F records at Bonneville Flats last year.

The four-cylinder, 1489 cc. engine of the A brings the horsepower rating up to 68 at 5,500 rpm., 13 more horses than the standard form of the TF. The engine is a twin carburetor version of the B.M.C. "B" series unit, driving through an hydraulically operated Borg and Beck 8 in. clutch and 4-speed synchromesh gear box, synchro being on the top three gears. An unmod-

ified version will yield upwards of 90 mph.

Built to give maximum strength and rigidity (remember—Safety Fast), the new MG A chassis has deep box-section side members. These members are outswept, permitting the driver and passenger to sit within the frame rather than above it. The factory promises exceptional roadability.

So much for genealogy and specs. This is an exciting development for the enthusiast. As can be seen, the new MG body is a beautiful example of the coachwork we've come to expect from across the sea. Retaining only the familiar design (if not shape) of the grill, the "A" boasts a two-seater streamlined body with enclosed luggage compartment: independently adjustable bucket seats with foam rubber cushions and backs that are fitted in leather (red, green, grey or black); and the usual MG extras in the way of side-screens, folding top, spare wheel, jack and tools.

The choice of exterior color ranges through black, Orient red, Tyrolite green, Glacier blue, and Old English white (that's what the man said).

This is a handsome job which should show up well in the road testing we have scheduled. There is a strong desire to shout, "The Prince is dead; Long live the Prince." We feel the heir apparent has a long and successful reign before him.

MG A SPORTS CAR SPECIFICATIONS

ENGINE: Four cylinders; bore 73.025 mm. (2.875 in.), stroke 89 mm. (3.5 in.), capacity 1489 c.c. (90.88 cu.in.); o.h.v. push-rod-operated; three-bearing counterbalanced crankshaft; compression ratio 8.3 to 1; b.h.p. 68 h.p. at 5,500; cooling by water pump and fan with thermostatic control; forced-feed engine lubrication by accentric rotor pump; external renewable element full-flow oil filter; oil capacity 8½ pints; filler on valve cover; aluminum alloy pistons with one oil control and three compression rings; 14mm. spark plugs; and pressed steel sump.
FUEL SYSTEM: Twin S.U. semi-downdraught carburetors with individual air cleaners; rear-mounted S.U. electric high-duty fuel pump; tank capacity 12½ gallons; fuel gauge on dash.
ELECTRICAL EQUIPMENT: Ignition by 12-volt oil-filled coil and fully automatic distributor with vacuum and centrifugal advance control; suppressor equipment; belt-driven dynamo; compensated voltage control; single-pole positive ground wiring system; dash-controlled started switch; twin-blade self-parking windshield wipers; twin stop-tail lamps with flashing direction indicators and rear reflector equipment; double dipping sealed beam headlamps; foot-operated dimming switch; separate sidelamps; twin Lucas batteries mounted in balance positions behind seats.
CHASSIS: Exceptionally sturdy box-section frame, specially braced for torsional rigidity; rear end of chassis swept over rear axle.
TRANSMISSION: Hydraulically operated single dry plate Borg and Beck clutch; 8 in. diameter; four speeds and reverse; synchromesh on second, third and fourth. Overall gear ratios: first 15.652, second 9.520, third 5.908, top 4.3, reverse 20.468. Central remote-control gear change. Tubular propeller shaft with needle-bearing universal joints.
AXLE: Three-quarter-floating rear axle with hypoid final reduction gears; ratio 4.3 to 1; semi-elliptic rear springs controlled by hydraulic dampers. Independent front suspension by coil springs and wishbone-type links controlled by hydraulic dampers.
STEERING: Direct rack-and-pinion steering with large-diameter spring-spoke, clear-view steering wheel.
BRAKES: Lockheed hydraulic fully compensated on all four wheels; 10 in. diameter brake-drums; central hand-brake lever with press-button "fly off" ratchet control.
TIRES AND WHEELS: Dunlop 5.60-15 tires on 4.00 x 15 well base, disc-type wheels with four-stud fixing.
INSTRUMENTS: Large speedometer with headlamp high-beam warning lamp; large revolution indicator with ignition warning light; oil pressure gauge; water temperature gauge; fuel indicator gauge; ignition switch; rheostat panel light switch; mixture control; map-reading light, direction indicator switch and warning light; lighting switch.
BODY DETAILS: Open two-seater streamlined body with enclosed luggage compartment; independently adjustable bucket-type seats with foam rubber cushions and backs covered in leather; door pockets; one-piece, curved safety glass windshield; folding, waterproof top with large rear transparent panel; two detachable side-screens with combined stowage and top cover; driving mirror centrally mounted; spare wheel, tools, jack and starting handle housed in rear compartment; quick-release gas filler cap; remote-control locks for hood and luggage compartment lid; one-piece hood hinged at rear, giving easy access to engine unit.

OPTIONAL EXTRAS

Heater and demister—complete.
White wall tires.
5.90 x 15 competition tires.
Adjustable telescopic steering column.
Center lock wire wheels.
Other special equipment also available.

DIMENSIONS

Wheel base—94″
Front track—Disc wheels 47½″—Wire wheels 47⅞″
Rear track—Disc wheels 48¾″ —Wire wheels 48¾″
Overall length—156″
Overall width—58″
Overall height (including top)—50″
Ground clearance—6″
Weight—1900 lbs.

Performance

0-40....6.2 seconds
0-60....13.8 seconds
0-80....25.8 seconds
Top Speed....106 mph (4.3 back axle)
Top Speeds gear (6000 rpm)
Max. Torque....4500 rpm
1st....28 mph.
2nd....49 mph.
3rd....78 mph.
4th....106 mph.

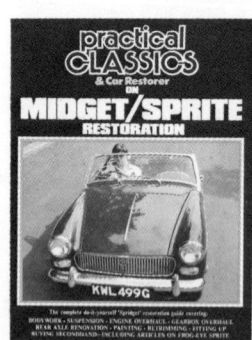

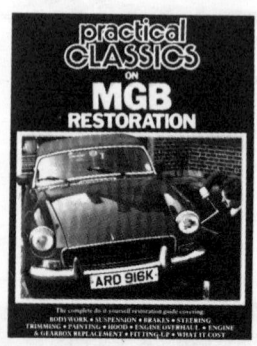

road testing the MG-A

By Jack Phelps and Robert Lee Behme

Upper Picture: The top on the new MG-A fits snugly and is designed to blend in with the car lines. Above: This is the MG lineup (left to right) MG-A, MG-TF, MG-TD, MG-TC.

▸ The MG for 1956 is not merely a new *looking* car, not a TF wrapped up in a new package. It is an entirely new automobile, the most complete model change ever made on any automobile in recent years. About the only traditional items remaining are the front suspension (introduced with the TD series) and the hexagonal MG emblem.

Even the ride is different. Gone is the masochistically beautiful belt in the seat of the pants as the car is barrelled over a dip or bump. Gone also is the nervously highstrung feeling at speeds over 60 mph. As a district service manager wonderingly remarked upon climbing out of the car after his first ride: "It doesn't even sound like an MG!"

Let's go for a ride.

The first thing you notice as you climb in is that you sit *in* it, not on it. Gone are the deep dips in the doors; the seats are set within the frame with the drive shaft tunnel riding high between the two very comfortable buckets. Within scant inches and directly down off the right hand side of the steering wheel is one of the shortest stump gearshift levers in the business. There is only a slight motion of the hand from wheel to lever.

Straight out from the seat are the swinging pedals of the clutch being somewhat like that of a well-oiled throttle rather than the stiff push of the earlier MG pedal. Just to the right and on a level with the brake is a very generously sized throttle, quite long and handy for heel-and-toe work. The steering wheel sits low in the driver's lap, giving a "feel" much like that of an Italian machine rather than like one made in Britain where the approach is usually more straight out from the shoulder.

A quick kick at the clutch and nothing more than a twitch of the fingers on the stumpy gear lever gets the car into first. The clutch is quick and low gear is very low, a combination which begets neck snapping starts until two or three standing starts are made. Once the knack is mastered, though, starts become as smooth as warm castor oil. If one is used to the earlier model MG, or to the Jaguar, the shift from first to second gear occurs with just about half the expected effort. For the first few times we found ourselves grabbing a second handful of gear, thinking the shift was not completed.

Second gear is a bit more satisfactory than low, a considerably longer wind-up being available in this range. Third gear is almost a direct diagonal push rather than a guiding from gate to gate and the same quick engagement is evident. There is a considerable split between second and third and a definite tendency to lug at engine speeds under about 2300 to 2500 rpm. As the tach hits 2500, though, it seems as if another two cylinders have cut in. From 2500 to 5000 the car moves out with the

COMPLETELY NEW DESIGN GIVES GREATER COMFORT AND LUGGAGE SPACE; PERFORMANCE UP SLIGHTLY

The new envelope body on the MG-A has smooth lines and the new luggage compartment is a great improvement over T's.

swift rush of a speed cop nailing an erring customer, smooth but surprisingly quick.

Top gear is much the same, a slight lugging tendency under 30 mph and then a sudden feeling of new power. It would seem from this that one would have to row the car around in traffic with the gearbox but things don't work out that way. Shifting with the new transmission is like working a paddle around in warm axle grease; the word "smooth" hardly connotes the real feeling. Further, third gear is adequate for any slow traffic from about 15 miles an hour on up and we drove the test car through Los Angeles rush-hour traffic with hardly a downshift except for an occasional dead stop for a light.

Out on the road the car is as pleasurable as it is new. Light but smooth, the car is rock steady at any speed up to its top speed of from 94 to 97 mph. There's none of the taut, nervous feeling associated with many of the earlier models and, strangely enough, scarcely any wind noise. All but the tightest curves are taken with almost no let-up.

When thrown into a drift the slight slide is absolutely even, neither the front nor the back wheels tending to break early, even on a down-hill bend. We tried a decreasing radius, down-hill curve several times. In the middle of the curve the road cambered sharply to either side and as long as the car was not run over on the reverse camber

Front end of the MG-A is very neat with an attractive rounded grille and a minimum of bright metal is used to emphasize the flowing lines of the entire design. Sloping hood provides good visibility ahead.

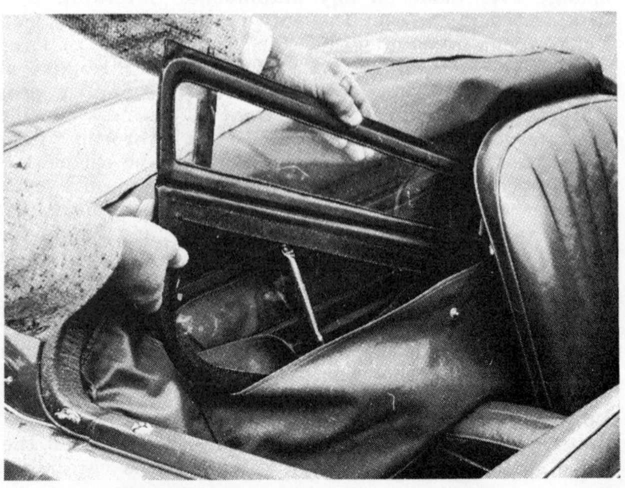

A real boon is the special storage space provided for the top and its components. Side curtains can be stored neatly and are right at hand when needed. It provides good package space when top is raised.

Roadtesting: MGA

side there was almost no drift at any speed up to about 50 mph, even when straddling the crown. Once we belted into the turn, pulled a quick downshift and stood on the loud-pedal. It broke loose as we expected but at no time was it out of control.

At first the steering seems a bit slow for these shenanigans but it actually isn't. The thing that makes it seem slow is the fact that it takes an extra half turn to go from lock to lock. However at each lock point the wheels are turned further than in the TF and the turning radius is much shorter than on any earlier MG.

Both acceleration and top speed have improved in the model change. Top speed is just about an even 10 mph over that of the 1500 TF and acceleration, even with the higher 4.3 to 1 gearing, is improved at the upper end. An average of four runs each gave the following results, using the fifth wheel:

0 — 30 — 5.1 seconds
0 — 45 — 9.2 seconds
0 — 60 —15.0 seconds
Standing ¼ mile—19.9
Top speed —94.75

Speeds from 0 to 30 are somewhat slower than for the TF 1500 by about two to three tenths of a second; about equal to 45 mph and almost a full second quicker to 60. The speedometer in the car tested was, at an actual 29.5 mph, almost dead accurate at an indicated 30 but fell off gradually to a true 56 mph at an indicated 60.

When it was first announced that the MG would have an envelope type body and the first dim photos were seen the conclusion was that the car would look somewhat like a sawed-off Healey 100. Nothing could be further from the truth; about the only Healey-like item on the car is the windshield. From the side the new A-type MG looks as if it were styled in the SIATA plant. The entire aspect is almost that of the SIATA 208-S. From the front the car is distinctively original.

Perhaps the utter finality of the style-change is the fact that the MG has finally blossomed out with a trunk. It's not a very large trunk to be sure but nonetheless it is capable of holding a spare tire, a set of tools and at least enough luggage for a conservative week-end.

The top, wonder of wonders, actually looks good. All too often the British approach to a top is that it doesn't matter how it looks as long as it holds back some of the rain. The result of this attitude in the past has been runny noses among the prideful and a peering squint among the prudent. The new top fits tightly and does its job well without detracting from the appearance of the car in the least.

From a styling standpoint wire wheels are almost a necessity it would seem. The Italian styling does not lend itself to the use of disc wheels, even at the $135 reduction in price of the car with pie-plate running gear. The change from disc to wire is not an easy one, either, in case one changes one's mind later. We'll make this clear in a moment when we discuss the rear axle.

The new frame design is strictly a development of the one used on the Eyston-Miles record-breaking EX-179 streamliner. The chassis side members are box sections made of light steel pressings welded along the center line to form a sort of squared oval tube. The chassis sweeps outward from a point forward of the rear wheels to just aft of the front wheels, allowing a very low seating position between the rails. A total of six tubular cross-members and a heavy steel bridge at the cowl line give extreme rigidity. Further stiffening is provided by two longitudinal members running from the rear engine mounting back to the cross-member nearest the rear axle. The whole thing is as solid as a concrete bridge abutment.

Front suspension is the only hold-over, being similar to that used on both the TD and TF series cars, independent with double A-arms and coil springs. No stabilizer (anti-roll) bar is used and shock absorbers are of the Armstrong double piston type. Rear suspension is by fairly soft semi-elliptic springs riding in very high frame kick-ups.

The brakes also are new and much bigger with a total of 134.4 square inches of area. The drums have been increased by an inch in diameter and ¼-inch in width, now being 10 inches by 1.75 inches respectively.

The rear axle is a complete design change. It is practically a quick-change unit in that the entire gear assembly, ring, pinion, differential carrier and attendant bearings can be removed as a unit merely by pulling the axle shafts out a few inches and dropping the drive shaft. By having several of these carrier units handy at a race in the options of 3.7, 3.19, 4.1 and 4.55 to 1 practically any course condition can be met in minutes instead of hours—if one is that serious. Two different types of axle shafts are used; heavy double splined units for use with wire wheels and knock-offs and standard flange type axles for use with the four-bolt disc wheels. It is this that makes for expensive switches in the matter of wheel choice.

The new engine is both old and new. The design is strictly BMC and bears almost no resemblance to the old faithful XPAG and XPEG plants used in the past. It was first introduced in the Morris Oxford, the MG-ZA Magnette sedan and the Austin A50. The new engine is lighter and more powerful by about five bhp than the XPEG 1500 engine. The change is largely to the good except for a few inherent faults of the BMC head design.

The engine is a four-cylinder unit of typical BMC construction with a bore of 73 mm (2.875 in.) and a stroke of 89 mm (3.50 in.) for a total displacement of 1489 cc or 90.88 cubic inches. The factory rates the engine at 68 bhp as against 63 bhp found in the XPEG plant. Although lighter, the new engine is a very rugged item with a .200-inch increase in crankpin diameter over the older engines. The main journals are .040-inch smaller than the mains in the XPEG. A large overlap between rod journals and mains coupled with a position high in the block make for a very rigid crank layout that should last indefinitely and stand up under rough treatment even from the "stress 'em till they groan" boys.

Lubrication is full pressure and full-flow. The pistons are of the concave type which should allow goodly increases in compression over the stock 8.3 to 1 ratio although for reasons soon to be apparent not the brutal c.r. tolerated by the earlier engines. The rods in the new engine will be a boon to do-it-yourself types since the rod caps are set at an angle, making it possible to remove the rod and piston assembly *in toto* from the top of the block instead of separating the piston from the rod.

The head design is the only weak point in the whole car. The original design has been around for years and was obsolescent when fitted to the Austin Healey. For the average motorist it will make little difference but for the competition enthusiast, or for one who is interested in top miles-per-gallon performance at cruising speed, there are problems.

The biggest problem is that of restriction through the strange port layout. Intake ports are skimpy and, worse, siamesed with one small port serving two fairly generous intake valves. This is a common practice in tractor engines where torque and not engine speed is the main requirement but has been considered more than passé in sports car engine design. The main problem lies in one cylinder robbing another's cylinder's charge of fuel since the manifold and port capacity are too small to carry a sufficient charge for both. The two center exhaust valves also share a single port, a fault that makes exhaust tuning almost impossible.

It is apparent that the MG people recognize this problem fully. The head used on the Le Mans cars was essentially the same design but with much larger ports and a unique method of alleviating the intake problem. This head has the intake ports bored completely through to the spark plug side and a large balance tube connected these right-hand ports. The result was far better intake breathing and a larger charge of fuel in the system. There are also some very interesting carburetion layouts possible with this head that would be unfeasible if not impossible with the stock layout.

Although compression ratio increases may be limited by the vertical valve layout and flat combustion chamber, an increased turbulence may make up for it. The earlier XPEG chamber utilized slanted valves and a semi-wedge chamber which would tolerate compression ratios up to 11 to 1 on gasoline. Whether the new one will go that far remains to be seen.

Valve springs too may present a problem in competition. Though the engine uses a much heavier valve, spring pressures have been decreased to 77 pounds shut and 130 pounds open. Pressures in earlier engines were 114 and 150 pounds open and shut. Too the BMC springs are much shorter, some say too short for long life, although a wider helix and slightly heavier wire might make up for it. Earlier springs were double while the BMC coils are single wound. Under-cutting the spring seats and use of either compound or longer single springs would appear to be a must if cam characteristics are to be changed.

Despite the foregoing slap in the eye, the MG-A is best described in one word: "satisfactory." Regardless of whether one is interested in full bore competition or just plain fun-type driving Abingdon has come up with a car that should satisfy almost anyone, especially considering the price. At a base price of $2190 and an average total including tax, delivery and handling charges *and* wire wheels at $2490 there can be little or no beef from the customer. Tank mileage is from 23 to 28 miles to the gallon depending on conditions and the amount of driver exuberance.

Speed and power cannot be considered sensational in comparison with such cars as the Porsche Super and the slightly larger TR-2 but it is more than adequate and no sass need be taken from anybody, particularly on the open road. Leading an ordinary car over a twisting down-hill stretch with this MG-A is like taking a lamb to the slaughter and in the handling department the car can be considered among the very best. So can the workmanship.

Incidentally, you can sell that set of Whitmore wrenches upon delivery of the A-type; all the nuts and bolts are made to American standard hex sizes. 'Nuff said?

All things considered, the MG-A is no OSCA but then it doesn't cost 10 grand either.

SPECIFICATIONS

Base price	$2190
Wheelbase	94 in.
Tread—front	47.5 in.
Tread—rear	48.75 in.
Length O.A.	156 in.
Width O.A.	58 in.
Height with top up	50 in.
Ground clearance	6 in.
Weight (dry)	1911 lbs.
Tire size	5.60 v 15
Wheel size	4.00 x 15
Engine	4 cyl. OHV
BHP	68 at 5500 rpm

O.A. Gear ratios: (with 4.3 axle ratio)
1st—15.652
2nd— 9.520
3rd— 5.908
4th— 4.3
Reverse—30.468

Optional extras:
Heater
White wall tires
5.90 x 15 competition tires
Wire wheels
Adjustable steering column
Speed equipment (to be announced)
Gear ratios (see text)

DRIVING AROUND

with WALT WORON

WHETHER OR NOT the people who yelled to me from the curb, called from other cars at intersections, and spoke to me whenever I stopped in the MG-A will ever buy this new car is one thing; it certainly indicates more than a passive interest in the appearance and popularity of this radically restyled marque. Typical comments: "Is that a special or the new MG?" "What is that? The new MG? Wow!" "That the '56 MG? What a terrific difference!"

Probably the outstanding thing (to me anyway) about the MG-A outside of its new cloak is its amazingly good handling qualities; there just don't seem to be many ways you can get into trouble. You can slide into a corner, thru a corner, drift into it, correct the drift with a tick of the wheel and force a slide — practically any combination — and you're into and thru the corner with no strain. Steering response is very quick and the feel is light. It certainly puts the fun back into driving.

Going pretty fast on choppy surfaces (like a dirt washboard) you won't get into trouble unless you let the rear end come around on you (which it has a slight tendency to do). You'll pretty much float over them tho, with little complaint from your passenger, somewhat more from the steering wheel which transmits its objection to you in the form of vibration.

On a straight road you'll whip along at 50, 60, 70 mph without having to saw at the wheel, nor will a gust of wind from behind a huge rock tend to throw you off course. Clear up to its top speed of 97.6 mph, you have complete mastery of the MG-A. At top speed it has some tendency to weave, because of its lightness (2000 pounds) and quick steering, but won't if you watch it; it never feels airborne.

The MG-A is fine for darting in and out of traffic's tightest spots. Parking places open up that never seemed to be there before. The steering is light and positive and you have to expend very little effort in driving, outside of pumping the clutch and pushing the gearshift around. Starts are quite easy at all times, most of the time without choking. (This test was made in early fall, and winter might change the story.) The 90-cubic-inch, 68-hp BMC engine is not as silent as the stock-car engines many of us are used to, but each power pulse of this sometimes violently-running 4 is quite pleasurable.

The transmission gate of the modified Magnette transmission has been changed in that reverse is to the left and alongside 2nd gear. Reverse does not require pressing or pulling of the

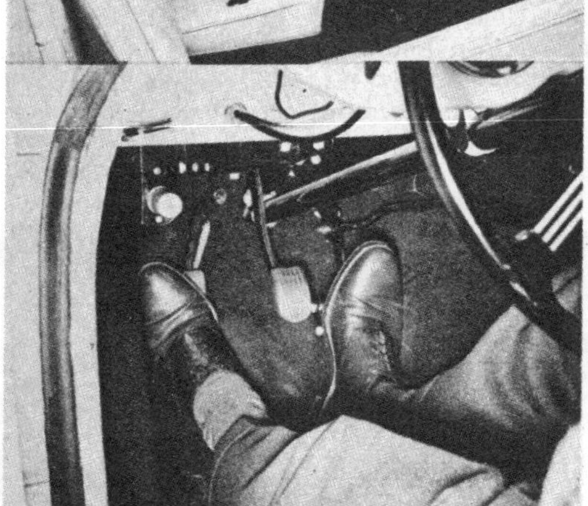

Engine compartment houses 91-cubic-inch, overhead-valve, 68-bhp engine using twin S.U. carburetors. Accessibility for servicing is now exceptional

PHOTOS BY BOB D'OLIVO

knob but takes some getting used to, as my 1st encounter with it at the MG gymkhana introduction pointed up. It also is not particularly easy to speedshift from 2nd to 3rd because of the narrow crossing of the H gate. After overcoming this, however, I was able to knock some time off the 1500 cc MG-TF which we tested last year. Here's the comparison:

	TF	A
Standing ¼-mile	20.8 (65.5 mph)	20.4 (68 mph)
0-60 mph	17.3	15.9
50-75 mph	6.8	6.5
50-75 mph	24.0	
50-80 mph		20.6

The fastest shifts were made by revving up to 4500 rpm, slowly engaging the clutch, razzing the throttle, then popping the clutch to get a quick bite and be on our way. I wound to 5500 rpm in 2nd and about the same in 3rd when I crossed the quarter-mile mark. (You could wind it tighter and *possibly* get a somewhat better time, but I certainly wouldn't recommend it as a general practice.) At the higher rpms, the engine had a peculiar whine, quite unlike the previous TF engine. The 30 to 50 mph checks were made in 2nd gear with a shift to 3rd at 5500 rpm. The 50 to 80 mph checks were made in 3rd gear up to 6000 rpm (just short of the red band on the tach) but with a shift into 4th, acceleration flattened out considerably. There just doesn't seem to be enough power to pull the 4.3 rear axle and give you any reserve for acceleration.

The brakes (last year's bigger Magnette brakes) feel particularly positive, stopping down from fast speeds with no strain and no swerve. After numerous acceleration checks, and later "road race driving" on our handling course, I encountered absolutely no indication of fade.

The side of the door is just below my shoulder and even during the most violent maneuvering, I was never thrown uncomfortably against it. The steering wheel sits down in my lap, at a good slant and in a convenient position for a stable 2-hand grip (see photo). The seats are thickly padded, extremely comfortable, molding well to your back. They both adjust back and forth on their tracks quite easily by means of a manual control, so your passenger can be comfortable too.

With the driver's seat all the way back I couldn't keep my legs out straight (which you sort-of come to expect in a sports car), but I found a comfortable resting place for my left knee against the door panel when I occasionally had to use the gears; when I was cruising on the highway I put my leg out straight, with my foot behind the clutch pedal. The brake and throttle are as close together as ever (see photo), causing me concern at times because the sole of my shoe would catch on the back of the brake pedal when I was trying to lift it quickly off the throttle. (The pedals are being moved farther apart on models now coming out.)

The white-on-black tachometer and speedometer are both immediately readable in their location on either side of the column (see photo), but I couldn't help getting the feeling that BMC was trying to economize by not providing more numbers on these 2 dials. Unfortunately, this feeling is bound to be heightened when you find that the panel is attached so flimsily that it moves when your knee hits it getting in or out. (John Beazley of Gough Industries, Los Angeles, tells me that the factory is going to provide bracing on future cars to prevent this.) The more important water temperature and oil pressure gauges (in one dial to the right of the centrally located radio speaker) could easily have been substituted for the fuel gauge (just right of the speedometer). The optional radio goes where the glove compartment could have gone at the right of the panel; Gough Industries has an optional locking compartment for the passenger's door.

With the doors now opening at the rear (hinged in front) instead of at the front as on previous MGs, it's not as easy to swing your legs in and out; your feet have a way of getting tangled up with the front part of the door. And on cars without a telescoping column (which is an optional extra now), you don't get any help from that quarter; instead you have to wrap yourself around the low wheel. With the top up, you double up and back in. Speaking of tops, I wish the British manufacturers would take a leaf out of Porsche's and DKW's book and provide tops that can be put up or down from the driver's seat instead of out in the rain and generally with the assist of another person.

There is no distortion thru the slightly curved windshield and the windshield posts are much too thin to create any blind spots. The hood drops off suddenly, so you're not apt to run over any sleeping pedestrians without seeing them. With top and/or side curtains up you needn't fear claustrophobia, for there is fair headroom and the outside world is still visible.

My one and only major complaint about the MG is directed at British sports-car builders in general: I hope that they will soon recognize the fact that performance (and more particularly, acceleration) is what the majority of the American motoring public desires. There seems to be little reason to saddle a potentially good-performing car like the MG with a 1½-liter engine that doesn't even allow it to hold its own against such cars as a '55 Chevy, Ford, or Plymouth when leaving a stoplight. Why not a bigger-displacement, more powerful engine —even if only for export? It certainly seems like it would help to up exports to the U. S. (which ranks only 4th in imports from the United Kingdom). And despite the fact that the Central Office of Information (London, Eng.) states that "there seems little doubt that these [sports-car race] successes have helped in the increased sales of this type of car in North America," what about their "race" against the U.S. stock car on every highway and (*Continued on page* 29)

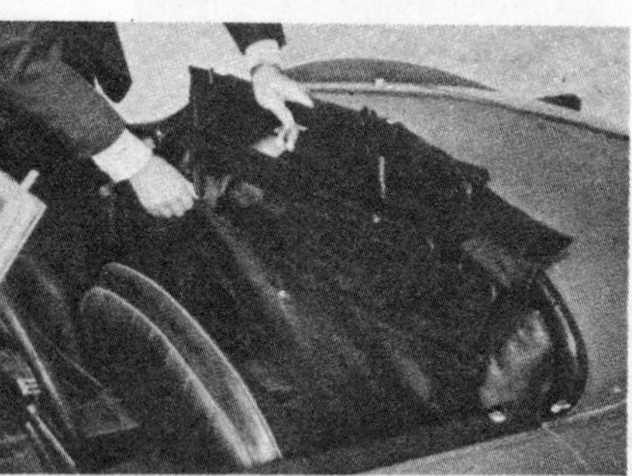
Good-fitting side curtains stow away in flap behind seats, are easy to install

Sleeker rear end includes shallow trunk compartment that holds spare tire, tools (standard equipment), and small amount of weekend luggage

MG and the Curves...

An Auto Age Staff Report

DO YOU REMEMBER what happened when the first MG-TD appeared on the American scene? Thousands of purists, remembering the truly classic lines of the older TC—with its huge wire wheels and sharply cutback front fenders and right-hand steering—cried that their favorite car had been ruined. Sure, the TD rode better, and it steered better, too, and handled just as well, but it just wasn't the same. There was an MG tradition, and it had been broken.

But before long there were even more TD lovers than you could shake a stick at and although the TC remained a collector's item, it was the TD that came to the fore in racing circles.

Then came that black day when the Porsche first made its appearance. It was immediately obvious that the MG would have to be faster to compete and suddenly the same purists who had bemoaned the passing of the TC now cried for a lighter, ultra-speedy streamlined MG to regain the honor of the *marque*.

But the British seemed to pay little attention. They had maintained all along that none of the MGs were intended for racing in the first place, and they saw no reason to redesign their car completely so that it could race successfully with the Porsches and similar ilk. They went along at their own quiet pace, bringing out a somewhat hotter TD called the Mark II, then a slightly modernized TF version with the Mark II engine, and finally a TF with a brand new 1,500-cc power plant. But by this time almost five years had passed and they were being threatened not only on the racing front but in the matter of sales. Something had to be done.

What *was* done surprised even the most avid of MG fans. First the factory announced that they were going back into active racing and before long they had produced a team of 1,500-cc prototype automobiles that were entered in the Le Mans race. There was never any attempt to win the race; all the directors hoped for was one or two finishers. That, they thought, would be a good start. At it turned out, they did quite well, placing two cars in 12th and 17th positions over-all.

Shortly after, it was announced that the new cars

MG designers thought they knew all the angles. And they did, for years. But suddenly the angles are gone—for good.

This is the way the "A" looked at the Frankfort, Germany, auto show, its first official public appearance in production form. Earlier, prototypes had performed extremely well at Le Mans.

were to be produced under the designation MG "A." We waited and waited and finally a few of the new cars drifted into this country. We grabbed one as soon as we could but in our hurry to get this report to you we had to settle on a car that was almost brand new—not the best thing for a real road test.

Before we had ever laid eyes on the new MG, we had heard some complaints strangely reminiscent of those that had accompanied the introduction of the TD model. Again some purists were sure it wasn't an MG at all. The *lines* were gone—replaced with (ugh) *curves.* Why, the new car looked like an Austin-Healey.

Actually the "A" does look like a Healey, but there's a good reason. Both cars were modeled after the original streamlined MG racing prototype—the Phillips MG —which ran at Le Mans in '52. You don't hear too many people complaining because American cars look alike these days. Why worry about the MG?

At any rate, we wanted to find out if this was truly an MG in every sense of the word. Here are our findings:

To begin with, this is the first MG ever built that really cradles the passengers. You sit *in* it rather than on it. The two bucket seats are extremely comfortable and leg room, especially for the driver, is vastly improved. There is, at last, a place to rest the previously neglected left foot and matters are made even better by the fact that the pedals are suspended. The whole car has amazing room for an MG. Pull the seats forward and you will find that the top folds neatly away behind them, out of sight. There is no glove compartment on the dash but both front doors contain generous map-and-utility pockets. The door cut-outs also serve to give more elbow room to driver and passenger. There is a fair-sized trunk, housing the spare tire and tools.

The dash panel itself is of a rather thin metal but equipped with a full range of instruments that are meant to be read, including a fuel gauge. Your right hand falls nicely on the gear lever.

Start the engine and you will hear a nicely muffled but unmistakable MG exhaust note. The "A" warms up quickly and you select first gear and take off, smoothly and with surprising snap. Perhaps the word "select" should not have been used in reference to first gear. There is often considerable trouble even finding first, and double-clutching is necessary at least half the time unless you think to slip the lever back into low just before coming to each dead stop. But once under way the gearbox proves to be a delight—short throw, rather good intermediate gearing—and shifts can be made so fast as to be almost unnoticed. Third gear is a very useful one, having a range between 10 and 70 mph.

When we thought we had our shifting down just right we made some acceleration runs and got rather good times in spite of the newness of the car. Zero to 30 mph time averaged a fraction over

Front end is a far cry from the old, boxy MG look; streamlining is excellent. Vents on hood near windshield exhaust heat from engine.

Passenger compartment is roomy, everything accessible. Note that defrosters are built in. Telescopic steering column is now optional.

Viewed from above, the A effectively shows off its beauty of line, heavily upholstered bucket-type seats. Windshield doesn't fold down.

Rear-end styling is particularly clean, there being no more external gas tanks or spare tires. Trunk is opened via an inside latch.

Road Test: MG and the Curves

5 seconds with two tries at 4.9. To 50 mph took 11.6 seconds and 60 mph was reached consistently in under 16 seconds with an average of 15.4. We did the standing quarter mile several times in 20 seconds flat. It is interesting to note that the "A" employs a 4.3 to one rear axle—obviously set up for speed rather than acceleration.

Top speed runs were somewhat less productive. We were able to squeeze no more than 91 mph out of the car but that was at 5,600 rpm and a well broken in MG "A" should be able to pull at least 6,000 rpm without any modifications. With the slightest degree of "tuning" this will be a genuine 100-mph car. Some of the boys will get a lot more than that out of it for racing.

When driven at speed on twisting roads the MG demonstrated its utter command of any situation in a relatively few miles. The steering wheel goes 2¾ turns from lock to lock and response on the road is so fast and positive that the driver is seldom conscious of having to do any steering at all. It is almost impossible to get "crossed up." As for cornering the car can be aimed once and then forgotten; it seems to guide itself around with absolutely no lean at all. This feels like an out-and-out competition car on corners, and the rest of the handling matches, even on fast bends that must be drifted under power. The car will set up its own drift; there is no need usually to snap it loose with a violent twist of the wheel as is the case with many softer-sprung automobiles. The ride is excellent. A nice amount of understeer, combined with ample power is usually enough to get you through most tough corners, even if you overplay your hand just a little coming in. Thus, many mistakes are forgiven. The MG is so stable that it gives the impression that you would be hard put to flip it. Over-all handling, in fact, was definitely superior to that of any other MG we have driven, excluding certain specials. It was interesting to note that while the "A" has the same wheelbase as all of the "T" series cars, the tread has been reduced by several inches.

We used the brakes brutally and there was never a trace of fade. Our tests may not have quite approached actual race conditions but they certainly exceeded any that are liable to pop up in normal—or even abnormal—touring. Our test car was equipped with knock-off wire wheels, a fact which probably helped to ward off brake fade, but these are optional equipment, the standard car being delivered with bored, bolt-on disc wheels. A heater and radio are available.

What did we like most about the car? Appearance, comfort and handling all rated high. There are a few annoying minor details, like a headlight dimmer switch that is almost impossible to reach unless your left leg is very long, too wide a gap in seat adjustment—from too close to too far away from the wheel and pedals in one jump—and a stupid little left-right indicator that is timed so that it never quite stays on long enough when you are waiting at a red light. But there has never been a car made that cannot be faulted and this MG has much on the pleasure side of the ledger. List price is only $2,195 and with its gas mileage of 28 mpg or better it will even make a first class economy car if that's what you're after. And if what you really want is a fine, dependable, beautiful sports-touring car this is your meat. ●

SPECIFICATIONS

ENGINE: four-cylinder, overhead valves; bore, 2.875 in.; stroke, 3.5 in.; total displacement, 90.88 cu. in. (1,489 cc); developed hp, 68 at 5,500 rpm; torque, 77.4 lb./ft. at 3,500 rpm; carburetors, twin 1½-in. SU; ignition, 12 volt; compression ratio, 8.3 to 1.

TRANSMISSION: clutch, single dry-plate 8-in. diameter; gearbox, four forward speeds and reverse with synchromesh on top three gears.

REAR AXLE RATIO: 4.3 to 1. (4.55 available as an optional).

SUSPENSION: front, independent with coils and wishbones; rear, semi-floating axle with semi-elliptic leaf springs; hydraulic piston-type shock absorbers all around.

BRAKES: Lockheed hydraulic on all four wheels with 10 in. brake drums; front, two-leading shoe; rear, leading and trailing; fly-off hand brake.

DIMENSIONS: wheelbase, 94 in.; track, 47½ in. front, 48¾ rear; width, 58 in.; height, 50 in. over-all; length, 156 in.; ground clearance, 6 in.; turning circle, 28 ft.; curb weight, 1,904 lbs.; tires, 5.60 x 15 disc wheels standard, wire knock-off type available at extra cost.

PERFORMANCE

ACCELERATION:
Zero to 30 mph: 5.0 seconds
Zero to 50 mph: 11.6 seconds
Zero to 60 mph: 15.4 seconds
Standing quarter mile: 20.0 seconds

TOP SPEED: 91 mph.

continued from page 26

Driving Around

city street? Everyone doesn't have a road course or mountainous road in his backyard (and wouldn't that be fun!).

ATTENTION: Uranium prospectors, farmers, hunters, miners, loggers, fishermen, service station owners, ranchers, plumbers, electricians — or anyone else who likes (or has) to traipse off the beaten track. If you're in need of a truck that will plow thru axle-deep mud or snow, and take you up the side of a hill where only motorcycle riders and fools dare tread, then you should get a Chevrolet truck fitted with Napco Powr-Pak 4-Wheel Drive (Napco Industries, Inc., Minneapolis, Minn.).

Rarely have I seen a person more enthusiastic than Chuck Lambert, who loaned me a half-ton truck. To hear him tell it, it would not only take a 70 per cent dirt trail in stride, but would do anything short of scaling a brick wall. (The Lambert Co., Ltd.—1202 E. Olympic Blvd., Los Angeles—distributors for Napco, supplying the bodies and 4-wheel conversions.)

Bill Babbitt (our Technical Editor) and I tried it up some of the roughest motorcycle hillclimb trails we could find. To the consternation of some 'cycle hounds, we scaled the hills with a minimum of effort. We took some extreme grades in 2nd gear with front-wheel drive engaged, and steeper ones in 1st gear, but **at no time were we peaked out in gear.** Nor does the truck buck or chatter when you lug down.

When we stalled out deliberately, the finger-tip-controlled vacuum brake (on the column) kept us from moving an inch backwards until we restarted and released it. The vacuum brake is extremely sensitive. The normal foot brake pedal is positioned a bit high off the floor.

Once you get onto the operation of the transfer case, there's no problem in shifting—even thru the 8 gears you can use with both front and rear drive. For a truck it is unusually easy to shift. You can shift in or out of 4-wheel drive at any speed, without clutching; you definitely want to watch your tach at all times tho, so you won't over-rev or lug the engine.

There was perceptibly more gear noise in high range than there was in 4-wheel drive. The quiet operation of the transfer case is probably due to its being mounted in rubber. Constant-velocity joints keep whip to an absolute minimum.

Another asset of the Napco Powr-Pak is the fact that it can be removed at trade-in time for use on your next truck; it takes no frame-cutting to install it.

My one unfulfilled desire was to mush thru snow to see if I could bog down the truck. The weatherman, however, did not cooperate—all he furnished was smog. With its amazing ability to push thru soft ground and tall weeds (it has 14 inches ground clearance), I seriously doubt if I would have bogged down in snow. But—it would have been fun to act like a snow rabbit. —**Walt Woron**

FAST AND FRIENDLY

The M.G.A. Offers Comfort and Performance at a Modest Price

WITH all the good will in the world, it is difficult, when trying to assess cars, to make fair allowances for differences in size, power and price. It is even more difficult to ignore personal preference and to try to gauge the probable reaction of that legendary character, the typical customer.

The brief notes on the new M.G.A. which follow are purely personal, but one has no fear of being alone when according it the praise which it deserves, because most present and future owners of the M.G.A. will be from the international group of drivers (its membership is still expanding rapidly in the United States) who almost instinctively take a smart and efficient little sports car to their bosoms.

The latest model in a long line has no mean reputation to uphold. It starts with the advantages of much good will and affection for its name, creditable racing performances by its prototypes, a very pleasant appearance and a modest price.

I first took over a production M.G.A. on a wet evening in London traffic. In spite of feeling tired and somewhat out of humour, it was not long before life again seemed worth while, and this was largely due to the infectious eagerness and the sweet handling qualities of the car.

What does the M.G.A. have to offer, bearing in mind that it has several potent competitors in the two-seater, open sports class? It is as good as or better looking than any of them, regardless of cost; it has a roomy and well-trimmed cockpit in relation to its size, its standard all-weather equipment is adequate and its price in the U.K. is under £900 total (its export price, ex works is only £595).

While the maximum speed and acceleration are not quite so high as those of larger engined rivals, so good are the steering and brakes that the usable performance under the very varied conditions encountered today is very little short of the faster, less economical cars and results in unexpectedly high averages with plenty of safety margin. Under the best conditions the standard model is capable of the 100 m.p.h. A somewhat inexperienced driver could learn with the M.G.A., with the certainty that it would treat him kindly and help him out of the occasional "tight corner."

Turning now from broad assessment to personal experience and preferences, there are small features both to praise and criticize. The cockpit is neat and comfortable and the seat can be adjusted to suit almost every reach. The seats themselves, of bucket type, are small but hold you well. Interior space is well utilized, giving plenty of elbow room and good big pockets in the doors. The shapely, slopeaway tail offers some interior luggage space, even though it contains also the spare wheel and fuel tank.

On the particular car which I drove, the gear box was on the stiff side and thus, with such a diminutive lever gear-changing was quite hard work, and as a result, reverse was too easy to snick by mistake. The gears engaged sweetly, very quick changes could be made between top and third, and all the ratios seemed to be well chosen. To obtain the full per-

The M.G.A. cockpit is well equipped and offers more than average space and comfort. Note the very short gear lever, fly-off handbrake and twin dials for engine and road speeds

formance the gears had to be used freely. I decided that I should have preferred an inch more lever and, having a rather short arm and a preference for steering "long" in a sports car, a slight rearward bend in it.

Large clear instruments are an asset, and the matched pair indicating speed and r.p.m. are easy to read and pleasant to look at. The positions of the panel light rheostat and the tell-tale light for the traffic indicators would be interchanged on my car; the former is inconvenient to twist between the main dials and the latter, with the driver holding the wheel, is obscured behind the right hand.

At the risk of appearing to pick on too many trivialities, I would add that switches dotted around the panel do not appeal to me, even if they are symmetrically placed, nor do I see any virtue in retaining the unconventional mid-panel horn push position. Again, a dip-switch situated well above the clutch pedal is not very convenient for a car in which gear changing is often likely to be very frequent. To my mind, a dip-switch for the right hand, placed Continental fashion on the steering column, would be preferable.

For a two-seater sports car of modest cost, quite lavish provision is made for both the small luxuries and the usual extras. This car carried in addition to the adjustable intensity panel lighting (which, for me, is a near essential) a separate map light, radio, heater, screen washer and twin horns.

A delicacy of curve and very pleasing proportions place this car ahead of most of its competitors in appearance

Standard all-weather equipment includes sturdy sidescreens, and the cockpit remained dry and free from draughts on the cold, wet evening on which I collected the car. There are no exterior door handles and it is not easy to reach through the heavily spring-loaded flaps at the bottom of the side screens and into the pockets to find the cords which operate the door latches.

With the hood up, visibility is still quite adequate. On the light coloured cars (this one was cream) reflections in the wide curved screen from the polished scuttle and chrome mirror and tonneau studs can be distracting.

It seems to me that the engine note which for so long has remained M.G. in spite of model changes, has altered a great deal in the case of the M.G.A. Although in certain export markets the right note is almost as important as the desired urge, I think we should err on the side of maturity rather than otherwise, in order to be considerate towards the many who do not share our enthusiasm for sports cars. The M.G.A. is not, however, high on my list of potential offenders in this respect.

In spite of the compactness of the car, the engine and components are accessible. This photograph tends to exaggerate the extent of the plumbing, much of which is concerned with the heater

When driving this model one is more conscious of the engine than was the case in the earlier series of cars, but it is most exhilarating—and the engine has no objection—when the r.p.m. needle shows better than 5,000. As an *aide memoire* may I mention that the capacity is 1,489 c.c., the stroke·89 mm, the compression ratio 8.15-1 and the maximum output 68 b.h.p. at 5,500 r.p.m. *The Autocar* road test fuel consumptions for gentle and hard driving were 38 and 25 m.p.g. respectively.

In case the criticism of several minor points may lead to an overall wrong impression, let me add that had I not been intrigued and very favourably impressed by the car, I should not have bothered to mention details at all. The important fact remains that this latest model—first of a new line—handles better than any of its predecessors and offers a safer, faster drive than anything else I have tried in its class. If I earned my bread and butter as an M.G.A. car salesman at home or abroad I would expect there to be jam on it most days of the week. I should also expect to find big smiles on the faces of customers when they checked in for routine service.

M. A. S.

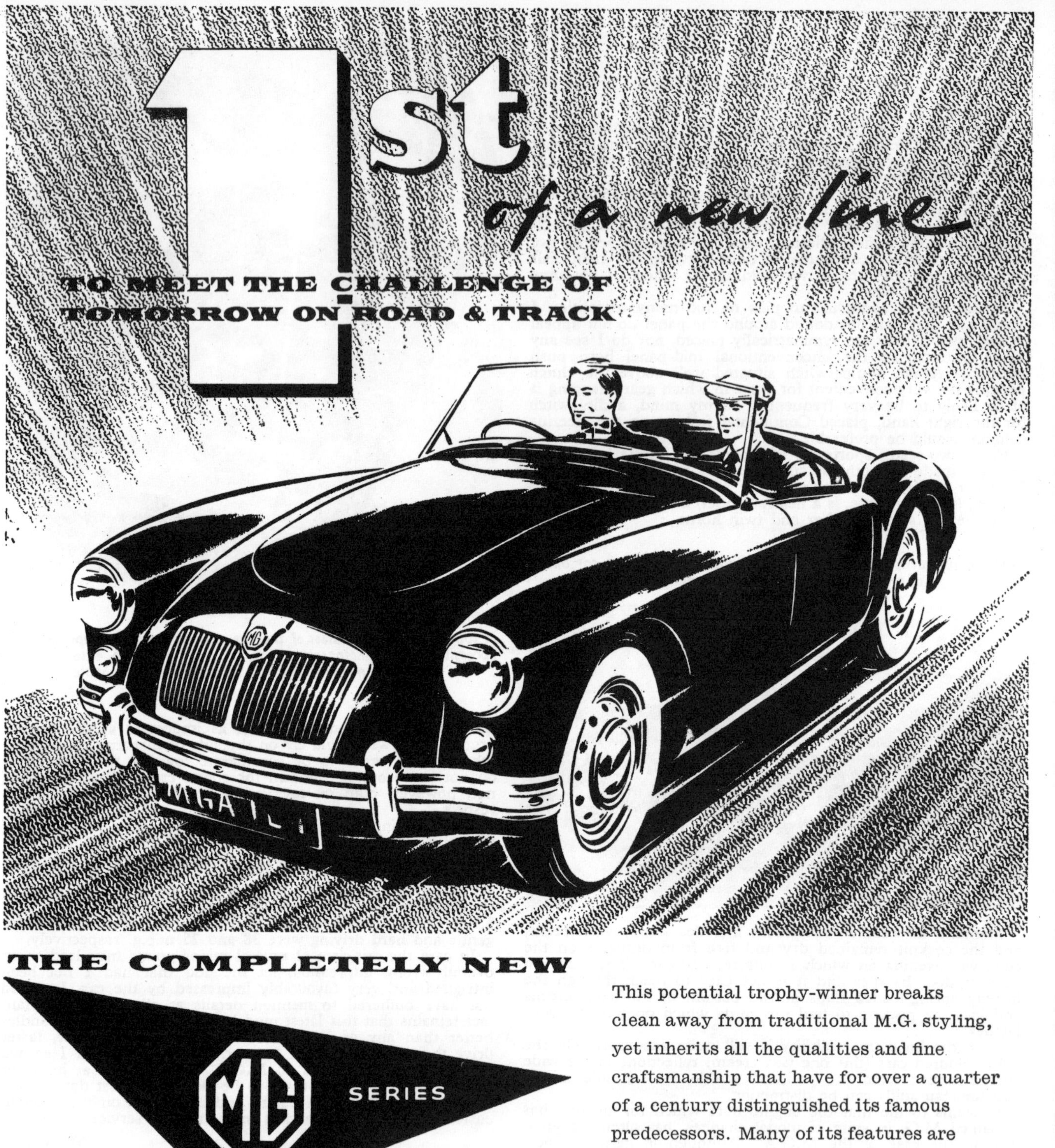

1st *of a new line*

TO MEET THE CHALLENGE OF TOMORROW ON ROAD & TRACK

£595. 0. 0. *Ex Works plus*
£249. 0. 10. *Purchase Tax*

This potential trophy-winner breaks clean away from traditional M.G. styling, yet inherits all the qualities and fine craftsmanship that have for over a quarter of a century distinguished its famous predecessors. Many of its features are identical to those embodied and tested in George Eyston's record-smashing M.G. Special. Faster . . . sturdier . . . safer, it holds the road like a limpet and its 1500 cc. O.H.V. engine puts up a performance that is quite exceptional.

Safety fast

PROFILED FOR PERFORMANCE

THE M.G. CAR COMPANY LIMITED, SALES DIVISION, COWLEY, OXFORD

London Showrooms: Stratton House, 80 Piccadilly, London, W.1
Overseas Business: Nuffield Exports Limited, Cowley, Oxford, and 41 Piccadilly, London, W.1

The roof of the coupé gives adequate headroom without spoiling the appearance. A wide wrap-round screen is used which, with very similar rear window and thin pillars, provides fair visibility. A badge bar runs across the handsome curved, but unmistakably M.G. grille

M.G.A. COUPÉ

SHORTLY before the 1955 London Show the traditional M.G. two-seater, which had been acknowledged for some twenty years as one of the world's pre-eminently successful, economical sports cars, emerged in a new form. Known as the Series A (or "A-type" among the sporting fraternity for whom it was and is built) it was the production version of prototypes proved at Le Mans in the classic 24 hours race, in which two of the three cars finished, the third having crashed.

The body, windcheating and handsome, was completely different from those of its forebears, and a low seating position was achieved by placing the floor level with the lower parts of the frame. This frame is made up of two main components of box-section shape, running longitudinally, and widely spaced to take full advantage of the body width and at the same time permit the sinking of the seats between them.

Now, with a basically similar but slightly improved specification comes the Series A fixed-head coupé, in which a smoother shape and a power increase are provided, with a modest increase in weight resulting from the additional coachwork. Owing in part to the enclosed body style, the top speed has now reached three figures. The 1½-litre (1,489 c.c.) B.M.C. engine remains much the same but, with the compression ratio still at 8.3 to 1, the brake horsepower has been raised from 68 to 72 at 5,500 r.p.m.

Instead of the fairly flat detachable screen of the open car, that of the coupé is considerably curved. It permits good upward vision in addition to a wide arc of view. The roof is high enough to provide plenty of headroom without appearing as an ugly bubble.

When the open car was tested, maximum speed data were obtained on one of the fine dual carriageway roads of the Continent, but the latest coupé felt more sprightly, even on first acquaintance, and it was decided to complete the test in England. This was made possible by the rapidity with which the model reaches 90 m.p.h., coupled with stability of a very high standard.

Average speeds are usually of little account, as traffic and road conditions vary so much in Britain, yet one or two are worth recording. For example, in a run from Winslow (Buckinghamshire) through Buckingham, Brackley, Bicester and Southam, heading north to by-pass Coventry on secondary roads, 52 miles were put in an hour in safety. On this run, which included 41 miles in the first hour getting clear of the heavy traffic of the London area, the m.p.g. proved to be 25—the lowest figure recorded during the test. On another run covering part of the same route but substituting some straighter stretches for the winding sections, an almost exactly similar average speed was recorded with an m.p.g. of 29.5.

From these examples, one can see that although the car is only a 1½-litre, it can cover the ground very quickly indeed, and in normal, fairly fast driving, about 28 m.p.g. might be expected. When the car was driven with fuel

Tail, braking, and indicator lamps are housed in a unit in each rear wing. There are substantial overriders; and swivelling ventilator windows are fitted in the sides. The locker lid is opened from inside the car

The gear lever is ideally placed on the transmission cover; there is an ashtray immediately behind it. Entry and exit are not easy even by sports car standards. The instruments are well placed but minor controls are scattered. There is a pocket on each side below the facia, and provision is made for radio

M.G.A. Coupé

top gear from speeds below 20 m.p.h., yet their characteristics are such that drivers would rarely, in fact, attempt to make such demands. With the A-type, however, one can and does leave the car in top when dawdling through city streets. Throughout the test, which covered a considerably greater mileage than has been possible with most other models tested during the fuel shortage, the car was made to work very hard; nevertheless, it kept its tune right up to the time it was returned to the factory, with the sole exception that an adjustment of the slow running became necessary.

There is little to fault in the engine itself, the unit being already well proved. The noise level is appreciable, yet provided the occupants are prepared to raise their voices a little, conversation may be carried on without difficulty at any speed. On the car tested some tappet noise could be heard. The overall note was rather harsh, giving the initial impression that the engine was working harder than it really was. It started well, hot or cold, and the water reached its normal running temperature very quickly.

The transmission proved free from vibration and, as far as could be judged, silent. The clutch is a happy compromise between the smooth take-up desired on normal road cars, and the bite required for fast getaways. On the car tested it was just a little slow in engaging, although there was no suggestion that it could not withstand hard use. For competition purposes a stronger unit might be preferred.

The gear box earns high praise as one of the best encountered. The central lever is perfectly placed where it comes immediately to hand, and, with the exception of reverse, all gears can be found smoothly. Reverse may be engaged simply by firm use of the lever, gentle pressure revealing some stickiness. For all normal road work the speed of the change is amply satisfactory. The position of the pedals is such that heel-and-toe changes are fairly easily made if the driver's foot is not unusually small; the ball of the foot remains on the brake pedal while the edge of the shoe may be used on the throttle. Positioning of the pedals for comfort is fair, but there is not quite enough room for the left foot to be slid easily off the clutch. The dip-switch position above the clutch pedal is very unsatisfactory. Its use at night while the car is being cornered quickly is difficult; there appears to be no reason why the switch should not be transferred to a more convenient site on the steering column.

The ride and adhesion of this latest car are so much better than those of nearly all its rivals that criticism may be made only with some hesitancy. It appeared on test that the spring dampers were set a little too firmly—a state

economy in mind, 35 m.p.g. could be exceeded. On a run cruising along gently at about 50-55 m.p.h., with the inclusion of some town driving, the m.p.g. was 33.8, this being achieved without any coasting.

The cruising speed in the United Kingdom is what the driver cares to make it in the prevailing circumstances. At 5,000 r.p.m. in top the road speed is 85 m.p.h.—well within the rev range. In practice, 80 m.p.h. is obtained so quickly (in less than half a minute even from a standstill) that it is seen very frequently even on short stretches of clear road. The unusually accurate speedometer will continue to climb quickly until 90 to 95 m.p.h. is reached, whereupon the acceleration tails off sharply. On the flat, two miles or more of clear road is required before one can be sure that the absolute maximum has been obtained.

Full-blooded in performance, the M.G. is yet the complete gentleman in town. The flexibility of the engine is outstanding. Many other cars are capable of pulling away in

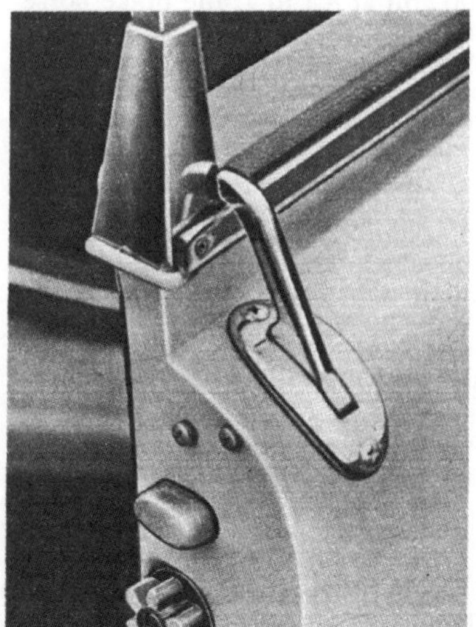

The unusual door handles are of a type most convenient on such a low-built car. In effect, one pulls the handles outwards to release the catches. In the closed position there are no projections which might catch in clothing

There is very little room in the locker for luggage, most of the available space being taken up by the spare wheel and the tool kit. On the car tested the locker lid had to be slammed hard before it closed securely. The large tool roll is held securely by two straps

of affairs which should be remedied easily. Apart from this harshness the ride and the stability are exceptionally good. If a bump is encountered on corners taken at relatively very high speed, there is slight wheel hop, but it must be emphasized that this occurs at speeds which few owners would want to achieve. The seats are well tailored, but slim occupants might wish to reduce the amount of lateral movement that their bodies are permitted in spite of the central armrest-cum-separator; the passenger would probably appreciate the addition of a grab handle. Also, slightly softer seat cushions would be welcome. The adhesion of the car on wet or dry roads is impressive; in fact, if any driver gets into difficulties he can blame himself and not the car.

The steering is light and sensitive; there are $2\frac{3}{4}$ turns from lock to lock which, with a turning circle of 28ft, make for easy manœuvring in confined spaces and instant response on the open road. There is little kick-back at the wheel in any circumstances; the driver may command the course with a light or heavy hand as he wishes, because there are no tricks with which he must become acquainted, no special techniques which must be employed to maintain accurate control.

Similar praise is not merited by the driver's position at the wheel, for if the seat is adjusted so that leg reach to the pedals is satisfactory, the chest is rather near the steering wheel, elbows having to be tucked in. Neither the door nor the armrest fouls the elbows, yet, as the steering column does not include an adjustment as a standard fitting, there would appear to be little reason why the column could not be shortened to bring the wheel a little closer to the facia.

It may be said fairly that the brakes are up to their task, in that they will slow or stop this fast car without any display of temperament. Their mechanisms are well protected against rain water, but their "bite" is not impressive, and the maximum retardation obtained was just under 85 per cent. Occasionally there was a little gentle pulling to one side or the other, and while no serious fade was encountered, one felt that a really fast Alpine descent would have to be undertaken with caution on this score. Few owners would have anything but praise for the braking system as a whole, yet the feeling exists that there is a limited margin of braking power for those who drive hard.

The hand brake lever is placed under the driver's left leg, where it is much more easily reached than might at first be thought. In a right-hand drive car, the driver's left hand falls on to it conveniently, and as the lever is of the fly-off type (in which the catch is pressed to secure the lever but not to release it) it may be used very easily to hold the car temporarily during traffic hold-ups on gradients.

While no criticism can be made of the general finish of the latest style coachwork, or of the materials used in its construction, it disappointed in two respects—there were draughts from the doors, and the wind-up windows shook at high speeds and on poor surfaces at other times.

All-round visibility is good, but not without fault. The windscreen is radiused so that the driver and passenger get a clear view through their own corners, but either suffers from distortion in the corner of the screen farthest from him. To this is added, for the driver, a badly sited rear view mirror which completely obstructs his view of the kerb-side wing. This is an inconvenience at any time, but would be an even more serious drawback on rallies where "round the pylons" driving tests are included. If no better mirror position can be found, most drivers would prefer an exterior fitting.

The arrangement of the minor controls leaves room for improvement. In the M.G. tradition the horn is mounted on the facia. Its position is central, where it may be reached by the passenger on rallies but (on a right-hand drive car) the driver's left hand can contact it instantly only if the wheel is in the straight-ahead position. A mounting on the steering wheel boss would be preferred. The lights are operated from the facia; again a switch near the steering wheel would be better. On the right of the facia is the control for the winking indicators; this, also, is not easy to reach and its mechanism is not precise. A tray under the facia would prevent the panel light reaching, and reflecting back from, the passenger's legs.

The car tested was fitted with some extras, including windscreen washers, wire wheels and a heater. The model

It would be difficult to provide first-class accessibility in such a compact, small car, but the filler caps, including that for the reservoir of the optionally extra windscreen washer, are easily reached. The twin carburettors have individual air cleaner-silencers. Fresh air is taken through a wide diameter pipe to the heater unit, mounted on the bulkhead, from the radiator grille

M.G.A. Coupé

also has provision for radio. The heater was tried out only in mild weather, but an impression was gained during some high-speed runs in a chilly dawn that its power was considerable, and that its efficiency was aided by the quick warming up of the cooling system. At any temperature it is not easy to obtain draught-free fresh-air ventilation.

Ease of entry and exit are poor even for a sports car. The driver has, of course, the extra obstruction of the steering wheel, and unless he can lean across the passenger seat while getting in he must disport himself with flexibility. The luggage space in the tail locker is limited to that sufficient for a shallow suitcase, most of the room being taken up by the spare wheel, but this coupé does have a little stowage space for soft articles behind the seats, the backrests of which may be folded forward. This extra space is not found in the open model, in which provision must be made for hood stowage.

The lighting system is good for about 80 to 85 m.p.h., and there is a map light on the passenger side. The top of the facia, in effect a continuation of the bonnet, is finished in polished cellulose and causes reflections in the screen. Underbonnet accessibility is not such as to inspire the amateur to great tasks of maintenance and repair, but filler caps, ignition equipment and carburettors are reached easily.

The M.G. coupé is as pleasant to drive as it is to look at. It is an excellent successor to a famous line, with fine road-holding and a performance which is worthy of the manufacturer. Where the going is tricky it should prove capable of holding its own against much more powerful rivals with larger engines.

M.G.A. COUPÉ

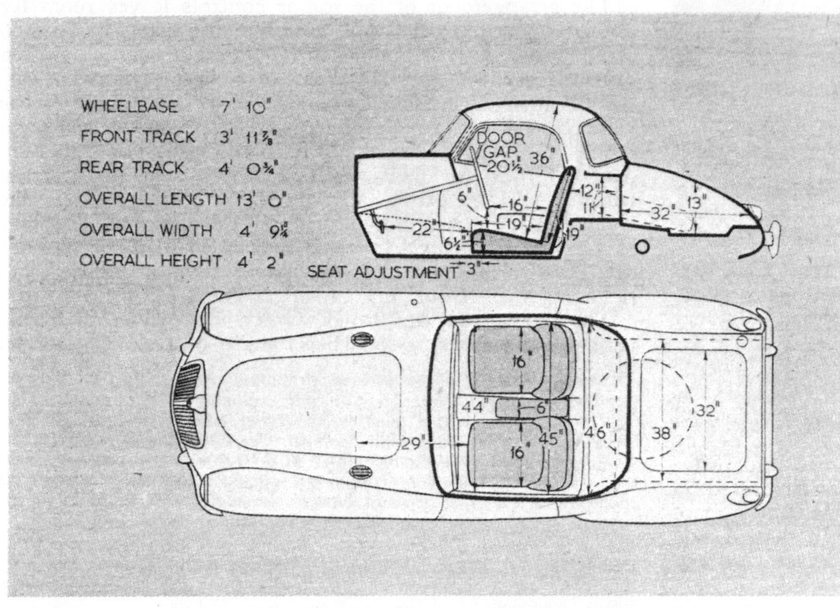

Measurements in these ¼in to 1ft scale body diagrams are taken with the driving seat in the central position of fore and aft adjustment and with the seat cushions uncompressed

DATA

PRICE (basic), with coupé body, **£699.**
Purchase tax, **£350 17s.**
Total (in Great Britain), **£1,049 17s.**
Extras: Wire wheels **£25 17s 6d** plus **£12 18s 9d** purchase tax. Heater **£11 15s** plus **£5 17s 6d** purchase tax. Adjustable steering column **£1 17s 6d** plus **18s 9d** purchase tax.

ENGINE: Capacity: 1,489 c.c. (90.88 cu in).
Number of cylinders: 4.
Bore and stroke: 73.025×88.9 mm (2.875×3.5 in).
Valve gear: o.h.v., pushrods.
Compression ratio: 8.3 to 1.
B.H.P.: 72 at 5,500 r.p.m. (B.H.P. per ton laden 66.0).
Torque: 77.4 lb ft at 3,500 r.p.m.
M.P.H. per 1,000 r.p.m. on top gear, 17.0.

WEIGHT (with 5 gal fuel): $18\frac{13}{16}$ cwt (2,107 lb).
Weight distribution (per cent): F, 52.2; R, 47.8.
Laden as tested: $21\frac{13}{16}$ cwt (2,443lb).
Lb per c.c. (laden): 1.64.

BRAKES: Type: Lockheed. F, two-leading shoe; R, leading and trailing.
Method of operation: hydraulic.
Drum dimensions: F, 10in diameter; 1¾in wide. R, 10in diameter; 1¾in wide.
Lining area: F, 67.2 sq in. R, 67.2 sq in (123.2 sq in per ton laden).

TYRES: 5.90-15in.
Pressures (lb per sq in): F, 17; R, 20 (normal). F, 21; R, 24 (for fast driving).

TANK CAPACITY: 10 Imperial gallons.
Oil sump: 7 pints.
Cooling system: 10 pints (plus 0.65 pints if heater is fitted).

TURNING CIRCLE: 28ft (L and R).
Steering wheel turns (lock to lock): 2¾.

DIMENSIONS: Wheelbase: 7ft 10in.
Track: F, 3ft 11⅞in; R, 4ft 0¾in.
Length (overall): 13ft.
Height: 4ft 2in.
Width: 4ft 9¼in.
Ground clearance: 6in.
Frontal area: 15.08 sq ft (approximately).

ELECTRICAL SYSTEM: 12-volt; 51 ampere-hour battery.
Head lights: Double dip; 42-36 watt bulbs.

SUSPENSION: Front, independent, coil springs. Rear, semi-elliptic.

PERFORMANCE

ACCELERATION: from constant speeds.
Speed Range, Gear Ratios and Time in sec.

M.P.H.	**4.3 to 1**	**5.908 to 1**	**9.520 to 1**	**15.652 to 1**
10—30	—	8.3	4.7	—
20—40	12.7	7.7	4.7	—
30—50	12.0	7.5	—	—
40—60	12.2	8.2	—	—
50—70	13.7	9.3	—	—
60—80	16.6	—	—	—

From rest through gears to:

M.P.H.	**sec.**
30	4.7
50	10.8
60	15.0
70	20.1
80	29.1
90	45.2

Standing quarter mile, 19.3 sec.

SPEEDS ON GEARS:

Gear		M.P.H. (normal and max.)	K.P.H. (normal and max.)
Top	(mean)	100.5	161.7
	(best)	102.0	164.2
3rd		58—78	93.3—125.5
2nd		38—47	61.2— 75.6
1st		20—26	32.2— 41.8

TRACTIVE RESISTANCE: 20 lb per ton at 10 M.P.H.

TRACTIVE EFFORT:

	Pull (lb per ton)	Equivalent Gradient
Top	226	1 in 9.8
Third	292	1 in 7.6
Second	444	1 in 5.0

BRAKES (at 30 m.p.h. in neutral):

Efficiency	Pedal Pressure (lb)
51 per cent	25
66 per cent	50
85 per cent	75

FUEL CONSUMPTION:
28 m.p.g. overall for 543 miles (10.1 litres per 100 km).
Approximate normal range 25-34 m.p.g. (11.3-8.3 litres per 100 km).
Fuel, premium grade.

WEATHER: Dry, slight breeze.
Air temperature 61 deg F.
Acceleration figures are the means of several runs in opposite directions.
Tractive effort and resistance obtained by Tapley meter.

SPEEDOMETER CORRECTION: M.P.H.

Car speedometer:	10	20	30	40	50	60	70	80	90	100
True speed:	10	20	30	40	50	60	70	80	90	99

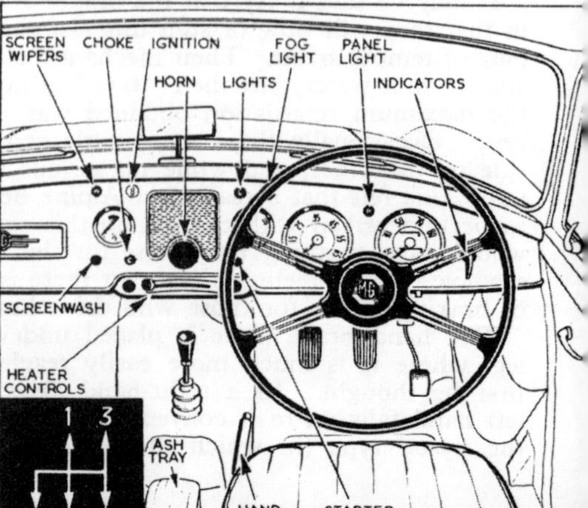

AS GOOD AS IT LOOKS..

New MG A bears out the promise of its appearance, says Bryan Hanrahan after road-testing it

THE Americans may not be able to build sports cars, but they have an unerring eye and those beckoning dollars for good British and Continental mounts.

So now more than half the production of the new MG A is being shipped from England straight across the Atlantic.

That means we don't get many at all—but it does not explain the shrinking violet tendencies of British Motors Corporation and the big MG distributors out here when it comes to the matter of a road test.

The A is a grand little car, and without going into the history of the MG breed, it certainly justifies the renowned "Safety First" slogan more than any of its predecessors have done.

Notwithstanding, this road test had to be done in a not quite run-in privately-owned vehicle. If the figures are a fraction behind what they should be, company interests and my nervous right foot under the eye of the owner are to blame.

With this reservation, I am satisfied that the data here gives a pretty accurate picture of this little beauty's performance.

A Preamble

If you are going to read this road test with the idea of getting some value out of it, a little exercise in perspective is necessary.

Don't compare the car's performance with either the Triumph or the Austin-Healey. Engine capacity is half-a-litre down on the Triumph and a full litre less than the Austin—and the price of the standard MG (£1256) gives away £200 to £300 to either of its bigger rivals.

On the road the MG has a personality all its delightful own. Breeding is the reason for this. Years of experience with small sports models

TAIL, tenacious on curves, responds instantly to the steering-wheel.

SEATS give excellent support, controls fall readily to hand, arm-rest on transmission tunnel adds extra comfort—but speedo, at extreme right, can't be seen by passenger. BELOW: Engine is readily accessible; so is the brake-and-clutch master cylinder (top left).

and record-breakers have gone into the design.

Prototypes first appeared in public at Le Mans in 1955. This was part of an extensive proving programme which embraced high-speed running at Montlhery, on the Nurburgring and in the Alps. Only recently production models scored well in their class in the Mille Miglia.

In standard trim it is not a true 100 m.p.h. car—95.8 was my flying quarter-mile speed—although only slightly favorable conditions will bring up the century.

However, special tuning data and equipment is available from the manufacturer, and I would imagine the car could be worked up to 105 m.p.h. or so with very little trouble.

Acceleration, as one would expect again falls off rather markedly after 80 m.p.h. (My word, what we demand from 1½-litres these days!)

On the Road

I slid into the driving seat and made my first acquaintance with the MG at 6 o'clock on a cold, windy morning.

After the first couple of miles I knew it was something specially good. There was never any hesitation in putting one's hand on to the necessary control—they happen to be placed just right. This is what I mean by breeding.

The seat is small, but gives excellent support. It is upholstered in leather—a minor but reassuring point.

Some five inches of gear lever sends instant and clear messages to the four-speed box through near-unbeatable synchromesh.

The engine had warmed by this time, and a couple of powerful headlights (it was still dark) urged the car along.

The first bend, well illuminated by the beam spread, came up. Brakes, gears and throttle worked together in inspiring harmony, and the car seemed to settle down even more firmly on the road as it went around.

Yes, it had to be steered. But no conscious effort was needed to do so, which is the highest tribute I can pay the rack-and-pinion mechanism, endowed with spot-on precision, directness and light action.

On the next corner I gently abused her. Dropping a cog too low, I trod on the acceleration as I entered. We proceeded broadside for a few feet, front and rear end balanced perfectly by that marvellous steering until the wheels gripped on a better patch of road.

Composed and orderly, the MG made off like a dart.

Needless to say, I had forgotten the owner in the first few exciting minutes at the wheel. He didn't seem to mind, though. He was good enough to allow a really thorough test to be carried out.

She was running so smoothly and

sweetly that I had to make a deliberate mental check of her qualities.

Nothing so far invited criticism except a small reflection in the curved screen. The hood was up, but I could see clearly in all important directions.

Speed and Brake Tests

At the test strip I consulted the rev counter as I ran the engine up to its useful maximum of just over 5000 r.p.m. in the intermediate gears in readiness for the first timed standing quarter.

Six runs were made in all. After four we checked the times—identical.

One would have expected a progressive improvement as the familiarisation process went on—but no. This MG had befriended me; there was no need to court her affections or allow for cranky ways.

So, the standing quarter stood at 19.9 seconds, and the watches returned a mean 95.8 m.p.h. for the flying quarter-mile.

Into the acceleration runs—0-50 in 9.9 sec. Not a trace of clutch slip, but wheelspin had to be watched.

Zero to 60, to 70, to 80 m.p.h.; that sweet little engine hammered out each figure four times.

Was it upset? Not a bit of it. The same remarkable consistency throughout.

The idling note never changed, and when switched off the engine died immediately: no fumes, no smells, no variation on the water temperature gauge.

The brakes had been punished on the acceleration runs to heat them up, so we immediately did the 30 m.p.h. to a stop—32 feet 3 inches on damp bitumen!

***HOOD** has generous rear window, fits well, and doesn't let in the weather; but, like most sports cars, MG A looks better without it.*

***CORD** in top of door recess releases the latch—there are no external door handles. Behind panel, it can't be worked accidentally.*

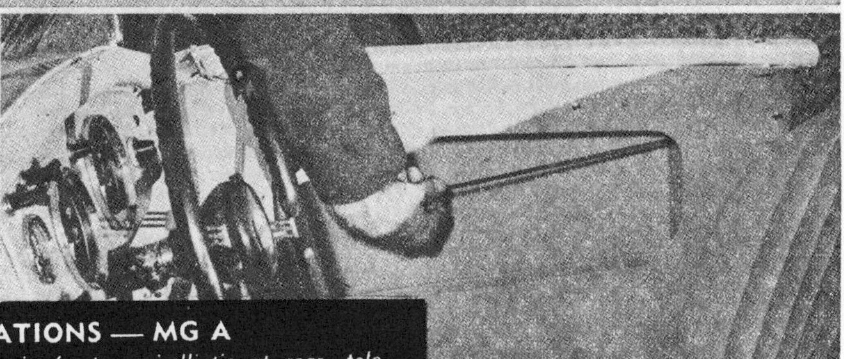

MAIN SPECIFICATIONS — MG A

ENGINE: 4-cylinder o.h.v.; bore 73.025 mm., stroke 89 mm., capacity 1489 c.c.; compression ratio, 8.15 to 1; rated h.p., 13.2, developed 68 at 5500 r.p.m.; twin SU semi-downdraught carburettors, electric fuel pump, 12-v. coil ignition.

TRANSMISSION: 4-speed gearbox, floor lever, synchromesh on top three; single dry-plate clutch; hypoid bevel final drive, 4.3 to 1 ratio.

CHASSIS: Separate, box-section.

SUSPENSION: Coil and wishbones in front, semi-elliptic at rear, telescopic hydraulic shock absorbers.

BRAKES: 10in. hydraulics, 2 leading shoes front; lining area, 134.4 sq. in.

STEERING: Rack-and-pinion, 2 2-3 turns lock-to-lock, 28ft. turning circle.

DIMENSIONS: Wheelbase 7ft. 10in.; track, front 3ft. 11½in., rear 4ft. 0¾in.; length 13ft., width 4ft. 10in., height 4ft. 2in.; ground clearance, 6in.; weight, 17cwt. unladen.

FUEL TANK: 10 gallons.

PERFORMANCE ON TEST

CONDITIONS: Cold, wet, damp bitumen, longitudinal breeze, two occupants, premium fuel.

MAXIMUM SPEED: 97 m.p.h.

FLYING quarter-mile: 95.8 m.p.h.

STANDING quarter-mile: 19.9sec.

MAXIMUM SPEEDS in gears: First, 27 m.p.h.; second, 44; third, 68; top, 97.

ACCELERATION from rest through gears: 0-30, 3.9sec.; 0-40, 6sec.; 0-50, 9.9sec.; 0-60, 12.6 sec.; 0-70, 18.9 sec.; 0-80, 24.8sec.

ACCELERATION in top and third gears (third in brackets): 10-30, 10.9 sec. (7); 20-40, 10.4sec. (5.2); 30-50, 10.6sec. (7); 40-60, 11.2sec. (8); 50-70, 12.8 sec. (—); 60-80, 16sec. (—).

BRAKING: 32ft. 3in. to stop from 30 m.p.h.

PETROL CONSUMPTION: 42 m.p.g. at 30 m.p.h.; 33 at 60; 36 m.p.g. overall.

SPEEDOMETER: Accurate at 30 m.p.h.; 3 percent fast at 60, 5 percent fast at 90.

PRICE: £1256 including tax

Nor did they at any time lose their smooth power, or cause the car to deviate off course.

We confirmed them with a 40-mile run through the hills, which was an exhilarating experience.

Pause for mental digging.

NOISE.—Engine extremely quiet, exhaust very fruity under load, wind not obtrusive up to almost 80 m.p.h.

HOOD.—Slight flapping on occasions, but not a drop of water inside and no draughts unless hand-signalling. Better stowed and erected by two people.

COMFORT.—Like being in bed.

WIPERS.—Cleared lots of screen, but two speeds would be welcome.

SMALL CONTROLS.—Horn push in traditional place on dash—not the best spot. Flashing indicator control on the dash, too.

SERIOUS FAULT. — Speedometer on right where passenger cannot see

(Continued on page 56)

The snow-capped peaks of the Alpes Dauphine made an impressive background as the M.G. was halted for photography on the long downhill run towards Poligny from the 4,000-ft. summit of the Col Bayard.

A GARLAND for a LADY

By E. H. ROW

THERE is a saying that a good big 'un will always beat a good little 'un; but it does not always apply in motoring. Take for example, reporting a Continental rally. While a big car may provide greater luxury and carry a lot of luggage, nine times out of ten it drinks more fuel, particularly if driven fast, and is far less easy to park on narrow mountain passes and other places where competitors need all the road there is. That was why, for an assignment to cover one of this year's major events, my mind immediately turned to something just big enough for two people and a minimum of luggage, fast enough to insure against "running out of rally" before the finish, and sufficiently economical at high cruising speeds to keep within the statutory car allowance.

A brief but brisk acquaintance with an M.G. A suggested that it should fill the bill, and a call to Abingdon clinched the deal—one of the cars which had already been used for the Circuit of Ireland Trial but was not eligible for the rally because open sports cars were barred. Despite very limited luggage room, the addition of a luggage rack on the boot lid and being very very firm about how much photographic gear could be taken, solved that problem; and to enable whoever was not driving to snatch a little sleep, a headrest was fixed to the passenger's seat.

Normally, after leaving the mid-day Dover-Boulogne ferry, the Bellevue at Montreuil makes a convenient lunch stop, but on this occasion, with the sun shining and the M.G. cruising nicely, well within itself, at 75-80 m.p.h., Montreuil went by, and Amiens and Breteuil; finally, at Meaux, we decided that this sort of thing was absurd—eating was a serious occupation on that side of the Channel, and when in France one should do as the French do. The size of the portions and the subsequent bill emphasized the advantages of our usual venue.

The Hotel des Roches at Nemours, some 15 km. down N7 from Fontainebleau, had been recommended as an unpretentious but worthwhile night stop, and thither we aimed ourselves. Leaving Boulogne at about midday, 204 miles is a reasonable run south, provided one does not tarry overmuch, and we arrived at this small, fairly simple hotel quite early in the evening. Spotlessly clean, hot water (out of the *froide* tap, as usual) really hot, and food in keeping with a Michelin cooking star, made a good impression, as also did the pleasantly reasonable *oddition*. High spot was when the chambermaid, who burst into my bedroom to make up the bed while I was in a state of considerable undress, shrugged the whole thing off with a "What does it matter? We are both married," and got on with her business.

Unpretentious night stop at Nemours, south of Fontainebleau on N.7, the Hotel des Roches provided comfortable quarters, good food and a lock-up garage for commendably few French francs.

do not run properly on any old fuel will once more instal a manual ignition control.

As the day wore on and the sun got hotter, *la famille Clot* in their 2CVs and assorted motorized two-wheelers, invaded the roads, intent upon Sunday picnic or fishing expedition. Perforce our progress was slower than planned, for your weekend accident, although probably of a different variety, is just as easy to have on a fine Sunday in France as it is in England.

Under such conditions it would have been foolish to follow N.6 right into Lyons where, in early evening, there is the inevitable embranglement with all the home-coming week-enders before getting to the right bridge across the Saône. So at Tournus we took N.75, which goes down through Bourg-en-Bresse and onto the Lyons by-pass on the outskirts of that city. In the event not much time was saved because, as in so many other places in France at the present time, a considerable amount of road development was going on. For long stretches, speed was reduced to a crawl over sections where the route had been stripped to its foundations.

Following competitors up the timed climbs of the various mountain passes provided some interesting studies of suspension behaviour. Here is the Thunnissen/Meartens Chevrolet on the climb to the Auberge du Pin near Valence.

With Valence our next objective, a cut across by secondary road was necessary next morning to join N6 at Sens. Although there was little fuel left in the M.G.'s tank, I reckoned it would be sufficient to get us on to the main road. Soon, however, the S.U. pump began to make thirsty sounds and one started to realize how few and far between are garages on the by-roads of this part of France. Hamlet after hamlet went by with not so much as a roadside pump and, when we eventually did strike a garage, it had commercial grade fuel only. With its 8.3 to 1 compression ratio, the M.G. does not care for such tipple, but it was that or nothing, if only in small quantities The anvil chorus which accompanied our further progress until something better offered, resurrected the hope that, some time, some manufacturer of cars that

What with the heat and the dust, a fine old thirst developed by the time we got to Bourg, but madame at the Hotel de l'Europe, who spent several years in Newcastle-on-Tyne, understands the brewing of a cup of real English tea. There was an even greater collection of exotic birds in the back garden than the last time I was there, including some Japanese ducks, which look exactly as ducks from that country might be expected to look. The son of the house also has a large indoor aviary, and by way of variety is thinking of adding an anaconda to his collection!

Once past Vienne traffic thinned out considerably and once again the M.G. could be motored at a cruising speed of around 80 m.p.h. Indeed, over the long, smooth straight between St. Rambert and St. Vallier, it was pushed hard

Considerable road work is going on throughout eastern France, particularly regarding major improvements to awkward sections. This example on N.85 south of Gap shows the viaduct which is being built to by-pass a dangerous S-bend.

just to "see what she'd do." The result was a 95 m.p.h. reading on a speedometer which, although unchecked, was known to be not far out. Considering the increased wind resistance induced by having the hood down and a largish suitcase strapped on the outside of the tail, this was not bad, especially as, hood up and otherwise unladen except for driver and passenger, a similar model, road tested in September 1955, had returned a mean maximum only 2.8 m.p.h. better. Subsequently, we learnt that "our" car had had little done to it in the way of mechanical adjustment since the Circuit of Ireland. In all, despite a multitude of assorted frustrations, the road average for that day (315 miles) worked out at 47.6 m.p.h. and fuel consumption 29 m.p.g.

In the Guide Michelin the Hotel de l'Europe at Valence is given a cooking star. It is also rated as "very comfortable," but being awakened several times during the night by an earthquake-like vibration due to the railway which runs under the hotel, we thought the appelation hardly justified: and it may have been because two hot and rather tired Englishmen expressed preference for the rather limited cold table, rather than the *specialités de la maison*, that the dining-room service was unspeakably poor.

A Study in Suspensions

As the rally came trickling in before dawn, the M.G. trickled out in the direction of the first daylight eliminating test—the climb to the Auberge du Pin. Like all the nine other tests which were to follow during the next couple of days, this was rather fun. The plot, in watching these timed hill-climbs, was to tuck in behind a competitor on the starting line, follow him up to some convenient space where the car could be pulled off the road while Maurice worked his camera and then, when sufficient exposures had been made, wait until another contestant hove in sight and follow him either to the next vantage point or to the finish of the climb. Actually, the M.G.'s full performance could seldom be used because, with the exception of the bigger Gran Turismo models at the head of the procession, it

The advantage of a small car in reporting a rally is the ease with which it can be parked in odd corners out of the way of competitors, in this instance by the communal washing trough in Saillans.

". . . when it came to converting miles per gallon into litres per 100 kilometres by mental arithmetic, I gave up."

A GARLAND for a LADY

was rather the competitors that obstructed us than we them. Nevertheless, plenty of opportunity was provided for studying the action of various forms of rear suspension when cornering at the limit—the advocates of i.r.s., and particularly the swing axle variety, appeared to have something.

Soon afterwards our navigation went wrong and we took a turning down a narrow pass not, apparently, even considered worthy of a name, but, as it turned out, a short cut. Down and down we went, hairpin following crazy hairpin, the surface mostly packed earth and the road never much more than a car's width. Mountain motoring in a hurry for the first time, Maurice remarked how fortunate it was that the Kwells were in the door pocket rather than in the luggage boot!

While the rally went down to Monte-Carlo for a night stop, we planned to stay put somewhere further north and meet the procession again as it came by the following day. So, after watching the tail-enders up the Col des Leques, including the touring class which, while not competing for the main awards, pressed on with as much verve as the rest, we debated the relative merits of an "early to bed and early to rise" at the Hermitage Napoléon at Digne, or a later retirement and lie-in at Gap. With the prospect of a 36-hour stretch ahead, the latter seemed the better idea.

One disadvantage of driving on the Continent in a car like the white M.G., particularly if one's French leaves something to be desired, is its attraction for onlookers wherever one stops. Between Die and Digne a group of roadmakers revealed a surprising knowledge of things automotive. In Gap, when the M.G. was refuelled, a similar thing occurred. But it was even worse on the Col Bayard. Parked in an orchard together with the fire brigade and gendarmerie, the M.G. was quickly surrounded by police and firemen who bombarded us with questions. With most of these I managed to cope, but when it came to converting miles per gallon into litres per 100 kilometres by mental arithmetic, I gave up.

The cost of high-speed hill-climbing and keeping the foot down over mile after mile of twisting mountain roads was well illustrated when we filled up at Grenoble, no more than 24.8 miles having been covered for each gallon of fuel, as compared with the previous day's figure for a far higher average speed, and 27.5 between Boulogne and Nemours —our fastest run to date.

From Grenoble to Belfort we forsook the rally route, cutting smartly up to Belfort via Lons-le-Saunier and Besançon, thereby narrowly escaping parting with a large number of francs. One understands that, by introducing their Code de la Route, the French mean to be obeyed. In one village, although speed was certainly below the prescribed limits, the sound of our passage in second gear was sufficient to rouse an unoccupied gendarme who stepped out, stopped us and, with much finger wagging, delivered a homily in which the word *doucement* occurred far too frequently for my peace of mind; in fact, by the time he eventually signalled us on, my wallet was almost at the ready.

Through the night, cruising speed down to 55-60 m.p.h., through Nancy, Metz and Luxembourg, and on to the Nürburgring, each of us in turn envying the one who slumbered by his side and mentally vowing "never again," as one is apt to do under such circumstances, the need for refuelling stops diminished as, at this reduced pace, the M.G. was covering no fewer than 44.6 miles to every gallon.

Wherever the M.G. halted it became a focal point of interest.

And so, from the Ring, down Eifel valleys strangely reminiscent of parts of Devonshire, even to the reddish earth, we came to the lowlands and the last flat stretch between vivid tulip fields and the bright, clean villages of Holland to Noordwijk and the finish—1,746 miles from our starting point in five days and at an overall fuel consumption of 31.1 m.p.g. As we crossed the Dutch frontier and the customary festoon of tulips was draped over the M.G.'s bumpers, a spectator who had been eyeing the car with obvious admiration, was heard to murmur *"Bloemenhulde voor een dame"*—"a garland for a lady."

How right he was.

The MG's side curtains snap on to give protection against storms or cold weather, but no window ventilation adjustment is possible

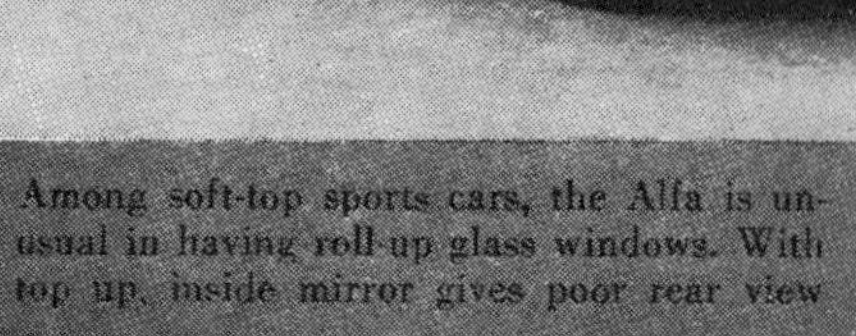

Among soft-top sports cars, the Alfa is unusual in having roll-up glass windows. With top up, inside mirror gives poor rear view

Sports cars, both imported and domestic, are achieving increasing popularity in the United States, and for good reason. As the family sedan grows more bulbous and less maneuverable, more and more drivers look for a car that's fun to drive, a vehicle that provides sprightly transportation with a minimum of metal and machinery. And, of course, as second—or third—cars become increasingly a part of the American family pattern, the sports car offers a tempting combination of virtues, while its deficiencies are largely offset by the availability of more conventional family vehicles.

The British *MG*, a sports car which has been seen in this country for many years, played a pioneering role in acquainting the American public with the sports-car type. This year, for the first time since its introduction, it has been completely redesigned and streamlined, and thus finally shorn of its old-fashioned "vintage" look.

For the current test report, CU's auto consultants have paired the new *MG "A"* with the Italian *Alfa-Romeo Giulietta Spyder*—to give the little vehicle its full and impressive title. The *Alfa*, about the same size as the *MG*, costs nearly a thousand dollars more.

Both cars have small four-cylinder engines, four-speed hand-shifted transmissions, and seats for two; both have curb weights just edging a ton; both have folding tops. But where the *MG* has side curtains, the *Alfa* has windows which crank up and down. Both cars have trunks too: the *Alfa's* is reasonable in size and quite useful, that of the *MG* (see photo page 484) houses the spare tire and has room for very little else.

Both cars are really small and light—four feet shorter overall and more than a foot narrower than a *Plymouth*, for instance, and three-quarters of a ton lighter in weight.

At its port-of-entry price of $2195, the *MG* is the lowest-

the MG "A" and Alfa-Romeo

The responsiveness of these two imported sports cars will win the admiration of discerning drivers

priced genuine sports car readily obtainable in the U. S.—and one of the handsomest at any price. It lacks many of the detail refinements of the *Alfa-Romeo* which, however, costs $900 more.

The *Alfa* (though it competes in a smaller-displacement category), is just as much a sports car as the *MG*; it handles and takes corners as well if not better; but it is much less austere in appointments, offers much more comfort, is of more advanced mechanical design.

As a result of CU's appraisal and testing of the two cars, its auto consultants feel that while the *MG* will appeal chiefly to sports car addicts, the *Alfa* will, in addition, please many motorists who want and can afford a small, high quality, personal pleasure car that takes up little room, handles like a dream, rides acceptably, and transforms into a snug and well-heated convertible.

Road behavior

The list of the "sports car virtues" is not a long one, but on it are items that every U. S. motorist ought to learn about—preferably at first hand. Stability on the road is one of these virtues, and oversized brakes (by American standards) constitute another (see photo page 484).

More important still, and virtually unobtainable in ordinary cars, is the sports car's extreme maneuverability. This is compounded of a great reduction in size coupled with exceedingly quick and precise steering, "eager" response to the steering on the car's part because of its light—and well-distributed—weight plus a tight-to-the-road feeling due to the sports car's low center of gravity, low seating, freedom from lean on curves, and relatively stiff springing.

The net result of these differences from conventional cars is, a feeling of release for the driver—like discarding his heavy winter clothing in the Spring. Governing the behavior of the car in relation to the road becomes a simple pleasure rather than a nose-to-the-grindstone chore.

Sports cars do, of course, differ widely in the degree to which they approach the ideal in their handling qualities, but both the *MG "A"* and the *Alfa-Romeo Giulietta Spyder* lie well toward the top of the list in these characteristics. Steering is easier, more sensitive, and slightly quicker on the *Alfa*, and the *MG's* tires squealed noticeably on corners, even at normal speeds, at the recommended air pressure.

Both cars had excellent brakes, and had no trouble with fade or in giving straight, quick stops on CU's downhill coasting test. Aside from grabbing when damp, the *MG* brakes behaved well, but the *Alfa* brakes rate special mention. (Italian cars in general have outstanding brakes, and one look at a relief map of mountainous Italy will show why.) The *Alfa* brakes are enormous for a one-ton car. The drums are of light alloy, with iron liners; the front brakes, which on all cars do more work than the rear, have drums with machined helical cooling fins, the rear drums have cast-in ribs. Brake pedal pressure is low, the brakes take hold gently and provide seemingly effortless stopping.

Neither car showed any lack of bounce control—as do the majority of U. S. sedans—when taken over CU's rough road loop at the standard test speed.

Performance

All that can be said of the acceleration, flexibility, and speed of the *MG "A"* and the *Alfa-Romeo Giulietta Spyder* is that both do very well considering the size (piston displacement) of their engines—91 and 79 cubic inches respectively. A *Chevrolet 6* will give them a hard time accelerationwise, while most any U. S. *V-8* will out-accelerate them with one hand tied behind its back.

Moreover, the maximum performance of the *MG* and the *Alfa* (in which, as the Facts and Figures show, the two cars are roughly equal) depends on frequent gearshifting and use of the high revolutions per minute of which both

Continued on next page

MG "A" AND ALFA-ROMEO continued

engines are capable. High engine speeds entail engine noise, of which the *Alfa* makes less than the *MG*.

There is a contrast in gear-shift operation between the two cars. Both have four forward speeds, and floor-mounted gear-shift levers. But the *MG's* gear lever is short, stiff to operate, and permits quick shifts. The *Alfa* has a longer, heavier lever that shifts the gears more easily but requires more movement. The *MG's* low gear is not synchronized; all *Alfa's* four forward speeds are.

Of the two cars, the *MG* is considerably more flexible, with more pulling power at moderate speeds in high gear, but the *Alfa* is the smoother-running powerplant—as indeed it ought to be, in the light of its construction. Compared with the *MG* engine, which is a "hotted-up" production four-cylinder job which, like most U.S. engines, has push-rod-operated overhead valves, the *Alfa* is an expensive-to-build piece of automotive jewelry.

The *Alfa* engine utilizes chain-driven double overhead camshafts, and has racing-type hemispherical combustion chambers. The bore and stroke are nearly equal—approximately 3 x 3 inches. Cylinder block, cylinder head, crankcase and transmission housing are of light alloy. Cylinder bores, as in many heavy-duty vehicles, are inserted cast-iron sleeves in direct contact with the cooling water. Nearly everything possible has been done to produce an engine capable of sustained high horsepower output per cubic inch and per pound of weight.

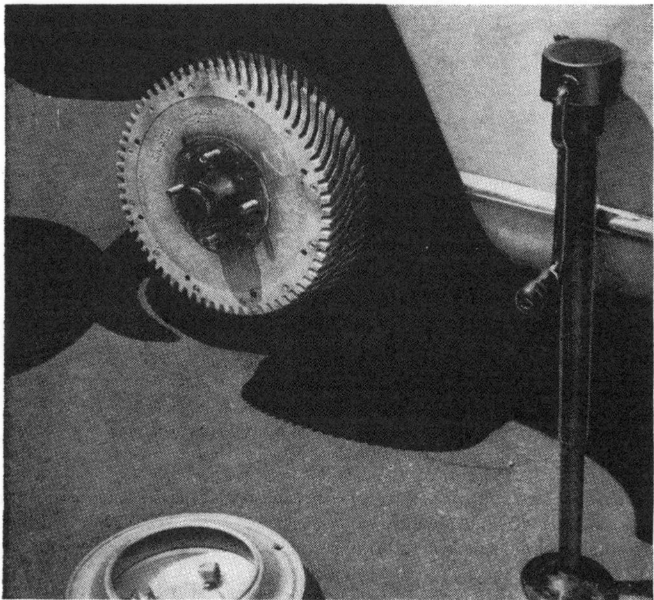

The cooling fins on the Alfa's big front brake drum help in preventing brake "fade." Alfa's fine jack is at right

Fuel economy

In addition to the contribution made by a small, lightweight engine to good car handling characteristics, the high cost of fuel in both Great Britain and Italy in part dictates the small engine displacement of both the *MG* and the *Alfa-Romeo*. Both give excellent gas mileage; the *Alfa* being the better of the two in about the proportion one would expect from its lesser cubic-feet-per-mile displacement. At 50 and 60 mph, however, the *Alfa's* superiority over the *MG* increased; in fact, at the latter speed, it gave better mileage than any other car CU has tested except one —the 1954 *Porsche* coupe.

To the American buyer of an *Alfa-Romeo*, in view of its price, any margin in gas mileage over a cheaper car is academic as far as overall costs are concerned, but outstanding gas mileage serves as an indicator of efficiency in design.

Comfort

While good handling should be paramount in a sports car, as much comfort should be built into it as is consistent with its small size, light weight and precise handling. The great majority of sports cars, in fact, are used as personal rather than sports cars most of the time, and their owners have every right to expect a reasonable degree of comfort. ***Continued on page 48***

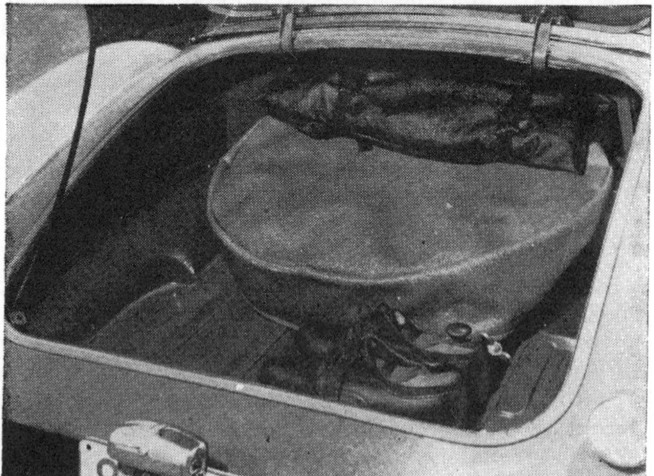

Golf shoes show the scale. MG's tiny trunk, loaded with spare tire and tools, leaves little space for additional luggage.

With top up, hand signals from the MG—or opening doors from outside—means fighting a stiff, springloaded flap

FACTS AND FIGURES

	Alfa Romeo	MG-A
PRICE		
AT COASTAL PORT OF ENTRY	$3230*	$2195
DIMENSIONS		
WHEELBASE	87 in.	94 in.
OVERALL LENGTH	152 in.	156 in.
OVERALL WIDTH	61 in.	58 in.
OVERALL HEIGHT, TOP UP	51 in.	50 in.
OVERALL HEIGHT,TOP DOWN	47 in.	46 in.
ROAD CLEARANCE	6.1 in.	5.4 in.
TURNING CIRCLE DIAMETER (wall-to-wall)	35 ft.	33 ft.
STEERING FACTOR	0.57	0.59
WEIGHT AND TIRES		
CURB WEIGHT	1955 lb.	2000 lb.
% WEIGHT ON REAR WHEELS	45%	49%
TIRE SIZE	6.00x15 in. (approx.)	5.60x15 in.
THEORETICAL TIRE CARRYING CAPACITY (above curb weight)	1095 lb. (approx.)	740 lb.
ENGINE		
TYPE	Double overhead camshaft 4	Overhead-valve 4
BORE AND STROKE	2.91x2.95 in.	2.88x3.50 in.
PISTON DISPLACEMENT	79 cu. in.	91 cu. in.
COMPRESSION RATIO	8.0	8.3
MAXIMUM ADVERTISED HORSEPOWER	65@6000rpm	68@5500rpm
ENGINE SPEEDS		
AXLE RATIO	4.55	4.30
ENGINE REVS PER MILE, HIGH GEAR	3772	3523
PISTON TRAVEL PER MILE, HIGH GEAR	1855 ft.	2055 ft.
PERFORMANCE		
LEVEL ACCELERATION		
0 to 60 mph	17.5 sec.	17.3 sec.
covered ¼ mile, standing start	21.3 sec.	21.8 sec.
45 to 65 mph (third gear)	10.9 sec.	10.6 sec.
ACCELERATION ON 9% GRADE (third gear)		
from 30 to 40 mph	15.8 sec.	13.7 sec.
from 30 to 50 mph	41.0 sec.	30.5 sec.
top speed attainable on grade	60 mph	62 mph
ECONOMY		
CONSTANT-SPEED GASOLINE MILEAGE		
at steady 30 mph	40.4 mpg	37.6 mpg
at steady 50 mph	39.3 mpg	35.3 mpg
at steady 40 mph	37.0 mpg	31.6 mpg
at steady 60 mph	34.4 mpg	29.1 mpg
TRAFFIC GAS MILEAGE (simulated traffic test)	23.7 mpg	21.2 mpg
HIGHWAY GAS MILEAGE	33.8 mpg	31.4 mpg
OVERALL GAS MILEAGE	26.4 mpg	24.2 mpg
OIL CONSUMPTION RATE AFTER BREAK-IN	for 2550 mi. 2100 mi./qt.	for 2600 mi. 725 mi./qt.

**Includes built-in fresh-air heater.*

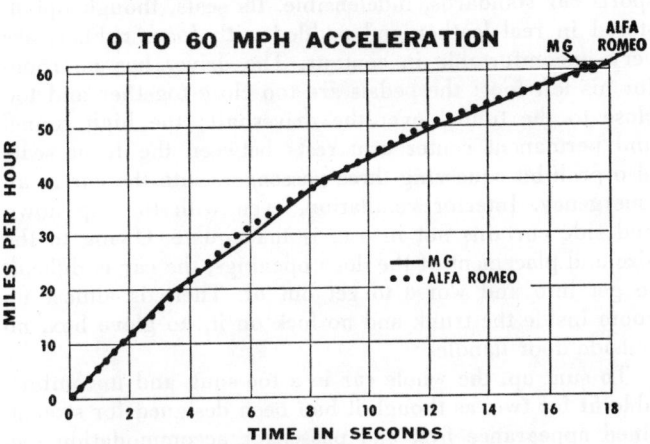

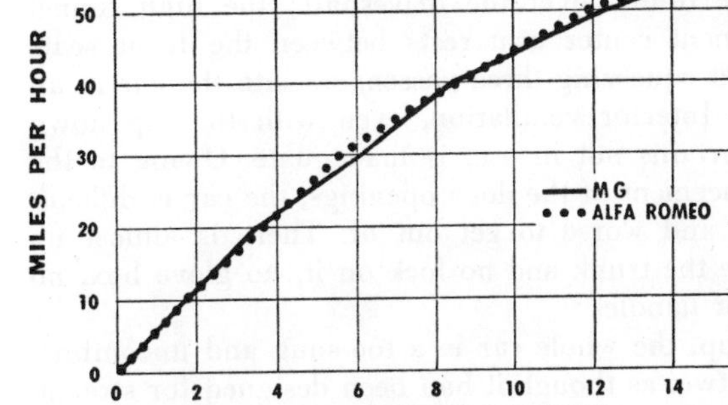

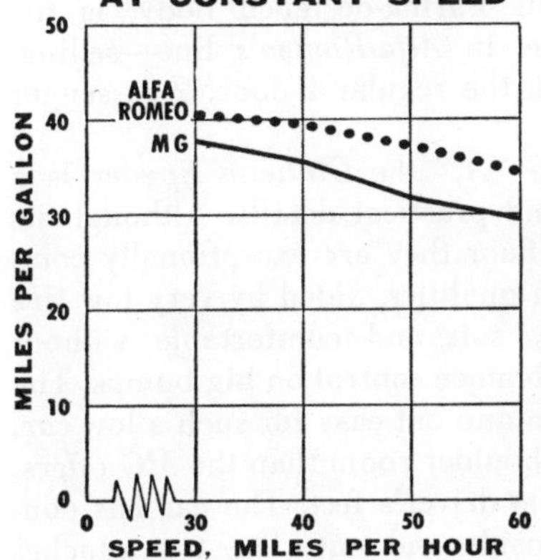

Mileage per gallon of fuel is recorded at various constant speeds for CU's test cars. The acceleration is measured at wide open throttle with the car moving from stand-still to 60 mph

A GUIDE TO THE FACTS AND FIGURES

PRICE AT COASTAL PORT OF ENTRY. Includes Federal tax, but not local taxes, freight, optional extras, accessories, or conditioning charges.

ROAD CLEARANCE. Distance from road surface to lowest part of car likely to hit high spots in the road.

TURNING CIRCLE. Path traced by outtermost tip of front bumper with wheels all the way to left, as for a tight U-turn. Some cars turn shorter to the right.

STEERING FACTOR. Number of turns of the steering wheel required to make a "right-angle" turn of 30-foot radius.

CURB WEIGHT. Weight of equipped car, full of gas, oil, and water, ready (at the curb) for occupants.

TIRE CAPACITY. Official but conservative load-carrying rating for the four tires, minus curb weight of car. Low capacity predisposes to more rapid tire wear.

ENGINE DATA. From factory figures.

PERFORMANCE. 0-60 mph, ¼ mile runs with all gears used to maximum advantage; 45-65 mph and 9% grade runs with floored accelerator but no manual shifting.

ECONOMY. Constant speed tests offer controlled comparison between cars. In normal driving at comparable average speeds mileage will be much lower. Traffic pattern involves moderate acceleration, 35 mph maximum, average speed for course of about 21 mph. Highway gas mileage is measured on a parkway, cruising at 55 mph, averaging about 51 mph. Mileage for most drivers will fall between Highway and Traffic Gas Mileage, depending on individual driving patterns.

MG "A" AND ALFA-ROMEO continued

Here, it seems to CU, is where the *MG "A"* falls down badly; its extremely hard riding qualities are, even by sports car standards, indefensible. Its seats, though upholstered in real leather and padded with foam rubber, are very uncomfortable in contour. The driver has no room for his left foot; the pedals are too close together and too close to the tunnel over the driveshaft; the high tunnel and permanent center arm rests between the front seats also prohibit squeezing three passengers into the car in an emergency. Interior ventilation, even with the top down and side curtains not in use, is inadequate. Owing to the size and placement of the door openings, the car is difficult to get into and worse to get out of. There is almost no room inside the trunk and no lock on it, no glove box, no outside door handles.

To sum up, the whole car is a too-snug and uncomfortable fit for two, as though it had been designed for streamlined appearance first and passenger accommodation second. The paint job and trim materials on the *MG*, however, are superior in quality to those of the *Giulietta Spyder*, which, notwithstanding its Farina-designed body, is the specially low-priced model in *Alfa-Romeo's* line—selling, in fact, for $900 less than the regular 2-door, 2-passenger *Giulietta Sprint* coupe.

Compared with the *MG "A,"* the *Giulietta Spyder* is a masterpiece of comfort and practical details. Although its seats are very low to the floor they are exceptionally comfortable. The *Alfa's* riding qualities, aided by very low tire pressures, are reasonably soft and comfortable without much sway or any loss of bounce control on big bumps. The wide doors make getting in and out easy for such a low car, and inside there is more shoulder room than the *MG* offers, and plenty of room for the driver's feet. The car has conventional door handles inside and out. The top attaches more easily to the windshield than the *MG* top and for some reason the fabric drums less at high speed. The *Alfa* has an effective built-in fresh-air heater and two ventilating ducts. Trunk space, while not large by American standards, is usable and efficient. Both car doors and trunk can be locked.

The little Alfa has faults, however. Maximum leg room is less than on the *MG*, and the distance between steering wheel rim and brake pedal is below average, which may bother the long-legged driver. Instrument panel chrome reflects in the windshield. The glove box has no door. Though located in the trunk, the battery is hard to service, and in CU's car, despite its being covered, it regurgitated acid solution over the trunk floor.

Summing up

To one who wants a solid and thoroughgoing sports car at a reasonable price, and is genuinely indifferent to major and minor discomforts in his vehicle, the *MG "A"* is a good buy. It is a handsome car, built for the most part of well-tried and simple components, which can be serviced with comparative ease, and, except for its seemingly springless ride, has no serious vices in its road behavior.

With the *Alfa-Romeo Giulietta Spyder*, to give it its full name for the last time, the owner will have more trouble vis-a-vis the *MG* getting service, but is much better off in the matter of comfort, and has a vehicle built, without penny-pinching, to very exacting standards in the matter of advanced mechanical design and road behavior.

The *Spyder* ("Spyder" is an obsolescent word for a "spidery," lightweight carriage) is, at present, the only imported sports car at its price that has roll-up windows, but it can lay no other claim to being a bargain. As a personal car it is an almost completely ingratiating connoisseur's item, and, although the sporting Italian drivers for whom the *Giulietta* was designed prefer the lighter, smoother-lined *Sprint* coupe to the convertible *Spyder*, it is hard to see how any knowledgeable motorist who gets acquainted with the *Alfa* can fail to respond to the facility with which the husky little plaything does what it was designed to do.

IN THE M.G. TRADITION

The Series-MGA Coupe Constitutes a Safe Fast Car, with First-Class Handling Qualities, Excellent Brakes and Decidedly Useful Performance

ANCIENT AND MODERN.—A camera-portrait emphasising the lasting beauty of old architecture and the pleasing appearance of the M.G. MGA coupe. For those who think of other things beside cars, the church is at Lavenham, Suffolk.

IT was MOTOR SPORT's pleasure during April to carry out a lengthy road-test of the modern M.G. sports car, in the form of a white MGA coupé with red upholstery. This little 1½-litre sports two-seater was driven by various experienced drivers for a total distance of over 1,200 miles and their collective opinions can be summarised by stating that the M.G. MGA is fun to drive, that it handles extremely well, possesses such adequate brakes as to fully justify the manufacturer's slogan "Safety Fast," and that the performance provided by the 72-b.h.p. engine in this 18½-cwt. coupé is sufficient to enable high average speeds to be maintained in a quite unobtrusive manner.

For the young man with a girl-friend but no children, or as a second-car to the family sedan the MGA fulfills a useful function and, as has been proved convincingly, it also constitutes an admirable rally car. It is, of course, available in two-seater and hard-top forms and, stripped of its full-width windscreen, it is by no means inadequate for club sprints and races.

TECHNICALITIES

The M.G. Series-MGA has evolved from a long line of descendants—M.G. Midgets of various types. The design is entirely conventional. The four-cylinder 1,489-c.c. long-stroke push-rod o.h.v. engine is provided with twin S.U. semi-downdraught carburetters and, with a compression-ratio of 8.3 to 1, pushes out 72 b.h.p. at its safe sustained speed of 5,500 r.p.m. The crankshaft is counterbalanced and runs in three bearings, cooling is by belt-driven pump and six-bladed fan, with thermostatic temperature control of the 10 pints of water, and the lubrication system incorporates an eccentric-rotor pump and full-flow oil filter, The pressed-steel sump has a capacity of seven pints. Ignition is looked after by a Lucas oil-filled 12-volt coil, fully-automatic distributor with vacuum and centrifugal advance control, and suppressed 14-mm. Champion sparking plugs.

This engine is in unit with a hydraulically-operated 8-in. single dry-plate Borg and Beck clutch and a four-speed and reverse gearbox having synchromesh on the three upper ratios and holding four pints of lubricant. The drive passes *via* an open propeller-shaft with needle-bearing universal joints to a ¾-floating hypoid-bevel 4.3-to-1 back axle, which contains 2¾ pints of lubricant.

The chassis is of box-section, upswept over the back axle, which is sprung on fairly stiff ½-elliptic hydraulically-damped leaf springs. At the front there is softer coil-spring and wishbone i.f.s., again damped hydraulically, and steering is by rack-and-pinion. Lockheed 10-in. hydraulic brakes are used all round and twin Lucas batteries behind the seats supply the 12-volt electrical system.

The body was re-vamped for the MGA, the "real" radiator shell and slab fuel tank giving way to a streamlined nose and a small, conventional luggage boot. This body is made by the Bodies Branch of Morris Motors, Ltd., in Coventry. The car is no longer festooned with M.G. octagon badges, but we are inclined to think that a small octagonal air-entry would make a better nose-piece than the existing oblong grille. (However, after witnessing with horror the vintage-looking radiator shell of a modern M.G. Magnette rise up into the air with the alligator-bonnet when the latter was opened while the owner looked at the dip-stick, we will not carp over the fixed radiator grille of the MGA !)

To reveal the engine a wire hook under the facia is pulled and after the safety-catch is released the bonnet panel can be raised, and supported on a prop. Its lid is liberally sound-proofed. Accessibility within the engine compartment is commendable, the oil-filler consisting of a (wire-secured) cap on the valve cover and the water-filler of a bayonet-cap on the radiator header-tank. The car tested had a Smith's heater-unit and its long, big-diameter hose-pipe is matched by a shorter piece on the opposite side, which rather casually conveys air from the nose-grille to somewhere in the vicinity of the carburetter air-intakes, which are fitted with individual air-cleaners. Throttle control is by a Bowden cable to a very dodgy-looking anchorage on a metal bracket on the inlet manifold, to which it is secured merely by a tiny split-pin. Fuel is fed efficiently from a 10-gallon rear tank by means of a rear-mounted S.U. electric pump, which primes adequately, if noisily, from a low level. The electrical fuses etc., are well placed on the bulkhead and there are plenty of under-bonnet data plates, but the dip-stick is rather short and the batteries are buried in the tail.

BEHIND THE WHEEL

The coupé version of the M.G. MGA is an attractive proposition for those who no longer enjoy large volumes of fresh air or for the business motorist who craves a sports car but who hasn't the time or inclination to erect a hood and sidescreens every time a shower falls to wet his City suit and the appurtenances of his trade.

It is difficult to provide a coupé top on a small car which is both practical and good to look upon. The M.G. stylists have got away with it reasonably well. The wrap-round screen is of Triplex laminated glass (praise be !) and does not normally distort the driver's vision; the large wrap-round back window is of Triplex toughened glass. The result is good forward and sideways vision, marred only slightly by the pillars behind the doors when glancing ¾-rearwards and more seriously because the large rear-view mirror, splendidly as it fulfills its function, is mounted on the facia-sill right in the near-side line of vision of a driver of average height. The obvious solution is to throw this inconveniently-sited mirror over the hedge and fit the wing-mirror offered as an extra.

The roof, of pressed-steel welded to the body, is not particularly thickly padded, so provides reasonable head room. The doors trail and have neat pull-up exterior handles. The windows wind down fully with 1½ turns of their handles, good hanging "pulls" are provided, and there are hinged ¼-lights with quite good, but not thief-proof, catches. The interior of the MGA coupé is tastefully upholstered in leather, the test car having red seats and trim, offset by white leather-cloth on the facia and door sills. The use of dull leather-cloth on the wide facia-sill obviates dazzle. The backs of the bucket seats fold, which facilitates the stowage of coats, etc., behind them but isn't really necessary. The seats, although small, are extremely comfortable and possess adequate adjustment for a tall driver and passenger. A "crash pad" lines the scuttle, as on many modern cars but the base of the rigid facia and the top of the screen, which cause just as much injury on impact, are not so protected.

Accommodation in this M.G. is strictly for two, as the spare wheel protrudes partially into the space behind the seats. No door pockets are provided, but there are generous open-topped scuttle stowages and the wide shelf behind the seats is lipped to retain parcels, etc. The luggage boot lid, released by pulling out a wire hook behind the passenger's seat, lifts to reveal a shallow boot in which the greater part of the spare wheel protrudes and the tool-roll is accommodated. Squig-bags rather than suitcases are the order of the day but, thus equipped, a week-end couple should be able to take adequate luggage, especially in these days of nylon undies. For longer-duration excursions an external luggage carrier is available. The boot lid has to be propped open with a stowable stay and requires slamming to shut it; the rubber sealing was already coming adrift from it.

The passenger's door carries a lock, which the ignition-key fits. Between the seats there is a padded rest which serves to hold the occupants securely and a lidded ash-tray can be provided on the propeller-shaft tunnel. The doors require a slam to shut them otherwise they tend to bounce open. Altogether this body earns good marks, for *chic* appearance and well-thought-out detail work, and it is commendably free from rattles. It scores a big black mark, however, when all but the more agile first try to enter it or leave it. The doors are large and quite properly trail, but they do not open more than about 45 deg., which, with the low floor and low roof line, renders dignified exit from an MGA virtually impossible for the elderly, who are in imminent danger of rupture or a slipped-disc unless care and thought is applied to the manoeuvre. Less anxiety is caused by the absence of anti-dazzle vizors, but there are times when they would be appreciated.

Although the test-car did not possess the telescopic steering column which may be ordered as an extra, the driving position is excellent and both front wings are in full view, or would be were the aforesaid mirror sensibly located. The pendant pedals, although small, are well placed and there is room for the left foot beneath clutch pedal. The accelerator action is light but not entirely consistent over the entire range.

The remote gear-lever is a delight, being 100 per cent. rigid, well placed, and ideal for really rapid cog-swopping. The movements are conventional and very short, especially across the gate. It is possible to beat the synchromesh, on which, however, few M.G. drivers will wish to rely; if any criticism is merited it is that the gear-change is slightly on the harsh side, possibly because the test-car had not completed 4,000 miles. Bottom gear, as on other B.M.C. gearboxes, is occasionally difficult to engage. The indirect gears are quiet and due to hydraulic actuation the clutch action is light; a trace of clutch slip is discernible when making snatch gear-changes, perhaps due to weak clutch springs.

The engine of the MGA was set to idle at 800 r.p.m. and begins to sound busy beyond 4,000 r.p.m. The rev.-counter has a warning area between 5,500 and 6,000 r.p.m. and to go beyond 6,000 r.p.m. is unwise. However, without exceeding 5,000 r.p.m. this M.G. provides adequate performance for fast travel on English roads. The maxima are about 26 m.p.h. in first gear, 44 m.p.h. in second and 74 m.p.h. in third gear. By using the lower gears excellent acceleration, in the order of 0-50 m.p.h. in 11 sec. and 0-70 m.p.h. in 20 sec., is available. So readily does the engine respond that the "red" is approached very quickly in second gear and a rapid change into third is necessary, which momentarily kills the surge of progressive acceleration. From this aspect second gear is rather too low but for all practical purposes the gear ratios are well chosen. Moreover, a higher second gear would kill some of punch available, which makes this gear so very useful for getting past slowly-moving

POWER FOR THE MGA.—The B.M.C. B-Series power unit with twin S.U. carburetters and remote gear-lever, etc., as installed in the M.G. sports cars.

obstructions. The overall ratios could be better chosen, however, but perhaps the use of standardised components constitutes a difficulty.

Although most owners will make very considerable use of the engine's willingness to run up to really high r.p.m., being encouraged to do so by the excellent gear-change, if an elderly parent borrows the M.G. to run down to the post he or she will find it perfectly amiable at an absurdly staid gait in top cog. Such sorry treatment brings to light that the engine is virtually "pink-proof" (only a trace occurring when picking up from low speed in second gear), but a more useful aspect of the MGA's docility is the absence of exhaust noise, so that, with the revs. kept within decent limits, this sports car will slip through towns without drawing unwanted attention to its presence. The tyres are less satisfactory in this respect, being prone to imitate an accident in the happening as the car is driven gently through a roundabout or acute bend. However, at higher speeds cornering fails to produce more than a murmur from the "Road Speeds." This is a matter of tyre pressures. The car was handed to us with these set for fast driving, with rather more air in the front tyres (rear 23 lb./sq. in., front 20 lb./sq. in.) than the handbook recommends. However, we found that by inflating the "Road "Speeds" on the back wheels to 30 lb. cold, tyre noise at lowspeed was cured completely, without impairing comfort on good roads it is possible that this might result in loss of adhesion on wet surfaces.

From the foregoing comments the reader will be left in no doubt as to the ability of the M.G. coupé to dispose of most things on the road and to make effective use of such gaps and opportunities as occur in the heavy traffic on our inadequate highways. Speed and acceleration are only half the battle when it comes to setting up satisfactory average speeds under such conditions, but the M.G. has other qualities equally as useful. For instance, roadholding is of a very high standard. The car inspires confidence from the outset but only by experimenting on open bends can a driver previously unacquainted with the MGA realise how very fast this car will go round corners. The suspension is firm, but not so stiff as to give an unpleasant ride, except over attrocious by-roads. The M.G. sits down well and hugs the verge round long bends in a manner which inspires immediate confidence, while the "quick" steering, asking

A FULL SIDE VIEW of the M.G. MGA coupe. Apparently it offers rather less drag than the two-seater, even when hood and side-screens are erect on the latter. As tested, the car costs £1,126 13s.

REAR VIEW.—The boot of the MGA is considerably restricted by the spare wheel. The lid is released by a control inside the car, so that a key is not required.

THE M.G. SERIES-MGA COUPÉ

Engine : Four cylinders, 73 by 89 mm. (1,489 c.c.). Push-rod operated o.h. valves. 8.3-to-1 compression-ratio; 72 b.h.p. at 5,500 r.p.m.
Gear ratios : First, 15.652 to 1; second, 9.520 to 1; third, 5.908 to 1; top, 4.3 to 1.
Tyres : 5.90 by 15 Dunlop " Road Speed " on centre-lock wire wheels.
Weight : 18 cwt. 2 qtr. (without occupants but ready for the road, with approximately half-a-gallon of petrol).
Fuel capacity : 10 gallons. Range approximately 275 miles.
Wheelbase : 7 ft. 10 in.
Track : Front, 3 ft. 11⅞ in.; rear, 4 ft. 0¾ in.
Dimensions : 13 ft. 0 in. by 4 ft. 10 in. by 4 ft. 2 in. (high).
Price (with extras as tested) : £751 11s. 6d. (£1,126 13s. inclusive of purchase tax).
Makers : The M.G. Car Company, Ltd., Cowley, Oxford, England.

only 2¾ turns lock-to-lock in conjunction with a small (28-ft.) turning circle, enables rapid changes of direction to be made. There is no pronounced over- or understeering tendency but if anything the former predominates. The steering is fairly light, free from sponginess or lost motion, and only just misses being 100 per cent. positive. The large-diameter (14½-in.) wheel with narrow-X spring spokes is pleasant to handle and there is no very pronounced column or scuttle shake, although considerable kick-back is transmitted to the driver's hands over rough roads. There is powerful castor self-centring action. Wheelspin can be provoked by vicious take-off in bottom gear; tail slides, if they occur, are instantly responsive to steering correction. There is so little roll and so responsive is the steering that quick changes of direction, so useful for rapid overtaking and essential in rally driving tests, are considerably facilitated. The stiff ½-elliptic springs locate the back axle effectively; even with the back tyres at high pressure bumps encountered on fast bends did not materially affect roadholding.

To these highly desirable handling characteristics add the impeccable braking provided by the Lockheed 2LS system. From maximum speed these brakes provide extremely powerful retardation and a straight-line stop in an emergency is possible not once, but repeatedly, because, at all events on the wire-wheel-equipped car, brake-fade is absent. So powerful are these brakes for so light a pedal pressure that they have to be used with discretion at low speeds or the passenger will be flung into the screen. Initial lost-motion on the pedal aggravated this fierce action. A slight squeal when applied lightly soon wore off and at the end of our strenuous test there was no loss of retardation from these very powerful and reassuring brakes. The hand-brake lever, nestling beside the tunnel by the driver's left leg, has the traditional M.G. fly-off action with push-button to lock it on, and thus ranks as one of the few really sensible hand-brakes found on modern cars. It held like a leech.

The foregoing represents an analysis of the M.G. MGA coupé as we came to know it under varied conditions of usage. On paper it is difficult to convey the charm of a long journey behind the wheel of this little sporting car. It does not possess the extreme of performance, but it steers and corners impeccably, with those splendid brakes in reserve should difficult situations arise. It has very useful acceleration, particularly as this can be maintained to well beyond 70 m.p.h. in third gear if desired; on the other hand, earlier upward changes may be made because after 50 m.p.h. or so the top-gear performance is excellent. Emphasis is lent to the M.G.'s top-gear abilities by an acceleration time in that ratio of 14 sec., from 50 to 70 m.p.h. Another aspect of the top-gear performance is an ability to cruise unconcernedly at 80 m.p.h. with the engine turning over at 4,700 r.p.m.—in comparison, sixty is a mere crawl, with the power unit idling at just beyond 3,500 r.p.m.

In sheer maximum speed this 1½-litre M.G. cannot compete with larger-engined sports cars which the flat-rate taxation system has encouraged. But on any reasonably straight piece of road the MGA is up to 80 m.p.h. as a matter of course and 85-90 m.p.h. is easily attained on British roads. The absolute maximum is of less importance but under favourable conditions it is a few m.p.h. over or under 100 m.p.h., depending on the run available.

Petrol consumption, driving hard but not abnormally hard, in a test which also embraced a cold start and some town-traffic, came out at 27½ m.p.g. The range is thus in the order of 275 miles. Gentle handling would no doubt lift these figures to around 30 m.p.g. and 300 miles. A later check confirmed that even under the exacting conditions of covering 350 miles in a day surveying a rally-route, in towns, very largely in country lanes and with really fast driving on main roads, the consumption did not rise above 27 m.p.g., using a variety of petrols. The engine had a slight tendency to run-on after a spell of slow driving when the ignition was cut. It always started very readily and showed a maximum of 70 lb./sq. in. oil pressure (pressure varies with engine speed) and a water temperature of 170 deg. F., rising to 190 deg. F. only when becalmed in Oxford Street, W., during the " April summer." The sump level fell to the danger level after the test had proceeded for some 700 miles, when three pints of Castrol XL brought the level back to " max." A later check after some fast driving confirmed that oil consumption is in the region of 2,000 m.p.g. No water was required. On the subject of fluids-replenishment, the petrol filler cap on the tail has a lift-up quick action, but is woefully small.

Going over the minor controls and detail work, they seem in keeping with the car's character and, as M.G. fans will realise, are in the Abingdon tradition.

Pendant pedals are used, with a heel-mat for the driver. Black (lettered) knobs on the leather-cloth-covered facia control the self-parking screen wipers, fog-lamp (not fitted on the test-car), starter, choke, and panel lighting, the last-named knob turning to provide rheostat control. Another knob on the extreme left switches on a useful map-lamp before the passenger. The choke can be held out in various degrees by locking it with its serrated stem, but this also opens the throttles, which can be inconvenient. There is a separate but uninformative fuel gauge and a combined oil-pressure and water-temperature dial. Before the driver and easily read are the matching 3½-in. Jaeger rev.-counter and speedometer, the former reading to 7,000 r.p.m. (but with the red area from 6,000 to 7,000 r.p.m.), the latter reading to 120 m.p.h. and possessing trip with decimal and total mileage readings. The needles of both these instruments are commendably steady and it is pleasing to find them travelling in the same plane. All the dials are, indeed, in good view of the driver; the steering wheel tends to blank the " flashers " warning light and if an M.G. badge is supplied with the ignition key this obscures the petrol gauge—which, these days, is no bad thing!

The gear-lever knob has the positions marked on it; reverse is back, outside second, and strongly spring-loaded. The horn button for the commendably loud horn is large and recessed in the centre of the facia; we prefer it in the centre of the steering wheel. No cubby-hole is provided but there is provision on the facia for radio, if required.

The car tested had a heater unit, controlled by a sliding knob set neatly below the centre of the facia, with knobs to left and right of it for air control and demist, respectively. The supply of cool air, even with the blower running, is insufficient, so that a choice has to be made between objectionable air noise with the windows open or a stuffy interior with them shut. An ignition warning light is incorporated in the rev.-counter, a headlamps-beam warning light in the speedometer dial. On the extreme right of the facia a rather wobbly but reasonably convenient lever operates the self-cancelling direction " flashers," with a warning light beside it. Another extra on the test-car was a screen-washer, which refused to function. Fluid for it is contained in a plastic bottle, which cannot freeze. The ignition key is separate and detachable; the wipers only function if the ignition is

Continued on page 63

SCI ROAD TEST: the MG a

MGA in profile measures 156 inches from bumper to bumper, and stands 2½ inches lower than the TF.

THE controversial "aerodynamic" MG is a true 100-mph sports car. Our best one-way speed of 101.1 mph was, to be sure, achieved with the help of a gentle zephyr at the rear, but off-setting this is the fact that we reached the full-century speed in only one mile. With a two-mile approach to the measured quarter, undoubtedly, we would have had a few more revs on the tach and a slightly quicker passage through the traps. What counts is that the "A" is an easy 15 mph faster than the TD, 10 mph faster than the TF1500, and stiff competition for such performance rivals as the Alfa Giulietta Sprint and the Porsche 1600 Speedster.

For most of us, nothing induces a friendly, responsive attitude toward a car—a willingness to be prejudiced in its favor—like a modest price. The "A" is a lot of sports car for its base price of $2195. It's almost entirely new mechanically; the only parts interchangeable with the TF are the steering rack and some front suspension components. Its body is sleek and suave and it has perhaps the first really stiff frame in the long evolution of the little hot rods from Abingdon-on-Thames.

But in spite of all the visible and hidden changes and improvements, you have only to drive the "A" around the block to recognize its old MG character. The engineer who designed the TC's noisy tappets, harsh ride, and loud exhaust system is apparently still bending over the drawing board. In spite of its contemporary look, better handling and thrustier performance, the "A" is still pure old-line MG Midget.

Like its ancestors it's a whole lot of fun to drive in spite of—or maybe because of—its imperfections. The steering as always is very quick over a large lock, and Detroit-conditioned drivers look somewhat palsied at the wheel until they sharpen their responses. Once they do, though, the alert steering naturally makes for excellent control of the machine. This steering is light, has a fairly strong self-centering action and is devoid of play. Minor road shocks are not felt through the steering wheel, but big bumps definitely are.

Another of the organs of the machine that retains the old MG's character is the gearbox. The remote shift lever is ideally at hand; stubby and short in travel, and the synchromesh is infallible. Pumping this lever through the cogs on our 5000 mile-old test car still took plenty of bicep power, but we understand that the transmission begins to limber up after seven or eight thousand miles.

Under the spare lies the battery. Luggage space is minimal after spare wheel has been set in place. Straps hold tool kit, missing here.

Most everything under the hood is accessible, but slightly cramped. Note large radiator for cooler running. Duct at right carries cool air to carbs

Car heads into SCI's familiar test curve at half throttle. Suspension worked a little hard, but kept the body fairly level.

The hydraulically-assisted clutch is light, strong and sure and upshifts can be made with lightning speed. Going down from third to second is slightly awkward and presents the possibility of crunching against reverse or even engaging it while moving forward at low speeds. Nevertheless, this is a good and very satisfying gearbox, despite the fact that low gear is overly low.

The "A's" ride is still another instance of blood telling. It's smooth on smooth pavement, and that's all. The rest of the time it's aggressively hard, in the spartan sports car tradition of the Thirties. Unlike a lot of modern light cars, which not only corner well but also absorb horrible bumps, the "A" and its occupants feel every surface ripple. Beyond about 80 or 85 mph, even on smooth pavement, the ride gets a little bouncy—this, in spite of the fact that a prototype of this chassis was run at better than 150 mph on the Bonneville Salt. (See pp. 32-37.)

But up to this point the car cruises free and easy and still retains pretty good acceleration. It has a solid, substantial, all-of-a-piece feel that's largely due to the "A's" new frame. The big, box-section rails are tied together by cross-members at something like two-foot intervals and to these are added a box-section superstructure that gives added

Drop-away hood offers little resistance to wind at speed, but protruding fenders may be little catch-alls.

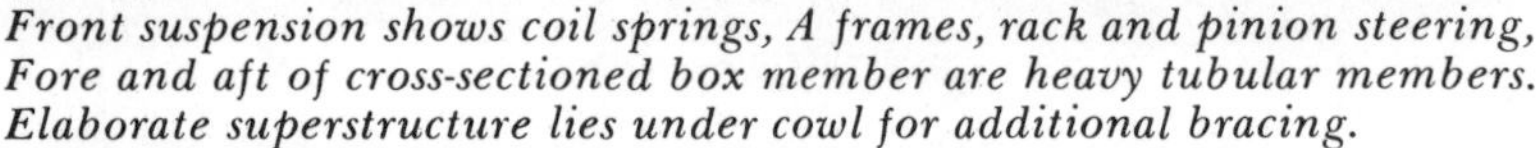

Front suspension shows coil springs, A frames, rack and pinion steering, Fore and aft of cross-sectioned box member are heavy tubular members. Elaborate superstructure lies under cowl for additional bracing.

The A's dash has a full complement of instruments. Tach is driven off camshaft instead of generator as before.

stiffness at the firewall line. This is a heavy frame but a very stiff one, and because of the reduced weight of the "A's" engine, transmission and rear axle, its chassis weighs just about the same as the TF's. The body is securely mounted to the frame and on the roughest surfaces there is no sign of frame twisting or of body panels "working" independently. The doors close with a solid sound and they stay closed, unlike those on some of the springier-framed MG's.

With a full tank of fuel the "A's" weight distribution is very close to 50-50, and this, combined with the stiff suspension and a close tread/wheelbase ratio helps give the car its well-balanced cornering qualities. Its bite in the turns is softer than the on-rails variety, but it sticks to the road very well—much better than its forebears did. Body roll and tire noise are slight. The rear tires begin to slide only when sorely tempted and then in a slow, controllable way.

As an accelerating machine the new MG goes much more briskly than the TF, in spite of nearly equal displacement and a 12 percent reduction in final drive ratio. Since horsepower and torque have gone up just 4.6 and 1.8 percent respectively, most of the gain in both acceleration and top speed has to be caused by the lower wind drag of the "A's" streamlined body. The acceleration curves of the "A" and the TF show that there's a big difference in the way that these similarly endowed cars penetrate the air.

The modified BMC B-type engine is basically the same as the one that powers the four-cylinder Morris, Wolsley and Austin except for its more sporting camshaft and dual carbs. The compact gauze-type air cleaners do little or no silencing and the moan of air being dragged into the cylinders gets really loud at about 70 mph. On the whole this is a pleasant sound, suggestive of gobs of power, but when the weather equipment is up it can get tiresome.

All the porting is on the left side of the engines. There are two intake ports and three for exhaust, feeding into a nicely contoured three-branch "header" type manifold. This style of porting is practically immune to the more advanced forms of intake and exhaust "ram" tuning, but since nobody is more aware of this than the factory, a simple remedy is undoubtedly already on the drawing boards. The throttle linkage is devious.

The throttle pedal is suspended from a shaft that extends to the right-hand side of the firewall. To a bracket on the far end of this shaft is attached a flexible cable that runs parallel to the right-hand side of the engine,

MG poses with its top up. Car looks clean with top in up or down position.

Trunk deck-lid releases from driver's compartment. Rear suspension is simple semi-elliptic with lever and piston type shocks. Ride is stiff.

then crosses over the top of it to connect with the throttle valves—which actually are no more than a few inches ahead of the foot pedal. Abingdon's engineers could have devised a more direct connection, but this one works very well.

During our warm-weather testing of the "A", the engine always fired up with no hesitation and quickly settled down to a somewhat rough idle at about 900 rpm. The engine revs willingly under load up about 4500 rpm, but at this point the tappets begin to chatter and you can feel the engine starting to work. The four-inch tachometer, now driven by the camshaft rather than the generator, has an orange pie-slice between 5500 and 6000. It also has a red warning slice from 6000 to 7000, but this is mainly decorative. The stock engine is wound very tight at 5500 in the indirect gears and the valve train protests politely but unmistakably. During acceleration runs we hit 5900 on a couple of occasions but retreated in haste. This is just about the limit. To venture into the red area on the tach is to invite the valves to come unglued. But at 5800 rpm in top gear (101.1 mph) the engine, though far from loafing, seems willing to sustain the pace indefinitely.

As it stands, this engine seems to be at the upper limit

MG-A

PERFORMANCE

TOP SPEED:
Two-way average................ 99.3 mph (top up)
Fastest one-way run............101.1 mph (top up); 96.7 (top down)

ACCELERATION: (Top down unless otherwise noted)

From Zero to	Seconds
30 mph	4.0
40 mph	6.3
50 mph	8.6
60 mph	14.1
70 mph	19.3; 18.5 (top up)
80 mph	26.5
Standing ¼ mile	19.6; 19.2 (top up)
Speed at end of quarter	73 mph

SPEED RANGES IN GEARS:

I	zero to indicated 30 mph.
II	15 to indicated 40 mph.
III	30 to indicated 60 mph.
IV	40 to indicated 90 mph.

SPEEDOMETER CORRECTION:

Indicated	Actual
30	30
40	38
50	47
60	57
70	67
80	77

FUEL CONSUMPTION:
Hard driving ....23.6 mpg during speed runs.
Average driving (under 60 mph)..32.4 mpg

BRAKING EFFICIENCY:

1st stop	86
2nd stop	86
3rd stop	86
4th stop	85 (left rear wheel locking)
5th stop	85 (left rear wheel locking)
6th stop	75 (left rear wheel locking)
7th stop	75 (left rear wheel locking)
8th stop	74 (left rear wheel locking)
9th stop	74 (left rear wheel locking)
10th stop	75 (left rear wheel locking)

SPECIFICATIONS

POWER UNIT:

Type	In-line four.
Valve Arrangement	Pushrod-operated ohv.
Bore & Stroke (Engl. & Met.)	2.875 x 3.50 ins.; 73.025 x 89.0 mm.
Bore/Stroke Ratio	1.22 to one.
Displacement (Engl. & Met.)	90.88 cu. ins.; 1489 cc.
Compression Ratio	8.3 to one.
Carburetion by	Two 1.5 in. semi-downdraft S.U.
Max bhp @ rpm	68 @ 5500
Max. Torque @ rpm	77.4 @ 3500
Idle Speed	900 rpm

DRIVE TRAIN:

Final drive ratio (test car)	4.3 to one.
Other available final drive ratio	3.7, 4.1, 4.13, 4.55 to one.
Axle torque taken by	Springs.

CHASSIS:

Wheelbase	94 ins.
Front Tread	47.4 ins.
Rear Tread	48.8 ins.
Suspension, front	Independent by coil springs and wishbones.
Suspension, rear	Semi-elliptic.
Shock absorbers	Lever-and-piston type.
Steering type	Rack and pinion.
Steering wheels turns L to L	2.75
Turning diameter	28 ft.
Brake type	Front: two leading shoe; Rear: leading and trailing.
Brake lining area	134.4 sq. ins.
Tire size	5.60 x 15.

GENERAL:

Length	156 ins.
Width	58 ins.
Height	50 ins.
Weight, test car	2080 lbs.
Weight distribution, F/R (full fuel tank)	49.8/50.2
Weight distribution, F/R, with driver	49.8/50.2
Fuel capacity	12 gallons

RATING FACTORS:

Bhp per cu. in.	.748
Bhp per sq. in. piston area	2.62
Torque (lb-ft) per cu. in.	.852
Pounds per bhp—test car	30.6
Piston speed @ 60 mph	2007 fpm
Piston speed @ max bhp	3208 fpm
Brake lining area per ton (test car)	129 sq. ins.

MGA —

of its compression ratio. It continues to fire for several revs after the ignition has been cut. But this is the only criticism we have to make of the "A's" power plant. It's a good combination of ruggedness, economy of operation and maintenance, and healthy output.

MG's old motto "Safety Fast" is highly appropriate for the "A". The machine's good steering, roadholding and acceleration are backed up by a set of genuinely outstanding brakes. The ten inch drums are heavy iron castings that show little tendency to expand. The retarding force of the brakes registered the unusual high of .86 g on our instruments, and over the ten-stop fade test they lost only 9.3 percent of their efficiency. (Some cars that Sports Cars Illustrated has tested have had fade losses of 25 percent and more.) From these figures it would seem that the "A's" perforated disc wheels do a good job of brake cooling which can be made still better if you use the optionally available wire wheels. For racing, the factory recommends the harder Ferodo BG95/1 lining, which gives even more fade-proof braking.

The body of the MG "A" is bound to be a controversial subject as long as there are still partisans of the old Thirties-styled models. The TC unquestionably deserves the much abused title of "classic" and the TD and TF proved to a lot of people that it was impossible to get a better looking car by "refining" the crisp, spidery TC.

As it is now, the "A" is a very attractive car from any angle, and downright beautiful from some. Its look and feel of quality closely approach those of some cars that cost twice as much money. The body feels and is very substantial. The quality of the painted finish is good, there's no skimping on the instrument panel, and the reinforced bumpers are very ade-

On the negative side, raising or lowering the top is a hassle, luggage space is minute, and the inside door panels are sub-standard compared to the quality of the rest of the machine. The 12-volt electrical system is fed by a pair of six-volt batteries in series, mounted behind the seats but accessible only if you haul the spare tire out of the luggage compartment!

In order to get the "A" 2½ inches lower than the TF, the frame rails have been bowed out enough to permit the occupants to ride between and alongside them. Sports Cars Illustrated's staff found the semi-reclining seating position perfectly comfortable, but criticized the seat-backs because they support only the shoulders. The driver sits with left leg extended to operate the clutch and right leg cocked to operate the throttle. This turns out to be a comfortable driving position, particularly since the high transmission tunnel provides good sup-

On the "A" the headlight dip-switch, which in previous MG's was on the instrument panel, is mounted on the firewall, which is stepped and lies in two planes, the higher portion roughly one foot farther aft than the lower. This means that to operate the switch you have to pull your leg back from its normal, relaxed, clutch-operating position and raise it high enough to prod the switch. Foot pedal room is better in the "A" than in earlier MG's but it's still easy to hook throttle foot on brake pedal, or hit the throttle pedal when you want to brake. This happened to most of our testing crew and made an unforgettable impression; it happened only once per driver.

The air flow around the car at speed with the top down is such that there is very little turbulence in the cockpit—the occupants get little wind buffeting, and conversation in normal tones can be carried on with ease except at high rpm's. With the top up engine noise is magnified, of course. And like most fabric tops the "A" rattles and booms against the wind. The side-screens are well designed, their lower third being a separate panel that can be pivoted outward against a spring-loaded plunger.

But ventilation is either all-off or all-on; there are no openings in the screens to permit the entry of outside air. There are also no external door handles, and reaching in through the spring-loaded flap and down to grasp the door-latch pull-cord can be fairly awkward.

With all its little irritations, this is a basically safe, friendly, likeable car —a genuine, well-built sports machine at a price that can't be considered anything but reasonable and fair. We'd be much surprised if the "A" sales situation were anything but what it is: demand fantastically ahead of supply. It's a very desireable car that will give years of economical driving pleasure and then have the high resale value that MG's have earned.

— *Griff Borgeson*

MG A TEST

(Continued from page 39)

it (unnoticed earlier because separate corrected speedo in use). Very silly mistake in a car which will be used a lot in competition work. All dials legible, though.

Through the hills the car was sure-footed as a cat. The tail, tenacious on curves, responds instantly to the steering wheel. Rough and loose going were handled ably by the suspension. Roll kept well in check. Firmish ride at low speeds. Good at speed over bumpy patches. Wise to remember ground clearance six inches.

Gearbox, steering and suspension combined to make the run sheer delight. Cornering powers are high even for a sporting mount. Third in the close ratios will take you up to 68 m.p.h.

On the way back we cruised quite happily at 80 m.p.h. Petrol worked out overall to 36 m.p.g.

Down to Details

But I picked one lovers' quarrel with the car when I went over it in daylight; the finish isn't quite what we have come to expect on MG's. Possibly the A's get churned out a little too fast, in view of the great demand for them.

When I say the trim is untidy, I mean by accepted MG standards—it would still do credit to many cars.

But the paint was not the best, and there is a hideous line of rivets low down on each side of the car.

The only spectacular thing about the engine is its performance. In design it is a straightforward o.h.v. four, inclined to reveal its numerical character only in low speeds.

Engine compartment, under a forward-opening bonnet, is well filled. Most regular maintenance points are not, however, difficult to get at.

Besides a reasonable boot by sporting standards there are useful door pockets and a glove locker, but no room behind the seats.

Standard wheels are pressed steel, bolted on. Knock-off wire wheels are extra. So, too, is a telescopic wheel column—but I think that, whatever your size and shape, a comfortable driving position can be found with the fixed wheel.

Detail equipment generally is generous; self-parking wipers; variable-intensity instrument lighting and fly-off handbrake—very efficient, too.

Independent front end is on coil springs, semi-elliptics at rear.

All in all, the "A" is a grand machine, in the best MG tradition.

"First of a new line," the manufacturers say. Let's hope it's a long one; and that import restrictions and a fine British product do not, paradoxically, continue for long to make one wish he was American. • • •

The safest, fastest MG ever engineered!

The Entirely New MG A

The MG A is a product of THE BRITISH MOTOR CORPORATION, LTD. Makers of MG, AUSTIN-HEALEY, MAGNETTE, MORRIS, AUSTIN AND RILEY CARS.

You'll gasp with admiration when you see the sleek new lines and brilliant new colors of the entirely new MG A. And, your appreciation of nimble performance and solid roadability will hit a new high when you take the wheel. Yes, in every design and engineering detail, this superb new model is the smartest, safest, fastest MG ever made.

Represented in the United States by

hambro

AUTOMOTIVE CORPORATION
27-29 W. 57th ST., NEW YORK 19, N.Y.

Sold and serviced through a nationwide network of distributors and dealers.

Road Test No. 30/57 (Continental)

Make: M.G. **Type:** MGA Coupé

Makers: M.G. Car Co. Ltd., Abingdon-on-Thames, Berkshire

Test Data

CONDITIONS: *Weather : Wind 10 to 15 m.p.h; showery. (Temperature 78°F., Barometer 29.6 in. Hg.). Surface : Concrete : Montlhery Track. Fuel : British and French Premium.*

INSTRUMENTS

Speedometer at 30 m.p.h.	3% fast
Speedometer at 60 m.p.h.	3% fast
Speedometer at 90 m.p.h.	4% fast
Speedometer at 100 m.p.h.	7% fast
Distance recorder	accurate

WEIGHT:

Kerb weight (unladen, but with oil, coolant and fuel for approx. 50 miles)	18½ cwt.
Front/rear distribution of kerb weight	52/48
Weight laden as tested	21¾ cwt.

MAXIMUM SPEEDS

Flying Montlhéry Lap	101.2 m.p.h.
Best one-way ½-km. time equals	103.8 m.p.h.

"Maximile" Speed. (Timed quarter-mile after one mile accelerating from rest.)

Mean of four runs	92.0 m.p.h.
Best one-way time equals	94.8 m.p.h.

Speed in Gears at recommended limit of 5,500 r.p.m.

Max. speed in third	68 m.p.h.
Max. speed in second	42 m.p.h.
Max. speed in first	26 m.p.h.

FUEL CONSUMPTION

47.0 m.p.g. at constant 40 m.p.h. on level.
43.2 m.p.g. at constant 50 m.p.h. on level.
35.4 m.p.g. at constant 60 m.p.h. on level.
31.2 m.p.g. at constant 70 m.p.h. on level.
28.8 m.p.g. at constant 80 m.p.h. on level.
24.8 m.p.g. at constant 90 m.p.h. on level.

Overall Fuel Consumption for 742 miles, 26.9 gallons, equals 27.6 m.p.g. (10.2 litres/100 km.).

Touring Fuel Consumption (m.p.g. at steady speed midway between 30 m.p.h. and maximum, less 5% allowance for acceleration) 31.5 m.p.g.

Fuel Tank Capacity (makers' figure) 10 gallons.

STEERING

Turning circle between kerbs :

Left	28½ feet
Right	29¼ feet
Turns of steering wheel from lock to lock	2¾

BRAKES from 30 m.p.h.

0.94g retardation (equivalent to 32 ft. stopping distance) with 90 lb. pedal pressure.
0.80g retardation (equivalent to 37½ ft. stopping distance) with 75 lb. pedal pressure.
0.52g retardation (equivalent to 58 ft. stopping distance) with 50 lb. pedal pressure.
0.27g retardation (equivalent to 115 ft. stopping distance) with 25 lb. pedal pressure.

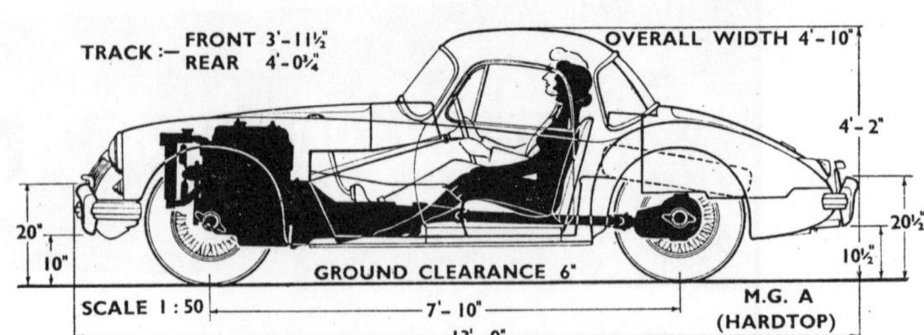

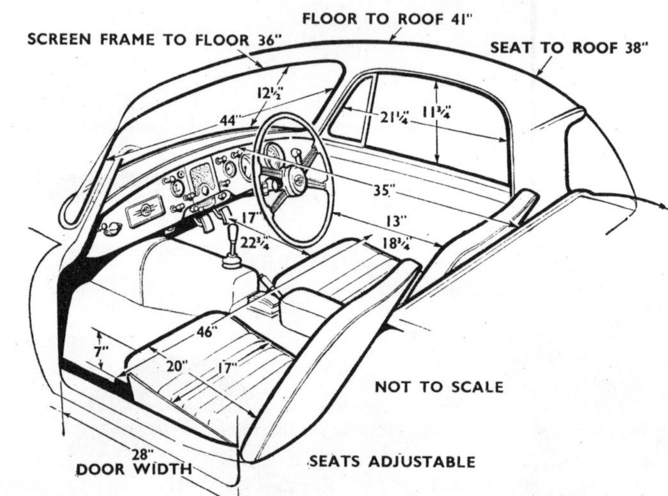

ACCELERATION TIMES from standstill

0-30 m.p.h.	5.0 sec.
0-40 m.p.h.	7.2 sec.
0-50 m.p.h.	10.8 sec.
0-60 m.p.h.	15.7 sec.
0-70 m.p.h.	21.4 sec.
0-80 m.p.h.	32.1 sec.
Standing quarter mile	19.8 sec.

ACCELERATION TIMES on upper ratios

	Top gear	3rd gear
10-30 m.p.h.	13.6 sec.	8.1 sec.
20-40 m.p.h.	13.6 sec.	7.9 sec.
30-50 m.p.h.	13.8 sec.	8.1 sec.
40-60 m.p.h.	12.6 sec.	8.7 sec.
50-70 m.p.h.	13.7 sec.	10.4 sec.
60-80 m.p.h.	17.6 sec.	—
70-90 m.p.h.	28.1 sec.	—

HILL CLIMBING at sustained steady speeds.

Max. gradient on top	1 in 10.7 (Tapley 210 lb./ton)
Max. gradient on third	1 in 7.3 (Tapley 305 lb./ton)
Max. gradient on second	1 in 4.75 (Tapley 472 lb./ton)

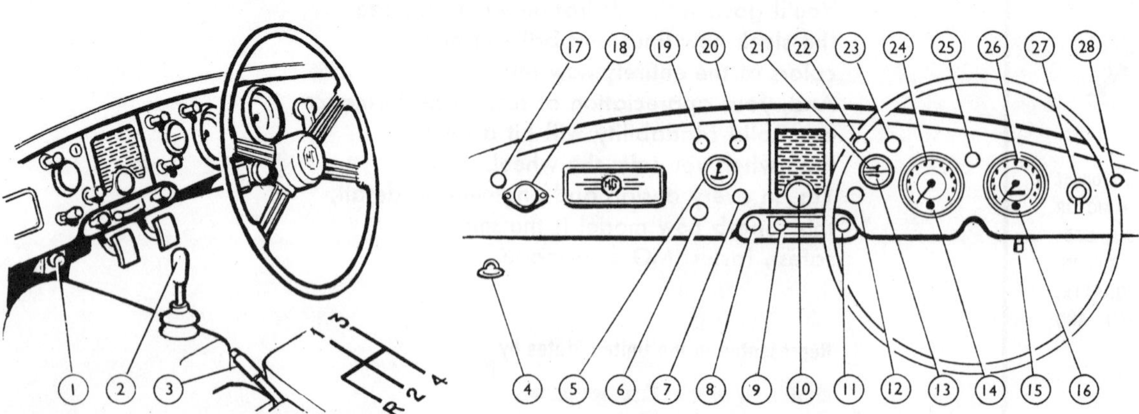

1, Headlamp dip switch. 2, Gear lever. 3, Handbrake. 4, Bonnet catch release. 5, Fuel contents gauge. 6, Windscreen washer control. 7, Choke control. 8, Ventilator control. 9, Temperature and heater fan switch. 10, Horn button. 11, Demisting control. 12, Starter button. 13, Water thermometer. 14, Dynamo charge warning light. 15, Trip re-setting knob. 16, Headlamp main beam indicator light. 17, Map reading light switch. 18, Map reading light. 19, Windscreen wipers switch. 20, Ignition switch. 21, Oil pressure gauge. 22, Lights switch. 23, Fog lamp switch. 24, Tachometer. 25, Panel light switch. 26, Speedometer and distance recorder. 27, Direction indicator switch. 28, Direction indicator warning light.

The M.G. A. Hardtop Coupé

An Economical 100 m.p.h. Car with Exceptional Roadworthiness

IN the world of motoring there are many cars capable of exceeding 100 m.p.h.; indeed, most current American productions are capable of this feat. In contrast, the majority of European cars place an accent on economical running as exemplified by a fuel consumption of, say, better than 25 m.p.g. Standing between these two extremes there is a choice of four cars, all of European origin, which will beat by a useful margin both the 100 m.p.h. and the 25 m.p.g. mark, the latest recruit to this select company being the M.G. A. model with the fixed-head coupé body.

Reference to our road test of the car in original form with open body but raised hood will show that the maximum speed on a flat and level road was 97.8 m.p.h., but the coupé model recently tested on the banked Montlhéry track displayed a sensibly superior performance by returning an overall lap time equivalent to 101.2 m.p.h. with a fastest half kilometre at 103.8 m.p.h. There is therefore no question of the ability of this car to exceed the three figure mark and anyone who questions the utility of this feat in itself should consider the implications thereof upon acceleration in the upper speed ranges and in the ability to cruise with the engine running on a modest throttle opening.

So far as acceleration is concerned, the figures show that making full use of the gearbox the M.G. will run up to 80 m.p.h. within 25 sec. from a speed of 40 m.p.h. and even if the driver remains in top gear between these two speeds the time needed is only 30 sec. A speed of 80 m.p.h. is therefore readily within the compass of the car on any reasonable section of road and in this condition the piston speed is only slightly in excess of 2,500 ft/min. and the engine is delivering little more than half maximum power.

The high acceleration of the car is perhaps of particular value on British roads; the aspect of a comfortable 80 m.p.h. cruising is of especial value abroad and it is perhaps significant that an extremely high proportion of M.G. A. production is exported.

Road surfaces abroad are notoriously poorer than they are in England and for this reason we were particularly impressed by the robustness of the car and the entire absence of chassis wave or body shake even when speeds considerably greater than 80 m.p.h. were being sustained on Continental highways. This high stiffness factor not only ensures freedom from deterioration of door windows, window frames and other small items in the general structure but also gives the driver and passenger a psychological impression that high speeds can be maintained in safety, whereas some more flimsily built vehicles suffer not only from mechanical disabilities but also impose strain and anxiety upon the occupants.

The impression of safety engendered by the M.G. is, fortunately, founded on fact. Although with the recommended tyre pressures, squeal is somewhat prevalent with high-speed cornering, with the higher pressures adopted on Montlhéry circuit, this annoyance disappears, and cornering power comes up into the racing car class which is not particularly surprising in view of the 30 years' continuous competition experience which lies behind the car.

Although automobile engineering has reached the point where the maximum speed, acceleration and fuel consumption of a new car will conform closely to predictions derived from the drawing board, this is by no means true in regard to steering and handling characteristics and the prototype M.G. A. models were developed on a special course to a point where the speed through a given series of corners was equal to the best obtainable irrespective of selling price.

The coupé displays almost neutral steering characteristics coupled with exceptional rapidity of response under the influence of the absolutely positive rack and pinion steering gear. The steering wheel itself might perhaps be placed farther from the driver for the benefit of those who prefer the modern straight-arm control position and over rough surfaces there is noticeable shake on the wheel which does not in any way affect the straight running of the vehicle. By the standards of the family car more than usual physical effort has to be exerted on the wheel, but this is a very small price to pay for that feeling of absolute mastery over the attitude of the vehicle which is one of the most desirable features a car

In Brief

Price (including wire wheels, heater, screen washer, etc., as tested), plus purchase tax: £1,158 15s. 9d.
Basic price of £724, with £363 7s. 0d. purchase tax equals £1,087 7s. 0d.

Capacity	1,489 c.c.
Unladen kerb weight ...	18½ cwt.
Acceleration:	
20-40 m.p.h. in top gear ...	13.6 sec.
0-50 m.p.h. through gears	10.8 sec.
Maximum direct top gear gradient	1 in 10.7
Maximum speed ...	...101.2 m.p.h.
"Maximile" speed	92 m.p.h.
Touring fuel consumption ...	31.5 m.p.g.

Gearing: 17 m.p.h. in top gear at 1,000 r.p.m.; 29 m.p.h. at 1,000 ft./min. piston speed.

SEATS which are rather low-set in relation to the scuttle are nevertheless very comfortable and give good lateral support; there is a central armrest on the transmission tunnel and, on the car tested, an optionally extra ashtray. Just forward of this is the stubby gearlever which gives very pleasant, positive use of the gearbox.

can have and yet is so rarely experienced.

The clutch gives a firm take up and very rapid gear changes can be made, despite the rather wide gap between top and third gear, the speed on the latter being restricted to 70 m.p.h. unless the driver is prepared to take the tachometer needle past the 5,500 r.p.m. mark into the red section. When the acceleration figures were obtained the needle was kept below this area and if the maximum r.p.m. had been increased to the competition limit of 6,000 r.p.m. slightly better times might have been recorded.

As a counterpart to the somewhat wide gap between top and third gear the latter is an excellent ratio to use either in traffic or on country roads as it gives very vivid acceleration between 10 and 60 m.p.h., some pinking from the engine however being noticeable below 2,000 r.p.m. unless 100 octane fuel is used.

The engine cannot be called mechanically quiet. There is a rattle from the pushrod valvegear which is an established characteristic of the type and does not denote mechanical defect but the gearbox and rear axle are free from objectionable noise. The attraction of the fully open car cannot be denied and the name M.G. is especially identified with this type. Nevertheless, from a strictly practical point of view it must be pointed out that despite the introduction of wind-down windows and wrapround rear window the coupé M.G. went on the scales only 32 lb. heavier than the open type; it is 3½ m.p.h. faster and returns a fuel consumption 1 m.p.g. better. Any resonant effects which may be introduced by the use of a closed body are more than offset by the reduced wind noise and buffeting which follow from the enclosure of the occupants and by reason of a well-designed and carefully positioned wrapround windscreen.

The overall fuel consumption was based upon hard driving (including some 50 laps of the Montlhéry circuit) but the M.G., by reason of the characteristics set out above encourages the driver to make full use of the performance available, this procedure being also wholly acceptable to the passenger.

Should it be necessary to drive really hard the brakes will be found equal to all demands made upon them, pedal pressures being reasonable, stopping consistent and free from the generation of smoke or smell, the drum temperatures being perhaps reduced by the wire wheels fitted.

It is clear from the very good figures recorded in the data panel and the remarks which have been so far made that the M.G. coupé is a car of considerable merit. It is also one which quickly commands affection by reason of those qualities of pleasure in driving and comfort in travelling which are not necessarily the outcome of good engineering. The suspension is on the hard side and this fact is the more noticeable if the tyres are run on the higher limits of pressure. If, however, bumps are somewhat more than usually noticeable neither pitch nor roll can normally be discerned and long high-speed journeys cause little physical and no mental fatigue.

Comfort could be further improved by raising the seats an inch or two which would at the same time give a better view over the rather high scuttle, as with the standard position a person of moderate height scarcely has both wings of the car in view. But the seats themselves are comfortable and give good support against side forces, a large fore and aft travel making it possible to accommodate small packages or even suitcases in the well at the back of the cockpit. The inboard mounting of the spare wheel causes an intrusion which is particularly noticeable in the somewhat shallow rear locker and for serious touring it would certainly be necessary to fit the optionally offered external luggage rack. Other minor matters which justify criticism are the somewhat limited arcs swept by the windscreen wipers and a rather haphazard layout of instruments and switches, although the principal items of road and

TWO inclined S.U. carburetters feed mixture to the four-cylinder o.h.v. engine. Plugs, coil, advance and retard unit, dipstick, carburetters and oil filler are easy to reach.

EXCELLENT rearward visibility follows from the use of a wrapround rear window which in conjunction with big door windows reduces the "blind" quarters to a near-minimum.

WITH spare wheel and tool roll carried in the boot, little room is left for luggage, but there is additional space behind the seats and an external luggage rack is available as an extra.

engine speed are clearly displayed immediately before the driver.

A nearside door lock is logical enough for the bulk of cars sold with left-hand drive but for the home market a lock on the driver's door would be more appropriate and, as in a closed car, the driver would probably not wear headgear, the absence of a sun vizor is hard to excuse.

The car tested had a built-in heater and ventilator which seemed more successful at supplying heated air, which was unwanted at this time of year, than fresh air at ambient temperature; which was more to be regretted as opening either the side windows or the ventilating panels permitted the entrance of rain water as well as raising the noise level.

No car is perfect and these minor criticisms must be viewed against the background that this is a car in which the exceptional performance, safety and pleasure are derived from simple mechanical components in large-scale production. In consequence, spares and maintenance costs are not out of line with ordinary commercial practice and no special mechanical skill or tuning aptitude is needed to keep the car in 100% mechanical condition. The accessibility of the engine components is adequate and an inspection of the chassis shows that the running gear is exceptionally robust and that the number of points needing regular lubrication has been reduced to nine.

Moderately priced, economical to run and maintain, remarkably fast, exceptionally safe and above all a constant pleasure to drive and be driven in, it is not surprising that the M.G. A. is beating all production records at Abingdon and that it has established itself as the most popular sports car in the world.

Specification

Engine

Cylinders	4
Bore	73.025 mm.
Stroke	89 mm.
Cubic capacity	1,489 c.c.
Piston area	25.97 sq. in.
Valves	Pushrod o.h.v.
Compression ratio	8.3/1
Carburetters	Two inclined S.U. 1½ in.
Fuel pump	S.U. electrical, rear-mounted
Ignition timing control	Vacuum
Oil filter	Full flow Tecalemit
Max. power (net)	72 b.h.p.
at	5,500 r.p.m.
Piston speed at max. b.h.p.	3,220 ft./min.

Transmission

Clutch	Single dry plate
Top gear (s/m)	4.3
3rd gear (s/m)	5.908
2nd gear (s/m)	9.52
1st gear	15.652
Reverse	20.468
Propeller shaft	Open
Final drive	Hypoid bevel
Top gear m.p.h. at 1,000 r.p.m.	17
Top gear m.p.h. at 1,000 ft./min. piston speed	29

Chassis

Brakes	Lockheed hydraulic (2 l.s. front)
Brake drum internal diameter	10 in.
Friction lining area	134.4 sq. in.
Suspension:	
Front	Coil and wishbone, i.f.s.
Rear	Semi-elliptic
Shock absorbers:	
Front	Armstrong incorporated in upper wishbone pivots
Rear	Armstrong hydraulic
Steering gear	Rack and pinion
Tyres	Dunlop 5.60—15

Coachwork and Equipment

Starting handle	Yes
Battery mounting	Behind seats
Jack	Screw-type
Jacking points	Front wishbones and rear springs

Standard tool kit: Ring-type tappet spanner, wheelbrace (copper hammer with wire wheels), tappet gauge, sparking plug spanner, pliers, grease gun, adjustable spanner, 2 tyre levers, cylinder head nut spanner, tyre valve spanner, distributor screwdriver and gauge, tyre pump, 3 box spanners, 3 o/e spanners, screwdriver, recessed screwdriver, tommy bar, jack, brake bleeder tube, gearbox plug spanner, touch-up paint-pencil, tool roll.

Exterior lights: 2 head, 2 side-indicator, 2 rear/brake/indicator.

Number of electrical fuses	Two
Direction indicators	Flashing type, self-cancelling
Windscreen wipers	Electric, self-parking
Windscreen washers	Optional
Sun vizors	No

Instruments: Speedometer with decimal trip distance recorder, rev. counter, oil pressure gauge, water thermometer.

Warning lights	Ignition, indicators, headlamp main beam
Locks:	
With ignition key	Ignition
With other keys	None
Glove lockers	None
Map pockets	Two
Parcel shelves	None
Ashtrays	One between seats
Cigar lighters	None
Interior lights	Instrument panel, map-reading light
Interior heater	Fresh-air type with de-mister
Car radio	Optional, Radiomobile

Extras available: Radio, heater, wire wheels, fog lamp, white-wall tyres, 4.55/1 axle gears, twin horns, external luggage carrier, radiator blind, rim embellishers, telescopic steering column, screen-washer, badge bar.

Upholstery material	Leather over foam rubber
Floor covering	Carpet
Exterior colours standardized	5
Alternative body styles	Open 2-seater

Maintenance

Sump	6½ pints, S.A.E. 30
Gearbox	4 pints, S.A.E. 30
Rear axle	2¾ pints, Hypoid 90
Steering gear lubricant	Hypoid 90
Cooling system capacity	10 pints (2 drain taps)
Chassis lubrication	By grease gun every 1,000 miles to 9 points
Ignition timing	7° b.t.d.c.
Contact-breaker gap	.014-.016 in.
Sparking plug gap	.019-.021 in.

Valve timing: i.o. 16° b.t.d.c.; i.c. 56° a.b.d.c.; e.o. 51° b.b.d.c.; e.c. 21° a.t.d.c.

Tappet clearances (hot)	.017 in.
Front wheel toe-in	Nil
Camber angle	1°
Castor angle	4°
Tyre pressures:	
Front	17 lb.
Rear	20 lb.
	(Fast driving, 18 lb. and 23 lb.)
Brake fluid	Lockheed
Battery type and capacity	Lucas SG9E, 12-v.

Miscellaneous: Tyre pressures as inflated for high speeds 22 lb. and 26 lb.

TWO SHAPELY MODELS are posed together at the Battersea Pleasure Gardens in London—the one on the left being the M.G.A Coupé. "Proper" wind-up windows, outside door handles and full interior trim are amongst the amenities provided. The girl is Australian ballet-dancer Toni Reece.

JOHN BOLSTER TESTS

The M.G.A Coupe

Fixed-head Coupe version of a Popular Abingdon 1½-litre Sports Car provides Saloon-Car Weather Protection and a Top Speed of over 102 m.p.h.

ON the Continent, the sports car is normally a 2-seater coupé. In England, in spite of our atrocious weather, most sports models are open, and there is a scarcity of hardtops except among the larger makers. Now, M.G. have produced a proper little coupé, and it will sell like hot cakes. It is of modern appearance and compact size, and its wrap-around screen and rear window avoid that "shut-in" feeling. Above all, it is a genuine closed car with wind-up windows, and not an open 2-seater with a hardtop attached.

The M.G.A is a well-known car and has, of course, been tested by AUTOSPORT in open form. Only a brief description is, therefore, required. The basis of the machine is a very sturdy box-section frame. The engine is the 1½-litre B.M.C. unit, tuned in this case to develop 72 b.h.p. at 5,500 r.p.m. There are twin S.U. carburetters and the Lucas distributor has centrifugal and vacuum control.

The four-speed gearbox has the traditional central remote-control lever, and one is delighted to find that the fly-off handbrake has been retained. Wishbone independent front suspension, with helical springs and rack and pinion steering, is mated with a hypoid rear axle on semi-elliptic springs.

The appearance is attractive and the car is nicely finished. The instrument panel is well arranged, and the octagon motif of the past is mercifully forgotten. Entry and exit are not particularly easy because the doors are curiously restricted in their opening. Once one is in, the driving position is found to be excellent, and the seats are comfortable, though some drivers would prefer a little more support for the thighs.

The M.G.A is astonishingly fast for a 1½-litre production car. The coupé is better streamlined than the open car, and I obtained the excellent timed speed of 102.27 m.p.h. Third gear gives a useful 74 m.p.h., but what is entirely unexpected is the flexibility in top gear, the car coming down to a crawl on that ratio and accelerating cleanly away. As the weight is fairly substantial, one does not expect slashing acceleration, but this is quite a lively vehicle nevertheless.

On the road, 80 m.p.h. is a suitable cruising speed. The engine does not become distressed at high speeds until valve bounce begins at 102 m.p.h. When driven hard it is by no means quiet, however, though the noise is not unpleasant to many sports car enthusiasts.

The old M.G. trouble of clutch slip has been eliminated, and this component is smooth in action but grips at once after a quick change. The gearbox is very pleasant indeed and requires no special skill. Although the suspension is fairly firm, this is only noticed on particularly bad roads.

Naturally, good steering is expected on a car of this class, and the M.G. rack and pinion gains full marks. It is very accurate and not too heavy, nor does the driver feel that he must "hang on" at three-figure speeds. The coupé perhaps rolls fractionally more than the open car, but it handles well and has fairly high cornering power. The rear wheels tend to bounce during a violent getaway, but one is not normally conscious of the weight of the rear axle on its semi-elliptic springs.

The M.G.A can put up a useful average speed when driven in enterprising fashion. Third gear permits hills to be stormed at a pretty impressive velocity. It is above all a sporting type of car, and the closed body in no way modifies this characteristic. The fuel consumption of 26 m.p.g. that I obtained was during really hard driving. No doubt something in the region of 30 m.p.g. could be achieved during Continental touring, which is a good argument for buying this in preference to a more powerful sports car. It is, nevertheless, a pity that the spare wheel occupies so much of the luggage compartment, for the M.G.A

SLEEK coupé top offers less wind resistance than the normal hood, and results in a higher top speed than the sports car although the all-up weight is slightly greater. Luggage space is largely occupied by the spare wheel.

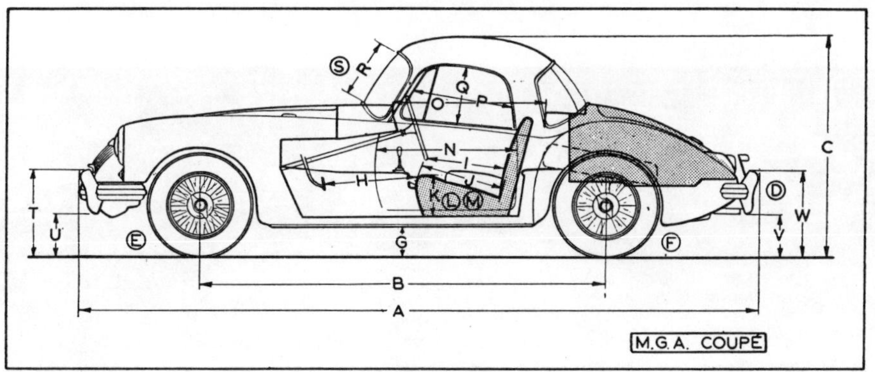

Dimensions

A Overall length, 13 ft.
B Wheelbase, 7 ft. 10 ins.
C Overall height, 4 ft. 2 ins.
D Overall width, 4 ft. 10 ins.
E Front track, 3 ft. 11¼ ins.
F Rear track, 4 ft. 0¾ in.
G Ground clearance, 6 ins.
H Seat to pedal, 1 ft. 5 ins. (min.), 1 ft. 10½ ins. (max.)
I Seat squab to steering wheel, 1 ft. 1 in. (min.), 1 ft. 6¾ ins. (max.)
J Depth of seat cushion, 1 ft. 8 ins.
K Height of seat cushion, 7 ins.
L Width of seat cushion, 1 ft. 5 ins.
M Overall width of seats, 3 ft. 10 ins.
N Door width, 2 ft. 4 ins.
O Instrument panel to rear screen ledge, 2 ft. 11 ins.
P Side screen width, 1 ft. 9¼ ins.
Q Side screen depth, 11¾ ins.
R Windscreen depth, 1 ft. 0½ in.
S Windscreen width, 3 ft. 8 ins.
T Height to top of front over-rider, 1 ft. 8 ins.
U Height to bottom of front over-rider, 10 ins.
V Height to bottom of rear over-rider, 10½ ins.
W Height to top of rear over-rider, 1 ft. 8½ ins.

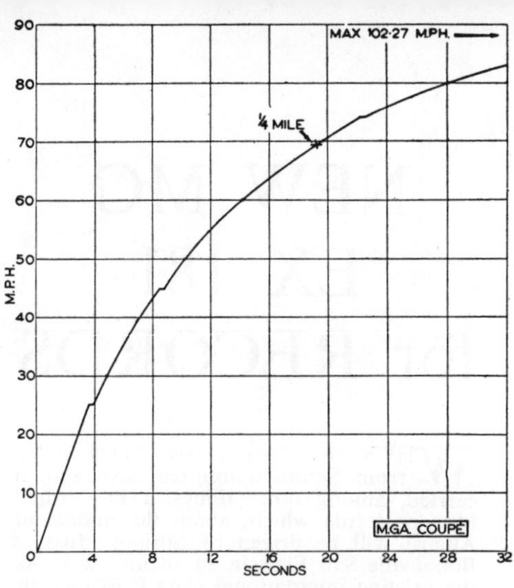

Acceleration Graph

their location particularly comfortable for my hands.

The M.G.A coupé is an extremely attractive small closed sports car. It forms a useful and reliable mode of everyday transport, but it also has a very real turn of speed. This is a British car with many of the attractions of the sporting Continentals.

★

ACCESSIBILITY under the bonnet hatch is quite good. The 1½-litre "B"-type B.M.C. engine is tuned in this case to develop 72 b.h.p. at 5,000 r.p.m.

★

is in other respects so suitable for long-distance touring.

Powerful Lockheed brakes are fitted and they stand up well to hard driving. The racing-type wire wheels of the test car probably helped to keep the drums cool, but in any case they are very much in keeping with the character of the machine and certainly enhance the appearance. There are many touches that will appeal to the fastidious sports car owner. The engine has an attractive appearance and the layout under the bonnet is neat. The headlamps permit a high cruising speed to be maintained at night.

In a car as low as the M.G.A, a very deep gearbox and shaft tunnel is unavoidable. As this is strictly a two-seater, it does not matter at all, except that some heat is radiated into the body during hot weather. The four spokes of the steering wheel are not evenly spaced, and I did not personally find

Specification and Performance Data

Car Tested: M.G.A 2-seater coupé. Price £1,087 7*s.* including P.T. Price with extras—wire wheels, screen washer, heater and demister—£1,158 15*s.* 9*d.*

Engine: Four-cylinders 73.025 mm. x 89 mm. (1,489 c.c.), pushrod operated overhead valves, 72 b.h.p. at 5,500 r.p.m., 8.3 to 1 compression ratio. Twin S.U. carburetters. Lucas coil and distributor.

Transmission: Borg and Beck 8 ins. single dry-plate clutch with hydraulic operation; four-speed gearbox with central remote control, ratios 4.3, 5.908, 9.520 and 15.652 to 1. Open propeller shaft. Hypoid rear axle.

Chassis: Box section frame. Independent front suspension by wishbones and helical springs. Rack and pinion steering. Rear axle on semi-elliptic springs. Piston-type hydraulic dampers, 10 ins. Lockheed hydraulic brakes with fly-off handbrake. Centre-lock wire wheels (extra), fitted 5.60-15 ins. tyres.

Equipment: 12-volt lighting and starting. Speedometer, rev. counter, fuel, oil pressure and water temperature gauges. Flashing indicators. Map light. Heater and demister (extra). Windscreen washer (extra).

Dimensions: Wheelbase 7 ft. 10 ins. Track, front 3 ft. 11¼ ins., rear 4 ft. 0¾ in. Overall length 13 ft. Width 4 ft. 10 ins. Weight 18½ cwt.

Performance: Maximum speed 102.27 m.p.h. Speeds in gears: 3rd 74 m.p.h.; 2nd 45 m.p.h.; 1st 25 m.p.h. Standing quarter-mile 19.2 secs. Acceleration: 0-30 m.p.h. 4.8 secs.; 0-50 m.p.h. 10.2 secs.; 0-60 m.p.h. 14.2 secs.; 0-70 m.p.h. 19.8 secs.; 0-80 m.p.h. 28 secs.

Fuel Consumption: Driven hard 26 m.p.g.

IN THE M.G. TRADITION—*continued from page* **51**

" on." The interior carpets have press-button fastenings and fit well where chassis members intrude, and the upholstery is securely attached.

The appearance of the car we borrowed for test was enhanced by centre-lock wire wheels. Besides these the M.G. owner has the choice of H.M.V. radio, whitewall tyres, a lower (4.55-to-1) back-axle ratio, twin horns, rim embellishers, radiator blind, and, for the two-seater, tonneau cover, badge bar, detachable hard-top, and de luxe sidescreens, besides the " extras " already mentioned, *i.e.*, demister and heater, ash-tray, telescopic steering-column, wire wheels, cockpit ventilator, " Road Speed " tyres, wing mirror, external luggage carrier, fog-lamp and windshield washer. He or she can specify black, orient red, tyrolite green, glacier blue or old English white finish, with various choice of upholstery colour.

Taking a last look at this convenient and economical fast car, which we returned with reluctance, naturally there are bumpers front and back, a badge-bar above the front one, the rear lamps rather vulnerable above the back one. On each side of the scuttle hot air escapes *via* apertures with MGA motifs and, naturally again, the Lucas headlamps are in-built. The lamps provide a good beam, but driving after dark brings the realisation that the nose dips to some extent under braking or over bad roads, whereas in the day-time this slight pitching is not apparent. The foot dipper is set too high, the foot having to leave the floor to operate it. This M.G. has a ground clearance of 6 in. and further details of the car as tested appear in the panel on page 296.

Summing up, the MGA is every inch an M.G. and Abingdon has obviously exercised considerable ingenuity in blending various standardised B.M.C. components into a sports car which is a worthy descendant of the race-bred cars which preceded it, inasmuch as it possesses impeccable road manners and adequate performance, combining these with an eye-stopping appearance. The starting price of the M.G. MGA coupé, before " extras " are ordered, is £699, which purchase tax inflates to £1,049 17s.; with " extras," as tested, the total price is £1,126 13s.—W. B.

NEW MG EX 181 for RECORDS

Front view of EX 181, latest of a long line of MG record-breakers, gives it a flying saucer appearance.

WHEN the liner Queen Mary sailed from Southampton ten days ago, it carried, among other things, a tiny bright blue projectile which, about the middle of August will be driven by Stirling Moss at Bonneville Salt Flats in an attempt to break the existing international class F flying mile record. Known as the EX 181, this latest in a long line of MG record-breakers, reveals much of the experience which the MG Car Company has amassed over the years in the design, production and preparation of cars of this type.

According to Sidney Enever, Chief Engineer of MG, this latest record breaker is as much as 37 per cent. more efficient aerodynamically than its immediate predecessor, so that with a supercharged 1500-cc engine, it is hoped to surpass the existing class F record by at least 36 mph. The record at presents stands to the credit of Goldie Gardner and the MG EX. 135, at 203.9 mph, this being the last record established before the outbreak of war in 1939, on the autobahn at Dessau, in Germany.

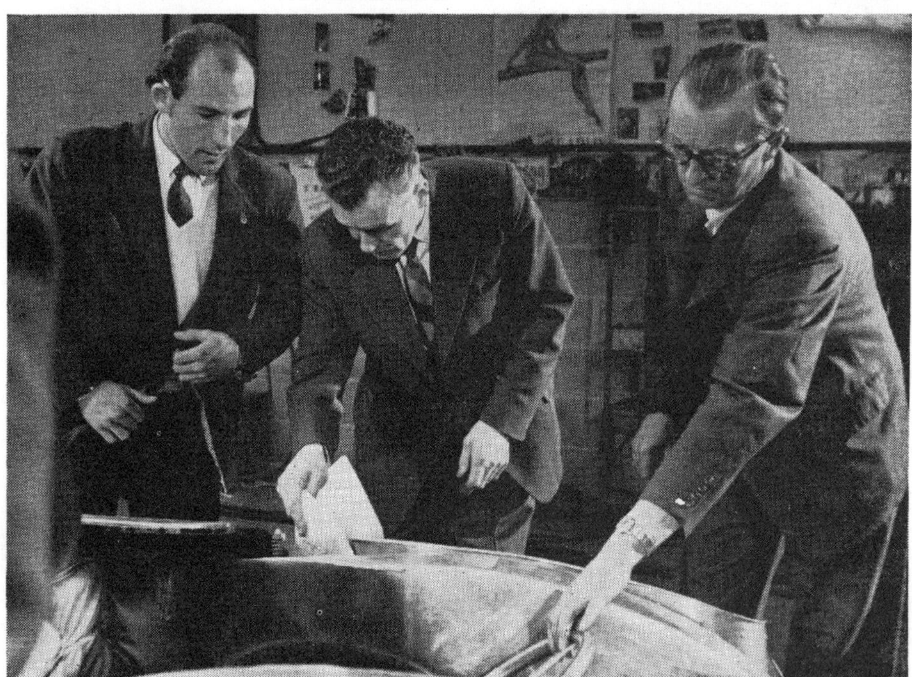

Driver Stirling Moss, designer Sidney Enever and MG Managing Director John Thornley discuss the seating position.

The EX. 181 bears at least some resemblance to its predecessors, except for the reduction in overall size which is quite striking. Frontal area has been greatly reduced, the major factor in this achievement being the location of the engine in the centre of the frame with the driver immediately in front and seated below the tubular frame side members. The layout thus follows the lines established by Reid Railton with the John Cobb Napier-Railton, but in place of a collection of aero-engines and assorted gearboxes, the power is provided by a developed version of the BMC B-series four-cylinder 1489 cc engine as used in the MGA, Magnette, Wolseley 15/50, 1500, Austin A55, Morris Oxford and Cowley and numerous light commercial vehicles. The engine has a similar twin-overhead camshaft cylinder head to that seen two years ago at the TT but undoubtedly has a stiffer crankshaft and bigger bearings.

Forced induction is provided by a large Shorrocks supercharger, and it is claimed that the engine produces over 260 bhp. Drive from the engine is through an MG TC gearbox to a chassis-mounted hypoid final drive unit in which the ratio is under 2 to 1. Full technical details of the EX. 181 are not being released until after the record attempts.

With its ultra-low build, the new MG appears aerodynamically efficient. Only a small amount of tyre tread near the ground is not faired on each wheel. Engine is mounted amidships.

With the driving seat below the frame and slightly ahead of the front wheels, it is clearly necessary to ensure that the driver has adequate visibility and room to operate the controls. Stirling Moss spent a day at Abingdon before the car left, to see that the " control room " met his requirements. The steering column pivots forward to allow access to the driving seat, in the same way as the front panelling which hinges forward complete with the acetate cockpit bubble. Only a few minor modifications were necessary to ensure a comfortable fit (a driving fit?) for Moss, who expressed confidence in the ability of the car to achieve 240 mph. Everyone will wish them luck in their joint efforts.

DISPATCH from UTAH

(Above) EX 181 streaks across the Utah salt in blinding early morning sunshine. Below, the tiny rear-engined car is prepared for the first run.

From Joseph Lowrey, Utah,
Sunday, August 18

SO it works. The speeds which U.S.A.C. timekeepers recorded officially this morning are an extremely tight secret, for it has been laid down that unless something goes wrong Stirling Moss will break the 1,500 c.c. class speed records when he arrives from his victory at Pescara. But this morning, after only one warm-up trip along the straight expanse of glaring white salt which should really be labelled Sunstroke Boulevard, Phil Hill did a one-way run at 6,500 r.p.m. in the rear-engined M.G. and went 100 r.p.m. faster on the way back, figures which seem to indicate a timed average very close to 240 m.p.h. It could hardly have been a more trouble-free morning's motoring.

Around 8.45 a.m. EX 181 was linked by tow-bar to an M.G. A, Australian Bill Pringle gave Alec Hounslow from Abingdon a tow start, the twin-camshaft supercharged engine was warmed up, and a set of hard plugs put in. At this point, shortage of observers led your correspondent to volunteer for duty on the telephone at the 5-mile timing ray, listening in on " party line " conferences between ends of the course instead of actually seeing the turn-arounds.

With a very modest rev. limit, the American driver Phil Hill took the car northwards for a warm-up run, reporting that everything was satisfactory. So, new tyres were put on the car (of very low profile on 14-in. rims, with a completely smooth tread) and at 9.20 he headed back towards Wendover, with the smoke from a crashed jet aircraft acting as an additional signpost and with orders to run at 6,500 r.p.m. The timing equipment, carefully checked a few minutes before to ensure that light-ray apparatus was coping with the glaring sunshine, worked perfectly, and the unorthodox little car with its forward driving seat, amidships engine and very narrow De Dion rear axle ran perfectly straight.

From this first high-speed run, however, there came news of inadequate cockpit ventilation, communication between the cockpit and the enclosed front-wheel arches producing a vacuum which drew in fumes of alcohol fuel. Tyres and plugs were checked but not changed, and a slit was made in a radiator air intake duct to blow more air on to the driver's face. Well within the permitted hour, the car made its third appearance on the smooth, straight track marked by central and side lines of black oil.

Over the telephone system, there came all too clearly the sound of misfiring as the car accelerated away from a push start in second gear. But, in sufficient time, all four cylinders cut in, and the driver came through the measured mile at 6,600 r.p.m., breathing comfortably this time. Slipping into neutral and shutting off the engine quite soon, he had no trouble stopping the car with the one disc-type rear brake, and reported that the car was completely stable although heavy to steer until it was moving fast.

On Tuesday night, Stirling Moss will arrive from Pescara if aircraft run to schedule, and he is due to make his runs on Wednesday (August 21). If all goes well, the record should be raised to over 240 m.p.h. EX 181 can obviously go much faster if required. Thunderstorms now rumbling in the mountains which surround this salt wilderness may, however, break over the dry lake and flood the track.

* * *

Storms did in fact flood the salt but, at dusk on Friday, August 23, Moss judged the conditions made an attempt possible. Five records (subject to F.I.A. ratification) resulted:—

INTERNATIONAL CLASS F (1,500 c.c.)

Records claimed for M.G. EX 181 (driver: Stirling Moss). All runs were with flying start. Previous records, held by Lt.-Col. A. T. Goldie-Gardner (M.G.), shown in brackets.

		m.p.h.
1 km.	(204.3 m.p.h., 1939)	245.64
1 mile	(203.9 m.p.h., 1939)	245.11
5 km.	(200.6 m.p.h., 1939)	243.08
5 miles	(189.5 m.p.h., 1952)	235.69
10 km.	(182.8 m.p.h., 1952)	224.7

BROOKS WINS BELGIAN GRAND PRIX

August 25. Spa-Francorchamps circuit, for sports cars. Duration: Three hours. 1 lap: 8.76 miles.

1, Tony Brooks (Aston Martin DBR1), 41 laps at 118.5 m.p.h.

2, Masten Gregory (3.5 Ferrari), 1 min. 27 sec. behind.

3, Olivier Gendebien (4.1 Ferrari), 1 min. 52 sec. behind.

4, Roy Salvadori (Aston Martin DBR1), 40 laps.

5, Brian Naylor (Jaguar D-type), 39 laps.

6, Graham Whitehead (Aston Martin DB3S), 39 laps.

7, Peter Whitehead (Aston Martin DB3S), 39 laps.

Fastest lap: Gendebien, 4 min. 10.4 sec., 126.1 m.p.h. (sports car record).

World's Fastest "Fifteen Hundred"

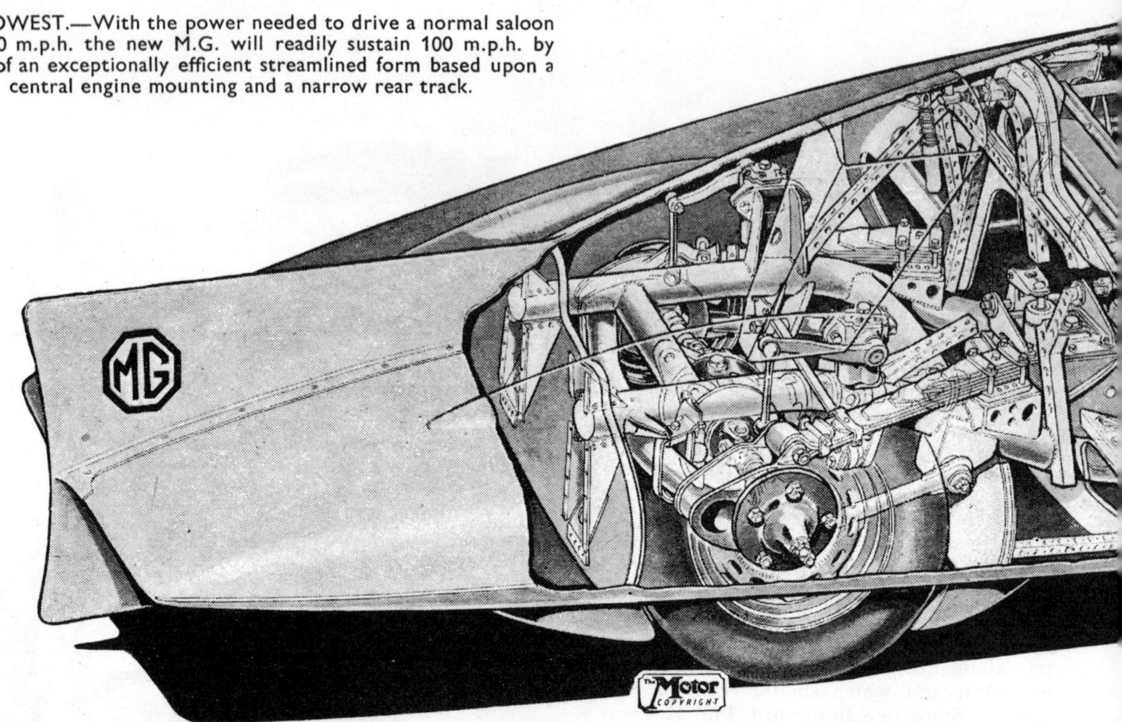

THE LOWEST.—With the power needed to drive a normal saloon car at 60 m.p.h. the new M.G. will readily sustain 100 m.p.h. by reason of an exceptionally efficient streamlined form based upon a central engine mounting and a narrow rear track.

WHEN the late Sir Malcolm Campbell broke the World Land Speed Record in 1931 at 246.09 m.p.h. and in 1932 at 253.96 m.p.h., he used an engine of 24 litres developing 1,450 b.h.p. in a car weighing some 4 tons. The special M.G. car, EX 181, in which records were recently broken on Bonneville Salt Flats, had an engine of only 1½ litres, which developed 290 b.h.p. in a car weighing a mere 14¾ cwt. dry. The comparison gives some idea of the progress made in a bare quarter of a century.

First details of EX 181 appeared in *The Motor* of April 24 this year and, from the side-elevation drawing published in that issue, readers will already be familiar with the general layout. Now it is possible to supplement the necessarily brief details then given with a full description and drawings.

When it was first decided by Mr. John Thornley, director and general manager of M.G., to build a car to replace the famous EX 135, in which no fewer than 34 International Records had been broken by Lieut-Col. A. T. Goldie-Gardner between 1938 and 1952 (not to mention 12 previous records achieved by George Eyston with the same chassis but an earlier type of body), the problem was soon found to be primarily one of shape, with power a vital, but nevertheless secondary, consideration.

The problem, in fact, revolved round the best way of accommodating a driver and an engine within an overall shell offering the least possible drag. Preliminary calculations soon showed that the conventional arrangement of seating the driver aft of the power unit had reached the worth-while limit and that although, given more power, a machine designed on the lines of Gardner's car could undoubtedly be made to go faster, the law of diminishing returns had already set in.

Thus, although 180 b.h.p. had been adequate for 200 m.p.h. on EX 135, no less than 295 b.h.p. would have been necessary for this car, or one like it, to reach the new M.G. target of 240 m.p.h. Accordingly, the present plan—first used on the late John Cobb's World's Land Speed Record car—of sitting the driver in the nose and locating the engine amidships was finally adopted after wind-tunnel tests of six different models.

This expedient, in conjunction with a very narrow rear track and small wheels, enabled a nearly ideal aerofoil shape of 10.99 sq. ft. frontal area to be obtained. How near can be gathered from the aerodynamic coefficient, or drag factor, K, which is only 0.000292. This is little more than one-tenth of that of an ordinary touring car. It also represented an improvement of 30 per cent. on EX 135 and (allowing for the fact that rolling resistance is not susceptible to similar improvement) lowered the power required to reach 200 m.p.h. to 145 b.h.p., and that needed for 240 m.p.h. to 240 b.h.p. leaving a margin of some 50 b.h.p. available over estimated target requirements.

Expressed baldly and briefly in this way, the achievement sounds all too easy and does less than justice to the genius of Sydney Enever, chief engineer of M.G., and his team in fitting the necessary "works" into so excellent a shell. In fact, of course, shell and chassis were parallel developments, each designed in conjunction with the requirements of the other. Before the construction of the body is dealt with in detail, therefore, something should be said about the chassis.

The main frame is a ladder-like fabrication of two 3½-in. diameter, 14-gauge mild-steel tubes, joined by 2½-in. 16-gauge cross-tubes and by the box-section front-suspension member, which is standard M.G. A except that a section of 5½ in. has been removed from the centre and the ends welded up to give a narrower track of 3 ft. 6 in. The side tubes are swept up slightly at the front and considerably at the rear, where the frame tapers to pass over the De Dion rear axle and between the wheels, with their narrow track of only 2 ft. 6¾ in.

Welded to the side members are brackets to take the engine mountings, shock absorbers, sharply splayed quarter-elliptic rear springs with their radius arms below, and also the framework for the front and rear bulkheads; these latter consist mainly of 1-in. square-section tubes, liberally drilled

The M.G. Record-breaker

A Full Technical Description of EX 181

where possible and reinforced additionally in the case of the front bulkhead by round-section tubes extending to the front-suspension cross-member. Extra rigidity is given to the whole structure by a further pair of bolt-on tubes connecting the two bulkheads and designed to be detachable for engine fitting or removal.

An interesting point is that the main frame is relatively short, terminating at the front suspension member and just aft of the rear wheels. The nose of the car and the pedals are carried on a light framework which supports the body, whilst the extended tail is a frameless stressed-skin structure.

The body itself is a beautiful example of the panel-beater's art in 18-gauge Hiduminium 33 light alloy and, apart from the detachable sections mentioned below, is welded in position as a complete shell. The detachable portions, all secured by Dzus clips, comprise (1) the front-hinged nose, which provides driver access; (2) the engine compartment cover, which includes most of the head fairing; (3) the panels for rear-wheel removal; and (4) the further small panels, below the "Plimsoll line," for front-wheel removal.

Points of unusual interest include wheel fairings bolted to the smooth belly and the fact that the road wheels each run in a separate wheel-box to reduce pumping losses. The whole body is set at a negative angle of incidence to the ground in the interests of stability and minimum drag; the shape provides a slight downward pressure on the front and a negative effect at the rear.

A considerable minor problem in the case of all high-speed machines is the admission and discharge of air without adding seriously to wind resistance, both in the actual passage through the car and in the disturbing effect of the discharge on the air flow past the body. In the case of the cooling system, air is taken from two small entries in the extreme nose and ducted on each side of the driver to a pair of segmental radiators located in the front bulkhead, whence further ducts lead to side exits placed to give some boundary-layer control of the airstream over the body. This arrangement, in conjunction with careful experiments with radiator thickness in relation to superficial area, results in a total calculated cooling-system drag of only 14 lb. at maximum speed.

Similar principles have been applied to the air inlet, to the carburetters and to the engine exhausts, which take the form of four fishtail exits. Pipe lengths have also been carefully graded to equalize the extractor effects on the four ports. Apart from the intake to the carburetters, the air in the engine compartment is stagnant, ventilation being considered unnecessary for the short runs involved.

The engine has an aluminium twin-camshaft cylinder head and a large-capacity Shorrock eccentric-vane supercharger, but the design of the remainder is based directly on the B.M.C. "B" Series engine of 73.025 mm. x 89 mm. bore and stroke (1,489 c.c.), so that many of the lessons learned can be applied to future development of the production unit and EX 181 can truly be regarded in the light of a mobile laboratory.

Extra stiffening webs are formed in the cast-iron block and crankcase, the crankshaft has nitrided pins running in lead-indium bearings and the connecting rods are steel forgings with fully floating gudgeon pins. No cylinder-head gasket is used, pressure rings being employed in the tops of the bores.

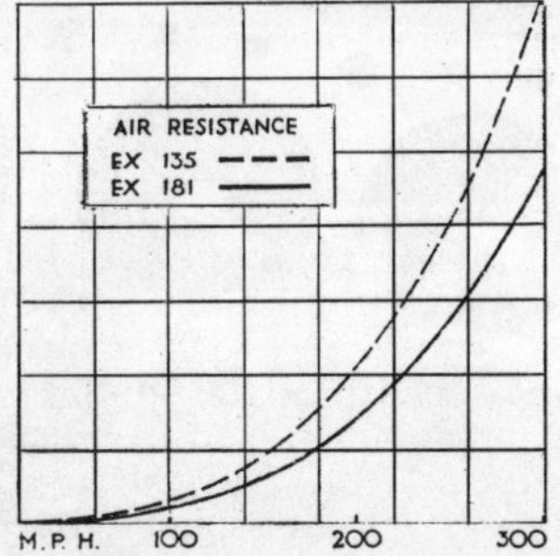

RELATIVE MERIT.—These two curves show the power needed at various speeds on the M.G. which held the records now broken by the vehicle having the wind resistance displayed in the lower curve.

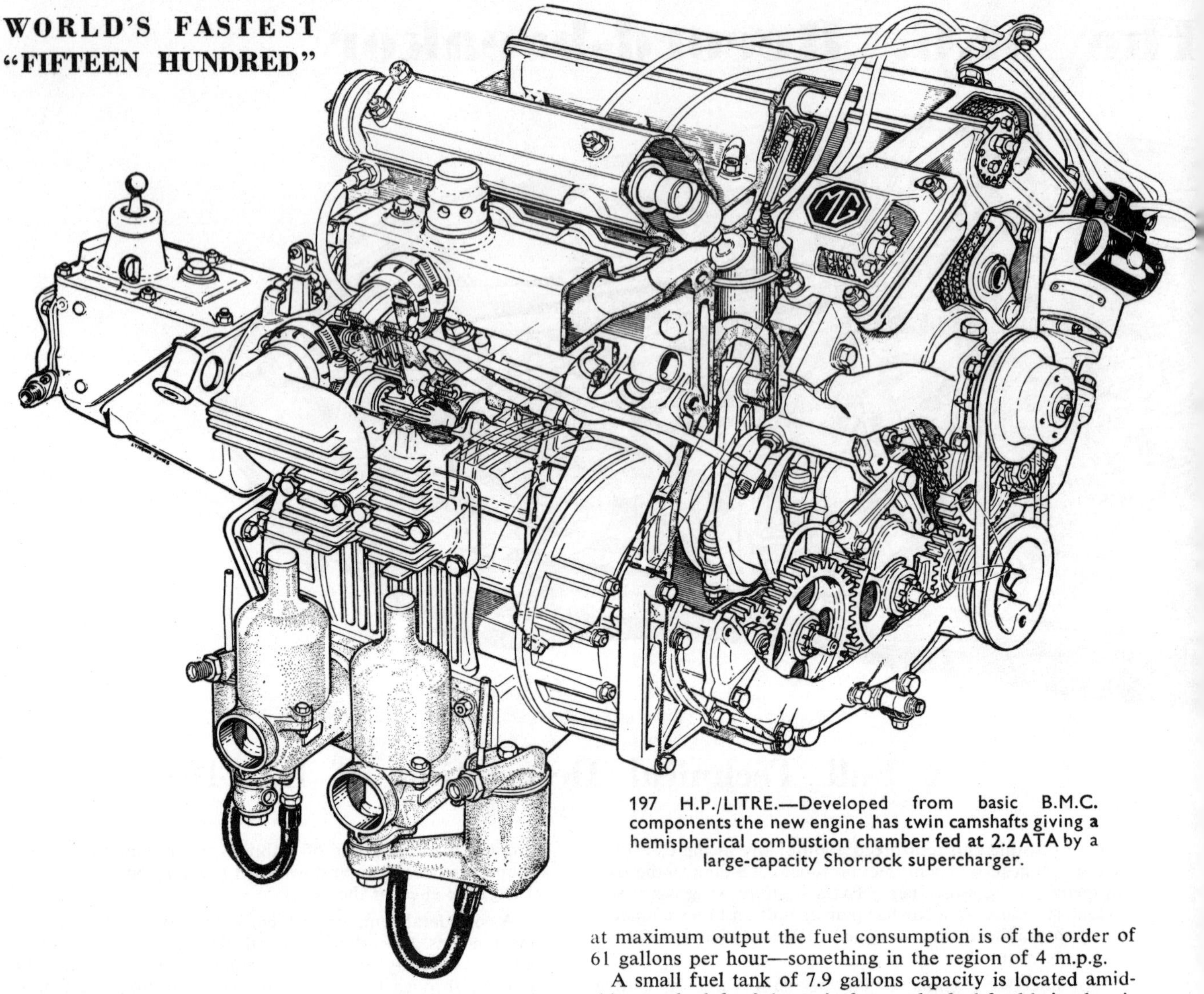

197 H.P./LITRE.—Developed from basic B.M.C. components the new engine has twin camshafts giving a hemispherical combustion chamber fed at 2.2 ATA by a large-capacity Shorrock supercharger.

A triangulated duplex roller chain drives the two o.h. camshafts, which operate the valves direct through inverted bucket-type tappets. The valves are inclined at an included angle of 80 degrees in hemispherical combustion chambers and seat on inserts in the light-alloy head. As one would expect, the inlets are larger than the exhausts, the latter being sodium cooled.

For the blower, a train of gears is used and the crankshaft also drives a secondary shaft, from which both the Lucas racing magneto and the Hobourn Eaton oil pump are driven by skew gearing. As already indicated, the blower is of very large capacity (5 litres per revolution) and, drawing mixture through two S.U. horizontal carburetters of $2\frac{3}{16}$-in. throat diameter, delivers it to the induction manifold at a maximum pressure of 32 lb./sq. in. Two blow-off valves are arranged in the manifold and a Ki-gass injector is provided for starting. The engine delivers 290 b.h.p. at 7,300 r.p.m. and at maximum output the fuel consumption is of the order of 61 gallons per hour—something in the region of 4 m.p.g.

A small fuel tank of 7.9 gallons capacity is located amidships on the left of the main frame, the fuel feed being by air pressure from a reservoir which is pumped up to 80 lb./sq. in. before the start of each run and, working through a reducing valve, feeds fuel to the carburetters at 5 lb./sq. in. A methanol-base fuel is used.

For the cooling system, a belt-driven water pump is employed and the block and head are fed separately. For the block, there are four inlets on the right-hand (inlet-valve) side and a single outlet on the left side at the front. The head is also supplied, at front and rear, on the inlet-valve side, the flow being ducted across to the exhaust-valve area and thence via an outlet between the camshafts to the single header tank in the fairing behind the driver's head.

In unit with the engine is a $7\frac{1}{4}$-in. Borg and Beck three-plate clutch and a straightforward four-speed synchromesh gearbox without reverse gear and with mechanical remote control carried past the side of the engine to a small lever

SIMPLE STRUCTURE.—Two large-diameter frame tubes are stiffened by front and rear arches welded to them which also give substantial protection in case of accident.

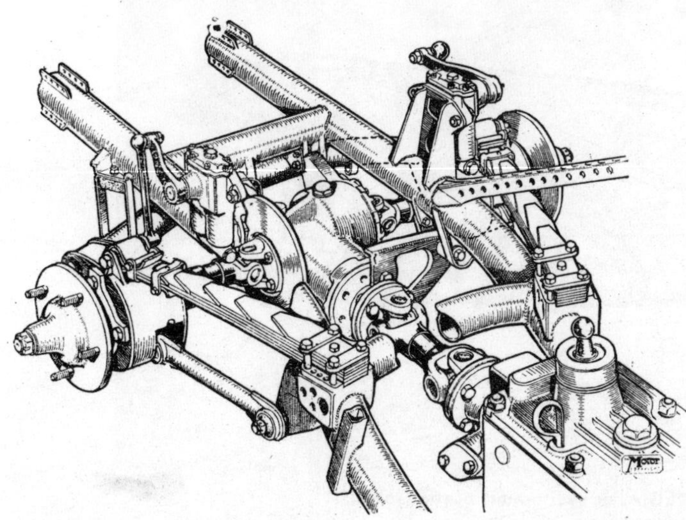

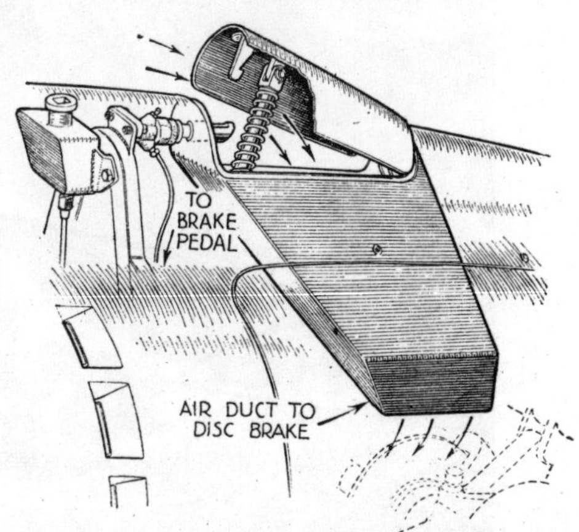

INGENIOUS DETAIL.—As the inboard Girling disc brake at the back is isolated from the airstream there is an ingenious interlock with the brake pedal so that air is fed into a cooling conduit when the car is being stopped. The left-hand drawing shows the splayed quarter-elliptic springs used in conjunction with the independent rear suspension.

on the driver's left. Hydraulic operation is used for the clutch.

A short open propeller shaft, only 6 in. between universals, leads to a spiral-bevel drive (contained in a light-alloy casing mounted on the frame), for which alternative ratios of 16/31 (1.94 to 1) and 17/31 (1.825) are available, the former giving 36.2 m.p.h. per 1,000 r.p.m. and the latter 38.6 m.p.h. Gear-changing speeds (at 6,500 r.p.m.) on the former axle are 59 m.p.h., 103 m.p.h. and 159 m.p.h. Very short universally jointed half-shafts transmit the drive to the hub assemblies, which are connected by a De Dion tube and located by short, splayed quarter-elliptic springs above and radius arms below. Control is by Armstrong piston-type dampers, which are also used at the front, where suspension is by a coil and parallel-wishbone system on M.G. A lines.

At the front, the spring rate is 150 lb./in. and at the rear 189 lb./in., total deflection in each case being only 3 in. between full bump and rebound.

As already mentioned, very small wheels are used for so fast a car, this expedient having been taken to avoid prominent bulges which would interfere with the smooth contours of the body. The rims are of only 15-in. size and in them are mounted tyres of 4.5-in. section having an overall diameter of 24 in. When it is borne in mind that, in addition to centrifugal loads, the rear tyres would also have to withstand a thrust which might reach 340 lb., the problems which faced the Dunlop concern in developing them will be appreciated. Pressures are of the order of 60-65 lb./sq. in.

Braking requirements are confined to bringing the car to rest from approximately half maximum speed and, in consequence, front brakes have been omitted to save weight. For the latter reason also, rear braking is confined to a single 10-in. diameter Girling disc system, inboard mounted and provided with cooling air from a special duct from the central fairing above the tail. This is normally closed by a flap, which springs open when the brake pedal is depressed. Although the flap itself inevitably acts to a minor degree as an air brake, this effect is incidental.

Steering is by rack and pinion, with a short column between the driver's legs surmounted by a 15-in. Bluemel wheel, of which the centre, spokes and inner portion of rim are cut from a single steel plate. To enable the driver to enter and alight, the column can be hinged forward.

Finally, some dimensions. Track details have already been given. The wheelbase is 8 ft. and the overall length 15 ft. 1½ in., these dimensions being originally determined by the frontal area which could be obtained and the optimum thickness/length ratio required to provide the desired aerodynamic shape. To the top of the driver's cowl, the height is only 3 ft. 2¼ in., and to the top of the main body shell only 2 ft. 6⅛ in., whilst the overall width is 5 ft. 4¼ in. The dry weight is 14 cwt. 3 qr. 3 lb. (front, 7 cwt. 1 qr. 12 lb.; rear, 7 cwt. 1 qr. 19 lb.) and the all-up weight with driver, 17 cwt. 0 qr. 6 lb., the front/rear weight distribution in the latter case being 51½/48½.

RESPONSIBLE MEN.—Seen here with the car are (left to right): J. Thompson, chief engineer of Morris Engines branch, who designed the engine, J. Goffin and E. Maher, assistant chief and chief experimental engineers of the Engines Branch, who developed and tested the power unit, S. Enever, M.G.'s chief engineer who designed the car, A. Hounslow (in car), foreman of the M.G. development shop which built the car, John Thornley (bending over), director and general manager of M.G. responsible for the whole project, G. Iley, M.G. assistant general manager, and T. Mitchell, M.G. designer who executed the detail design.

High altitude: the M.G.A. at the summit of the Gavia.

HIGH ALTITUDE

A PROVING TRIP OVER EUROPE'S HIGHEST PASSES *by JOHN GOTT*

ONE of the most valuable things a manufacturer gains from competing in Continental rallies is technical information upon his cars' reaction to extreme Continental conditions. The "emasculation" of this year's Alpine Rally by the suppression of the Gavia and of the Dolomite Cup Circuit prevented full technical value being obtained from the event, while crews tired by the strain of Liège-Rome-Liège (see "Blues in the Night," in *The Motor* of September 12 and 19) are usually physically incapable of driving their cars to the extreme and then making an accurate technical report on them.

Thus I was not altogether surprised when Marcus Chambers, B.M.C.'s genial Competitions Manager, casually inquired if I would be interested in a little 'mountaineering' on the same M.G.A. 'hardtop' which had carried me in the Alpine and Liège-Rome-Liège. Once I had accepted, he shook me somewhat by stating that the 'mountaineering' would consist of what he cheerfully described as 'destruction tests' and timed runs over the Stelvio and Gavia Passes, and that they would take place almost immediately before snow closed the passes.

Now the Stelvio is about the best-known pass in Europe, as its height of 9,042 feet entitles the souvenir-sellers at the summit to claim it as Europe's highest—although France's Col d'Iseran just shades it—but the Gavia is quite another kettle of fish! Although its height of 8,599 feet makes it about Europe's third highest pass it is shunned by most tourists on account of its indifferent surface and extreme narrowness flanked by fearsome drops. Indeed, near the summit there is a beautiful crucifix erected by a party of tourists in devout thankfulness for getting safely off it.

True—this was in 1929, but even nowadays hardened rally-drivers tend to heave sighs of relief on hearing that it is not on the Alpine or Liège-Rome-Liège routes. Was it not here that Niedermeyer crashed in '56; that Meier went over the edge in '55; and that 'Gatso' dropped 20 feet into a stream bed in '53?

The phrase 'destruction tests' consequently had an ominous ring until Marcus made it clear that these related to certain components on the car (the engine of which had only had a decoke since L-R-L), and not to its crew! To offset this, however, he also made it clear that the driver would be expected to lend a hand in changing the axle and gearbox ratios which were to be the subject of timed tests.

Thus the late afternoon of September 30 found the B.M.C. party of Marcus, Ernie Giles of the Competitions Department and myself on the summit of the Stelvio.

It was a glorious Indian Summer day and the rain and mist of Dunkerque, which we had left the morning before, seemed but a bad dream. However, the weatherwise locals told us that snow was not far away, so while Marcus parked our tender car, Austin A90, SOL 125 (erstwhile winner of the highest Concours prizes in this year's Monte and victor of the British and French Economy Rallies, but now weighed down with tools and spares), and prepared to enjoy a glass of wine preparatory to timing us up the *lacets*, Ernie and I took the M.G.A. down the 48 hairpins to Gomagoi, whence start the Alpine climbs.

Friendly interest at Ponte di Legno.

Grim memory: The monument on the Gavia to the 36 men of the Alpinieri who plunged over the edge at this point in July, 1954.

(*Below*) Marcus and SOL triumphantly cresting the Stelvio's summit with the Volkswagen on tow.

For us both the run up was vital.

If Ernie, who had only once before been on the Continent and who had never been driven over a real pass at speed, doubted my ability to keep the M.G.A. on track or if I queried the accuracy of his timing, the value of the sortie would be largely lost.

We need not have worried; at Gomagoi we were just two men in a car, but at the summit we were a mutually confident crew.

Incidentally it is interesting to note that Ernie reckoned that the climbs were more nerve-racking than the descents, whereas most rallyists hold diametrically opposed views.

In planning the sortie Marcus had selected as our base Bormio which lies in the Sondrio valley at the foot of the passes. We chose the Hotel Posta e Bormio solely because it was recommended in a brochure which had been thrust into the car as we hurriedly clocked into the Bormio control on L-R-L.

The recommendation was fully justified, as the proprietor, Signor Renzo Pelosi, went out of his way to be helpful, even though our routine—we made the runs around dawn, siesta time and dusk, when traffic was at a minimum—called for meals at odd hours. Nor did this seem strange to the enthusiastic Italians who came to look at us, and to whom we were always introduced in the strict mechanical order of precedence as the Engineer (Marcus), the Meccanico (Ernie), and the Pilota (myself). Indeed, almost everywhere we encountered interest and enthusiasm. Road repair gangs were out on the passes, working feverishly to beat the snow, but they never failed to wave cheerfully as we went past, and Ernie and I wondered if one of them was running a book on our progress. The foreman of the Gavia gang, once he had seen our L-R-L transfer, was particularly helpful, and indeed this transfer was a sort of talisman, for L-R-L is an important event in the lives of some of the more remote mountain-dwellers at the summit of the Gavia, one of whom stopped us to ask if more cars were coming and seemed disappointed to hear that there weren't.

The chief drawback to this intense interest was that almost everyone insisted on telling us, at some length, about gruesome crashes in past years, which was a little unsettling.

That these were not unfounded is proved by the beautiful marble monument to the Alpinieri who plunged to their death in July, 1954, when their truck swayed over the edge on the most dangerous part of the descent. However, as a result of this appalling accident the pass was widened and the sheer drop fenced by strong iron posts. According to our friendly foreman these saved the lives of Niedermeyer and Brunner when their Porsche crashed in L-R-L of 1956, and he showed us the bend in the rails in proof of his assertion.

To get the Gavia into a true perspective, however, it should always be remembered that it is not a main link of tourist communications, but, as monuments at the summit bear witness,

The foreman of the Gavia repair gang has a word with Ernie Giles whilst his men clear a rockfall.

Crew's-eye-view as the M.G.A. sweeps down the Gavia.

primarily a military road, for which purposes it is quite adequate. Actually at touring speeds on a fine summer's day I do not think that the Gavia's ferocious reputation need deter anyone with a good car from attempting the pass from the Bormio side. This climb is not unduly difficult nor is the gradient severe although the surface is very rough towards the summit.

The really dangerous section is the first five kilometres of the descent to Ponte di Legno, but it is easy to turn round at the summit and to return to Bormio, so avoiding this.

Certainly any tourist with a sense of adventure who tackles the climb successfully will be rewarded not only with some wonderful views of wild mountain lakes but also with a feeling of real achievement. Nevertheless, familiarity with the Pass certainly did not breed a contempt of it in Ernie and me, for it was on the Gavia that we had most of our 'moments'. It was here that we shot over the summit to find cloud right down, which reduced visibility to a matter of feet; it was here that we unexpectedly came on a rock-fall blocking the road; it was here that a razor-edged rock slashed through a tyre-wall and the resulting immediate flat caused some interesting swerves in the narrowest section of all.

In my opinion—which is borne out by the fact that in this year's L-R-L only three drivers from a field comprising the pick of Europe's mountain rally drivers managed the pass without penalty—at rally (or racing) speeds, the Gavia will always remain the supremely dangerous pass, to be done 'clean' only by a crack driver on the top of his (or her) form mounted on an extremely potent car.

The Stelvio, on the other hand, is probably one of the best maintained of all passes for the repair gangs literally live on the job, i.e. on the pass, while its excellent surface and superbly engineered concrete hairpins make it a climb that any tourist can tackle with confidence from the north-east or Merano side.

This should not be taken to imply that the descent to Bormio is unduly difficult, but the surface is much looser and the six rock tunnels should be treated with respect as the drips of icy water from their roofs make them very slippery. One year in L-R-L a tunnel was blocked by a fantastic scrapheap of cars reaching almost to the roof—so the moral is, 'Slow in with full lights on for a safe exit.'

The only trouble likely to be met on the climb is altitude lock (fuel starvation) caused by the long drag in bottom gear. Now how often have *you* heard the so-called

A last view of the Stelvio as the snow-clouds come sweeping wildly in.

knowledgeable say, "Foreign cars never suffer from altitude lock. That's a fault of British cars, Old Boy!" Yet one of my happiest memories is of Marcus grinning cheerfully as gallant SOL 125 tugged a Volkswagen over the Stelvio's crest. This he had found stranded with altitude lock on the steepest part of the pass and triumphantly towed round six hairpins to the summit.

Gear Changes

Marcus and SOL certainly did a grand day's work on that occasion, but I do not think that it could fairly be claimed that any of us were idle during daylight hours. When we were not climbing either the Gavia or the Stelvio (in all, the M.G.A., Ernie and I made eight climbs over each, usually at around a steady 5,900 r.p.m.) we all three rang the changes of the axle and gearbox ratios. We found that we could change the axle in under an hour and the gearbox—which necessitated slinging the engine from the hotel garage roof—in about four and a half.

After nightfall we wandered round the little town and received a most friendly welcome. We found that for a ridiculously small expenditure on 'Grappa" we could lay the foundations of an hilarious evening but that the local liqueur, a ferocious drink known as Braulio, had unpleasing laxative effects. We met many interesting people such as the former partisan who still had always to wear his hat to hide the trademark of Buchenwald and the enterprising young trader behind the collective scheme to build a ski-hoist and put Bormio really on the map as a winter sports centre.

But always our last routine before retiring was to inspect the public weather instruments and note their forecast. On our last night they were ominous and in the morning the Stelvio's summit was under snow. The Indian Summer was over and we had just completed our schedule before the snow clouds came up in force. To plagiarize the Iron Duke—It had been a d....d close-run thing!

We had 'destroyed' nothing, had learnt a lot, and the M.G.A. still did its r.p.m. equivalent of a 'ton' on the run back to the dampness of an English autumn.

And finally, if you have the leisure (and the pocket) for a real epicure's meal, we can recommend Veltingers Keller, off Zurich's Schlüsselgasse beneath the shadow of St. Peter's Church, which it is claimed has the largest clockface in Europe (did you also think that belonged to our Big Ben?).

TWIN CAMS for MGA

DISC BRAKES, CENTRE LOCK DISC WHEELS STANDARDIZED

TWIN camshafts, apart from increasing the top end performance of an engine, have a known sales appeal. The M.G. Car Company, of Abingdon, raced a prototype B series engine so equipped in the T.T. race at Dundrod in 1955, followed a year later by the fitting of the same experimental engine in the famous car EX 179 which broke many International Class F world records at Utah, and finally last year fitted it in the new streamlined record-breaker EX 181 with a supercharger. Enthusiasts for the marque took these as portents of a future production car.

This is now confirmed by an announcement from M.G. that a twin camshaft model is added to the MGA range. It will not replace the current push-rod MGA models, which will continue unchanged. The two styles of body for the current and new twin-cam models—open and coupé—are identical. The extra cost on basic price is £180, so that inclusive of purchase tax the extra price in the United Kingdom is £270. In addition to the new engine, Dunlop disc brakes and centre-lock disc wheels are fitted all round as standard equipment. It must be emphasized that because of the different installation, it is impossible to convert a standard MGA to the specification of the Twin Cam model, and that disc brakes will not be made available for the basic MGA.

The chassis of the new car is identical with that of the push-rod model, except for minor changes dictated by the installation. For instance, the rack-and-pinion steering gear is approximately 1in farther forward to clear the front of the power unit, and slightly longer and stiffened

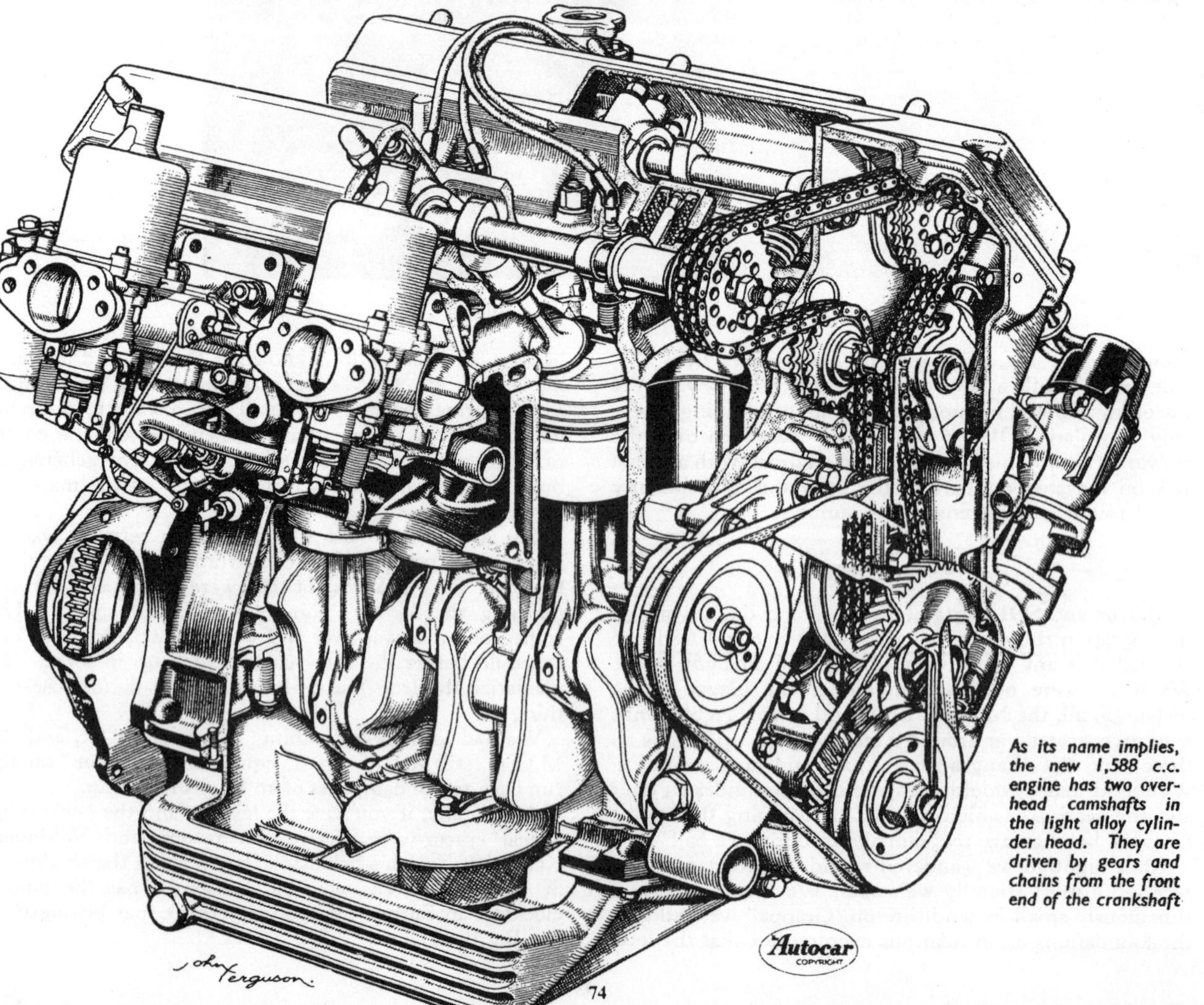

As its name implies, the new 1,588 c.c. engine has two overhead camshafts in the light alloy cylinder head. They are driven by gears and chains from the front end of the crankshaft

John Ferguson

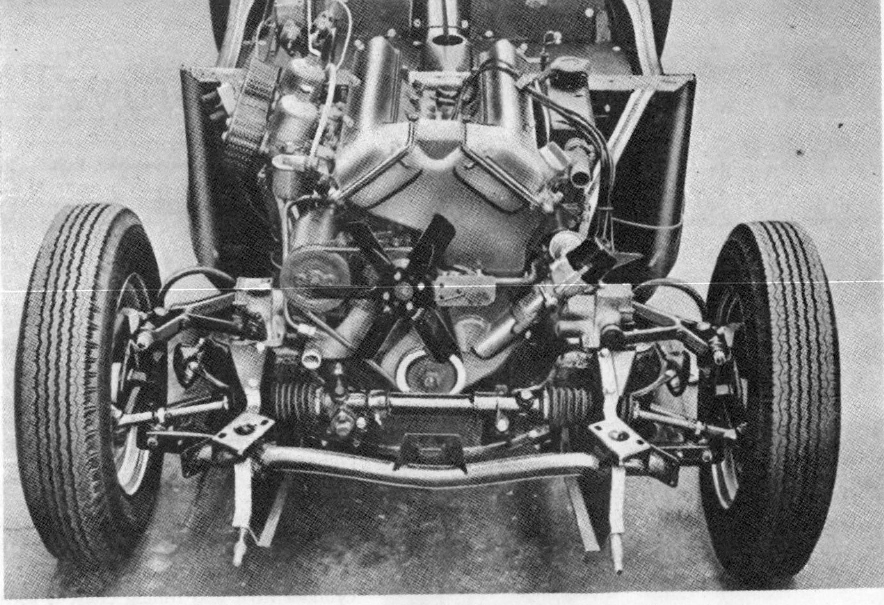

Left: Induction side of the engine, showing the full-flow filter, and water connection from the pump direct into the rear of the cylinder head. Right: Engine installed in the chassis. The box-section frame is well braced to minimise torsional deflections. Compared with the push-rod model, tyre sections have been increased from 5.60 to 5.90—both use 15in wheels

steering arms are used. A modification in the front wheel hubs arising from the adoption of disc brakes and disc wheels is the substitution of taper roller bearings for ball races, and the front track is fractionally wider. Steering swivel pins have been slightly increased in the length between pivot centres, and the rate of the front suspension springs increased to allow for the additional weight of the twin-camshaft engine. Other basic dimensions are as for the current MGA push-rod model.

As many M.G. owners compete in sporting events, the capacity of the new engine has been increased to take full advantage of the classifications laid down in appendix J of the International Sporting Code. Thus the engine displacement, as compared with the push-rod model, has been raised from 1,489 c.c. to 1,588 c.c., by enlarging the bore from 73.02mm to 75.4mm, retaining the same stroke of 88.9mm. This increase in bore size has entailed sacrifice of the water space between Nos. 1 and 2 and Nos. 3 and 4 cylinders.

For ease of production, certain parameters were placed on the design of the cylinder block which, although outwardly resembling the standard B series unit, is made from entirely new pattern equipment. Location of main faces from the crankshaft centre line, and main bearing bores are identical. Thus the basic machining can be undertaken on the transfer-matic machines of the production line at the Austin works at Longbridge (with consequent reduction in costs), and the units are then despatched for finishing at the Morris engine works at Coventry where, in fact, the design and development was undertaken.

Main- and big-end bearing sizes are unchanged—the mains being 2in dia by 1½in wide, and the big-ends 1⅞in dia by 1¼in wide. To accommodate the higher loads involved, all bearings are copper-lead, indium-infused. A completely new design of con. rod has been introduced, but the big-end bearing is still offset from the centre line of the piston by 0.109in.

To enable the rod to pass through the cylinder bore, the big-end is split at an angle of 45 deg, with the cap positively located on the rod by a saddle joint, and retained by set bolts locked by tab washers. The fully floating gudgeon pin is retained by circlips in the piston, the crown of which is domed to provide the 9.9 to 1 compression ratio; there are three narrow compression rings (the top one chromium plated) and a slotted oil control ring, all above the gudgeon pin.

Drive to the camshafts is in two stages, the first being by gears and the second by a duplex roller chain. Replacing the camshaft of the push-rod engine is a jack shaft in the same position, driven at half engine speed by single helical, case-hardened and shaved steel gears from the front end of the crankshaft. On the front end of this jack shaft is a spiral gear drive for the distributor, at its mid-point another set of gears for the vertically mounted Holburn Eaton type oil pump, and at the rear a third set for the rev counter drive.

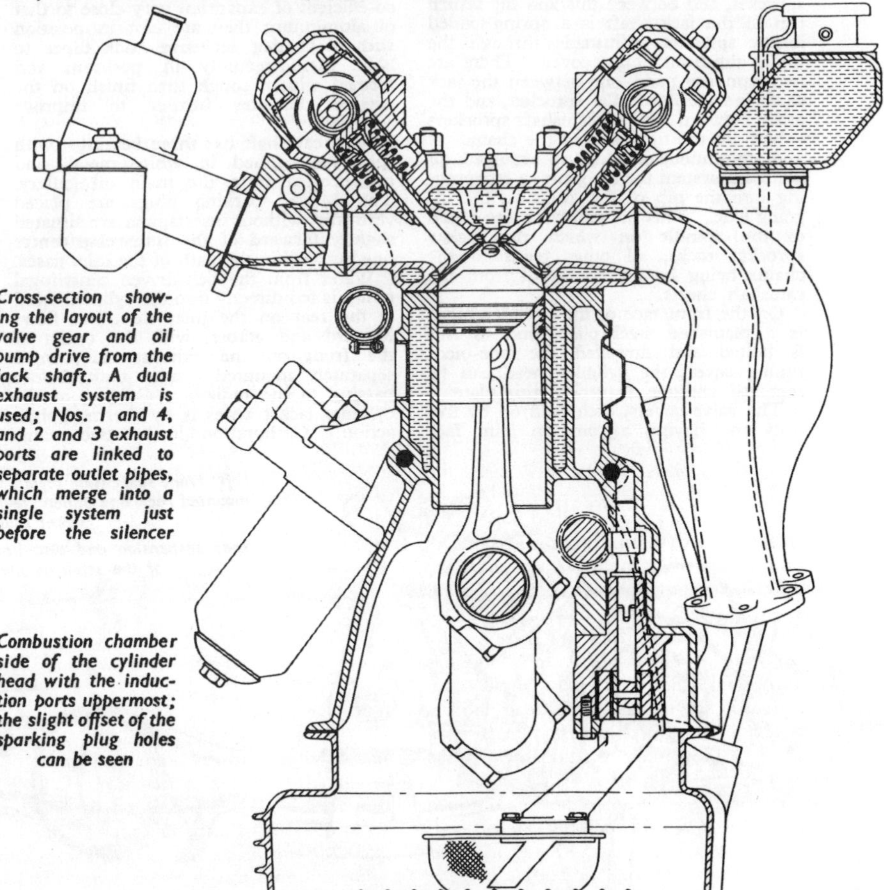

Cross-section showing the layout of the valve gear and oil pump drive from the jack shaft. A dual exhaust system is used; Nos. 1 and 4, and 2 and 3 exhaust ports are linked to separate outlet pipes, which merge into a single system just before the silencer

Combustion chamber side of the cylinder head with the induction ports uppermost; the slight offset of the sparking plug holes can be seen

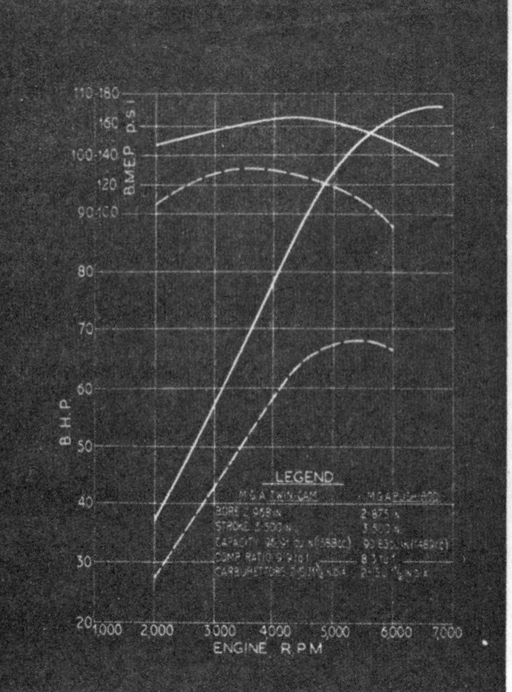

A comparison of the power curves for the 1,489 c.c. push-rod engine and the new, 1,588 c.c. twin-cam unit, emphasizing the improved breathing which is permitted by the twin camshaft layout

PRICES: Open two-seater, basic price in U.K. £843, plus purchase tax £422 17s, total £1,265 17s; coupé, basic price in U.K. £904, plus purchase tax £453 7s, total £1,357 7s.

TWIN CAM MGA

In tandem with the jack shaft gear is the primary sprocket of the chain drive. Running in an anti-clockwise direction, it connects first of all with the inlet camshaft, the chain passing over a fixed idler sprocket to form a right-angle run. Next in the sequence is the exhaust camshaft sprocket, and between this and the return run to the jack shaft is a spring-loaded jockey sprocket, adjustable through the top of the front timing cover. There are two damping pads, one between the jack shaft and the fixed idler sprocket, and the other between the two camshaft sprockets—both on the tight side of the chain.

A continuous oil feed is arranged off the main system for the gears, a jet spraying into the nip of the gears on the ingoing side. This oil supply is also piped to the spindle on which the jockey sprocket rocks, all other feeds to the chains being by the over-spill from the camshaft chests.

On the front face of the cylinder block is a planished steel plate, and to this is bolted and dowelled the one-piece timing cover; the cylinder head can be removed without disturbing this plate.

The valve covers, each held on by five nuts and having a common joint face with the head and front timing cover, are first removed, to expose the camshaft and chain drive. Each camshaft sprocket is held on by two fitting bolts and located on a spigot; these bolts are removed. In addition, there is a central locating bolt; unscrewing this withdraws the sprocket and, at the same time, the front end of the central bolt enters a threaded keep plate attached to the timing cover, to prevent the sprockets and chains falling into the timing chest.

Each sprocket has 25 teeth, and there are 12 holes for the fitting bolts, so that by a suitable combination of tooth-and-hole, 2½ crankshaft degrees, i.e., 1¼ deg on the camshaft, of vernier timing can be obtained. An oil joint between the cylinder head and timing chest is formed by a half-round synthetic rubber ring which seats in a corresponding cradle in the timing cover plate and is compressed when the cylinder head is tightened.

What must now be regarded as the classical design for an overhead camshaft is utilized. This consists of inverted, bucket-type tappets, valve clearances being set by a selected range of case-hardened and ground biscuits interposed between the tappet and the end of the valve stem, and retained radially by the valve collar. Head material is aluminium alloy, with seat inserts for each of the valves, which are disposed equally on either side of the cylinder centre line at an included angle of 80 deg. The tappets, which are manufactured in Brimol cast iron, run directly in the aluminium casting; the shouldered valve guides also are of cast iron. The valve seats are of austenitic cast iron having a co-efficient of expansion very close to that of aluminium; they are cast in position with a 14 deg inclusive back taper tc hold them securely in position, and formed with a rough turn finish on the outside diameter further to improve adhesion.

Each camshaft has three bearings, with split shells lined in white metal, and pressure-fed from the main oil gallery. The 14mm sparking plugs are placed vertically, without inserts, and are situated slightly forward of the transverse centre line but well in the path of the inlet gases.

Water from the belt-driven centrifugal pump is fed directly into the cylinder head at the rear on the inlet side, and flows forward and across, with the outlet at the front on the exhaust side, to a separately mounted header tank, before passing to the radiator. Cooling of the cylinder jacket bores is by thermosyphon action. Carburation is by two semi-downdraught 1¾in dia S.U. carburettors, and no manifold heating is provided.

For an extra weight penalty of approximately 50 lb the twin-camshaft engine produces 58 per cent more power, and the engine speed at which it peaks has been raised from 5,500 to 6,700 r.p.m. Similarly, the maximum torque has been increased by 35 per cent, and the point in the engine range at which it occurs extended from 3,500 to 4,500 r.p.m. Examination of the b.m.e.p. curves on the left, which are directly proportional to the torque, shows that filling at the bottom end of the speed range has been maintained, and that the fall-off up to maximum speed is very moderate, indicating good filling throughout the range.

To match this increased engine performance, Dunlop disc brakes are fitted all round. In the M.G. installation no servo assistance is provided; by using discs of large diameter, pedal loads have been kept reasonable, as the accompanying road test reveals. Because the disc brakes have no self-servo action as in a normal drum and shoe installation, pedal ratios have been increased. With many drum type brakes this could result in a lot of free pedal travel with frequent adjustment; but as an inherent feature of the Dunlop discs is automatic maintenance of a constant running clearance, this problem is obviated. Additionally, discs do not expand away from the friction pads at temperature as do drum brakes, so that a fairly consistent amount of free pedal travel should be maintained. The centrally mounted, fly-off hand brake is linked to the rear wheels, which have a separate set of pads for the mechanical hook-up.

Among the extra items available are de luxe seats, a shallow competition windscreen, windscreen washer, a wood-rimmed steering wheel, adjustable steering column, an oil cooler for competition work, radiator blind, tonneau cover, twin horns, heater, fog lamps and radio.

Experience of several push-rod MGA models has convinced us that the road-holding and steering is of a very high order. Much of this arises from the use of a very stiff—albeit rather heavy—box section frame, well braced at the scuttle to minimize deflection against suspension loads. These desirable features are retained in the new MGA Twin Cam. The price to be paid for the extra performance and increased braking is not unreasonable, and this latest product from Abingdon must rank among the world's outstanding sports cars.

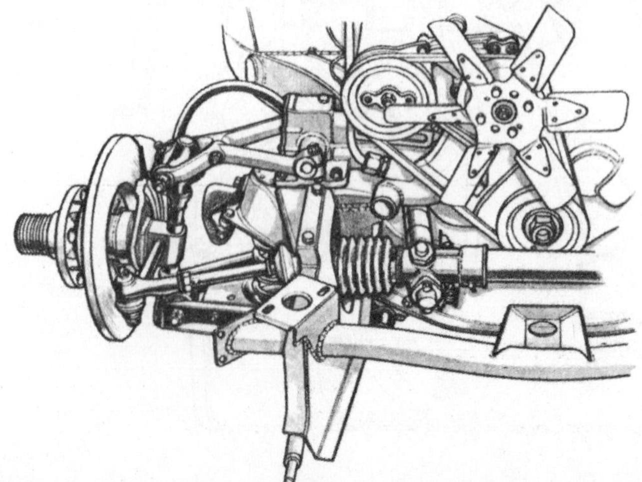

Left: Front suspension layout showing the Dunlop disc brakes and the forward-mounted rack and pinion steering. The dynamo, and the fan on the end of the water pump shaft run at engine speed

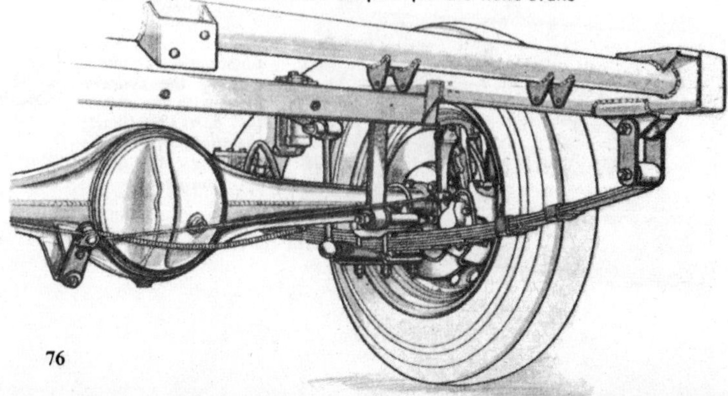

Rear suspension and disc brakes, showing the cable and conduit operation of the separate mechanical calipers for the hand-brake

The radiator grille bears the well-known M.G. octagonal motif. On each side of the bonnet are vents to allow hot air to escape from the engine compartment. Direction indicators are combined with the side lights

M.G. TWIN CAM MGA

OPEN TWO-SEATER

BY producing a high-performance model to partner the successful MGA two-seater, the M.G. Car Company, Ltd., has filled a gap which has been evident to overseas and competition-minded motorists; the new 1,588 c.c. twin overhead camshaft engine will enable the car to compete on equal terms in the 1,300-1,600 c.c. class with Continental-built cars. As described in preceding pages, this engine is a development of the special power unit used in the record-breaking M.G. EX 181.

The new model also has Dunlop 10¾in disc brakes, centre-lock steel wheels and Road Speed tyres, which are not fitted to the standard MGA. The road test car was an open model equipped with hood and side screens and all optionally extra equipment. A coupé version of the car is available.

Powered by the twin carburettor version of the 1½-litre B series engine, the standard MGA coupé is capable of slightly more than 100 m.p.h.; the new 1,600 c.c. unit gives the open car, with hood and side curtains in position, a maximum of 114 m.p.h. It is faster than the 1½-litre car by 1.7sec to 60 m.p.h., and by 15sec to 90 m.p.h.

The engine starts easily and quickly reaches working temperature. It revs freely, and the limit marking on the tachometer is 7,000 r.p.m.; it was taken up to this limit repeatedly during the test.

Engine vibration was noticed at 2,500 and 5,500 r.p.m.; at maximum speed in top gear the tachometer reading was 6,500 r.p.m., and this was held for approximately 5 miles on a level stretch of *autoroute*.

Power builds up noticeably after the engine tops 3,500 r.p.m.; by the time 4,000 r.p.m. is reached it really takes hold and the little car begins to show its potential performance. In first gear it gets very quickly to 30 m.p.h., and a fast change to second gear is needed to avoid exceeding the rev. limit. The comfortable minimum speed in top is 18-20 m.p.h., and in traffic, second and third gears are most used. In open road cruising, 80-90 m.p.h. can be held indefinitely, with plenty in hand for use when required. The car was quite happy at 100 m.p.h. for long stretches on Continental roads, although to maintain high engine speeds has a marked effect on the fuel consumption, of course, and above 90 m.p.h. the driver has the feeling that the engine is working much harder.

There is a constant, rather obtrusive background of mechanical noise; most of this can be traced to the valve gear, particularly the tappets, which have a recommended clearance of 0.018in, but there is also a "ring" associated with the first stage of the timing gears. Nor can it be said that the engine is smooth or silky. Exhaust-wise, the car is not objectionable, and it can be driven through city traffic without attracting undue attention. This car had a loose silencer baffle. Carburettor intake noise is not noticeable, although only small flame-trap type air cleaners are fitted.

From the performance and maintenance angles, the MGA has an enthusiast's engine. Many of the ancillary units are not easy to reach, as the underbonnet space is filled by the engine itself. The distributor is located below a camshaft housing (it became covered in oil during the test), and the coil is tucked away under the heater trunking. The oil level dipstick would be easier to replace if its containing tube were a little longer. An oil cooler, which is an optional extra, was mounted in front of the radiator, but no oil temperature gauge was supplied.

All maximum speed and acceleration tests were carried

When the side curtains alone are used, the crew can enjoy fresh air motoring with some measure of protection from draughts. The Twin Cam insignia appears beneath the motif on the tail panel

M.G. Twin Cam MGA . . . .

The hood and side curtains are a snug fit and follow closely the contours of the body. There is no exterior door handle. Three large windows at the back of the hood are made of flexible Vybak. Bumper over-riders are standard

out with 100 octane petrol. With this, and Belgian premium petrol (89 research octane rating), the engine tended to "run on" after being switched off. It also used a considerable amount of oil; five pints were added to the sump during one journey of 800 miles, and an overall oil consumption figure of 1,020 m.p.g. was recorded—approximately one quart of oil each time the petrol tank (capacity 10 gallons) was refilled.

Once accustomed to the controls, an experienced driver can get off the mark with very little wheel spin, but it was felt that more suitable gear box ratios would give an even more sparkling getaway, without losing the benefit of easy fast cruising—there is a very noticeable interval between first and second, and between second and third. An owner using the car for circuit racing would, no doubt, prefer a gear box with closer ratios. A 4.55 to 1 axle ratio can be fitted in place of the standard 4.3 to 1 ratio at an extra cost of £10 2s 6d.

Apart from occasional difficulty in selecting first gear when the car is stationary, the gear box is generally pleasant to use. The short, remote control lever has precise movements between the ratios, and very fast changes can be made. One notices a slight difficulty—not uncommon in B-series gear boxes—in getting through the gate transversely, particularly when the gear box is hot. This sometimes makes difficult the change from third into second, and there is a risk that the lever may overshoot into the reverse quadrant. The top of the lever is close to the steering wheel when the latter is set near the facia; it is also well placed in relation to the driving seat. There was no vibration from the transmission, and the axle was silent.

Free from slip during full-bore gear changes, the clutch transmitted the engine power without judder under all conditions. Some adjustment was found necessary to take up pedal movement, but once attended to the need did not recur. Positioning of the pedals is good, although to clear the clutch pedal, the left foot has to be placed beneath it rather than to the left. The accelerator, which is connected to the throttle by a cable, works smoothly, and delicate, progressive control can be achieved.

Among the most delightful features of the MGA are its road-holding and cornering. The manufacturers' well-known motto—Safety Fast—is particularly pertinent to this new model. Changes in road surface have little effect on the manner in which the car sits firmly on the road, and its behaviour on a streaming wet road is equally good, although the tail will swing slightly if the throttle is opened suddenly when cornering. Power can be used judiciously to help the car round a corner, in fact progress on a winding road is all the better if this technique is applied.

There is strong self-centring of the steering, and there is no lost motion to impair its accuracy; from lock to lock requires only $2\frac{3}{4}$ turns of the wheel, and although the turning circle is greater by 4ft 6in than that of the $1\frac{1}{2}$-litre-engined car, the Twin Cam model can be manœuvred easily in narrow streets.

A slight heaviness in the steering was noticed with the tyres inflated to the normal recommended 18 lb front and 20 lb rear; when pressures were raised by 4 lb sq in, this heaviness disappeared and the ride was not uncomfortable.

With full load, or with the driver only in the car, there is a satisfactory firmness about the suspension, which reaches an excellent compromise in a car which may be called upon to take the owner to work during the week, and yet be driven in races at the weekend. Stability is first class and there is no heeling-over on corners, although brisk progress is marked by excessive tyre squeal; the latest pattern Road Speed tyres were not fitted to the test car.

The driving position is well suited to most drivers, but a person of small stature would be happier with a higher seat cushion. The steering wheel can be set close to the facia, by a lock-nut and bolt fitting; in this position of adjustment the driver has fingertip control of the horn button and indicator switch. The thin-rimmed wheel is set at an ideal angle for control, being almost vertical; it does not obscure the instruments.

Fitted to the test car were the competition-type seats, which have a padded roll round the edge of the back rest, and long cushion; they proved most comfortable and provided firm support at a good angle. Driver and passenger are well held when cornering fast, and long distances can be covered without fatigue. The proximity of the engine and gear box can bring about an uncomfortably high temperature around the legs and feet; it is probable that owners in hot climates will call for separate fresh air ventilators. On the other hand, the warmth would be appreciated in winter conditions.

All the advantages which this car affords for fast motoring would be wasted if the braking system was not up to the same standards. It is becoming increasingly the practice for 100 m.p.h. cars, whether they are large saloons or agile two-seaters, to be fitted with disc brakes. The Dunlop $10\frac{3}{4}$in diameter discs fitted to the Twin Cam MGA are adequate to all they are called upon to do in wet or dry. The pedal has a good feel to it, being neither spongy nor too hard, though loads are rather high in normal traffic stops; this is normal with discs, which have no self-servo effect, and is noticeable

A cover encloses the spare wheel, on top of which is strapped the tool kit. The petrol filler has a quick release cap

The polished aluminium covers of the camshaft housings dominate the under-bonnet view

when there is no external servo assistance, as in the case of the MGA. Maximum braking brought the car to a standstill all square, and the brakes could be applied hard when the car was being driven fast on wet roads. There was no noticeable increase in pedal travel after 800 miles of fast driving. The front discs did show signs of scoring, which has not been noticed on other cars.

The parking brake is controlled by a fly-off-pattern lever, in which the button is pressed to lock the brake on. The lever is placed between the transmission cover and the driving seat, and the hand falls readily on it.

At night reasonable use can be made of the car's performance, although more powerful head lamps would be appreciated for speeds close to 100 m.p.h.; the dipped beam did not inconvenience oncoming traffic. The Twin Cam MGA is one of the cars which really do require a hand dipper switch. When driving on the open road at night, one needs two left feet to operate the clutch and the foot dipper, for the driver always seems to need to change gear and alter the light setting at the same moment. The positioning of the pedal and switch are such that the changeover cannot be made on the instant.

Facia instruments are well lit, and the switch is fitted with a rheostat. There is a small map light, with a separate switch on the left side of the facia. Self-parking wipers are fitted, and although they are powerful and silent, they are up against an unusual handicap—in heavy rain, water is blown off the bonnet on to the screen and the wipers have difficulty in clearing it. An owner could perhaps prevent this by fitting a shallow Perspex deflector across the bonnet to deflect the air stream up and over the screen.

With the hood and side curtains erected, the car proved weatherproof except at speeds over 90 m.p.h., when wind pressure tended to lift the hood above the middle of the windscreen; rain found its way in there, and also through the scuttle on to the passenger's legs. Although there were gaps between the windscreen frame and the side screens, rain did not penetrate here. The hood is comparatively simple to erect and can be folded away neatly behind the seat backrests. A plastic bag, secured to the bodywork behind the seats, provided stowage for the side curtains.

With the hood and side curtains erected, a tall driver has no difficulty in getting into or out of the car, and there is ample headroom. In this condition, the occupants find the interior rather warm, and it was not possible to obtain a flow of cool air through the vent above the gear box cover. A heater—part of the extra equipment—proved amply efficient in the moderate temperatures encountered during the test.

Accommodation for maps and small articles is provided by a deep pocket in each door, but as the doors cannot be locked, it is not advisable to stow valuables in these pockets if the car is left unattended. Only the Twin Cam models and the 1½-litre coupé are supplied with a leather-covered facia. A large proportion of the luggage compartment is occupied by the spare wheel and tool kit, and it is not easy to find room for a large suitcase, but a number of small bags and boxes can be stowed away. If coats and soft travelling bags are fitted in carefully, more can be carried than at first appears likely.

The tool kit includes a starting handle and, surprisingly, an old-fashioned, screw-type lifting jack. Two 6-volt batteries are located just forward of the rear axle; to service them the spare wheel and a panel in the floor behind the seats must be removed. The high-pressure electric fuel pump is close to the battery on the right side of the frame. Nine lubrication points require grease gun attention every 1,000 miles.

In the road test of the 1½-litre MGA coupé it was stated in summary that the car was capable of holding its own against more powerful vehicles; this applies even more markedly to the 1,600 c.c. Twin Cam model. The extra performance is matched by the road-holding, steering and brakes, and this car maintains the M.G. tradition of good looks coupled with a very fine performance.

Left: Competition seats, an optional extra, are contoured to give extra support in cornering, and under the thighs. Right: This is a functional facia, with neat, easily read dials. The main switches come quickly to hand. The steering wheel is shown in its nearest adjustment to the facia. The plated support on the left of the windscreen forms a useful grab handle for the passenger

SPECIFICATION

ENGINE

No. of cylinders ...	4 in line
Bore and stroke ...	75.4 x 88.9 mm (2.97 x 3.5in)
Displacement... ...	1.588 c.c. (96.91 cu in)
Valve position ...	Twin O.H.C. Hemispherical combustion chamber
Compression ratio ...	9.9 to 1
Max. b.h.p. (nett) ...	108 at 6,700 r.p.m.
Max. b.m.e.p. (nett)...	163 lb sq in at 4,500 r. p.m.
Max. torque (nett) ...	104 lb ft at 4,500 r.p.m.
Carburettors... ...	Twin 1¾in dia S.U. type H.6
Fuel pump	S.U. high pressure
Tank capacity... ...	10 Imp. gallons (37.8 litres)
Sump capacity ...	12 pints max. (5.7 litres) 7¾ pints min. (3.6 litres)
Oil filter	Full flow
Cooling system ...	Pump, fan and thermostat
Battery	12 volt, 51 ampère hour

TRANSMISSION

Clutch	B and B. 8in dia single dry plate
Gear box	4 speeds and reverse, synchromesh on top, 3rd and 2nd. Central lever
Overall ratios ...	Top 4.30; 3rd 5.91; 2nd 9.52; 1st 15.65; reverse 20.47 to 1.
Final drive	Hypoid bevel, 4.3 to 1.

CHASSIS

Brakes	Dunlop disc. Hydraulic operation. Mechanical calipers for hand brake on rear wheels
Disc dia, pad width ...	10¾in outside dia (2⅛ x 1⅞in pads)
Suspension: front ...	Independent, coil springs and wishbones
rear ...	Live axle, half-elliptic leaf springs
Dampers: front ...	Armstrong in unit with wishbone pivots
rear ...	Armstrong lever arm, chassis-mounted
Wheels	Dunlop centre-lock steel disc type
Tyre size	5.90—15in Dunlop R.S.4
Steering	Rack and pinion
Steering wheel ...	16½in dia four spoke
Turns, lock to lock ...	2¾

DIMENSIONS

Wheelbase	7ft 10in (239 cm)
Track: front	3ft 11.9in (121 cm)
rear	4ft 0.87in (124 cm)
Overall length ...	13ft (396 cm)
Overall width ...	4ft 10in (147 cm)
Overall height ...	4ft 2in (127 cm)
Ground clearance ...	6in (15 cm)
Turning circle ...	31ft 4in (9.55 m)
Kerb weight	2,156 lb (19¼ cwt) (977 kg)

PERFORMANCE DATA

Top gear m.p.h. per 1,000 r.p.m. ...	17.3
Torque lb ft per cu in engine capacity	1.083
Brake surface area swept by linings ...	494.8 sq in
Weight distribution (dry)	F, 54.6 per cent R, 45.4 per cent

M.G. TWIN CAM MGA

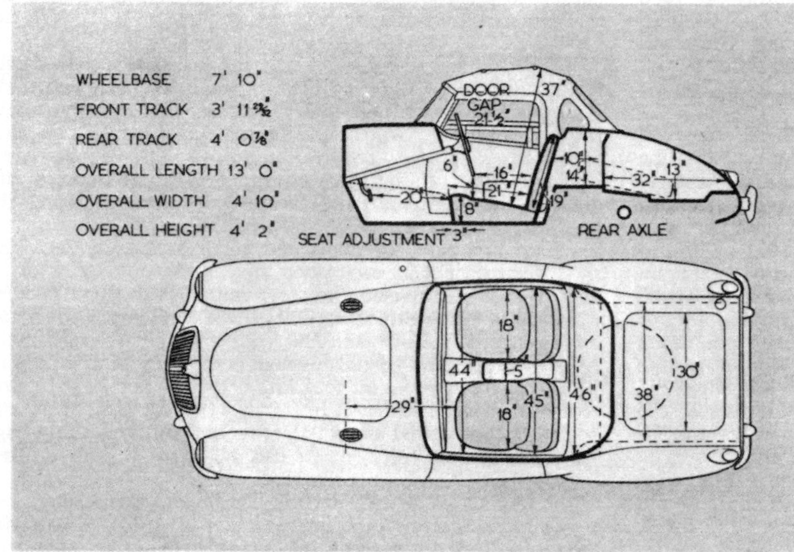

Scale ¼in to 1ft. Driving seat in central position. Cushions uncompressed

PERFORMANCE

ACCELERATION:

Speed Range, Gear Ratios and Time in sec.

M.P.H.	4.30 to 1	5.91 to 1	9.52 to 1	15.65 to 1
10—30..	—	—	4.5	3.3
20—40..	11.0	7.1	4.5	—
30—50..	10.2	7.4	4.9	—
40—60..	10.5	7.5	—	—
50—70..	11.7	7.6	—	—
60—80..	11.7	8.9	—	—
70—90..	13.6	—	—	—
80—100	18.7	—	—	—

From rest through gears to:

M.P.H.	sec.
30	4.3
40	6.9
50	9.4
60	13.3
70	17.3
80	22.5
90	30.0
100	41.1

Standing quarter mile, 18.6 sec.

MAXIMUM SPEEDS ON GEARS:

Gear		M.P.H.	K.P.H.
Top ..	**(mean)**	**113.5**	182.7
	(best)	**114.0**	183.5
3rd ..	.. ..	**86**	138
2nd ..	.. ..	**53**	85
1st ..	.. ..	**32**	51

TRACTIVE EFFORT:

	Pull (lb per ton)	Equivalent Gradient
Top	232	1 in 9.6
Third	315	1 in 7.0
Second..	486	1 in 4.5

BRAKES (at 30 m.p.h. in neutral)

Pedal load in lb	Retardation	Equivalent stopping distance in ft
25	0.45g	67.2
50	0.62g	48.7
75	0.81g	37.4
90	0.92g	32.8

FUEL CONSUMPTION:

M.P.G. at steady speeds

M.P.H.	Direct Top
30	42.4
40	40.0
50	35.6
60	31.7
70	27.4
80	23.6
90	20.2
100	18.1

Overall fuel consumption for 1,117 miles, 21.8 m.p.g. (12.9 litres per 100 km).

Approximate normal range 18-30 m.p.g. (15.7-9.4 litres per 100 km).

Fuel: Super premium.

TEST CONDITIONS: Weather: overcast, raining. Slight breeze. Acceleration and braking tests on dry surface.

Air temperature, 55–65 deg F.

Acceleration figures are the means of several runs in opposite directions.

Tractive effort obtained by Tapley meter.

SPEEDOMETER CORRECTION: M.P.H.

Car speedometer:	10	20	30	40	50	60	70	80	90	100	110	114
True speed:	11	20	28.5	38.5	48	58	69	80	91	101	112	114

DATA

PRICE (basic), with two-seater body, **£843.**
British purchase tax, **£422 17s.**
Total (in Great Britain), **£1,265 17s.**

Extras:	£	s	d
Screen washer	3	0	0
Heater	18	7	6
Adjustable steering column	3	0	0
Oil cooler	13	10	0
Competition seats	9	18	9
Twin horns	2	1	3

ENGINE: Capacity, 1,588 c.c. (96.91 cu in).
Number of cylinders, 4.
Bore and stroke, 75.4 × 88.9 mm (2.97 × 3.5in).
Valve gear, twin overhead camshafts.
Compression ratio, 9.9 to 1.
B.H.P. 108 (nett) at 6,700 r.p.m. (B.H.P. per ton laden 96.5).
Torque, 104 lb ft at 4,500 r.p.m.
M.P.H. per 1,000 r.p.m. in top gear, 17.3

WEIGHT: (with 5 gals. fuel), 19¼ cwt (2,156 lb).
Distribution (per cent): F, 53.9; R, 46.1.
Laden as tested, 22¼ cwt (2,506 lb).
Lb per c.c. (laden), 1.6.

BRAKES: Type, Dunlop disc.
Method of operation, hydraulic.
Disc diameter: F, 10¾in; R, 10¾in.
Lining swept area: F, 247.4 sq in; R, 247.4 sq in.

TYRES: 5.90—15in.
Pressures (lb sq in); F, 18; R, 20 (normal). F, 22; R, 24 (fast driving).

TANK CAPACITY: 10 Imperial gallons.
Oil sump, 12 pints.
Cooling system, 13⅝ pints (plus 1 pint if heater fitted).

STEERING: Turning circle, 32ft 6in.
Between kerbs, 31ft 4in.
Between walls, 33ft 5in.
Turns of steering wheel from lock to lock, 2¾.

DIMENSIONS: Wheelbase, 7ft 10in.
Track: F, 3ft 11 29/32in; R, 4ft 0⅞in.
Length (overall), 13ft.
Height, 4ft 2in.
Width, 4ft 10in.
Ground clearance, 6in.
Frontal area, 13.8 sq ft (approximately).

ELECTRICAL SYSTEM: 12-volt; 51 ampère-hour battery.
Head lamps, Double dip; 50–40 watt bulbs.

SUSPENSION: Front, independent, coil spring and wishbones. Rear, half-elliptic leaf springs with live axle.

TRYING THE "TWIN CAM"

SPORTS CARS ILLUSTRATED in company with other motoring journals and newspapers was recently privileged to briefly try the new M.G.A. "Twin Cam" on the F.V.R.D.E. banked circuit at Chobham, Surrey. Although hardly suited to assessing the maximum speed of this promising little car, the circuit certainly served to demonstrate its high-speed handling and braking qualities.

The new car is understandably a little noiser mechanically than the "pushrod" model but this disappears as the car gathers speed—which it does in a very convincing manner. Unfortunately the stipulated three laps of this very tricky circuit did not lend itself to extending the maximum performance—the first two laps being used to learn something of its bends and intricacies, the last lap being the only one when anything like full power could be applied.

Similarly, it was not possible to take acceleration tests in fairness to other journalists who were dispatching themselves on the "saucer". It is however quite safe to say that the acceleration figures of the "Twin Cam" far surpass those of the standard model, and that its maximum is well over 100 m.p.h., it being possible to "break the ton" on the small Chobham track, in spite of all driving being done with the hood furled.

Perhaps the most impressive feature of the "Twin Cam" is its superb Dunlop disc brakes. Of non-servo type and with 10½ in. discs the power of the brakes is immense, no fade being evident even after a whole day of "Press Grand Prix" work.

Although the new car retains a live axle the handling is impressive and typically M.G., bends being managed at high speed without anxiety. It was noticed that the day's high-speed motoring prompted the M.G. staff to keep a very watchful eye on the oil level, the dipstick being checked on an average every other three-lap stint. The engines of all three test cars were obviously running with a rich mixture setting, presumably to safeguard against any risk of "drying up" or overheating. If the mixture had been *au point* it would probably have been possible to exceed the 102 m.p.h., best speed recorded at Chobham.

The customary excellent M.G. gearbox provided quick precise changes although the movement tended to become stiff after such strenuous use. Ratios are identical to the standard M.G.A. The clutch remained sweet throughout the tests—a tribute to its efficiency.

All test cars were fitted with the optional equipment, "competition" seats with padded-edge back rests. These gave excellent support even at high cornering speeds. There is ample legroom for a "six-footer". A pleasant feeling of being "in" rather than "on" the car springs from its low seating position and high door sides and the deep pockets give sufficient arm movement for high-speed motoring.

It is unfortunate for U.K. motorists that this worthy follower of the Abingdon tradition will, for the time being, be almost 100 per cent for export.—D.A. ★

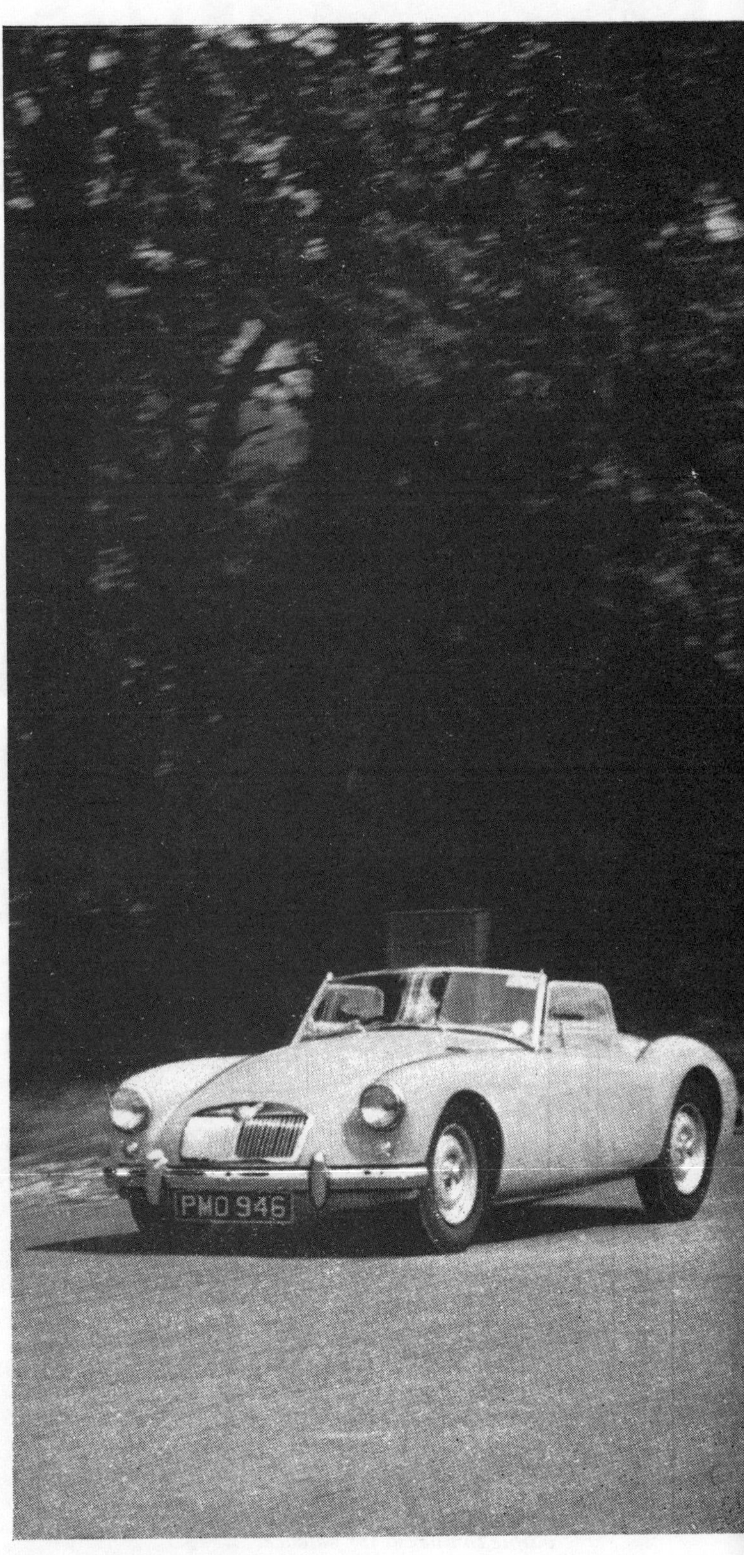

With nose well down under the impressive Dunlop disc brakes the M.G. "Twin Cam" is slowed from 100 m.p.h. for part of the banked section of the Chobham F.V.R.D.E. track

SCI builds an MGA TWIN CAM for competition

The potential was there — all it needed was coaxing. Here is how it was done.

by John Christy

LEFT — New type of piston is seen at right. Rings are closer together and there are no vent holes visible. In the SCI MG the top chrome ring was replaced with an iron ring similar to second and third units. RIGHT — Pins are palm-push fit at room temperature. Large ridges visible can be cut for balance.

SUBSCRIBERS and regular SCI readers who were with us for the October and December, 1958, issues will remember a certain black MG Twin Cam, New York license number 6N 3298. This particular MG was one of the first Twin Cam cars off the boat and it had, from the moment of its landing, anything but a life of tender loving care.

For the October issue it was tested as delivered. The results, while good were not terribly impressive. Performance was on the order of that of a Stage 4 MGA but with more docility than is found in the stage-tuned rocker box car. In short, a good car but no class F winner.

In the December issue we told how we attempted to improve the raceability of the car without going into the engine. In brief we stiffened up the suspension in front, changed the Dunlop Roadspeed tires for Dunlop R-3 racing rubber and removed about 80 of the 150-plus legally removable pounds of weight. Lap times around the Lime Rock Park course dropped from 1:20 to 1:18.5. For the earlier October issue runs we had already experimented with gears, dropping the original 4.3 to 1 rear end in favor of 4.55 to 1 final drive gears, one of three standard sets available with the car. Also installed at that time was the optional close-ratio gearbox with ratios of 2.45, 1.62, 1.27 and 1.00 to 1 respectively in first, second, third and fourth. As we said, all these little things added up to about two seconds worth of lap time. At this point we could pursue this tack no further without actual body and chassis modifications that would have nullified the "production" status of the automobile.

The obvious succeeding step was to check out the engine. There isn't a true production power plant in the world that is perfect — the exigencies of a production line won't permit the hand fitting and careful tool setting that must be used if the final product is to fit the designers plans perfectly in all respects. For that matter, many racing enignes are built up and then carefully torn down and reassembled before ever appearing on the race course.

It was obvious by this time that this particular MG was no exception. In the first place it had been well and truly pushed from the start and it was now showing the strain of many fast laps and acceleration runs. Power was very obviously down, oil consumption was up, water temperature stayed high, it pinged piteously at any but the lowest ignition setting and it "ran on" like a berserk diesel. It would still turn 7000 revs without clattering but there just didn't seem to be any power coming through the flywheel. It didn't have the willingness that two cams, nearly 10 to 1 compression and 1600 cc's would lead one to believe was there. In short, it was a very unhappy, unhealthy engine.

The one problem here was that the car was not the property of SCI. It belonged to Hambro Automotive Corporation, the importers of all BMC products in the U.S. A call to Hambro management elicited the necessary permission to delve into the engine with two provisions. First the car must remain a legal production machine and second, that the results must not be listed as official recommendations of either Hambro or of the MG Car Company. The first provision was already part of the plan and the second was absolutely standard procedure in any case.

The car was then taken to Imported and Domestic Service, Ridgefield, Connecticut where master mechanic Joe Virag makes good machinery better. Virag had already reworked a Sprite for SCI with considerable success so we were familiar with his brand of craftsmanship. DOHC equipment is also a specialty of the house. The obvious first move was to pull the engine, a task more easily talked about than accomplished. We were to learn many things about MG's new road-eater and the engine pulling lesson was the first. The Twin Cam engine is not only wider than its rocker-arm cousin across the head, but there is considerably more girth at the bottom. The result was that the increased size of the cast alloy sump hits the front cross member when an attempt is made to remove the engine in the normal way. Either one of two alternate procedures must be used; the gearbox can be unshipped from its mounts and slid back carefully, or the sump can be removed. Of the two, the sump removal tends to be more tedious but, in the long run, easier. In any case one doesn't just unbolt the engine and lift. The long, tuned exhaust system must also be dismounted in either instance.

Next, the engine was mounted on an engine stand and all manifolding was removed as were the two angular cam covers. Here the dissassembly was halted and a degree wheel was mounted on the crank nose. Every cam lobe and every valve was then checked out.

At this point and because of what follows it is only fair to point out that this particular car was one of the first 40 produced in a pilot run. The engine was not put together at Abingdon but was run through the production line at BMC's huge Engines Branch plant. The pilot run, we understand was a check to see if it was feasible to produce the Twin Cam in quantity on a production line.

But back to the valve check-out. Correct valve clearances are specified as .018 to .019 of an inch. The clearances on this particular pilot model were from .016 on

Combustion chambers were relieved of all sharp edges left in production machining operations. Special attention must be paid to sparkplug holes.

Head assembly from the front shows the straightforward layout. Cams are clamped in 3 bearings.

one valve to .021 on another and all points in between for the rest. The cam timing also gave a clue to why we hadn't been getting the power we had expected. The intake cam checked out at four degrees late and the exhaust cam proved to be seven degrees early. In other words the intake valves were opening and closing later in the cycle and the exhaust valves were operating much too soon. The net result was that most of the fire was going out the exhaust instead of pushing the pistons down like it should.

Lesson number two. If you have one of the early series Twin Cam units and are not getting the wallop you should, set the cams by use of a degree wheel and depending on the camshaft numbers use the following figures:

Intake opens 20 degrees BTDC
Intake closes 50 degrees ABDC
Exhaust opens 50 degrees BBDC
Exhaust closes 20 degrees ATDC

In addition to the above, the first production run Twin Cam engines had cams which degree out at 280 degrees with the same lift and slightly milder acceleration than the 250° units. Check yours with a dial indicator and degree wheel. If you have the 280° cams the timing is:

Intake opens:	35 degrees BTDC
Intake closes:	65 degrees ABDC
Exhaust opens:	65 degrees BBDC
Exhaust closes:	35 degrees ATDC

After, and only after, all the valve data was gathered, dismantling proceeded by the book. The cam sprockets were unbolted and slid forward into their locks and the cams lifted. Piece by piece in strict accordance with the factory manual the engine came apart.

The bearings, both rods and mains, were in fair shape, all things considered, but were worn enough to be replaced and so set aside. The crank was absolutely unscored and brightly clean which attests to the quality of material that goes into the Twin Cam when the pounding this engine took is remembered. The big, sturdy rods were checked and proved unflawed and in perfect alignment. This last item is important. In rebuilding any engine, especially if competition is the goal, any and

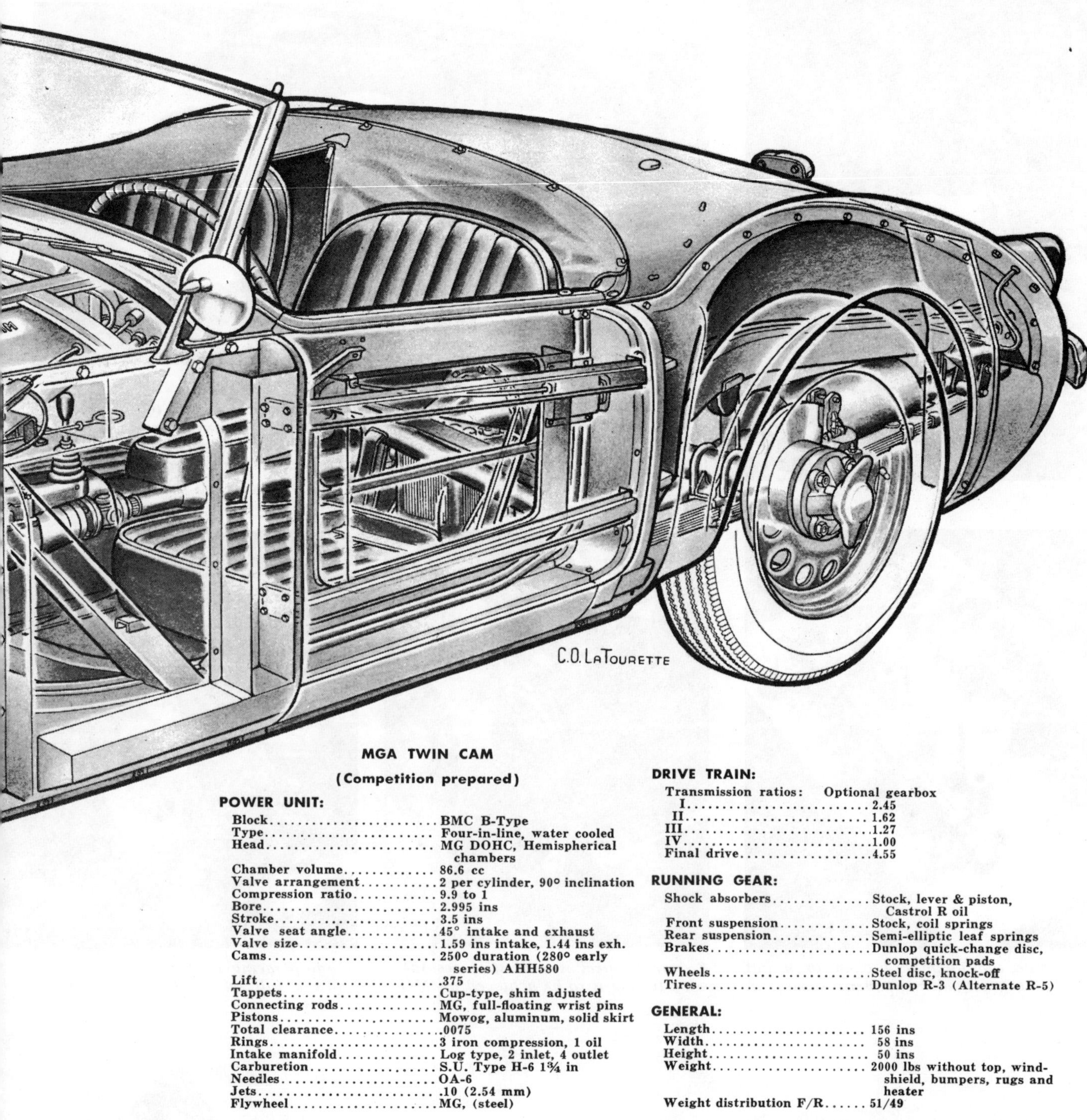

MGA TWIN CAM

(Competition prepared)

POWER UNIT:

Block	BMC B-Type
Type	Four-in-line, water cooled
Head	MG DOHC, Hemispherical chambers
Chamber volume	86.6 cc
Valve arrangement	2 per cylinder, 90° inclination
Compression ratio	9.9 to 1
Bore	2.995 ins
Stroke	3.5 ins
Valve seat angle	45° intake and exhaust
Valve size	1.59 ins intake, 1.44 ins exh.
Cams	250° duration (280° early series) AHH580
Lift	.375
Tappets	Cup-type, shim adjusted
Connecting rods	MG, full-floating wrist pins
Pistons	Mowog, aluminum, solid skirt
Total clearance	.0075
Rings	3 iron compression, 1 oil
Intake manifold	Log type, 2 inlet, 4 outlet
Carburetion	S.U. Type H-6 1¾ in
Needles	OA-6
Jets	.10 (2.54 mm)
Flywheel	MG, (steel)

DRIVE TRAIN:

Transmission ratios:	Optional gearbox
I	2.45
II	1.62
III	1.27
IV	1.00
Final drive	4.55

RUNNING GEAR:

Shock absorbers	Stock, lever & piston, Castrol R oil
Front suspension	Stock, coil springs
Rear suspension	Semi-elliptic leaf springs
Brakes	Dunlop quick-change disc, competition pads
Wheels	Steel disc, knock-off
Tires	Dunlop R-3 (Alternate R-5)

GENERAL:

Length	156 ins
Width	58 ins
Height	50 ins
Weight	2000 lbs without top, windshield, bumpers, rugs and heater
Weight distribution F/R	51/49

all rods should be checked for flaws and set in perfect alignment. One bad rod can wipe out the whole engine in less time than it takes to tell about it, and it can do it with no warning whatsoever.

It was when we came to the pistons that we discovered just what had been going on inside this particular MG. The standard minimum clearance for pistons in the BMC B-Type engine block is .0035 of an inch. This is all very well in a passenger car engine that is to be broken in over thousands of miles and is meant to give years of service after that break-in. It is just sufficient clearance, tight but all right with *split skirt pistons* such as those used in the ordinary B-Type engine. But the Twin Cam is not an ordinary B-Type—the block is the same casting but that is about as far as it goes. The Twin Cam is equipped with sturdy *solid* skirt racing type pistons which have an expansion factor much greater than that of the split skirt type in which the split or slot takes up the swelling when the piston is hot. To further complicate matters the car had been run in with Castrol R #40. The combination of what amounted to virtually nil clearance on the hot pistons and the heavy racing oil left no room for oil on the cylinder walls. The result was a set of four badly scuffed racing pistons and, worse, a four-thousandths taper in the bore. The hard chrome top ring had acted like a cutting tool when pressed by the expanding piston on the oil-less wall and had chewed the upper bore out by over .004 of an inch. The wonder was that the tops hadn't been pulled right off the pistons. Strong stuff, these Mowog racing slugs.

The wear was too great to be cleaned out with a simple honing. The decision had to be made and it was. Virag bored the cylinders out an additional .020 of an inch and ordered a set of pistons for that oversize. Two cuts were made for each cylinder. First a rough cut to plus .019 was made and then a finish cut to bring the bore out .0085 of an inch further completed that particular hole. Between each cut for each cylinder the tools were dressed so that separate bores were absolutely accurate to the ability of the micrometer to measure. A fast hone in a diamond pattern finished the job. The new pistons are of the latest type with the oil vents behind

LEFT — Joe Virag checks out the valves with a dial indicator prior to disassembly of the engine. All timing was carefully checked during dismantling and assembly. ABOVE — Ports on exhaust side are huge and virtually straight through. No enlargement necessary but all ports were matched to manifolds and equalized in size.

Valve, cam assembly broken down and laid out with all components separated.

A degree wheel is a must if accurate valve timing is to be achieved on MG.

Dunlop racing tires accounted for almost a full second lap-time in tests.

BELOW — Dynamic balance tests of the sturdy crankshaft showed only one small balance drilling was needed (arrow). The same applied to flywheel and clutch. RIGHT — Short stiff rods are similar to those in Stage 4 MGA fitted with solid skirt pistons. Large bosses on caps and little end may be ground for balance.

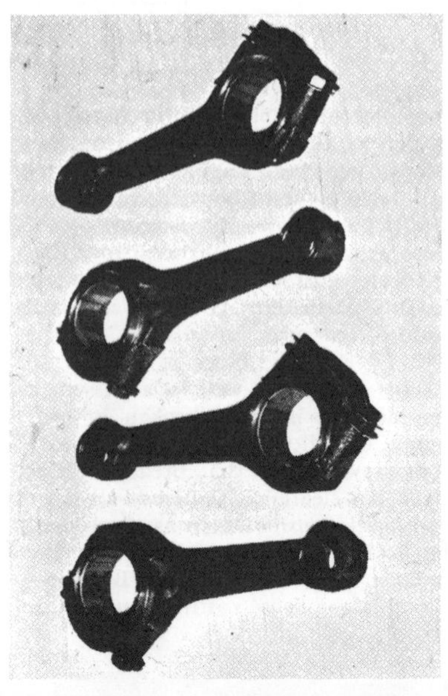

the oil ring only and none in the piston wall. The rings are also spaced closer together on these later replacements for a better seal. The pistons were measured and found to be exactly on size and the bores — as outlined above — were then honed out carefully to give a skirt to wall clearance of .007 instead of the original .0035 of an inch. When fitted to the bore without rings the new pistons dropped through freely but with no sign of cocking or wobble — a perfect fit.

Next came the balancing act.

Each rod, piston and the bearings to go with that particular rod were carefully weighed and balanced against each other. The weights were marked down and the crank, flywheel and new clutch assembly were sent out for dynamic balancing. Only one small balance hole had to be drilled in each item but they *did* need the drilling. This balancing comes easy on the Twin Cam — or any MGA for that matter. The rods have large, meaty sections at the lower end of the caps and on the little ends so they can be slightly ground to gain the necessary end-for-end and overall balance. The pistons also have internal ridges at the bottom of the skirts from which metal can be carved if found necessary. In all cases it is vital that the bearings to be used in the final assembly be clamped in the rods when the weighing is done. It is also a good idea at this point to tamp the locating tang on each bearing shell into its recess in the rod big-end. These are *not* full floating bearings and must be well and securely located. The rods in the Twin Cam are virtually the same as the Stage Four rods for the MGA in that the wrist pins are of the full floating, push-fit type rather than the clamped pins found in the standard MGA and other B-Type engine units. These wristpins should be (and were in our case) an easy palm-push fit in both the rod and the piston at about 70 degree temperature, Fahrenheit. Location is by circlips in the piston at either end of the pin.

The crank, rods, pistons with rings and flywheel were then mounted in the bare block and cinched down to the various torque readings specified in the manual. A solid spin of the flywheel produced nearly six complete revolutions with no clicking noises. Although we had been afraid at first that there might be some piston noise with a cold engine due to the large clearances we had allowed there was none when the engine was later fired up. Thus while the clearances we had used were somewhat larger than those specified in the manual they were still within the range of silent running even using the Castrol R-20 with which the engine is being run-in.

During the wait for the necessary block components and the balancing operation the head and valves were given close attention. The inlet manifold showed the usual bumps, lumps and casting ridges found in any production casting and was cleaned up without hogging immediately, a process made easy by the short, very wide passages. When bolted to the head for checking it was found that the outlets at the mating surface were offset downward in relation to the inlet ports in the head so the ports were scribed and tapered to a perfect match. On other engines this offset could be up, down, right or left or even non-existent in some cases. In these cases not too much worry need result but if the offset is downward as in our case there is a problem since there is not too much metal in the bottom lip of the port. The angularity of the taper must be watched and controlled to avoid weakening this lower lip. The ports in the Twin Cam need not and should not be enlarged but they must be cleaned and matched one against the other. Some attempt at equalization is made at the factory but the speed of production line prevents really accurate port equalizing. The result is that in the non-machined portions no two ports are exactly alike as they should be if the potential inherent in the MG is to be realized.

Other than the port matching and cleaning the major work in the head is the relief of hot spots in the form of sharp edges left by machining and doming operations. The major source of trouble and the one that probably caused the running-on and preignition in our engine was the sparkplug area. Apparently the dome cutting was done after the plug inlet was drilled and threaded and the resulting knife edges made ideal glow points. Such faults as these are not necessarily the private property of MG Twin Cams but are found in many other marques as well and cause much of the running-on character that is usually associated with four cylinder engines tending to cause the mistaken impression that running on and preignition is one of the characteristics of the four-barrel. All such edges and the edges of the combustion chamber as well were rounded off in our Twin Cam. Where it once dingled, pinged and chugged on with the switch off it now runs smoothly and quietly under load and shuts off instantly with the key. Combustion now takes place when the sparkplug tells it to and not when the fuel and air are shoved up against some evilly glowing piece of metal.

The valves, which were found to be in good shape were lapped into place after the valve seats had been refaced and slightly narrowed and new guides installed, the old ones being just worn enough to warrant replacement. Each spring, both inner and outer, was checked against the others and all found to be within half a pound of each other fully compressed. After this the assemblies were installed at exactly the .018 of an inch clearance the book calls for.

Now came the tedious part. Virag is a nut on absolutely accurate valve timing. With his Offenhauser the job is made simpler since the cams are gear-driven but with most sports cars chains are used in the interests of silence and economy. The MG Twin Cam falls into this latter category and the chain is long indeed. The major problem is to keep enough tension on the chain so that it doesn't slip off the lower sprocket while the adjustments are made at the cam sprockets. Once the tensioner is backed all the way off or removed the chain is quite likely to skip a tooth and anything from three degrees on up can be lost. The main points to watch are contacts at each cam sprocket and at the half-speed shaft and the tension in between these points. The workshop manual gives the adjustment procedure in great detail and it would be repetitious to cover it here since the use of this manual is an absolute must for anyone delving into the innards of the Twin Cam. You can bumble through a rocker-head and make it run but the Twin Cam is not a rockerbox. Either a thorough course of instruction or meticulous use of the book and succeeding bulletins are as necessary as proper tools.

Next came the outside accessories. When the engine was first removed it was discovered that the generator bracket had cracked at the generator swivel point. The original bracket is made of bent flat stock and this form of breakage is not unique to the Twin Cam but is fairly common. A reinforcement plate was made, doubling the thickness of the bracket. The generator was then mounted and shim washers placed between the bracket and the mounting flanges on the generator so that tightening would not displace or strain either the flanges or the bracket.

The original carburetors, H-6, 1¾ inch S.U. instruments, were used in their standard trim with OA6 needles and 2.54 millimeter main jets. No richening was deemed necessary. The ignition distributor was equipped with new points, the springs of which have been changed metallurgically since the earlier models since it was found that the former metal tended to fatigue. The distributor on the Twin Cam is rather hard to get at, being down on the left side of the engine so the rubbing blocks on the points were run in for several hours on an ignition strobe machine. This imparts a high, hard polish and retards the tendency for these blocks to wear, which causes the points to open with a progressively shorter gap as time goes on.

What does all this do?

We've indicated that we have a smooth, virtually trouble-free engine. It also goes. As might be expected torque at the bottom end is low. At anything under about 3000 rpm the push is just not there. As the tach needle swings past 3500 rpm, though, you begin to realize just what this engine can do—it appears as though someone added two more cylinders. At one point, motoring happily along at 3600 rpm in third gear we saw a clear stretch of road ahead. Half a mile up was another car also motoring along at about 40 mph. A quarter of a mile ahead of him was a bend. Feeling that he'd be well around the bend before we got there we poked the throttle. We were on top of him, backing off and dragging brakes, before he got halfway to the curve!

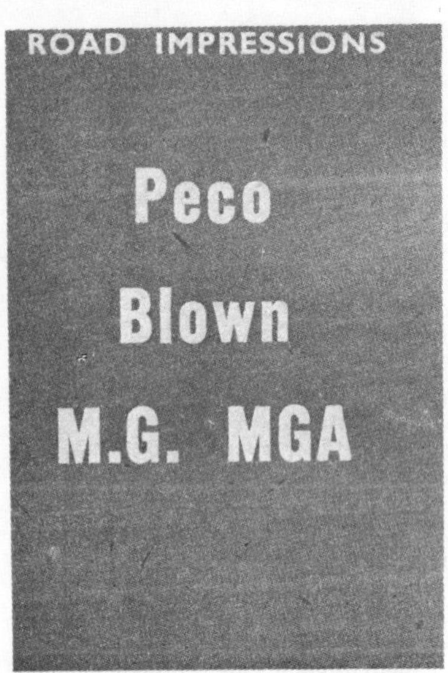

Outwardly, the only sign on the body that the car is something special is a tiny winged transfer fore and aft

Bolt-on Supercharger and Exhaust System Transforms Performance

TAKE a standard M.G. MGA engine and bolt on an entirely new exhaust and intake system, using 6lb sq in induction supercharge, and what have you got? The outcome, determined over 500 miles of road and a day of performance testing at the M.I.R.A. circuit, is quite exhilarating, as the figures show.

But first the installation.

The Performance Equipment Company, of Tower Buildings, Water Street, Liverpool, 3, whose stand was seen at the London Show for the first time this year, has come a long way in a short time. It is an offshoot of V. L. Farthing and Co., who are consultant engineers, designing such things as special gas compressors for the Atomic Energy Research Establishment. Managing director of the Peco firm is Mr. Vernon H. Farthing, who besides being an enthusiast for fast motoring, is an authority on gas flow and can call on the resources of Liverpool University for research (and on their computer for the complex mathematics of the science). He is also a member of the Aintree Circuit Club, which gives him a field test circuit right on the doorstep.

He reasoned that a low-pressure supercharger, plus a straight-through silencer with a special built-in resonating chamber, and finally a Peco booster to eliminate pulsation effect (not ordinary back pressure, but the reverse shock wave that travels back up the exhaust at often supersonic speed), would give a performance up to 100 m.p.h. and outdo that of the Twin-Cam. His own figures substantiate this, and those recorded by *The Autocar*, taken in not-very-favourable circumstances, show the keenest rivalry between the two versions of the already well-loved M.G.

The supercharger fits neatly in the existing bonnet space on the intake side, discharging through a Peco manifold into the ports. The single carburettor has the intake facing aft; an air filter-silencer is optional

Design problems involved the accommodation of the blower, often a difficult matter, the building-in of reliability, and the provision of ease of maintenance. Well aware of the suspicion with which "specials" are regarded by secondhand buyers, Peco have made no vital alteration to the MGA as it comes from the factory—even compression ratio is unchanged—so that anyone buying the equipment can remove it when desired, refit the exhaust and second carburettor and sell the car as a standard MGA. They can then, of course, utilize the Peco installation on another M.G. if they wish.

Accommodation proved easy, the Roots-type blower, supplied by Sir G. Godfrey and Partners, fitting snugly on the port side of the engine and involving no ugly bonnet bulge; similar units are supplied to the Rolls-Royce Oil Engine division. No internal lubrication is required by this supercharger, and the gears need only a little. Peco have arranged a positive oil feed from the engine, however, draining into the dipstick hole, the stick being stowed in a clip-on rubber sheath inside the bonnet. To check oil level, the flexible oil discharge tube is withdrawn and the stick inserted, with the same simplicity as is involved in taking an ordinary reading, and the additional virtue of always inserting a clean stick.

With this arrangement, the supercharger should need only routine maintenance at the end of, say, a year's usage. When the time comes to replace the belt drive, great assistance is provided by the divided nose pulley, which permits the new belt to be rigged without radiator removal. Belt life should be twelve months or about 20,000 miles, and a spare belt is supplied with each kit.

Maximum boost is 5 to 6lb sq in, although the blower speed can be adjusted to give up to 10. The mixture is fed into a Peco cast manifold mounted on the engine's existing twin ports, and the single S.U. carburettor is on the after end of the blower, drawing air from a reasonably clean and warm part of the under-bonnet space. An intake air filter-silencer will be optional; one was not fitted on the car tested.

The S.U. carburettor is the standard product, but it has a special Peco needle; the recommended fuel, 100-octane, was used throughout the test.

M.G. have been making good fast cars so long that it goes without saying that the strange driver forgets his strangeness the moment he sits behind the wheel. But the blown M.G. had more than the usual cosy Abingdon familiarity. As soon as the car was on the move the right foot seemed master of all situations, for the power under the sole of one's shoe was right out of the ordinary reckoning for this size of car.

A non-standard brute of a competition clutch (special to this car) made first gear merely first, but second was a gear to be reckoned with, showing 10-30 m.p.h. in 4.0sec against the Twin-Cam's 4.5 and the normal MGA's 5.0sec. Third and top soon proved to be the two working gears for road use.

The car's speed—with the moral and physical support of superlative brakes—was the speed of the road, even on the 90 m.p.h. East Lancashire road, or the equally fast switchback straight of A515 between Buxton and Ashbourne (which would have been embraced by the abortive Peak District road circuit).

Tested for maximum on the M.I.R.A. banked high-speed circuit, the M.G. held just over 100 m.p.h. but Peco stress that this rev. point—5,900 or 6,000 r.p.m.—is much more critical with the blown engine than with the standard car, because the combustion chambers are still well filled with mixture. This provides almost a furnace blast when, with the onset of valve bounce at 6,000 r.p.m., the gases no longer get away efficiently, and there is consequent liability of severe over-heating. An unsupercharged engine has only partial filling at this speed. The recommended r.p.m. limit on the MGA is 5,800, and owners of the blown version will be warned not to exceed it; a yellow light directly ahead of the driver is a reminder, flashing when 5,800 is reached.

The critical nature of maximum revs proved somewhat of a handicap in taking the acceleration figures. The car was also too new, having done only 4,500 miles, for best results; additionally, it was difficult to prevent wheelspin on a wet surface, while the competition clutch was a disability in getting away from rest. Even so, the figures are commendable and are compared with those of the standard MGA and the Twin-Cam in the panel.

Only with 0-50 m.p.h. is there a disappointing discrepancy, but this is explained by the rev limit. Peco, knowing the car intimately, take it through 50 m.p.h. in second, but *The Autocar*, having decided that 49 m.p.h. was the utmost it cared to risk in that ratio, changed up between 49 and 50, with consequent delay.

Naturally, the better breathing of the B.M.C. B engine was also noisier. On the intake side there was a scissors-grinding noise at around 1,000 r.p.m., giving place to an eerie whistle for a further 200 r.p.m. or so. The noise disappeared in the rising exhaust note as r.p.m. mounted. It was distinctly loud to ears tuned to, say, Jaguar standards, but was calculated to delight the heart of the sort of buyer Peco have in mind. It left behind no drumming in the ears after a long day of it, and settled to a pleasant, almost melodious, burble under a light throttle at 30 m.p.h., even in confined city streets. As the road speed exceeded the sixties, the fabric roof flap almost drowned the exhaust note, and the two combined effectively to subdue the noise of the intake air, and of the blower gears themselves, which by now was a scream so high-pitched as to be hardly detectable.

The tail end of the exhaust is the familiar twin-outlet Peco pulse rectifier, but the silencer also is a special straight-through design

Such a description may tend to suggest the harshness of bygone sports car performance, which would be a pity, for the M.G. was docile, flexible, and extremely agreeable. It would pull away smoothly in top from 20 m.p.h. It climbed like a rocket, taking the double hairpin at the foot of Holme Moss at 30 m.p.h. in second, and careering up the two miles to the summit and the B.B.C.'s famous mast in a mixure of third and top that set the Pennines roaring, and even caused the grazing sheep to raise an eyebrow.

Starting from cold was instantaneous, the blower promoting turbulence, and hardly any use of the choke was required even in late November. Fuel consumption over the whole period, including the performance testing, was 31 m.p.g., compared with 21.8 for the Twin-Cam and 27 m.p.g. for the standard MGA. While increased combustion efficiency plays its part in this commendable figure, it was also helped by one long-distance run made in a fog which limited maximum speed to 50 m.p.h. Peco themselves claim that 30 m.p.g. can be achieved, and an absolute minimum of 22.5 using all the performance.

Cost of the installation has not yet been finalized, orders being taken at present with "Less than £100" stipulated. Production will begin in January and is earmarked to the end of February.

The installation could be made by a motorist who is also an engineer by instinct if not by profession, the vitally important factor being the aligning of the drive pulleys. Otherwise a competent garage should be briefed, of the kind where the words "Grand Prix" excite more than a blank stare. The job should take about half a day and no special tools are required. The special exhaust system is an integral part of the kit, playing its part in the performance, though how big that part is has not yet been determined.

MICHAEL BROWN.

PERFORMANCE

Acceleration:

Speed Range M.P.H.	Ratio to 1	Peco	Twin-Cam*	Two-seater†
		Time in Sec.		
10—30	9.52	4.0	4.5	5.0
20—40	5.908	5.7	7.1	8.0
20—40	4.3	8.1	11.0	12.2
30—50	5.908	5.5	7.4	8.4
30—50	4.3	8.1	10.2	12.3
40—60	5.908	6.2	7.5	9.1
40—60	4.3	8.1	10.5	13.1
50—70	5.908	7.0	7.6	10.7
50—70	4.3	8.7	11.7	15.0
60—80	4.3	9.7	11.7	18.1
70—90	4.3	12.7	13.6	—

From rest through gears to:

M.P.H.	Peco	Twin-Cam	Two-seater
30	4.7	4.3	4.9
40	6.5	6.9	—
50	9.9	9.4	11.0
60	13.1	13.3	15.6
70	17.1	17.3	21.4
80	23.1	22.5	32.1
90	30.6	30.0	50.1
Standing quarter-mile	19.0	18.6	20.2

MAXIMUM SPEEDS ON GEARS:

Gear	M.P.H. (max.)	K.P.H. (max.)
Top (best)	102	164.2
3rd	74	118
2nd	44	71

FUEL CONSUMPTION:
31 m.p.g. overall for 479 miles (9.12 litres per 100 km)'

TEST CONDITIONS: Drizzle, wet surface.
Air temperature 45 deg F.

SPEEDOMETER CORRECTION: M.P.H.

Car speedometer	10	20	30	40	50	60	70	80	90	100
True speed	10	19	29	37	48	58	68	77	86	97

*18 July 1958. †23 September 1955.

The Motor Road Test No. 22/58 (Continental)

Make: M.G. **Type:** M.G. A Twin Cam Two-seater

Makers: M.G. Car Co., Ltd., Abingdon-on-Thames, Berkshire.

Test Data

World copyright reserved; no unauthorized reproduction in whole or in part.

CONDITIONS: *Weather: Warm and dry, light wind. (Temperature 52°-61° F., Barometer 30.0-30.1 in. Hg.) Surface: Dry concrete Autobahn (acceleration and maximum speed tests). Dry concrete banked track for fuel consumption tests. Fuel: German pump fuel, approx. 97 Research Method Octane Number (acceleration and maximum speed tests), 100 R.M.O.N. elsewhere.*

INSTRUMENTS

Speedometer at 30 m.p.h.	2% fast
Speedometer at 60 m.p.h.	6% slow
Speedometer at 90 m.p.h.	4% slow
Distance recorder	3% slow

WEIGHT

Kerb weight (unladen, but with oil, coolant and fuel for approx. 50 miles)...	19½ cwt.
Front/rear distribution of kerb weight	53½/46½
Weight laden as tested	23 cwt.

MAXIMUM SPEEDS

Flying Quarter Mile

Mean of four opposite runs ...	...113.0 m.p.h.
Best one-way time equals ...	...115.0 m.p.h.

"Maximile" Speed. (Timed quarter mile after one mile accelerating from rest.)

Mean of four opposite runs ...	...101.3 m.p.h.
Best one-way time equals ...	...104.2 m.p.h.

Speed in Gears. (at 6,500 r.p.m. recommended limit).

Max. speed in 3rd gear	81 m.p.h.
Max. speed in 2nd gear	50 m.p.h.
Max. speed in 1st gear	31 m.p.h.

FUEL CONSUMPTION

Top gear

37 m.p.g. at constant 30 m.p.h. on level.
36½ m.p.g. at constant 40 m.p.h. on level.
33½ m.p.g. at constant 50 m.p.h. on level.
32½ m.p.g. at constant 60 m.p.h. on level.
29½ m.p.g. at constant 70 m.p.h. on level.
26½ m.p.g. at constant 80 m.p.h. on level.
22 m.p.g. at constant 90 m.p.h. on level.
17½ m.p.g. at constant 100 m.p.h. on level.

Overall Fuel Consumption for 1,593 miles, 71.7 gallons, equals 22.2 m.p.g. (12.7 litres/100 km.).

Touring Fuel Consumption (m.p.g. at steady speed midway between 30 m.p.h. and maximum, less 5% allowance for acceleration) 27.6.

Fuel tank capacity (maker's figure) 10 gallons.

STEERING

Turning circle between kerbs:

Left	31 feet
Right	30 feet
Turns of steering wheel from lock to lock	2¾

BRAKES from 30 m.p.h.

0.90g retardation (equivalent to 33½ ft. stopping distance) with 100 lb. pedal pressure.
0.80g retardation (equivalent to 37½ ft. stopping distance) with 80 lb. pedal pressure.
0.51g retardation (equivalent to 59 ft. stopping distance) with 50 lb. pedal pressure.
0.32g retardation (equivalent to 94 ft. stopping distance) with 25 lb. pedal pressure.

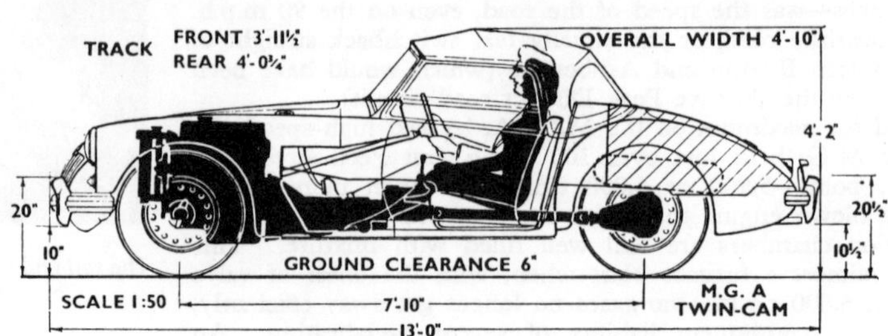

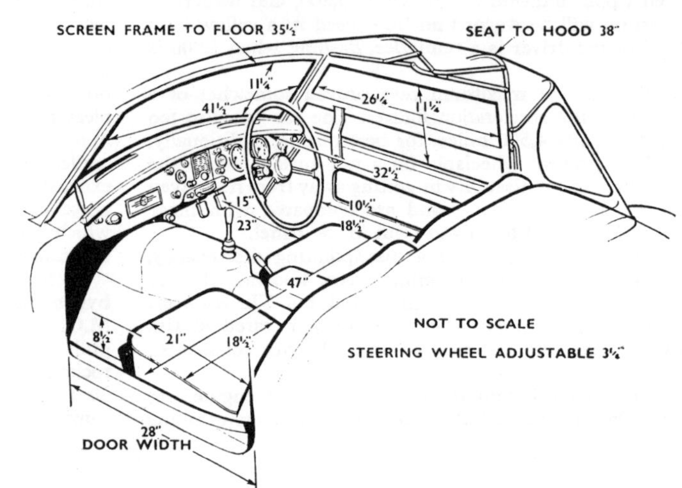

ACCELERATION TIMES from standstill

0-30 m.p.h.	2.6 sec.
0-40 m.p.h.	4.4 sec.
0-50 m.p.h.	7.3 sec.
0-60 m.p.h.	9.1 sec.
0-70 m.p.h.	12.3 sec.
0-80 m.p.h.	16.2 sec.
0-90 m.p.h.	24.6 sec.
0-100 m.p.h.	40.3 sec.
Standing quarter mile	18.1 sec.

ACCELERATION TIMES on upper ratios

	Top gear	3rd gear
10-30 m.p.h.	—	8.3 sec.
20-40 m.p.h.	10.7 sec.	6.5 sec.
30-50 m.p.h.	9.7 sec.	6.5 sec.
40-60 m.p.h.	8.8 sec.	5.5 sec.
50-70 m.p.h.	9.4 sec.	5.5 sec.
60-80 m.p.h.	13.9 sec.	8.3 sec.
70-90 m.p.h.	15.2 sec.	—
80-100 m.p.h....	23.1 sec.	—
90-110 m.p.h....	—	—

HILL CLIMBING at sustained steady speeds

Max. gradient on top gear	1 in 9.3 (Tapley 240 lb./ton)
Max. gradient on 3rd gear	1 in 6.6 (Tapley 335 lb./ton)
Max. gradient on 2nd gear	1 in 4.0 (Tapley 545 lb./ton)

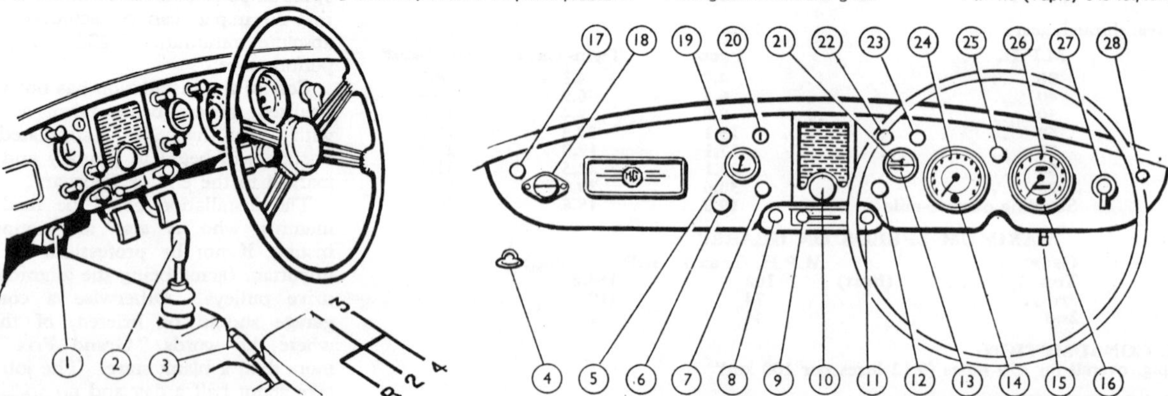

1, Headlamp dip switch. 2, Gear lever. 3, Handbrake. 4, Bonnet catch release. 5, Fuel contents gauge. 6, Windscreen washer button. 7, Choke control. 8, Ventilator control. 9, Heater control and fan switch. 10, Horn button. 11, Demister control. 12, Starter switch. 13, Water thermometer. 14, Dynamo charge warning light. 15, Trip resetting knob. 16, Headlamp main beam indicator. 17, Map reading light switch. 18, Map reading light. 19, Windscreen wipers switch. 20, Ignition switch. 21, Oil pressure gauge. 22, Lights switch. 23, Foglamp switch. 24, Rev. counter. 25, Panel light switch. 26, Speedometer and distance recorder. 27, Direction indicator switch. 28, Direction indicator warning light.

The M.G. A Twin Cam Two-seater

A Roadworthy Sports Car of Very High Performance

ONE hundred and eight net horsepower from an unsupercharged engine of 1.6 litres swept volume is a figure which only a very short time ago would have inspired a picture of a noisy, intractable and probably temperamental racing machine. As the power (together with the disc brakes) is the feature of paramount importance in the latest M.G., one may as well sum up the car to begin with by stating that it is relatively noisy, entirely tractable, quite untemperamental and will probably appeal in the main to owners who wish to win races.

Apart from minor details of trim, these two mechanical features are the only departures made by the "Twin Cam" M.G. A from its less expensive and very well known counterpart. It seems justifiable to leave for a moment a recapitulation of familiar virtues and vices, and concentrate for once upon a straight comparison figures between the old and the new.

In Brief

Price (including oil cooler, as tested) £854 10s. plus purchase tax £428 12s. equals £1,283 2s.

Capacity	1,588 c.c.
Unladen kerb weight ...	19½ cwt.
Acceleration:	
20-40 m.p.h. in top gear ...	10.7 sec.
0-50 m.p.h. through gears	7.3 sec.
Maximum direct top gear gradient	1 in 9.3
Maximum speed ...	...113.0 m.p.h.
"Maximile" speed ...	...101.3 m.p.h.
Touring fuel consumption ...	27.6 m.p.g.

Gearing: 17.2 m.p.h. in top gear at 1,000 r.p.m.; 19.4 m.p.h. at 1,000 ft./min. piston speed.

In respect of maximum speed a comparison with the last M.G. A tested by *The Motor* cannot be exact, owing to the slightly greater drag effect of a fabric hood and sidescreens. An increase in net power output of exactly 50% has however raised the mean speed by 12% and the best one-way run to a creditable 115 m.p.h., the latter figure corresponding precisely to the peak engine speed of 6,700 r.p.m. This is by no means all. It might be supposed that the main advantage of a twin overhead camshaft design would be to increase performance at the upper end of the speed range, without comparable gains at lower revolutions. The only extent to which this is true is that, with the new car running on German pump fuel of approximately 97 Octane instead of its preferred 100 Octane, the rather academic acceleration test for 10 to 30 m.p.h. in top gear had to be omitted. Thenceforward the improvement in acceleration times is so marked as to warrant a table of direct comparisons between the standing-start figures for two cars.

Rest to:	Twin Cam	Normal
30 m.p.h.	2.6 sec.	5.0 sec.
40 m.p.h.	4.4 sec.	7.2 sec.
50 m.p.h.	7.3 sec.	10.8 sec.
60 m.p.h.	9.1 sec.	15.6 sec.
70 m.p.h.	12.3 sec.	21.4 sec.
80 m.p.h.	16.2 sec.	32.1 sec.

Perhaps the most revealing way to sum up this performance is to say that of all the cars so far tested by *The Motor* only machines built specifically for sports-car racing would keep pace with this 1,600 c.c. touring two-seater in a standing start match to speeds of 60, 70 or 80 m.p.h.

Observant readers will have noticed that although racing cars are excluded from this comparison the "Twin-Cam" has already been referred to as a potential winner of competitions. To what extent has racing performance been bought at the cost of inconvenience? There is, to begin with, a considerable increase in noise, both mechanically from the engine and from the tailpipe when the throttle is opened at all wide. Neither is particularly objectionable at the speeds of normal traffic, but both can become tiring with the prolonged cruising at 90 m.p.h. or so which is a very practicable possibility with this type of car.

So long as 100 Octane fuel can be obtained the engine is extremely docile at low revolutions and extremely smooth at high ones. On slightly lower grades it pinks only when pulling hard at low speeds, but has a very definite tendency to run-on after the ignition has been switched off. A fairly rich mixture setting of the twin S.U. carburetters was indicated by the fact that after a mild night under cover there was no need of the "choke" for starting, although steady speed fuel consumption tests bear out the reasonable economy achieved in fast Autobahn cruising. Under typical English conditions, indirect gears and high engine speeds are used as a matter of course to hustle the M.G. from point to point, and treatment of this sort has to be paid for. A check over 170 miles, using a good deal of full-throttle acceleration with a rev. limit of between 5,500 r.p.m. and 6,000 r.p.m., showed a fraction under 20 m.p.g., which

Accessibility is not the strongest point of the new and appreciably more bulky engine. The distributor cannot be reached without removing the heater air duct, just visible to the right of the top radiator hose. The camshaft covers are chrome-plated.

Cockpit layout is unchanged from the normal M.G. A., but the seats are more heavily padded and better shaped, while the instrument panel is covered in leather.

puts a sharp restriction on the range of a 10-gallon fuel tank. Different styles of driving, on the other hand, do not appear to affect an oil consumption in the region of one pint for every 120 miles. The test car was fitted with the external oil cooler which is an optional extra, and which lies between the radiator and grille.

To continue the review of new features, the highest praise can be given to the Dunlop disc brakes, which are fitted in conjunction with centre-lock, perforated steel disc wheels. Really high average speeds, whether on busy motor roads or ordinary fast highways, make demands upon a braking system quite different from those of day-to-day driving. Consistent performance from disc brakes is by no means universal, yet the Dunlops combine smooth and progressive action right down to zero speed with a reassuring ability to slow the M.G. quite abruptly from 100 m.p.h. as often as small saloons hold their course in the fast lane of an Autobahn—which can be very frequently. They appear, moreover, to be unaffected by rain as well as heat.

Having dealt with those components by which, in return for some £180 of basic price, the owner of the "Twin Cam" M.G. obtains a considerable edge over his fellows, it would not be quite accurate to say that the car as supplied for test was in other respects just like its predecessor. The M.G. A has built up an enviable reputation for roadholding and sensitive handling, largely because it is, so to speak, stronger than it is fast. It must be recorded that the faster model, after 500 miles in England and 1,000 on the Continent, was virtually without front shock absorbers and suffering accordingly. In particular quite severe scuttle shake and reaction through the steering wheel would build up at speeds between about 70 m.p.h. and 85 m.p.h.

Whilst the shock absorbers are operative—and presumably after a more robust pattern has been adopted—the handling of the car is in the excellent M.G. A tradition. The steering is neither especially light nor especially heavy, but absolutely positive and responsible in a manner which is rare. Just sufficient understeer is present to make the car straight running and insensitive to cross-winds, without requiring efforts of skill or strength on a winding road. The cornering power of the new Dunlop Road Speed RS4 tyres is exceptional on a dry surface, provided that higher pressures are adopted than the 18 lb. front and 20 lb. rear recommended for "normal" driving—at least 24 lb. and 26 lb. seems to be desirable. In the wet these tyres favour enterprising use of the accelerator if corners are to be taken fast, when the rear wheels break away very easily, but at the same time very controllably. The embarrassing and much more dangerous phenomenon of a front-wheel slide is happily unknown to the M.G. driver.

Stated thus baldly, the plain facts of roadholding behaviour may not convey to a reader unfamiliar as yet with the M.G. A its most endearing characteristic: that of being fun to drive. This quality as a whole is hard to pin down, yet instantly recognizable by anyone coming fresh to the car, and is probably owed to the obvious but not universal circumstance of a set of controls which all work perfectly. The steering and brakes have been remarked upon. An essential of any sports car is a really good gearbox and that of the M.G. is first class, with a light and completely positive movement of the short lever but no obstruction to snatched changes from tl synchromesh. The only objections are a reverse position located

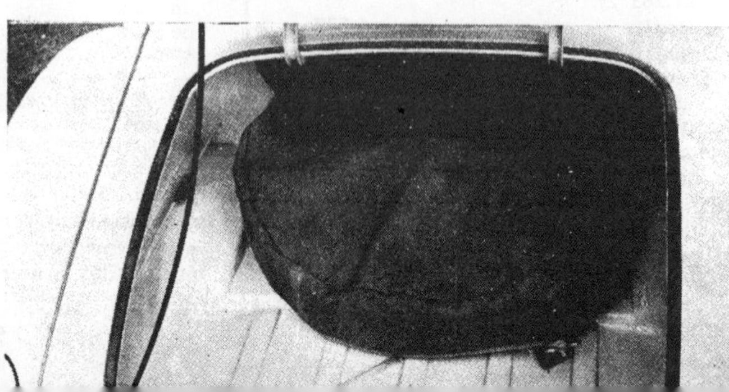

Space in the boot is limited by the necessity to fit in a spare wheel, but a couple of soft grips can be carried without much difficulty. On top of the wheel is a full set of tools.

next to second and therefore provided with rather too strong a guard spring for convenience, and a biggish gap between the second and third ratios which allow speeds of approximately 81 and 50 m.p.h. respectively at 6,500 r.p.m. The clutch is completely without slip, and befits a car which will readily spin its wheels during getaway on a dry road. The accelerator, in spite of a flexible cable connection, works well and is placed so that it is easy to blip the throttle with the side of the foot to synchronize engine and transmission speeds while braking.

In a car with slower steering, requiring more arm work, the bucket seats might be uncomfortably close up to the steering wheel even for the long-legged. As it is, shorter drivers move in a rather restricted space, but the seats themselves are comfortable, well padded, more upright than most and excellent in holding the driver in place. At medium tyre pressures—high enough to ensure good roadholding, but below the 30-32 lb. requested for maximum runs—the suspension provides a much more comfortable ride than might be expected of so solid-feeling a car, possibly on account of softer sidewalls in the new tyres. Even over really bad pave, jarring through the steering wheel was the only unpleasant sensation.

The seats are fairly low slung between the chassis side-rails, with the advantage of greater protection against the elements from high doors and the corresponding disadvantage of slightly reduced visibility. Nevertheless, any driver tall enough to see over the scuttle has a clear view of both front wings, while transparent panels now sewn into the hood fabric allow almost 350-degree vision even when it is raised. The latter operation is one requiring a good deal of perseverance for one man to complete it in less than four or five minutes, although the hood offers the compensation of being one of the most weatherproof of its kind when erect. No drop of water entered in quite heavy rain, and the windscreen is kept well clear outside by electric wipers and inside by a powerful fresh-air heater and demister. Plated studs on the scuttle, for attaching the tonneau cover, produce rather trying reflections in the windscreen.

The hood, although rather cumbersome to erect, is extremely efficient in keeping out rain and draughts. Centre-lock pressed steel wheels are standard equipment.

Stowage of the hood, complete with its folding frame, behind the seats, considerably reduces the limited space available for luggage, the greater part of the boot (whose lid is released by a concealed toggle inside the car) being occupied by the spare wheel and tools. A couple of soft grips, together with small articles which can be wedged into odd spaces or the door pockets, just about complete the possible payload when two people are carried. It would appear that an enterprising accessory manufacturer might produce a lockable glove box to make use of the part of the facia panel now occupied alternatively by a decorative emblem or the optional car radio controls.

Quarts into pint pots frequently take up a lot of the available space. The extra width of a twin o.h.c. cylinder head has filled the bonnet to very near its capacity, and the engine is by no means as accessible as formerly. The dipstick, requiring as it does frequent attention, is almost completely hidden from view; a fault which could be most easily cured by fitting a long tube rising to the top of the engine. Similarly the distributor cannot be reached at all without first uncoupling the air duct to the interior heater.

The "Twin Cam" M.G. A is not intended for very large scale production, and such details as these may well be unimportant to the comparatively few people who, by their choice of the more costly model, indicate that performance is their first consideration. When one or two matters have been attended to there is little doubt that numerous competition successes will come the way of the M.G., the more so because of its favourable situation in the 1,600 c.c. category.

Specification

Engine

Cylinders	4
Bore	75.4 mm.
Stroke	89.0 mm.
Cubic capacity	1,588 c.c.
Piston area	27.7 sq. in.
Valves	Overhead (twin o.h.c.)
Compression ratio	9.9/1
Carburetters	Two S.U. H6
Fuel pump	S.U. electric
Ignition timing control	Centrifugal and vacuum
Oil filter	Tecalemit full flow
Max. power (net)	108 b.h.p.
at	6,700 r.p.m.
Piston speed at max. b.h.p.	3,910 ft./min.

Transmission

Clutch	Borg and Beck 8 in. s.d.p.
Top gear (s/m)	4.3
3rd gear (s/m)	5.908
2nd gear (s/m)	9.520
1st gear	15.652
Reverse	20.468
Propeller shaft	Hardy Spicer open
Final drive	Hypoid
Top gear m.p.h. at 1,000 r.p.m.	17.2
Top gear m.p.h. at 1,000 ft./min. piston speed	19.4

Chassis

Brakes	Dunlop disc
Friction lining area	32 sq. in.
Suspension:	
Front	Coil springs and wishbones
Rear	Semi-elliptic
Shock absorbers:	
Front and rear	Armstrong lever
Steering gear	Cam Gears rack and pinion
Tyres	Dunlop Road Speed 5.90-15 tubed

Coachwork and Equipment

Starting handle	Yes
Battery mounting	One each side behind seats
Jack	Screw
Jacking points	No fixed points

Standard tool kit: 3 double-ended spanners, 4 box spanners, tommy bar, feeler gauge, grease gun, adjustable spanner, pliers, Phillips screwdriver, tool roll, wheel nut hammer, screwdriver, tyre pump.

Exterior lights: 2 head, 2 side/indicator, 2 stop/tail/indicator, rear number plate.

Number of electrical fuses	2
Direction indicators	Flashing, self-cancelling
Windscreen wipers	Lucas electric
Windscreen washers	Optional, Tudor
Sun vizors	None

Instruments: Speedometer with decimal trip distance recorder, rev. counter, oil pressure gauge, fuel gauge, water thermometer.

Warning lights: Indicators, dynamo charge, headlamp main beam.

Locks:	
With ignition key	Ignition only
With other keys	None
Glove lockers	None
Map pockets	Two in doors
Parcel shelves	One behind seats (with hood up)
Ashtrays	Optional
Cigar lighters	Optional
Interior lights	Optional
Interior heater	Optional, Smiths 3½kw. fresh air type
Car radio	Optional, Radiomobile

Extras available: Heater and demister, cold air ventilation, cigar lighter, adjustable steering column, luggage grid, wing mirror, tonneau cover, radiator blind, horn, foglamp, radio, competition windscreen, ashtray, windscreen washer, hardtop, sliding sidescreens, badge bar, sun vizor, seats, oilcooler, tonneau cover.

Upholstery material	Leather and leathercloth
Floor covering	Carpet
Exterior colours standardized	Five
Alternative body styles	Coupe

Maintenance

Sump	12 pints, S.A.E. 30 (below 32° F. S.A.E. 20)
Gearbox	4 pints, S.A.E. 30
Rear axle	2¾ pints, S.A.E. 90 (extreme cold, S.A.E. 80)
Steering gear lubricant	S.A.E. 90 oil (extreme cold, S.A.E. 80)
Cooling system capacity	13⅜ pints (1 drain tap)
Chassis lubrication	By grease gun every 1,000 miles to 9 points
Ignition timing	t.d.c.
Contact-breaker gap	0.015 in.
Sparking plug type	Champion No. 3
Sparking plug gap	0.024-0.026 in.

Valve timing: Inlet opens 20° b.t.d.c., closes 50° a.b.d.c.; exhaust opens, 50° b.b.d.c., closes 20° a.t.d.c.

Tappet clearances (hot)	
Inlet	0.018 in.
Exhaust	0.018 in.
Front wheel toe-in	Nil
Camber angle	1°
Castor angle	4°
Steering swivel pin inclination	9°
Tyre pressures:	
Normal, Front	18 lb.
Rear	20 lb. (see text)
Fast, Front	22 lb.
Rear	24 lb.
Competition, Front	24 lb.
Rear	26 lb.
Brake fluid	Lockheed No. 103
Battery type and capacity	Lucas SG9E 12v., 51 amp./hr.

more power for the MGA

more driving power . . . more braking power

Now . . . more punch and more liveliness from a bigger capacity 1588 c.c. engine, power-packed for exhilarating performance. And increased safety from front-wheel disc brakes —smooth-acting and instantly responsive. Other new developments include a re-styled hood with full-vision wrap-around rear window and sliding side-screens. Separate amber flasher-lights are now fitted fore and aft.

1600

Price £663.0.0 plus £277.7.6 P.T.

Twelve Months' Warranty and backed by B.M.C. Service – the most comprehensive in Europe.

Safety fast!

161

THE M.G. CAR COMPANY LIMITED, SALES DIVISION, COWLEY, OXFORD

London Showrooms: Stratton House, 80 Piccadilly, London, W.1

Overseas Business: Nuffield Exports Limited, Cowley, Oxford and 41 Piccadilly, London, W.1

MORE GO FOR MG

Exterior appearance of competition MG-A resembles its more placid brother. The big changes are under its hood.

Dunlop disc brakes are fitted to all four wheels of "Twin Cam". Photo shows disc and caliper behind knock-on wheel mount.

Twin overhead camshaft engine has been bored out to 1588 cc, develops 107 bhp at 6500 rpm. Engine came from BMC "B" unit.

HEARTILY tired of their product looking down the twin tailpipes of Porsches on the world's road circuits, the men of Abingdon-on-Thames have turned their popular but innocuous MGA into what bids fair to become a raging Porsche-killer.

With a bored-out, twin-cam power plant that crams the engine compartment like that of an American V-8, the new competition MGA develops 107 brake horsepower and is capable of blasting down the straightaways at over 120 mph. It will reach 100 mph from rest in 31 seconds, 110 mph in 38 seconds, according to BMC officials, who are confident that it will outperform any machine on the road at anywhere near its price.

The price will be in the $3,500 range at U.S. ports of entry. It's about $1,000 more than the price of the standard MGA, but still a good deal cheaper than any other serious contender in the under-1600 cc production category.

Officially known as the "Twin Cam," the new machine can be distinguished visually from the standard MGA only by the new knock-on disc wheels and the words "Twin Cam" on the trunk lid and by the air vents just forward of the windshield.

But under the hood is the new engine. Developed from the tried-and-true BMC "B" series unit which powers the MGA, the Magnette and several other BMC cars, it has been bored out to 1,588 cc (75.4 mm by 88.9 mm) to take full advantage of the International Touring Car Classification. The twin overhead camshafts, driven by a duplex chain from a half-speed shaft gear-driven from the crankshaft, operate the valves at an angle of 80 degrees.

With compression increased to 9.9:1, the engine develops 107 bhp at 6,500 rpm. Torque peaks out around 5,000 rpm at 92 lbs./ft. With the standard 4.3:1 rear axle ratio and standard 5.90 x 15 tires, top speed works out to over 120 mph. Best acceleration is achieved by using 6,500 rpm as the gear shift point.

To give the "Twin Cam" stopping power in keeping with its acceleration and speed, the Abingdon engineers fitted it with the latest Dunlop disc brakes on all four wheels. ●

HOW TO DRIVE THE

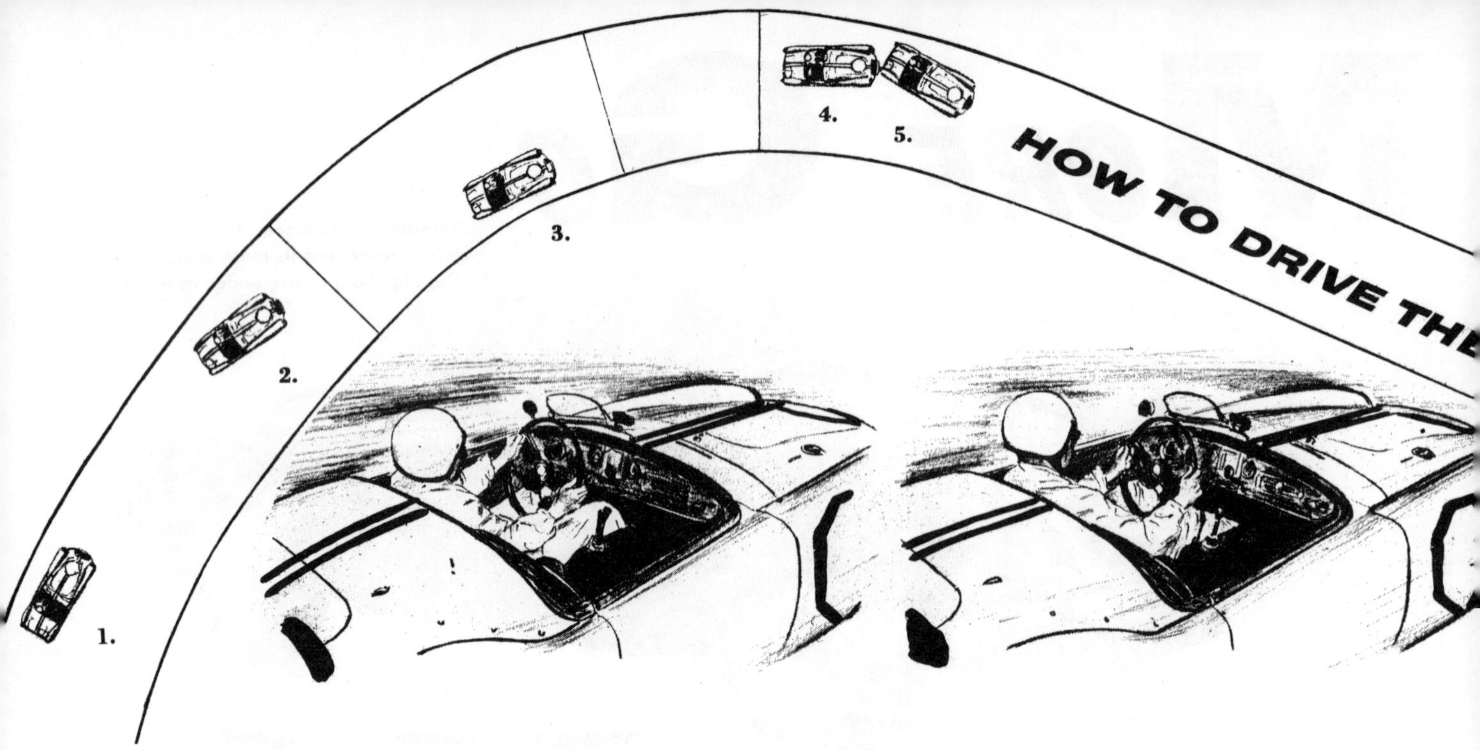

or the fastest way through two corners in Abingdon's latest competition car.

NOT LONG ago a young friend of mine asked me if I could name a typical road racing circuit where he might learn something about competition driving. (He already owns an MG and is a pretty fair touring driver.) I thought for a while and finally realized that there is no such thing as a "typical" road racing circuit. Furthermore, it occured to me that this is a very good thing for experienced race drivers and beginners alike. I say this because if any one course could be truly typical this would mean that all of the courses were pretty much the same—that road widths and surfaces, grading, curve lengths and angles, etc., were all standardized. Obviously this is impossible, but even if it were possible it would be an exceedingly bad thing for the sport because it would soon eliminate all of the challenge and most of the fun from sports car racing. In other words, it is the very differences that exist from one course to another, from one bend to another, that make road racing challenging. And it is these same differences and the necessity to cope with them, that face both beginners and experts. To develop into highly

One of the most interesting, and challenging, road racing circuits in the East, and therefore one of the best to learn on, is Lime Rock Park, in Connecticut. The section of the Lime Rock Course that we used in connection with this article comprises just two turns (although I will discuss two others that are inter-connected) that are *a*typical enough to give you a good idea of the type of problems that are encountered on a road race circuit.

In depicting the "line" through the turns in question I broke the whole process down into 10 basic steps. Artist J. George Janes has covered these steps in his drawings from three angles; if you follow the corresponding numbers as I go over each step in detail you will be able to see (a) the proper positioning of the steering wheel, (b) the path taken by the car, as seen from overhead, and (c) the attitude of the vehicle itself on the road at each point. There is a map of the entire course on pages 62 and 63 that will give you the over-all picture.

As I drive down the pit straight, maximum speed in the twin-overhead-cam MG (about 112 mph) is achieved just as I approach the marker that is placed 100 yards from the first turn. At this point I am in high gear, driving about five feet from the left-hand edge of the road. With the excellent disc brakes of the twin-cam MG I am able to delay my braking until just past the 100-yard marker, and then, as I apply the brakes hard, I shift down to third gear. (I stay in third all the way around the rest of the circuit, until I come back onto the main straight again). The first turn, which is not included in our step-by-step diagrams, is *part* of what is known as the Hook. Actually a separate turn in itself, this first part of the Hook is more or less a constant-radius bend and is taken in "classic" style. That is, when I have gotten the speed of the car down to about 6000 rpm in third gear (4.55-1 axle ratio) (about 70 mph) I begin to steer across from the left-hand side of the road, heading for the apex of the turn on the inside. This is a critical point because from here the car has to be positioned properly for the short approach to the second part of the Hook. I like to enter the first turn just fast enough so that I will *tend* to be carried by centrifugal

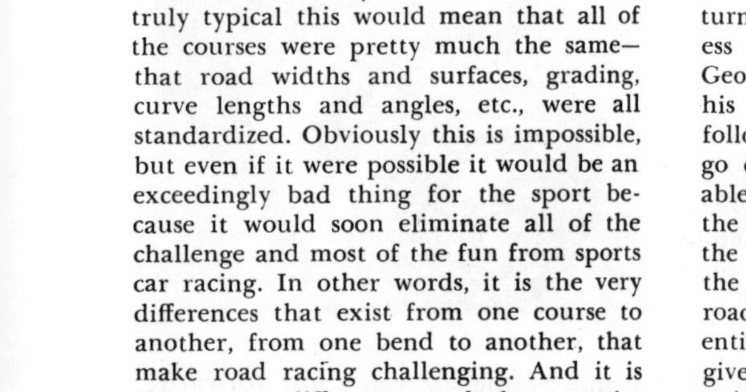

By Dave Ash & George Janes

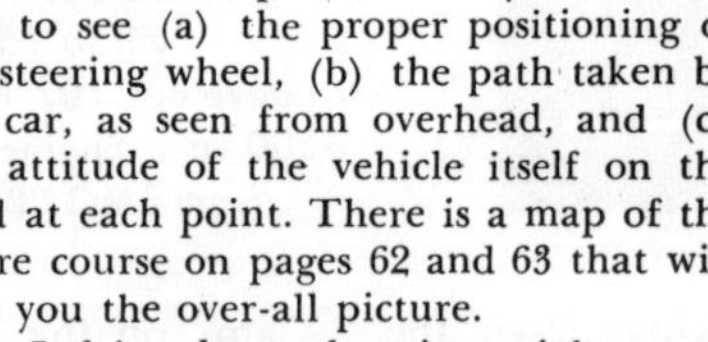

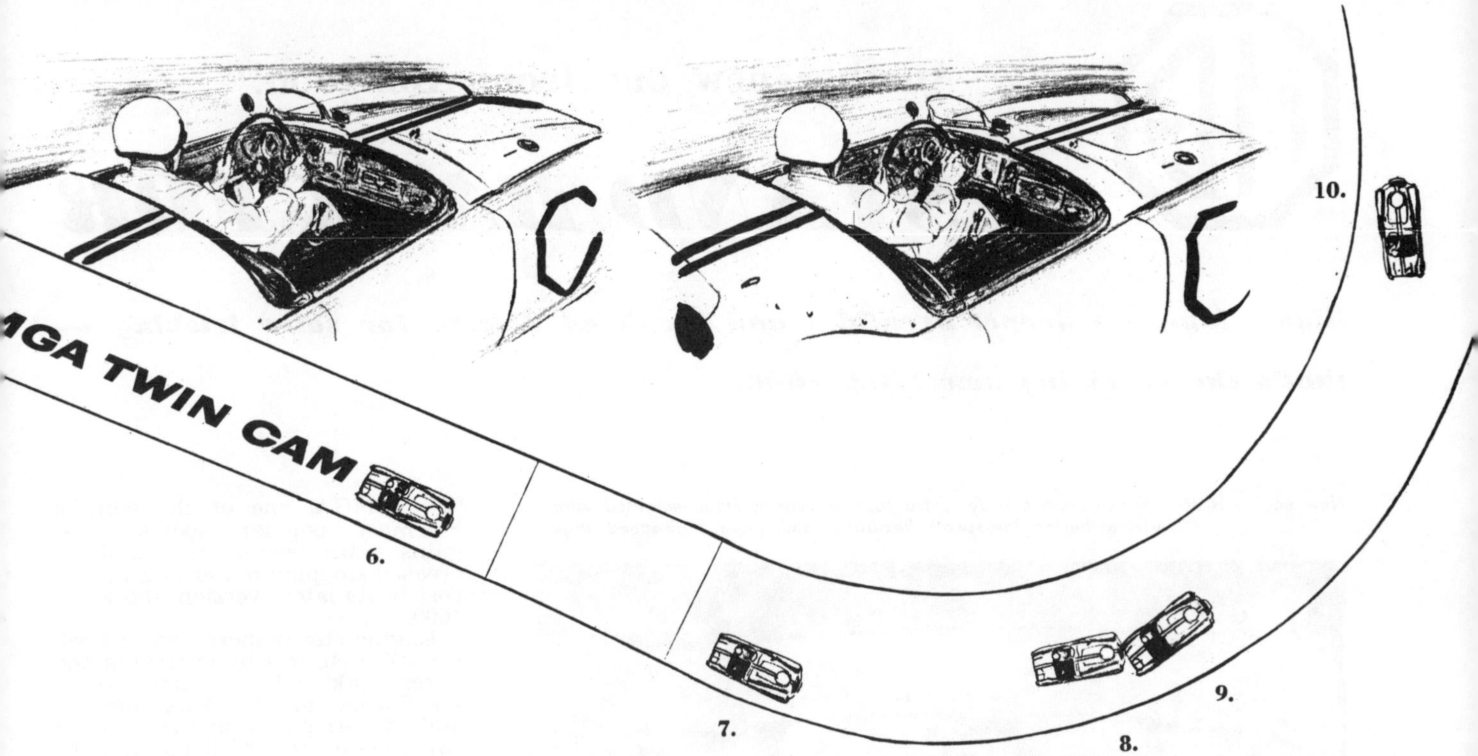

MGA TWIN CAM

6.

7.

8.

9.

10.

force, sliding slightly, to the left side of the road. If I drove into this turn too fast I would slide too violently and might go off the road altogether on the left-hand side. Or, if I managed to stay on the road, the corrective action needed to accomplish this would slow the car. In this case the engine revs would fall off so much that I would not have enough power available to take the next turn properly; a downshift to second gear might be necessary, and this is certainly to be avoided. On the other hand I would find if I took the first turn too slowly, that I was too far to the right to go into the second part of the Hook correctly. I would have to *drive* across to the left and then my engine revs would still be too low.

Assuming, however, that I have driven through the first turn perfectly, and at optimum speed, I now find myself, at position #1 in our step-by-step series. The car is just shy of being half-way between the first and second turns of the Hook, about three feet from the left-hand side of the track. Here, for a brief instant, the wheels are pointed straight ahead. Then I steer slightly to the right and drive (not slide) ahead for about two-car lengths. For these few feet I am driving on what might be called a "trailing throttle" — not quite applying enough power to make the rear wheels begin to break loose. Then, at point #2, without changing the steering wheel position, I begin to apply more power so that the traction is broken slightly on the rear wheels, causing them to slide out. Thus the car is actually oversteering a bit, whereas the MG normally will understeer. This oversteer accomplishes two things. It keeps the car from sliding too far out to the left, nose first, and it keeps the car pointed more and more into the turn which, from its apex, begins to decrease in radius. This decreasing radius, in which the turn gets tighter and tighter as we go around it, is what makes it tricky. In position #3 I am between two and three feet from the right-hand edge of the road. The front wheels are hardly sliding at all; the rear wheels are sliding out just enough to keep the car heading into the turn. Since the steering wheel is held steady, to maintain the correct line I must, as the radius tightens, apply just enough power to keep the car more or less parallel with the sides of the road. If I am applying too much power the rear wheels will swing out too far, pointing the nose of the car too far to the right. The car will be forced to sideslip too much and this will waste time, not to mention rubber and engine revs. If I have not applied enough power I will tend to slide too far to the left, again creating too much sideslip, but in another direction. From this you can see that one of the secrets of driving the MG properly and smoothly is delicate throttle work, with a minimum of exaggerated steering-wheel twisting. It is, however, better as a rule to come into a corner a little too slowly rather than a little too fast; it is easier and usually less wasteful to apply more gas than to have to correct for a mistake resulting from too much speed. The big trick in motor racing is to come *out* of corners quickly so as to take best advantage of the straightaways. If you go into a corner way over your head you will invariably come out of it slowly, if you are fortunate enough not to fall off the road altogether. Even if your average speed through that particular bend is no lower than the driver

(Continued on page **100**)

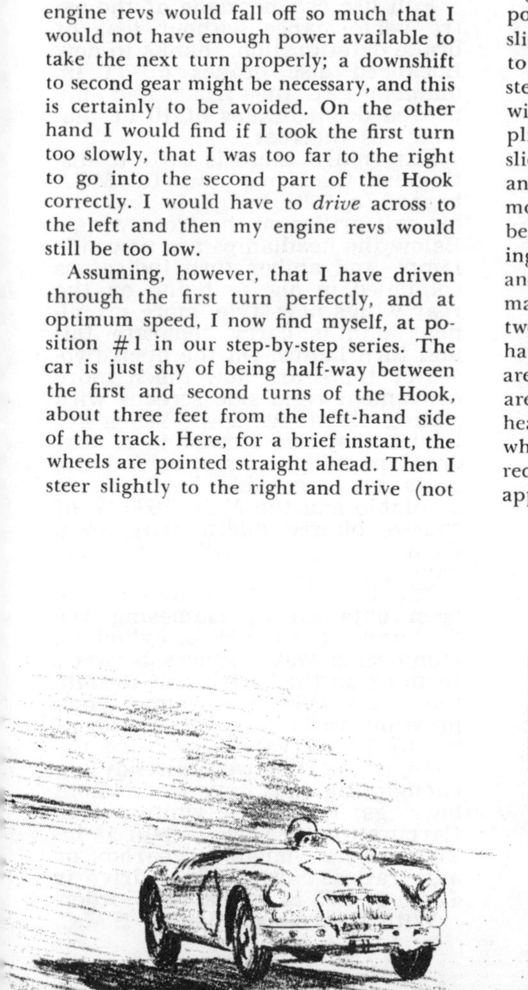

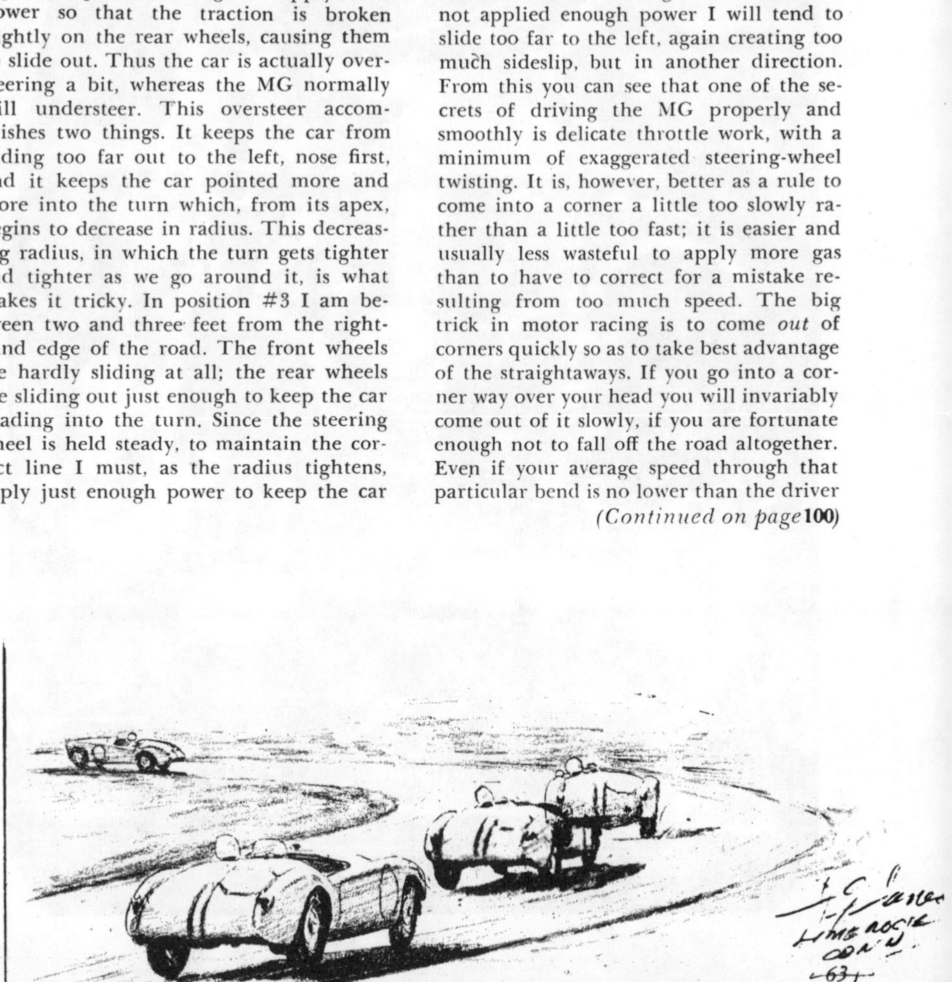

Another new one from Abingdon!

STAND BACK FOR

Bigger lungs for deeper breathing and Lockheed discing for safer frisking — that's the sparkling new MGA 1600.

New engine is no different from outside. Extra capacity comes from increased bore, giving better low-speed flexibility and more high-speed urge.

THE MGA, one of the world's most popular sports cars, gains extra performance and increased stopping power at no extra cost in its latest version, the MGA 1600.

Engine size is increased to 1,588 c.c. (96.9 cu. in.) by enlarging the bores, making it the same size as the Twin-Cam unit. Maximum installed nett power in the pushrod car goes up to 79.5 b.h.p. at 5,600 r.p.m. and maximum torque to 87 lb. ft. at 3,800 r.p.m. An increase of 6½ per cent. in swept volume has, therefore, produced a rise of 10 per cent. in power and 12½ per cent. in maximum torque, giving quicker acceleration and a maximum speed around a genuine 100 m.p.h.

Full use can be made of the extra performance without fear of brake deterioration, thanks to new Lockheed disc brakes of 11 in. diameter at the front and improved drum brakes of 10 in. diameter at the rear.

Externally, there is little to distinguish the more powerful MGA beyond a 1600 badge behind the air exit grilles on the front wings. Below the headlamps are new side lamps and amber turn indicators combined in one unit and on the rear wings new-style, more prominent plinths carry separate tail and turn lamps. On the open two-seater there are now much more convenient rigid side screens with sliding plastic windows. When not in use they are stowed in a neat envelope which hangs behind the seats. A detachable hard top is available and the MGA 1600 is, of course, offered additionally as a fixed head coupe with glass side windows.

The larger cylinder bores have been obtained by siamesing the first and second pairs of cylinders, eliminating water spaces between them as on the Twin-Cam. Despite the extra cylinder volume, compression ratio has been held at 8.3 to 1 and valve sizes are unchanged, as they were already big enough. Big ends have lead-indium bearings; mains are white metal. Carburettors are two SUs of 1½ in. There is no change in gearbox or axle ratios. Normal final drive is 4.3 to 1; 4.55 is available to order.

With the co-operation of B.M.C.

THE

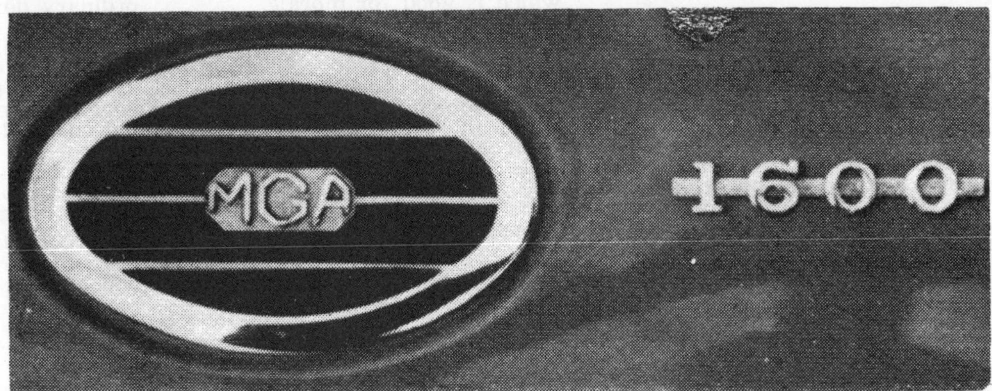

I was able to pick up one of the new MGAs at Lyon and give it a hard 250-mile run over the Route Napoleon via Grenoble, the Col des Leques, Castellane, the Col de Luens, and Cannes to Antibes. It is a route which begins with some fast straights but soon gets involved in interminable twists, turns, climbs and descents through the mountains — it certainly showed the qualities of the new M.G. at their best. It is better balanced and nicer to handle than ever. The chassis has a margin of roadholding which can use all the extra power and torque and it never seems to be an embarrassment. Slipping into second for the sharp corners, you can really send the car tearing around with a sharp bark from the exhaust.

Taking the tachometer round to 6,000 r.p.m., where the red warning sector now begins, maximum speeds in the gears are first, 27 m.p.h., second 44 m.p.h., third 71 m.p.h.

Although the car was not yet fully free, it averaged about 46 m.p.h. over the difficult mountain section from Digne to Castellane, and the brakes were given a real work-out on the tortuous descent of the Col des Leques (well-known to Monte Carlo rally drivers), but they showed no sign of fade or even of any appreciable increase in pedal travel.

These new Lockheeds are progressive and need no heavy pedal pressure. At low speeds they seem to be more decisive than some other discs.

The car had done only about 1,000 miles when I took some performance checks and it was running open, so that air drag began to affect acceleration at the higher speeds. But all the same it knocked about a second off the time taken from 0 to 50 m.p.h. by a closed 1500 and recorded a comparable standing quarter mile.

At present about 520 people a week are buying MGAs and they obviously have a lot of fun with them, but I must admit that for my own driving there are things I would like to change in the driving position. If the seat is adjusted comfortably in relation to the pedals, the wheel comes too close to the chest to permit a really fluent driving style. The accelerator pedal is too high to allow easy heel and toe action when braking and changing down, so the right foot goes hopping from brake to accelerator and my downward gear shifts tend to be jerky in urgent moments on mountain roads.

Bigger sidelamps with flat lenses are almost the only frontal recognition points on M.G.'s latest, the MGA 1600. Other detail differences are modified side-screens allowing better ventilation, name tags, flanks and altered tail light assemblies.

STAND BACK FOR 1600

The starter control is a pull-out knob rather awkwardly placed behind the wheel. A key starter or press button would be easier to use.

Placement of the horn button in the centre of the instrument panel seems odd at first, but it demands less hand movement than one in the middle of the wheel and in rallies the passenger can use it, which is good for morale.

The speedometer (calibrated in kilometres on the test car) was four per cent. fast at 30 m.p.h., 9-11 per cent fast at 50-80 m.p.h. The odometer was accurate to within one per cent.

On straight open highways, the little car goes singing along at 5,000 r.p.m. in top, which represents a very useful cruising speed of just over 85 m.p.h. At the other end of the scale it shows extraordinary flexibility. Put your foot hard down at 12-14 m.p.h. in top and it will pull away quite smoothly without audible protest. The extra power has given the performance new sparkle but has not changed the sound, solid character which has made the MGA so popular. With the new disc brakes, it lives up still better to the famous slogan "Safety Fast".

Optional items at extra cost include the special competition seats, which are already ordered on 50 per cent. of all Twin-Cam models and nearly 70 per cent. of all coupes. Other options: a very effective heater and demister, twin horns, windshield washer, cold air ventilation, competition windshield, roll bar for driver protection, headlamp flasher switch and relay, cockpit cover, adjustable telescopic steering column, centre lock wire wheels.

Performance, M.G.A. 1600 Roadster

Acceleration:	
0-30 m.p.h.	4.0 sec.
0-45 m.p.h.	7.8 sec.
0-50 m.p.h.	15.3 sec.
0-60 m.p.h.	15.3 sec.
Standing ¼ mile	19.5 sec.
Acceleration in gears:	
2nd Gear, 20-40 m.p.h.	4.2 sec.
3rd Gear, 20-40 m.p.h.	7.1 sec.
30-50 m.p.h.	7.7 sec.
Top Gear, 20-40 m.p.h.	12.2 sec.
30-50 m.p.h.	13.0 sec.
Gearing	17.16 m.p.h. at 1,000 r.p.m. in top gear

(B.M.C. Australia has told S.C.W. that no MGA 1600 will reach this country until late this year or early next. B.M.C. also says the new car has Dunlop discs, but specifications could have been changed without their knowledge. It seems to us, on comparison with our own 1500 test figures, that Wilkins' car probably had the optional high final drive gearing—Ed.) #

Driving The MG Twin Cam

(Continued from page 97)

who came into it slowly and dug out faster than you did, he will be able to get up to a higher speed more rapidly on the straight (in an equal car), and will breeze right past you.

I have found that if I allow the MG to go no closer than 10-feet from the outside of the road coming out of the Hook (position #4) I automatically come into the straight properly positioned and at optimum speed. Then in the next instant—I have gone only about 10 or 12-feet past position #4—I give the steering wheel a slight twitch to the left, get off the throttle a hair and then stand on it hard. This action stops the car from sliding and it sort of "uncocks" it, eliminating the slight leaning angle to the left. Now (this is position #5) the wheels are pointed straight ahead and the car is pointed down the short straight and to the right-hand side of the road, just at the beginning of the next turn. Note that I do not have to steer the car across the road; it is already facing at a slight angle to the right from position #5. By the time I have reached point #6 I am only two or three-feet from the right side of the road, still going in a straight line.

After the short straight you encounter two long bends—the first to the left and the next to the right—known as the Esses. Only the left-hander is covered in our step-by-step diagrams—for reasons of space and because it is the more difficult of the two—but the right-hander is equally important and I will explain why in a moment.

The first turn in the Esses is difficult because it is a perfect example of a turn that is deliberately taken "wrong" to set the next one up "right." To explain this I will have to jump ahead to describe the approach for the right-hand part of the Esses. Remember I indicated earlier that your line through a corner is important mostly because it allows you to enter a straightaway following it at the highest possible speed. Well, there *is* a short straight section between the left and right sweeps of the Esses, but this is so short that unless we are properly set up coming out of the left-hander—that is, on the left side of the road at position #10—we will not be able to get into the right line for the right-hander. And if we don't go into this second curve properly we can't hope to come out "bombing" into the back stretch which, although it may look a bit twisty on the complete course diagram, is taken almost in a straight line.

Therefore we must "think ahead" and drive through the left-hand part of the Esses "wrong," or at least differently than we would if a long straightaway and not a right-hand bend followed. Instead of cutting to the extreme left at the apex of the turn and then allowing the car to slide to the right (the classic "outside-inside-outside") we must set up an artificial line that will bring us, with a minimum waste of time and engine revs, to the left side of the road at point #10. Here is how I do it.

At point #7 I am about one-foot from the edge of the road. Here I hit the brake slightly just to steady the car so that the tires will be on the biting side rather than the sliding side of traction. And since I do not want to let up on the throttle I usually touch the brake pedal with my left foot at this point. You might prefer to "heel and toe," but I find my method much easier although some practice is required before the move can be made naturally.

After I have applied the brakes I begin to steer slightly to the left, following the curvature of the road until, at point #8, I am about four to six-feet from the right side of the track (which, by the way, widens at this point). Right here I snap the steering wheel sharply (but only a couple of inches) to the left, at the same time applying more power. This throws the tail of the car abruptly out and, to a lesser degree, breaks traction on the front wheels as well. Thus, at position #9, I have "turned" a 45-degree corner that isn't actually there. This is the critical point in my artificial line. As soon as I have "thrown" the car I return the steering wheel to its original position (from point #7) and ease off slightly on the throttle. Again, as it was in the latter part of the Hook, the car is oversteering slightly and, as you can see from the overhead diagram, all I need do is to drive, almost in a straight line, to position #10, allowing the car to slide just a bit to the right between there and point #9. I consider that I am in perfect position at point #10 if the left front wheel is about six-feet from the left side of the road and the car is pointed dead ahead, into the short straight that separates the two sections of the Esses.

And that, my friends, is the lesson for today. It *won't* make a race driver out of you overnight, but if you are really serious about going into competition you should begin to see, from the above description, that it is a complicated business—oops, sport—one that requires a great deal of practice and experience. Before you go out to race, you should be certain that you are complete master of your car, and have confidence in your ability to handle any situation.

—da

In the Alps with the M.G.-A 1600 and the Austin-Healey 3000

On a cold and wet morning in June a party of journalists assembled at the R.A.C. in Pall Mall at the invitation of the British Motor Corporation to take part in a trip to the South of France to test the Austin-Healey 3000 which was announced in July and the M.G.-A 1600 which is announced today.

From the R.A.C. we were driven to Gatwick Airport where a chartered Transair Viscount waited to transport us in silence and comfort to Lyon where six M.G.s and six Healeys awaited our attention. There was little time to examine the cars as the 300-mile drive to Cap d'Antibes near Cannes had to be completed in time for dinner. I selected a red M.G.-A and like everyone else spent some time trying to open the boot to stow some luggage, but once the hidden catch behind the seats had been located the boot opened easily enough. A route had been selected by B.M.C. avoiding the N.7 and going via Grenoble, Gap, Digne, and Grasse along the N.85 known as the *Route des Alpes* but as much of this would have to be covered in darkness I decided to head the M.G. along the almost deserted N.7 in company with Gregor Grant of *Autosport* who had selected an Austin-Healey.

At the first of several stops for liquid refreshment we examined the specifications of the new cars and found that the major changes occurred in the engine and braking departments. On the M.G.-A 1600 the " B " Series engine has been bored out to a capacity of 1,588 c.c. (the same as the Twin-cam) and with an 8.3 : 1 compression ratio now gives 79.5 b.h.p. at 5,600 r.p.m. as compared with the 72 b.h.p. of the previous model. Following the general trend the M.G. 1600 is fitted with disc brakes on the front wheels combined with drums at the rear. Lockheed discs have been chosen for the M.G. while improved linings are used at the rear. Externally the only differences are the use of sliding sidescreens as standard equipment and a slight re-styling of the rear lights to accommodate separate flasher lamps.

Turning to the Healey we found that the " C " type engine has been enlarged to 2,912 c.c. and now develops 130 b.h.p. (gross), 124 b.h.p. net at 4,600 r.p.m., on a compression ratio of 9.03:1. This increase in capacity has been obtained by the use of a new cylinder block casting having a bore of 83.36 mm. and a stroke of 89 mm. The torque has gone up to 175 lb./ft. at 3,000 r.p.m. from its previous 149 lb./ft. and a strengthened gear cluster has been designed to cope with the increased power. The 3000 is the first model to be equipped with Girling disc brakes on the front wheels as standard equipment. The rear drums brakes have dimensions of 11 in. x 2¼-in.

This then is the sum total of noticeable changes to these two cars. The pleasing note for potential M.G.-A buyers is that prices remain the same—£940 7s. 6d. for the open model and £1,026 15s. 10d. for the coupé. The Healey 3000 is only a matter of £10 dearer than the 100-Six at £1168 9s. 2d. for the two-seater and £1,175 10s. 10d. for the occasional four-seater.

Having discovered these differences we headed the cars out on to the N.7 once more. All the cars were French-registered left-hand drive models destined for the Paris distributor and were brand new, some of them not having been fully run-in owing to the short notice given for the trip. Nevertheless the M.G.-A 1600 had a smooth flow of power and lost surprisingly little ground to the Healey on acceleration. The orange band on the rev.-counter runs from 5,500 to 6,000 r.p.m. and the red band from 6,000 to 7,000 r.p.m. In the lower gears the needle could be pushed well into the orange section without trouble but in top gear the engine could not be made to exceed 5,000 r.p.m., but since this showed exactly 160 k.p.h. (99 m.p.h.) on the speedometer no great trouble was found in keeping the Healey in sight. The steering of the M.G. is commendably light whilst gear changes can be made almost as quickly as the hand can move, although the synchromesh can be beaten if very fast changes are made.

The run to Cannes was uneventful, stops being made in Montelimar for the inevitable *Nougat* and at Avignon for petrol. The route from Aix-en-Provence to Cannes runs over some bumpy roads with enough mountain corners to test the suspension and roadholding of any car.

The M.G. survived the test with flying colours. If a corner was taken too ambitiously the rear end would slide out most controllably and could always be corrected with ease while the disc brakes could be relied on in an emergency and no trace of fade was noticed at any time. The pedal pressure required was higher than that needed for drum brakes but this was amply compensated for by the complete lack of fade which would have certainly been apparent with drums all round.

Next day a gastronomic expedition was planned to Vence which included some more mountain driving and for this trip I selected an occasional four-seater Healey fitted with overdrive. The transition from the fleet M.G. to the rather ponderous Healey is rather startling at first as all controls are much heavier than those fitted to the M.G. Owing apparently to carburation difficulties the car proved rather difficult to start at times, the engine having to be " caught " with the throttle. The throttle pedal itself was not above criticism as on all cars at least two inches of lost motion was apparent before the revs. began to rise. It was also placed higher than the brake pedal making heel-and-toe gear changes out of the question, but this fault should be merely a matter of adjustment. The gear-lever is bent sharply backwards about 2 inches from its base in order to bring the knob near the driver's hand and combined with a gearbox which was still rather stiff gear changing was nothing like as easy as on the M.G. This spoilt the otherwise excellent characteristics of the car because on mountain roads one had to be sure that the car was in gear before taking a bend at any speed and very often the gearbox would find neutral instead of the required gear. I arrived at a compromise by using third and overdrive third for much of the journey. Overdrive third was useful for the few straights encountered and by flicking the dashboard-mounted switch third gear was easily obtained. On corners up to around 50 m.p.h. the Healey could be slid quite comfortably and appeared to be very stable. The 3-litre engine of the Healey is of course given a much easier time than that of the M.G. and this aspect undoubtedly appeals to a great number of sports car buyers. In overdrive top at 4,000 r.p.m. the theoretical speed is 92.4 m.p.h., going up to 115.5 m.p.h. at 5,000 r.p.m. Owing to the stiffness of the gearbox we felt it unfair to take performance figures but the manufacturers claim that the car will reach 60 m.p.h. from a standstill in under 11 seconds and 100 m.p.h. in 31 seconds.

In the two days which followed we were able to thrash the cars about in the mountains or on shopping expeditions at will and most of the cars stood up to the test very well. Pottering through towns one's leg becomes rather weary if the brakes have to be used much because of the traditional reluctance of disc brakes to operate at low speeds.

Just as several journalists were becoming proficient at water-skiing the time came for us to return to England and leave the sunshine of the Riviera. The cars were driven to Nice Airport for the last time and we embarked on an Air France flight for London having a healthy respect for the latest versions of the M.G. and Austin-Healey. Full marks to the manufacturers for organising this rigorous test.—M. L. T.

ROAD TEST MGA 1600

► It wasn't too many years ago that a long cross country haul in an MG could be looked upon as an adventure in frustration if much throughway or turnpike travel were on the itinerary. Secondary road travel was, and still is, another thing —the MG came into its own, sticking like glue and maintaining an average well above the capabilities of more staid machinery. But long straight turnpikes with their high constant speeds and, from a sports car standpoint, hundred mph bends were not the MG's dish of tea. Then it became a case of constant hours-long buzzing at a sustained engine speed that seemed positively painful to the sensitive ear while domestic machinery went whooshing past.

That day, gentlemen, is past—we guarantee it. It actually died with the TD and TF series but not entirely. The MG-A 1500 still retained some of the feeling that cruising speeds of 70 were somehow to be lumped under the various anti-cruelty acts. Not that the ubiquitous A won't do 70 — it will and much more, 20-odd miles an hour more, in fact — but it still didn't seem right. A steady speed of 65 or 70 in the 1500 is a matter of a bit more than half throttle. One knew one's foot was pushing the gasworks.

No longer. With the 1600 things are different. So much so in fact that it seems unbelievable that only 100 cc's are behind the difference. With a properly broken-in 1600 a steady speed of 70 mph is a matter of keeping one's foot out of it rather than pushing. It's not a matter of higher gearing and flat country either. Long grades that had trucks dropping down several gears and American automatics going into passing gear were nothing more than a mere eighth of an inch more throttle to Abingdon's latest offering.

These things we know from experience. The experience was gained from a round trip of some two thousand miles most of which was on the recently opened network of turnpikes and tollways that run through New York, New Jersey, Pennsylvania, Ohio, Indiana and Illinois with a side trip to Detroit over what is now considered secondary highway for comparison.

The car was run-in but not thoroughly broken-in when we picked it up from Hambro Automotive Corporation. The odometer showed a bit over 800 miles at the start of the trip. The first day's run started late in the afternoon and ran the length of the Jersey Turnpike and the Pennsylvania turnpike over a period of about eight hours total time including gas and food stops. A cruising speed of 60 felt right so it was the speed we traveled —all questions of legal rates of speed aside, especially since the legal limit in Pennsylvania is 65.

The next day's run started early. The only other car on the road was a well known two-liter roadster noted for its vim and vigor on the road. It was only after we sailed easily by the other car that any attention was paid to the speedometer, an exceedingly accurate instrument about which more later. This device claimed we were in the process of putting 75 miles into the hour. Not that 75 mph was any great surprise, it was just that, driving by the seat of the pants, we had been using the same throttle pressure that had, a few miles back, produced a shade over 60. The odometer showed 1273 miles. Obviously the previous day's run at a steady temperature and speed, the overnight stop and the short morning run had combined to bring about the perfect break-in. Water temperature which had been running at an even 185 on the cool day before was now down, on a much warmer day, to 175 and the oil pressure was up 5 to 10 psi due to an obviously cooler running engine. It was here, then, that the previously mentioned light foot on the throttle became necessary — half throttle would have been more than sufficient to bring down the wrath of the local gendarmerie. The remaining six hours into Chicago were run with the constant feeling that a case of shin-splints in the right leg was imminent from the conscious effort not to get too heavy on the throttle.

This ability to cruise seemingly forever at high speeds is not the only point at which MG's new star shines, either. There are several other items, some major, some minor in which the difference is felt. The biggest item is in the stopping department. New for this year is the disc-*cum*-drum brake set-up similar to that used on the Triumph TR-3 and the new Austin-Healey 3000 and like those units it works wonders. No-fade stop after no-fade stop can be made with these brakes with no loss of pedal or seemingly any need for higher pedal pressure. The BMC competitions department has for some time been using disc brakes all around and has offered these as an extra cost option (standard on MG Twin Cam). Unless one plans all-out competition there is now no need for these, the new Lockheed units being more than sufficient for club and regional racing. For those planning full-bore competition or major modification, the competition Dunlop brakes are still available but the average owner need not feel as if he has been left out of the running if he hasn't spent the extra money for the conversion. The major difference in "feel" between the new Lockheeds and the older drum brakes is one of slightly increased pedal pressure, especially on a wet day. It's just a matter of pushing a little further and a shade harder, though. On a wet day it is a good idea to tap the brake, release it and then push the pedal again when coming to a planned stop such as a stop-light or a toll booth but it's not vitally necessary since a slightly harder push will accomplish the same thing. The light, first tap merely accomplishes a cleaning and warming of the disc and makes the second tap a lighter effort. Straight line emergency stops can be made with no preliminaries. In fact the only reason we mention the preliminary tap at all is that cleaning the disc before a harder application is easier on the caliper pads and disc material.

We had occasion to be thankful for all this stopping power at one point in the test trip. Happily cruising along the Indiana Tollroad just at dusk one day we were startled to see a large, brown shape bound out from the ditched center island onto the roadway directly in the path of the MG. It was a large mule deer and not more than 30 feet away when it decided to leap. We hit the brakes, hard, and cut to the left. In an ordinary car or one with inadequate brakes we would have wound up with a large amount of venison in the cockpit by

SPORTS CARS ILLUSTRATED ROAD TEST
MGA 1600 ROADSTER

ACCELERATION:

From zero to	seconds
30 mph	4.6
40 mph	6.7
50 mph	10.3
60 mph	13.7
70 mph	17.8
80 mph	23.4
Standing ¼ mile	19.8
Speed at end of quarter	73 mph

SPEED RANGES IN GEARS:

(800-5500 rpm)

I	0-27
II	5-44
III	9-71
IV	12-top

SPEEDOMETER CORRECTION:

Indicated Speed	Timed Speed
30	30
40	40
50	50
60	60
70	70
80	80

FUEL CONSUMPTION:

22 mpg

SPECIFICATIONS

POWER UNIT:

BMC "B" series ....four water-cooled, in-line
Valve Arrangement ....pushrod ohv, in-line
Bore & Stroke............2.97x3.50 in (75.4x88.9mm)
Stroke/Bore Ratio 1.18/1
Displacement..96.9 cu in (1588 cc)
Compression Ratio 8.3/1
Carburetion by ....Two SU H6
Max. Power...................79½ bhp @ 5600 rpm
Idle Speed ....800 rpm

DRIVE TRAIN:

Transmission ratios		overall	optional ratios
I	3.64	15.66	(2.45)
II	2.21	9.50	(1.62)
III	1.38	5.94	(1.27)
IV	1.00	4.30	(1.00)
Final drive ratio		4.30	(4.55, 4.88, 5.12)

Axle torque taken by leaf springs

CHASSIS:

Frame ....Box section
Wheelbase ....94 in
Tread, front and rear..47½, 49 in
Front Suspension........Coil springs, unequal wishbones
Rear Suspension ....Rigid axle, semi-elliptic leaf springs
Shock absorbers..Armstrong lever and piston type
Steering type......Rack and pinion
Steering wheel turns L to L....2.7
Turning diameter, curb to curb 32 feet
Brakes..Lockheed 11 in discs front, 10 in drums rear
Tire size...........................5.90x15

GENERAL:

Length ....156 in
Width ....58 in
Height ....50 in
Weight, curb, full tank....2040 lbs
Weight, as tested (two up) 2360 lbs
Weight distribution, F/R as tested...................49/51
Fuel capacity........12 U.S. gallons

RATING FACTORS:

Specific Power Output 0.82 bhp/cu in
Power to Weight Ratio, as tested ....29.7 lbs/hp
Piston speed @ 60 mph 2020 ft/min
Speed @ 1000 rpm in top gear ....17.3 mph

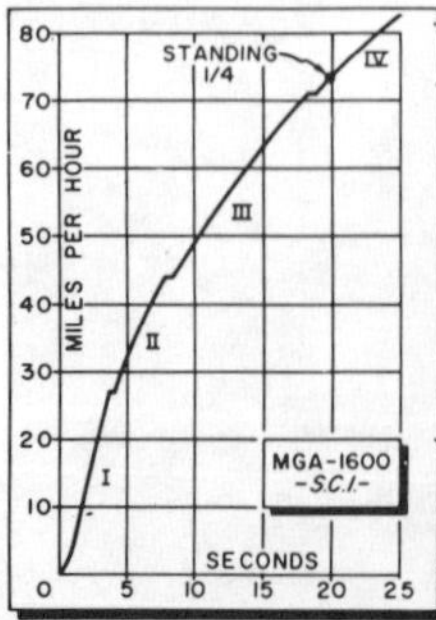

Right, the trunk lid still cannot be locked. Helping safeguard contents is well-hidden latch-pull in back of driver's seat. A lock and more space would both be welcome.

Safety Fast is MG's long-standing slogan; with Lockheed discs on the front and 100 more cc's under the hood, they've added to both.

Above: "When in doubt, bore it out." Though it looks the same on the surface, tenth-inch bigger bore inside makes a big difference. Right: X-spoked wheel combines strength with dashboard visibility. From left to right: tachometer, speedometer, fuel gauge and combined oil pressure-water temperature gauge. Far right: the single-wing nut, a holdover from at least the TC, has finally given way to this round knob for holding the side-screens in place. New, too, are sliding panels in the latter, one less accessory to purchase.

way of the hood and windshield. As it was, the deer clobbered the right headlight with a hind hoof and that was all. The state of Indiana had a sore-footed deer and we replaced a sealed beam headlamp at the next service pavilion and were on our way after reporting the incident to an amused Trooper.

Another major, although subtle, change is in the suspension. It's *different* somehow. There is less lean in the front and less dive on hard braking for one thing. This is due to minor changes: the springs are those used in the Twin Cam and therefore a slight bit stiffer and minor valving changes in the shock absorbers have been made to take the added spring beef. The rear end behavior is slightly different too. This is noticeable mainly on hard acceleration; where the earlier versions had a tendency toward rear end "walk" or alternate wheel slip this one lays a smooth strip and then bites in solidly. Strangely enough, the ride hasn't stiffened perceptibly, in fact, if anything it is a bit smoother with less of the well-known MG "chop" over small bumps.

Handling is excellent as can be expected. The steering has no play, moderate return and a smooth travel from lock to lock. Road feel is there but there is none of the kick-back felt in the very early versions of the rack and pinion steering. Tracking on the straight is fair though with a slight tendency to wander with hands off the wheel. If you want to light a cigarette it's best to steady things with a knee. Like previous models of the MG-A this one has a mild final understeer built in. The rear end can be kicked loose but breakaway is even and predictable. This last we found out on the Meadowdale Raceway where we gave the car a thorough workout. Much of the course was covered with a layer of dried mud washed down by a recent rain. This was in the slow, lower part and had no effect on the upper, high speed sections. It was actually a help more than a hindrance since it gave us an opportunity to barrel the car under less than ideal conditions without endangering life and property and still use the high speed banking and straight for performance tests.

This new MG, as we pointed out earlier, gets up and goes. There isn't too much difference between this one and the 1500 in 0-30 and 0-40 times but as the terminal speeds for each run went higher the times it took to reach these speeds dropped startlingly. The difference to 60 is over one-and-a-half-seconds, and the difference between the two in getting to 70 is three seconds exactly; to eighty it is about seven seconds difference. The speed reached at the end of standing quarter was 73 mph, some five miles an hour faster than earlier versions. This was reached in 18.8 seconds on at least one of several runs, a second quicker. Top speed on the best of several runs was 102 with the top down and with a full windshield. To reach this we had to head down the back stretch and into the famous bumpy banking at a shade better than 85 which the car would hold all the way around, accelerating as it came off and reaching terminal velocity at about a quarter mile down the straight. We saw a good bit more on the speedometer further along but had to discount it because of the downgrade which began just a little more than a quarter of a mile from the banking. The figure we saw, for what it was worth, was 112 before we shut off for the dropping turn at the end of the straight. If you go off this one you land on highway 31 at a highly illegal rate of speed and in somewhat the wrong direction for continued good health so 112 indicated downhill is all we can vouch for.

Speaking of indications, we mentioned earlier the accuracy of the speedometer in this particular car. Beyond a doubt this is the most accurate speedometer we have yet seen in any test car. It indicated true speed throughout a range from 30 mph to 80 mph over distances from one measured mile to five measured miles. At one point, still tending to doubt the accuracy of any mechanical speedometer we held a steady 80 over a twenty mile stretch of road and did the twenty miles in fifteen minutes almost to the second. This is accuracy of a high order when one considers the optimism with which most speedometers record time and distance, usually with an error of several miles per hour at that speed over a single mile.

There are other changes made to the new MG that can be classed as minor but make themselves apparent as one lives with the car. There is, for instance, a clip at the top center of the windshield to hold the center of the front top bow which aids in weather sealing. Side curtains now have sliding panels instead of the miserable spring-loaded flaps on earlier models. The trunk lid no longer conducts rain water down into the trunk and onto the one thing you don't want to get wet. The one meaningless change is a new taillight grouping that seems out of keeping with the otherwise clean design of the car. Bulbous and jutting, this bit of work looks like a project of an overzealous home customizer who wasn't really sure of what he was doing. The battery and fuel pump are still hidden away out of sight and out of mind until something happens.

But these are minor considerations only brought to attention because of the overall excellence of the rest of the car. Beyond a shadow of a doubt, this is the best touring MG yet. *—jpc*

The Motor Road Test No. 21/59

Make: M.G. **Type:** M.G. A 1600

Makers: M.G. Car Co., Ltd., Abingdon-on-Thames, Berkshire.

Test Data

CONDITIONS: Weather: *Warm and dry, gusty 10 m.p.h. cross wind. (Temperature 59°-63° F., Barometer 29.6-29.7 in. Hg.)* Surface: *Dry tar macadam and concrete.* Fuel: *Premium grade pump petrol (approx. 96 Research Method Octane rating).*

INSTRUMENTS

Speedometer at 30 m.p.h.	accurate
Speedometer at 60 m.p.h.	3% fast
Speedometer at 90 m.p.h.	4% fast
Distance recorder	accurate

WEIGHT

Kerb weight (unladen, but with oil, coolant and fuel for approx. 50 miles)	18¼ cwt.
Front/rear distribution of kerb weight	53/47
Weight laden as tested	22 cwt.

MAXIMUM SPEEDS

Flying Lap of Banked Circuit	96.1 m.p.h.
Best one-way ¼-mile on straight	100 m.p.h.

"Maximile" Speed (Timed quarter mile after one mile accelerating from rest).

Mean of four opposite runs	94.1 m.p.h.
Best ¼ mile time equals	96.3 m.p.h.

Speed in Gears (at 6,000 r.p.m. recommended limit).

Max. speed in 3rd gear	74 m.p.h.
Max. speed in 2nd gear	46 m.p.h.
Max. speed in 1st gear	28 m.p.h.

FUEL CONSUMPTION

39¼ m.p.g. at constant 30 m.p.h. on level
37 m.p.g. at constant 40 m.p.h. on level
34½ m.p.g. at constant 50 m.p.h. on level
32 m.p.g. at constant 60 m.p.h. on level
29½ m.p.g. at constant 70 m.p.h. on level
27 m.p.g. at constant 80 m.p.h. on level
23 m.p.g. at constant 90 m.p.h. on level

Overall Fuel Consumption for 1,028 miles, 42.2 gallons equals 24.4 m.p.g. (11.6 litres/100 km.).

Touring Fuel Consumption (m.p.g. at steady speed midway between 30 m.p.h. and maximum, less 5% allowance for acceleration) 29.7 m.p.g.

Fuel tank capacity (maker's figure) 10 gallons.

STEERING

Turning circle between kerbs:

Left	29¼ ft.
Right	28¼ ft.
Turns of steering wheel from lock to lock	2¾

BRAKES from 30 m.p.h.

1.00 g retardation (equivalent to 30 ft. stopping distance) with 100 lb. pedal pressure.
0.82 g retardation (equivalent to 36¾ ft. stopping distance) with 75 lb. pedal pressure.
0.53 g retardation (equivalent to 56¾ ft. stopping distance) with 50 lb. pedal pressure.
0.29 g retardation (equivalent to 104 ft. stopping distance) with 25 lb. pedal prersure.

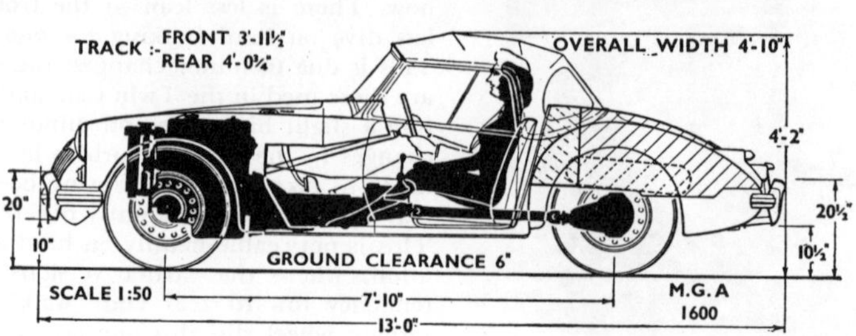

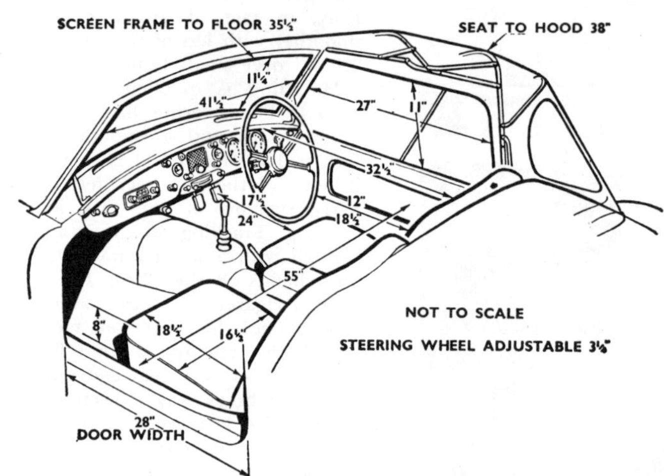

ACCELERATION TIMES from standstill

0–30 m.p.h.	4.3 sec.
0–40 m.p.h.	6.4 sec.
0–50 m.p.h.	9.1 sec.
0–60 m.p.h.	13.3 sec.
0–70 m.p.h.	17.7 sec.
0–80 m.p.h.	25.1 sec.
Standing quarter mile	19.8 sec.

ACCELERATION TIMES on Upper Ratios

	Top gear	3rd gear
10–30 m.p.h.	12.1 sec.	8.0 sec.
20–40 m.p.h.	11.0 sec.	6.9 sec.
30–50 m.p.h.	10.6 sec.	6.8 sec.
40–60 m.p.h.	11.2 sec.	7.4 sec.
50–70 m.p.h.	13.3 sec.	9.0 sec.
60–80 m.p.h.	15.0 sec.	—

HILL CLIMBING at sustained steady speeds

Max. gradient on top gear	1 in 10.9 (Tapley 205 lb./ton)
Max. gradient on 3rd gear	1 in 7.3 (Tapley 305 lb./ton)
Max. gradient on 2nd gear	1 in 4.5 (Tapley 485 lb./ton)

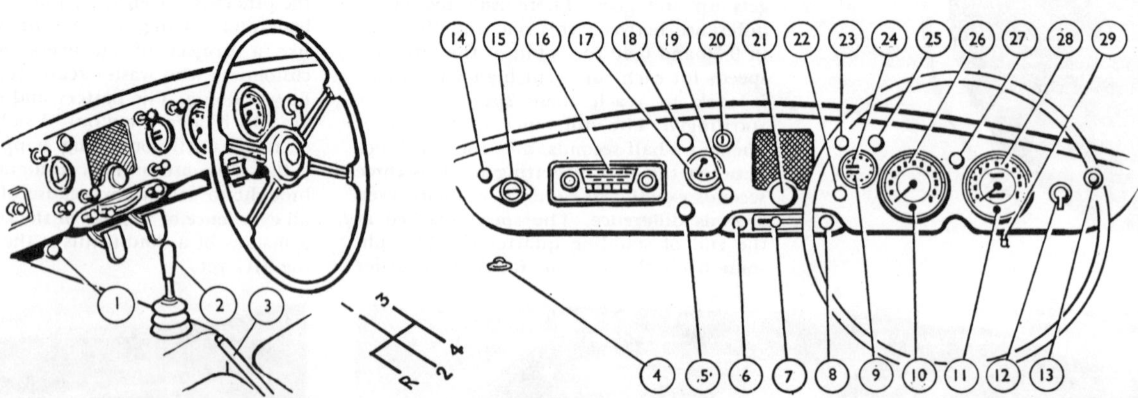

1, Headlamp dipswitch. 2, Gear lever. 3, Handbrake. 4, Bonnet catch release. 5, Windscreen washer button. 6, Heater air-intake control. 7, Heater temperature control. 8, Demister control. 9, Water thermometer. 10, Dynamo charge warning light. 11, Headlamp main beam indicator lamp. 12, Direction indicator switch. 13, Direction indicator warning light. 14, Map-reading light switch. 15, Map-reading light. 16, Radio controls. 17, Fuel contents gauge. 18, Windscreen wipers switch. 19, Choke control. 20, Ignition switch. 21, Horn button. 22, Starter button. 23, Lights switch. 24, Oil pressure gauge. 25, Switch for optional fog-lamp. 26, Tachometer. 27, Panel light rheostat. 28, Speedometer and distance recorder. 29, Trip adjuster.

The M.G. A 1600 Two-Seater

Extra Acceleration and Retardation for a Popular Sporting Car

FAMILIAR since the autumn of 1955 as a sporting two-seater of notable strength and roadworthiness, the M.G. A has now been endowed with extra acceleration by an increase in cylinder bore, and with improved retardation by disc-pattern Lockheed front brakes. Involving no price increase whatever, and accompanied by other minor refinements, these two important changes increase the attractiveness of what is already a very popular model.

Enlargement of the engine by 6½% without any alteration in the 4.3/1 axle ratio has produced a welcome improvement in the acceleration of the M.G. A which extends throughout its speed range. From 30 m.p.h. to 50 m.p.h. in top gear, the latest car took 10.6 sec., whereas the original M.G. A of September 1955 took 11.4 sec., and the M.G. A Coupé which we tested in August 1957 took 13.8 sec.; from 50 to 70 m.p.h. the latest car takes 13.3 sec. as against 14.9 sec. for the 2-seater in 1955 and 13.7 sec. for the hardtop in 1955. Acceleration from a standstill through the gears benefits very markedly from the extra engine torque, rest to 50 m.p.h. and 70 m.p.h. times of 9.1 sec. and 17.7 sec. comparing with 10.8 sec. and 21.9 sec. for the earlier 2-seater, 10.8 sec. and 21.4 sec. for the former coupé.

It may at first glance seem surprising that the engine changes which have resulted in such markedly improved acceleration through the gears have not raised the top speed of the car. With full silencing as installed in the car, however, the new engine develops peak power at 5,300 r.p.m. corresponding to approximately 89-90 m.p.h. in top gear, the timed mean speed of just over 96 m.p.h. being well within the 6,000 r.p.m. limit suggested by a red sector on the tachometer dial but 7% beyond the peak of the power curve. Raised tyre pressures, and/or the use of Road Speed tyres which are an optional extra, in place of the tubeless touring-quality tyres fitted to our test model, would no doubt have reduced drag and lifted the top speed—so, judging by our experience of other M.G. cars, would some additional running-in of an engine which was quiet mechanically and used very little oil indeed. What matters about the M.G. A 1600 is not, however, its ultimate speed, but the ease and rapidity with which 80 m.p.h. can be reached and exceeded whenever there is a slight break in the traffic on ordinary main roads.

Complete docility characterizes the enlarged engine, as witness our recording of top gear acceleration times from a mere 10 m.p.h., and it runs happily on ordinary Premium grades of petrol without demanding 100-octane, but it does not feel to pull its full weight below 2,500 r.p.m. In the warm summer weather which prevailed during our test, the choke was never needed for starting from cold, even after the car had stood in the open throughout rainy nights. The engine can seem rather harsh when accelerated hard in the gears, an effect which is difficult to define exactly as neither exhaust nor mechanical noise levels are high for a sports car. Fuel economy proved rather inferior to smaller-engined preceding models, our checks showing between 23½ m.p.g. and 25½ m.p.g. in varied (but always fast) road driving.

In Brief

Price £663 plus purchase tax £277 7s. 6d., equals £940 7s. 6d.

Capacity	1,588 c.c.
Unladen kerb weight ...	18¼ cwt.
Acceleration:	
20-40 m.p.h. in top gear ...	11.0 sec.
0-50 m.p.h. through gears	9.1 sec.
Maximum top gear gradient	1 in 10.9
Maximum speed	96.1 m.p.h.
"Maximile" speed	94.1 m.p.h.
Touring fuel consumption ...	29.7 m.p.g.

Gearing: 17.0 m.p.h. in top gear at 1,000 r.p.m.; 29.1 m.p.h. at 1,000 ft./min. piston speed.

COMFORT and convenience have been well studied in the layout and equipment of the cockpit; the two bucket seats have a central armrest between them on the propeller-shaft tunnel, just to the rear of the short gear lever. Rev. counter and speedometer are two large circular dials immediately in front of the driver, with smaller dials for fuel gauge, oil pressure and water thermometer on the left.

Provision of Lockheed 11-inch disc brakes behind the bolt-on front wheels has given this car an immense reserve of stopping power. There is outstandingly good balance between front and rear brakes, so that the car can be checked from 95 m.p.h. down to a standstill at virtually the limit of tyre adhesion without any fuss or excitement whatever. An extended series of stops from 60 m.p.h., at the closest intervals permitted by very good acceleration, produced no perceptible fade but merely a slight and entirely temporary loss of the usual perfect balance between the four brakes. As we have noted on some other disc-braked cars, a form of brake squeal could be induced by extremely gentle brake application at town speeds, a trivial price to pay for smoothly progressive stopping power which inspired utter confidence at all times. The fly-off hand-brake works very effectively upon the rear drums, location of the pull-up lever on the right of the transmission tunnel being reasonably convenient for tall drivers but awkward when the driving seat was adjusted further forwards.

Apart from the new braking system, no chassis changes in this model have been announced, nor was there any reason to expect them. Exceptional strength characterizes a box-section frame of which the scuttle structure is an integral part, and although 18¼ cwt. is thought rather heavy for a 1.6-litre sports 2-seater, stamina is known to go with the appreciable weight, and if the gearbox is used properly, acceleration can be very brisk indeed. Factory recommendations on the subject of tyre pressures cover rather a wide range, but we found the highest recommended pressures to be best suited to everyday use of this sporting car, which otherwise took town corners to an accompaniment of loud tyre squeal.

ALTHOUGH the smooth bonnet falls away to a very low front, the engine compartment is not cramped and access for routine maintenance is good.

Even with quite high tyre pressures, the coil-spring I.F.S. and semi-elliptic rear springs are very far from harsh, and in fact a certain amount of body roll is evident during fast cornering, despite the low build of the M.G. A. Around town, there is not quite the same cushioned ride as many present-day touring cars provide, but the suspension is extremely well suited to comfortably "flat" riding at the brisk pace which is natural to this car on country roads of all kinds. There is certainly no cause to be shy of taking the M.G. A onto really rough surfaces.

Like other M.G. two-seaters for a considerable number of years past, this model has a rack-and-pinion steering gear which is extremely positive in action, without any of the backlash or flexibility which spoil the precision of all too many steering installations based upon worm or screw gearing. In conjunction with a chassis which seems never to "put a foot wrong," steering gear precision makes this a very brisk car from point to point, especially on the secondary roads which in Britain often serve as traffic avoiders.

At the extremes of the speed range, it must be noted that the fully reversible rack-and-pinion steering, slightly damped by a friction device which makes it self-adjusting for wear, does reveal shortcomings. Below 25 m.p.h. the friction is evident enough to cause a slight amount of "wander," and above 60 m.p.h. road reaction begins to reach the driver's hands, of small amplitude but persistent enough to leave his fingers tingling after a fast non-stop hundred miles. Whilst it has strong self-centering action, the steering never becomes very heavy, and a turning circle of below 30 feet diameter is extremely convenient on many occasions.

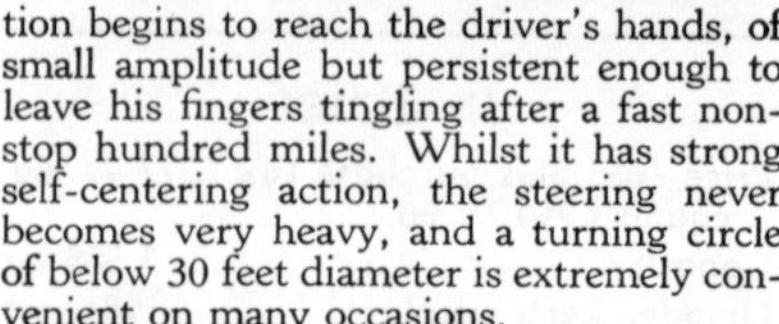

Set just about as conveniently close to the steering wheel rim as it could possibly be without getting in the way is the knob of a central remote-control gear lever, controlling an excellent four-speed gearbox. Faults can be found with the transmission, some people finding the small across-the-gate movement needed for a 3rd-to-2nd change awkward at first, and others tending to make audible changes into top gear when in a hurry, due to not depressing the clutch pedal through the whole of its travel. With familiarity these points cease

HOLDING the spare wheel, the boot has room only for soft luggage; those contemplating serious touring can obtain a grid to fit the boot lid.

Seater

DISTINGUISHED from earlier models by rigid sliding sidescreens and deeper plinths to accommodate flasher units separate from the rear lamps, the M.G. A 1600 retains such useful features as a large rear window and quarter lights in the hood, stout bumpers and smooth, easy-to-clean bodywork.

to obtrude, but a rather wide gap between 3rd and 2nd gears (which, at the 6,000 r.p.m. where a red sector of the tachometer begins, respectively, give speeds of about 74 m.p.h. and 45 m.p.h.) remains evident, the designers presumably not wishing changes down into an unsynchronized 1st gear to be needed very often. But, regardless of these imperfections, the smoothly firm clutch and quiet, easy-to-use gearbox are thoroughly appropriate to the car.

Purely and simply a two-seater, the sleek body of this car is no more difficult to enter than most comparable low-built models. The floor is flat and the doors open down to floor level, but the sturdy structure of the car does not let the doors extend far enough forward for utmost ease of entry. Once entered, this car offers an exceptionally high standard of comfort and convenience, the individual seats with their "wrap around" backrests having an adjustment range which even the very tall find satisfactory. Between the seats, a cushioned armrest covers the propeller shaft tunnel, and hollowed-out doors provide quite generous elbow width in the cockpit as well as two very capacious pockets. The facia is a metal panel onto which instruments and controls have been crowded with little pretence at "styling" but with a great deal of practical common sense—the speedometer and matching tachometer face the driver directly, a combined oil pressure gauge and coolant thermometer is close beside them and the fuel gauge not far away. Unusual but convenient once a driver is accustomed to them, are facia-panel locations of the horn button (on the driver's left) and turn-indicator time switch (on the driver's right), the horn button being touch-sensitive so that either a gentle cautionary note or a strident warning can be given at will. Rheostat-controlled lighting is provided for the instruments, a map reading light is in front of the passenger, and a spare switch is provided for a foglamp if this extra is specified.

All-weather equipment takes the form of two sidescreens and a hood, all of which ean in fine weather be stowed safely and invisibly behind the seats. These removable items really do keep out wet weather, and stay firmly in place at the car's maximum speed—the curved-glass windscreen has bracing struts which serve also as grab handles, the hood fastens to the windscreen at three points, and when the doors are closed, rubber-cushioned fittings on the sidescreens hold them in rattle-free contact with the windscreen. Each sidescreen has a sliding half panel to provide ventilation, and in striking contrast with the one-time austerity of sporting cars is the inclusion of a fresh air cockpit heater and windscreen de-mister in this competitively-priced model's extensive range of optional built-in extras.

The two criticisms which must be made of the hood are, that the car becomes very much noisier to drive when it is in use owing to wind-induced flutter of the roof fabric, and that the multiple joints which let a really rigid hood frame fold away so neatly make reasonably rapid erection or folding of the hood a skilled task. By some people's standards of judgement, the luggage locker also is criticized as being of rather modest size.

With its share of the imperfections from which no car ever altogether escapes, this remains a very attractive and versatile sporting two-seater. Sturdy, well furnished and probably built with more thorough care than most of its contemporaries, it travels fast and is enjoyable to drive or ride in, yet can also serve as a reliable and weatherproof form of everyday transportation.

Specification

Engine

Cylinders	4
Bore	75.39 mm.
Stroke	88.9 mm.
Cubic capacity	1,588 c.c.
Piston area	27.68 sq. in.
Valves	Push-rod o.h.v.
Compression ratio	8.3/1
Carburetters	Twin S.U. type H4
Fuel pump	S.U. electrical
Ignition timing control	Vacuum and centrifugal
Oil filter	Full flow Tecalemit or Purolator
Max. power (net)	75.5 b.h.p.
at	5,300 r.p.m.
Piston speed at max. b.h.p.	3,090 ft./min.

Transmission

Clutch	Borg and Beck 8 in. s.d.p.
Top gear (s/m)	4.3
3rd gear (s/m)	5.908
2nd gear (s/m)	9.520
1st gear	15.652
Reverse	20.468
Propeller shaft	Hardy Spicer, open
Final drive	Hypoid bevel
Top gear m.p.h. at 1,000 r.p.m.	17.0
Top gear m.p.h. at 1,000 ft./min. piston speed	29.1

Chassis

Brakes	Lockheed hydraulic—disc front, drum rear
Brake diameter	Disc 11 in., drum 10 in.
Friction lining area	87 sq. in.
Suspension:	
Front	Independent coil springs and wishbones
Rear	Rigid axle with half-elliptic leaf springs
Shock absorbers	Armstrong, hydraulic lever arm
Steering gear	Rack and pinion
Tyres	Dunlop 5.60—15 tubeless

Coachwork and Equipment

Starting handle	Yes
Battery mounting	One each side behind seats
Jack	Screw-type
Jacking points	Front wishbones and rear springs

Standard tool kit: Jack, wheelbrace and hub cap lever (combined), starting handle, 1 box and 3 open-ended or box spanners, sparking plug spanner, tommy bar, cylinder head spanner, ring-type tappet spanner, adjustable spanner, tappet feeler gauge, screwdriver grease gun, tyre pump, No. 2 screwdriver, pliers, brake bleeder tube, distributor screwdriver and gauge, tyre lever, tyre valve spanner, rear axle drain plug key, tool roll.

Exterior lights	2 head, 2 side, 2 stop and tail
Number of electrical fuses	2
Direction indicators	Flashing type, self-cancelling
Windscreen wipers	Electrical two-blade, self-parking
Windscreen washers	Optional
Sun vizors	None

Instruments: Speedometer with decimal trip recorder, tachometer, oil pressure gauge, water temperature gauge, fuel gauge.

Warning lights ... Dynamo charge, turn indicators, headlamp main beam

Locks:	
With ignition key	Ignition switch
With other keys	None
Glove lockers	None
Map pockets	In each door
Parcel shelves	None
Ashtrays	None
Cigar lighters	None
Interior lights	Instrument panel

Interior heater: Optional extra: Smith's $3\frac{1}{2}$ kW. fresh-air-type with de-misters.

Car radio ... Optional, H.M.V.

Extras available: Heater, radio, wire wheels, whitewall tyres, 5.90—15 Road Speed tyres, alternative 4.55:1 axle ratio, adjustable steering column, tonneau cover, radiator blind, twin horns, anti-roll bar, fog lamp battery cover, badge bar, screen washers, detachable hardtop, competition windscreen, luggage carrier, wing mirror, cold air ventilation, ashtray, competition de luxe seats.

Upholstery material: Leather on wearing parts, leathercloth borders.

Floor covering	Carpet
Exterior colours standardized	6
Alternative body styles	Fixed-head coupe or detachable hardtop

Maintenance

Sump	8 pints, S.A.E. 30 (winter 20W)
Gearbox	$4\frac{1}{2}$ pints, S.A.E. 30
Rear axle	2 pints, S.A.E. 90 Hypoid
Steering gear lubricant	90 Hypoid
Cooling system capacity	10 pints (2 drain taps)
Chassis lubrication	By grease gun every 1,000 miles to 10 points
Ignition timing	6° b.t.d.c.
Contact-breaker gap	0.015 in.
Sparking plug type	Champion N5
Sparking plug gap	0.025 in.

Valve timing: Inlet opens 16° b.t.d.c. and closes 56° a.t.d.c.; exhaust opens 51° b.b.d.c. and closes 21° a.t.d.c.

Tappet clearances (hot)	Inlet and exhaust 0.015 in.
Front wheel toe-in	Parallel
Camber angle	$\frac{1}{2}$°-1°
Castor angle	4°
Steering swivel pin inclination	9°-$10\frac{1}{2}$°
Tyre pressures:	
Front	17-23 lb.
Rear	20-26 lb. according to speed
Brake fluid	Lockheed grade 103 (S.A.E. 70-R-1)
Battery type and capacity	Two 6-volt Lucas SG9E, 51 amp. hr.

MORE FROM THE MGA

H.R.G.-Derrington Modifications to the B-type Engine

Polished heart-shaped combustion chambers with valve seat inserts in the light alloy head. Plugs located at each side of the paired induction ports are directed at the exhaust valves. A special spanner is available

ENGINES in a high state of tune in standard form require fundamental changes if they are to yield an appreciable increase in power. Such an engine is the B.M.C. B-type 4-cylinder, 1,489 c.c. unit installed in the M.G. MGA, and a 1955 model recently tested was fitted with special light-alloy cylinder head designed by S. R. Proctor, engineering director of the H.R.G. Engineering Co., Ltd. This firm manufacture the head, and marketing is in the hands of V. W. Derrington, Ltd., 159-161, London Road, Kingston-on-Thames, Surrey, who also provide a swept exhaust manifold.

In the standard cast iron head, exhaust ports and siamesed inlet ports are on the same side, whereas in the light alloy head they are on opposite sides, each inlet valve having a separate induction tract. All ports and the heart-shaped combustion chambers are machined, and seat inserts are fitted for the standard M.G. valves. The guides and the remainder of the valve gear also are unchanged. Special pistons raise the compression ratio to 9.3 to 1 and a pair of induction stubs joined by a balance pipe complete the equipment, the existing twin S.U. carburettors being retained.

Although the standard exhaust manifold may be used, the Derrington system was fitted on the car tested (giving an extra 2 b.h.p. or so at mid-speeds), bringing the cost to £88 12s.

Where the conversion scores is in the appreciable increase of power at high engine speeds, but this is not at the expense of low speed torque, so that flexibility is excellent; it is possible to accelerate from as low as 10 m.p.h. in top gear. As the comparative performance table shows, improvement in acceleration is most striking above 50 m.p.h., power being so well sustained that the 0 to 90 m.p.h. figure was bettered by no less than 16.2sec.

Conditions were against measurement of the absolute maximum speed, but a speedometer 110 m.p.h. (a true 105.5) was easily attained on a level road, with no wind and something still in hand. The engine exhibited no more than the usual harshness of the MGA unit at medium revs, and smoothness was improved beyond this up to 6,000 r.p.m.

There was pinking at low speeds during full-throttle acceleration and some running-on after performance testing, but subsequently it was found that the ignition was slightly too much advanced for the premium fuel used. All testing was carried out with hood up and side screens in position. A damp surface made get-away during standing start testing slower than it could have been but, to help comparison, it was also wet during the testing of the standard car.

Oil pressure was maintained at a steady 60 lb sq in. During 400 miles of mainly hard driving, fuel consumption was 30.4 m.p.g., compared with 27 m.p.g. for the standard car similarly driven over 672 miles—a significant improvement.

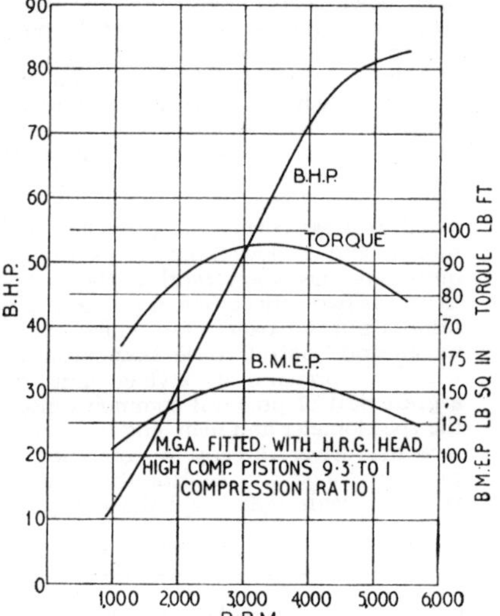

Below: Induction and exhaust ports are on opposite sides of the head, and a new three-branch exhaust manifold was fitted. The air box for the carburettor intakes is not part of the equipment. The distributor is difficult to reach below the carburettors. Right: Nett B.H.P., b.m.e.p. and torque curves of the modified engine

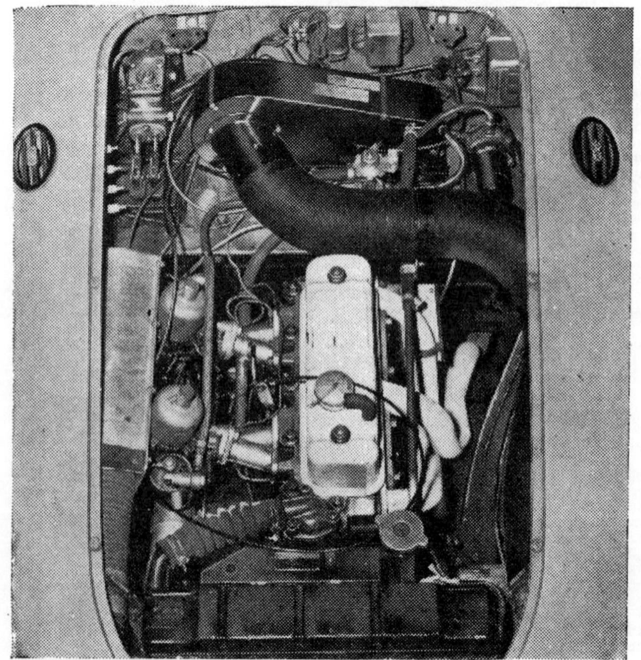

PERFORMANCE DATA

Acceleration from rest through gears to: M.P.H.	H.R.G. Derrington conversion sec	Standard* MGA sec
30	5.6	4.9
50	10.6	11.0
60	12.8	15.6
70	18.3	21.4
80	24.2	32.1
90	33.9	50.1
Standing start quarter-mile	19.0	20.2
30—50 m.p.h. in 3rd ..	7.3	8.4
30—50 m.p.h. in top ..	10.2	12.3
40—60 m.p.h. in 3rd ..	7.5	9.1
40—60 m.p.h. in top ..	11.4	13.1
50—70 m.p.h. in 3rd ..	8.1	10.7
50—70 m.p.h. in top ..	12.1	15.0
60—80 m.p.h. in top ..	13.2	18.1
70—90 m.p.h. in top ..	16.1	—
Fuel consumption	m.p.g. 30.4	27.0

Typically British, this new MGA will almost certainly be as popular in foreign markets as the previous models

M.G. MGA 1600

IN the tradition of maintaining the breed, the new M.G. MGA 1600 is a direct successor to the MGA which, in its comparatively short existence, has become one of the most popular sports cars not only in England but also abroad. Indeed, as a dollar earner there are few cars which have done better. This new MGA is virtually identical except for an increase in engine capacity, the adoption of disc brakes at the front, and minor restyling attention to the body, including little 1600 motifs secured at either side near the bonnet louvres and on the boot lid.

With an engine capacity of 1,588 c.c. in place of 1,489 c.c., the gross power has been raised from 72 b.h.p. at 5,500 r.p.m. to 79.5 b.h.p. at 5,600 r.p.m. The effect of this increase is apparent as soon as one starts to drive the car, and there is no need of a stop-watch for evidence of the enhanced performance. Acceleration figures have improved over those of the previous model, and this is particularly noticeable in top gear at the higher cruising speeds. The figure for 50-70 m.p.h. in top gear has improved by almost 2sec, and the 60-80 m.p.h. figure by over 3sec. The car is capable of holding a genuine 100 m.p.h., but after several flat-out laps on a high-speed circuit it was noticed that the oil pressure was gradually dropping.

At 80 m.p.h., which appears very quickly on the quite accurate speedometer, the car moves happily at a natural and comfortable gait. There was a tendency for the engine of the test car to become rough and to vibrate at about 5,000 r.p.m., but if the throttle pedal was held down this disappeared as engine speed continued to mount. Members of the staff with experience of the previous MGA feel the more powerful engine to be rather more noisy and harsh. This is unlikely to deter the true sports car enthusiast; nor is the exhaust note. While not obtrusive at lower engine speeds, at 4,000 r.p.m. and above it is, perhaps, a little loud for town use, although the occupants of the car do not suffer from this so much as onlookers.

One of the greatest advantages of the new MGA is that the increased power has improved the flexibility of the engine, and where previously one had to use first and second while crawling in heavy traffic, one can now employ second and third gears quite comfortably. In fact, it was found that the car would pull away from under 10 m.p.h. in top gear, though, of course, it is unlikely that any driver of this type of car would do so.

One has to pay a price for these various benefits in a slightly greater fuel consumption—24 m.p.g. overall for the 1,590 miles of the test. A gentle touring consumption which involved keeping the speed below 60 m.p.h. and avoiding high engine speeds in the intermediate gears returned a figure better than 31 m.p.g. During the test the car used three pints of engine oil, and the radiator needed considerable topping-up on two occasions.

When the car was delivered, the gear box proved to be extremely stiff; quite often it was necessary to employ both hands to engage reverse gear, and more effort than expected was required to select the other gears. Towards the end of the test, however, the movement had freed itself quite considerably, and it was obvious that in a thousand miles or so this would be a pleasant box to manipulate. Ratios are the same as those on the 1500 MGA, and one gained the impression that this car could have coped adequately with a slightly higher final drive ratio. Smooth to operate, the hydraulically actuated clutch could contend comfortably with violent acceleration from a standstill with a minimum of slip.

While our previous experience of the MGA left us in

Increased in capacity by 82 c.c. and in power by 7.5 b.h.p., the 1600 MGA engine appears identical with its predecessor

M.G. MGA 1600

Sleek, attractive lines of the MGA are not affected by the minor body alterations. Wire wheels and whitewall tyres are optional extras

slight doubt about the adequacy of the brakes relative to maximum performance, there is no doubt that the brakes of the 1600 are of a very high standard indeed. With Lockheed discs on the front and 10in drums on the rear, the car can be stopped repeatedly from its high cruising speeds very quickly without any trace of fade or loss of directional stability. For a maximum retardation stop a fair amount of pedal pressure is needed, but a mean efficiency of 98 per cent, without any tendency for the wheels to lock, is highly commendable. The comparatively high pedal loads arise because the braking system is not provided with servo assistance. The hand brake, of the fly-off type, is also powerful and held the car without trouble on a 1 in 3 gradient, from which incline the car moved away with plenty of power in hand.

By modern standards the suspension must be considered firm; on smooth roads this is, of course, no disadvantage, and the car could be really hurtled into corners, when it would go round with minimum fuss, sitting squarely on the road and feeling very safe and controllable during the whole performance. This did not apply on rougher surfaces, however, and a feeling that the wheels were hopping and jumping, accompanied by intermittent tyre squeal, indicated that the tyres were not maintaining full contact with the road. With standard tyre pressures there was some oversteer, but an increase in the rear pressures reduced this to a bare trace at the sacrifice of a little ride comfort. The steering—rack and pinion—had little self-centring action, but was commendably direct and precise. A degree of road shock was transmitted to the driver through the steering.

Body alterations centre round the restyling of the side, tail and turn indicator lights in order to bring them into conformity with new regulations in this country. The flasher lights on the front have been coloured amber, while at the rear the wing light units have been changed so that the turn indicators and rear lights are separate.

Side screens are now of the sliding panel type, and the manufacturers claim that these, with the hood up, give as much protection as a saloon car body. During the period that this car was on test the weather remained very fine and sunny, so that it was never possible to ascertain if rain would enter through the largish gap between the body and the leading lower edge of the side screen. A series of pastel shades of paintwork is available for the 1600; the test car was finished in an attractive beige called Alamo.

Since no alterations have been made to the interior, much of what had been said before still applies—the space provided inside is still cramped for a car of its dimensions. Well upholstered, leather-trimmed seats give moderately good support, and only for a very slim person is there any possibility of being insufficiently braced. A grab handle, incorporated in the windscreen mount, is provided for the passenger. An average-sized person found that he needed the driving seat in the fully back position to be comfortable, so that even with an adjustable steering wheel a tall person never seemed really at home in the driving position, his arms being bent considerably at the elbow. A fairly tall driver, however, has the advantage that his view of the nearside wing is unobscured by the centrally mounted driving mirror. Gear change lever and handbrake are conveniently placed, but the facia-mounted horn button—old M.G. practice—is not always found when needed suddenly. Also it is unusual today to find the ignition switch not incorporated with the starter control.

Mounted rather high, the dip switch needed a full stretch of the foot to operate, and the main beam warning light was obscured by the steering wheel. For normal cruising speeds the head lamps are entirely adequate, but if one were in a hurry more powerful beams would be desirable. The commodious door pockets are entirely adequate for all the odds and ends that normally find their way into motor cars, but it is a pity when manufacturers do not provide in an open car which cannot be locked up, a thief-proof facia compartment. On the M.G. this facia space was occupied by a radio; although pleasant at town speeds, the

Instruments on the facia include speedometer, rev counter, water thermometer, oil pressure gauge and fuel gauge. On the extreme left there is a map-reading light

set became practically inaudible as one accelerated away from speed limits. Wind noise on this car was marked when in open form, but became an irritating roar with the hood up; in the latter trim, visibility was not greatly restricted.

One person can erect the hood, but it is much easier for two; even then it is wise to anticipate rain if one is not to get wet. With hood and sidescreens stowed behind the seats it was rather difficult to reach the boot catch. Much of the small boot capacity is taken up by the spare wheel and tool roll—a flattish suitcase and an air travel bag are about the limit for stowable baggage, and they would have to be taken out to get to the spare wheel.

A quick glance beneath the bonnet would not encourage the private owner to carry out minor adjustments himself, but in fact most of the components which might need servicing or adjustment are fairly accessible.

The M.G., with its powerful, responsive engine, combined with a moderately heavy but low-slung chassis, adequate steering and superlative brakes, and without any little vices or unpredictable traits in behaviour, maintains the traditional high standards of performance and safety of the marque.

M.G. MGA 1600

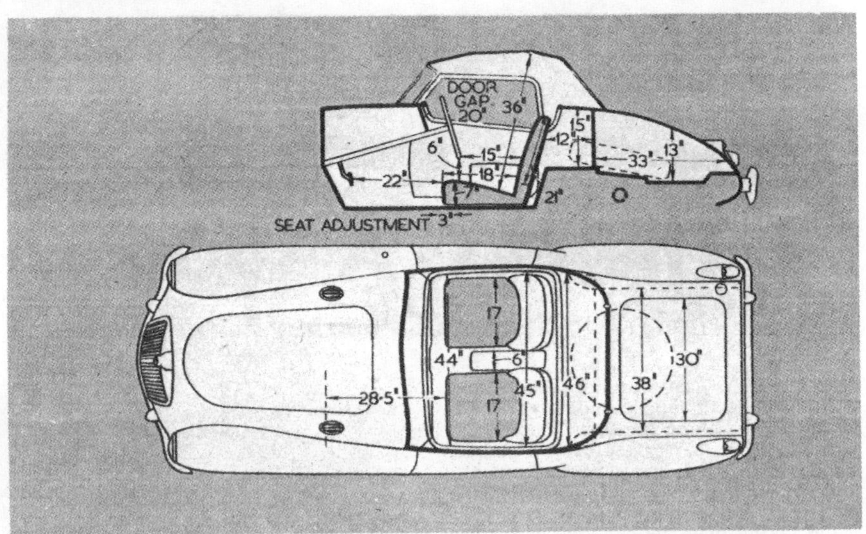

Scale ¼in to 1ft. Driving seat in central position. Cushions uncompressed.

DATA

PRICE (basic), with two seater body and hood, **£663.**
British purchase tax, **£277 7s 6d.**
Total (in Great Britain), **£940 7s 6d.**
Extras: Radio **£24 5s (£34 7s 1d** with tax).
Heater **£12 5s (£17 7s 1d** with tax).
Windscreen washer **£2 (£2 16s 8d** with tax).

ENGINE: Capacity, 1,588 c.c. (96.9 cu in).
Number of cylinders, 4.
Bore and stroke, 75.39 × 88.9 mm (2.968 × 3.5in).
Valve gear, o.h.v. pushrods.
Compression ratio, 8.3 to 1.
B.h.p. 79.5 (gross) at 5,600 r.p.m. (b.h.p. per ton laden 75.3).
Torque, 87lb ft at 3,800 r.p.m.
M.p.h. per 1,000 r.p.m. in top gear, 17.16.

WEIGHT: (With 5 gals fuel), 18.12 cwt (2,030lb).
Weight distribution (per cent): F, 53, R, 47.
Laden as tested, 21.12 cwt (2,366 lb).
Lb per c.c. (laden), 1.49.

BRAKES: Type, Lockheed. F Discs. R, Drums.
Method of operation, hydraulic.
Drum dimensions: 10in diameter; 1.75in wide.
Disc diameter, 11in.
Swept area: F, 240 sq in; R, 110 sq in.

TYRES: 5.60—15in.
Pressures (lb sq in): F, 17; R, 20 (normal). F, 21; R, 24 (fast driving).

TANK CAPACITY: 10 Imp. gallons.
Oil sump, 8 pints (including filter).
Cooling system, 10 pints (plus 0.65 pint if heater fitted).

DIMENSIONS: Wheelbase, 7ft 10in.
Track: F, 3ft 11.5in; R, 4ft 0.75in.
Length (overall), 13ft.
Width, 4ft 10in.
Height, 4ft 2in.
Ground clearance, 6in.
Frontal area, 13.77 sq ft (approximately) (hood up).

ELECTRICAL SYSTEM: 12-volt: two 6-volt, 58 ampère-hour batteries.
Head lights: Double dip; 50—40 watt bulbs.

SUSPENSION: Front, coil springs.
Rear, semi-elliptic leaf springs.

PERFORMANCE

ACCELERATION (mean):

Speed range, Gear Ratios and Time in Sec.

m.p.h.	**4.3 to 1**	**5.91 to 1**	**9.52 to 1**	**15.65 to 1**
10—30	—	8.7	4.7	—
20—40	11.0	7.8	4.6	—
30—50	10.9	6.9	—	—
40—60	10.5	7.5	—	—
50—70	11.9	8.3	—	—
60—80	13.2	—	—	—
70—90	17.0	—	—	—

From rest through gears to:

30 m.p.h. ..	**4.6 sec.**
40 " ..	**6.7 "**
50 " ..	**10.3 "**
60 " ..	**14.2 "**
70 " ..	**18.5 "**
80 " ..	**26.6 "**
90 " ..	**36.4 "**

Standing quarter mile, 19.3 sec.

MAXIMUM SPEEDS ON GEARS:

Gear		m.p.h.	k.p.h.
Top ..	(mean)	100.9	162.4
	(best)	101.4	163.2
3rd		77.0	123.9
2nd		46.0	74.0
1st		27.0	43.4

TEST CONDITIONS: Weather: dry, overcast. 5-15 m.p.h. wind.
Air temperature: 69 deg. F.

BRAKES (at 30 m.p.h. in neutral):

Pedal load in lb	Retardation	Equivalent stopping distance in ft
25	0.22g	137
50	0.42g	70
75	0.74g	41
94	0.98g	30.8

FUEL CONSUMPTION:

Steady speeds in top

30 m.p.h.	40.0 m.p.g.
40 "	36.3 "
50 "	33.3 "
60 "	30.7 "
70 "	28.5 "
80 "	26.0 "
90 "	22.3 "

Overall fuel consumption for 1,590 miles, 24.1 m.p.g. (11.72 litres per 100 km).
Approximate normal range 24-31 m.p.g. (11.7-9.2 litres per 100 km).
Fuel: Premium grade.

TRACTIVE EFFORT (by Tapley meter):

	Pull (lb per ton)	Equivalent Gradient
Top	245	1 in 9.1
Third	345	1 in 6.4
Second	550	1 in 3.9

STEERING: Turning circle.
Between kerbs, L, 31ft 2¾in, R, 31ft 5in.
Between walls, L, 32ft 8in, R, 33ft.
Turns of steering wheel, lock to lock, 2¾.

SPEEDOMETER CORRECTION: M.P.H.

Car speedometer:	10	20	30	40	50	60	70	80	90	100
True speed:	11	20	30	39	49	59	68	77	87	97

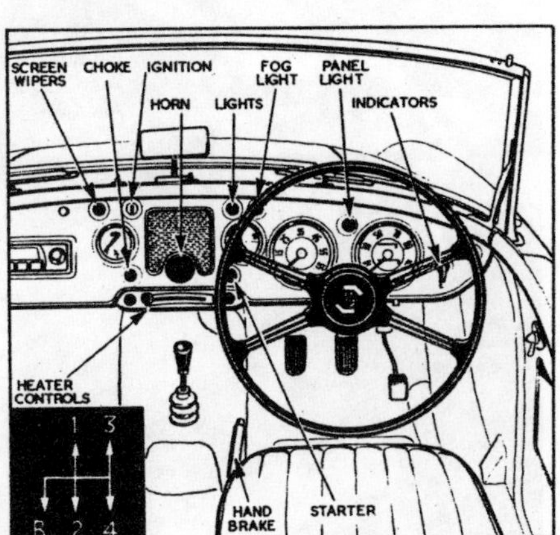

THE WELL-LOVED M.G.A has had a face lift and the engine capacity has been increased to 1,588 c.c. Disc brakes have been standardized for the front wheels.

THE M.G.A is an old friend to the readers of AUTOSPORT. I tested the original prototype EX182 long before it was in production, and the 1,500 c.c. version of the car was tried in open and coupé form. Now, this well-loved model has had a face lift, and the engine has been stretched to the 1,600 c.c. class, which is a popular category for competition purposes. Disc brakes have been standardized for the front wheels, and the sidescreens now incorporate sliding windows.

The M.G. is completely conventional. It has a rugged box-section frame, suspended in front on wishbones and helical springs, and the steering is by rack and pinion. The Lockheed hydraulic brakes

JOHN BOLSTER TESTS

The M.G.A 1600

A Lively Two-Seater of Pleasing Performance

are of disc type, 11 ins. diameter in front, and the rear 10 ins. drums are on a hypoid axle, suspended on semi-elliptic springs.

Based on the B.M.C. "A" series unit, the engine is a conventional four-cylinder with pushrod operated overhead valves. A small increase in the bore has put the capacity up from 1,489 c.c. to 1,588 c.c. A power bonus of some 6 b.h.p. has been secured, but more important is the raising of the torque curve in the middle range of revolutions. The twin SU carburetters are of the H4 size, and an 8 ins. Borg and Beck clutch is well able to handle the power output. The gearbox, with its traditional short remote control lever, gives a high third speed, which has for long been an M.G. feature.

The steel body has modern lines, and it is very solidly constructed. The driver and passenger sit right down inside it on their separate seats, divided by a very deep propeller shaft tunnel. The hood is attractive in appearance and folds neatly away behind the seats, this operation being best performed by two people. There is a good array of instruments, and the bumpers give real protection, the overriders being quite massive.

On taking over the car, one is at once impressed by the long, low appearance, the attractive finish, and the many practical details. Accessibility for normal maintenance is generally satisfactory, though this does not apply to the battery. Unfortunately, I must once again award a black mark to the luggage boot, which has insufficient capacity for normal touring unless one leaves the spare wheel behind.

As one expects of an M.G., the driving position is good. The gear lever is ideally placed, and the all-round visibility belies the low driving position.

CONVENTIONAL four-cylinder pushrod engine powers the car, with twin carburetters. LEFT: Driving position is good, the gear lever being ideally placed. Visibility is excellent.

The seats are comfortable for long journeys, though a little better lateral location would be appreciated. The instruments are well situated and legible, and the pedal arrangement makes the best use of the limited space available.

The engine is an instant starter and pulls well almost at once. The extra torque of the slightly bigger unit renders the car more flexible, and one makes less use of the gear lever than formerly during normal touring. Considered as a fast touring car, the M.G. must be rated very highly indeed. The occupants are well protected and the machine is comfortably sprung. It covers the ground in an effortless manner, and useful average speeds may be maintained without any feeling of strain.

At low speeds the steering feels rather dead and is perhaps heavier than would be expected. At higher velocities, however, it comes into its own, being

COCKPIT is well laid out, all instruments being easily readable. Curiously, no ammeter is fitted in spite of the full instrumentation.

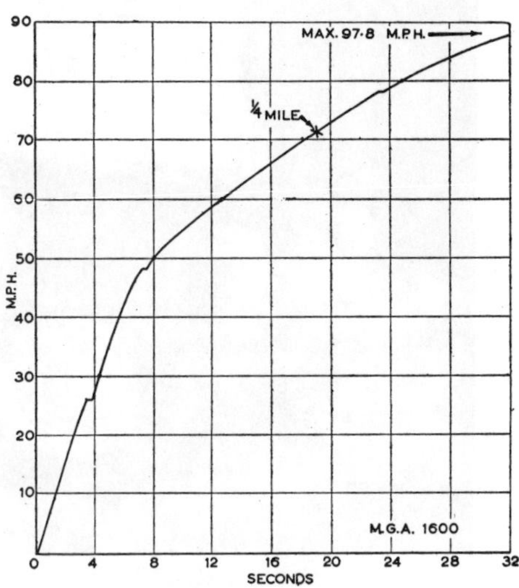

ACCELERATION GRAPH

delightfully accurate and affording a fine sense of control. The gearbox is a splendid component, and it would be hard to better the easy and precise operation of that short and rigid lever. The clutch is well able to cope with the bigger engine; the brakes also are entirely free from vice and cannot be made to fade.

The engine cruises at high speeds or revs happily on the indirect gears with equal aplomb. However, as the maximum speed of the car is approached it does go through a rough period when both noise and vibration become somewhat pronounced. The test car failed to reach a genuine 100 m.p.h., but with a smooth hard top that figure should be attained without difficulty. The hood is not ideally streamlined and tends to flap at high speeds, so the wind resistance must be fairly high.

The car is definitely livelier than its predecessor, and perhaps the acceleration figures scarcely do justice to the increase in performance. This is because there is a rather marked tendency for one rear wheel to spin at the getaway, even on dry concrete. It is, in fact, necessary to be well on the move before full throttle can be applied on first gear. When the speed begins to rise, however, the very real benefit of the powerful engine can be felt.

Although the M.G. is primarily a sports-touring car of the high speed variety, many amateur drivers will employ it for club racing. Accordingly, I drove the car to its limit on a racing circuit. Under these conditions it remains very controllable at all times, and it would take a clumsy driver indeed to run out of road. The cornering power is not outstandingly high by competition standards, the M.G. being somewhat heavily built for such capers. For the man who primarily wants a fast road car, and does the odd club event on the side, this machine will provide an acceptable compromise.

The very solidity of the car's construction is apparent to driver and passenger alike, and is somewhat reassuring under modern traffic conditions. The whole basis of the vehicle is its immensely rigid chassis, and this no doubt has a great deal to do with its accurate steering and controllability. The doors are wide, to give reasonably easy entry to the low car, and there are no outside door handles, it being necessary to slide the window forward and find the cord inside the door. The test car had pierced bolt-on disc wheels, but the knock-on type may be specified as an optional extra.

The M.G.A 1600 is a fast sports car that may almost be described as luxurious. It is lively, flexible, and a pleasure to drive, responding admirably to the proper use of that delightful gear lever but being perfectly willing to co-operate if one is in a lazy mood. It is, in fact, as practical a mode of everyday transport as many more staid vehicles, and its fade-free brakes, snappy acceleration and good road-holding are all important safety features.

SPECIFICATION AND PERFORMANCE DATA

Car Tested: M.G.A 1600 sports 2-seater. Price £940 7*s.* 6*d.* (including P.T.). Radio and heater extra.

Engine: Four cylinders 75.39 mm. x 88.9 mm. (1,588 c.c.), pushrod operated overhead valves. Compression ratio 8.3 to 1. 78 b.h.p. at 5,500 r.p.m. Twin SU carburetters. Lucas coil and distributor.

Transmission: Borg and Beck 8 ins. clutch. Four-speed gearbox with synchromesh on upper three speeds and central remote control lever, ratios 4.3, 5.908, 9.52, and 15.652 to 1. Open Hardy Spicer propeller shaft. Hypoid rear axle.

Chassis: Box-section frame. Independent front suspension by wishbones and helical springs. Rear axle on semi-elliptic springs. Piston-type hydraulic dampers. Lockheed hydraulic brakes with 11 ins. front discs and 10 ins. rear drums with fly-off hand brake. Bolt-on disc wheels fitted 5.60-15 ins. tyres.

Equipment: 12-volt lighting and starting. Speedometer. Rev. counter. Fuel, oil pressure, and water temperature gauges. Flashing indicators. Heater and radio (extra).

Dimensions: Wheelbase, 7 ft. 10 ins. Track, front 3 ft. 11½ ins., rear 4 ft. 0¼ in. Overall length 13 ft. Width 4 ft. 10 ins. Weight 18 cwt.

Performance: Maximum speed 97.8 m.p.h. Speeds in gears, 3rd 77 m.p.h., 2nd 50 m.p.h., 1st 26 m.p.h. Standing quarter-mile 19.2 secs. Acceleration: 0-30 m.p.h., 4.4 secs.; 0-50 m.p.h., 8 secs.; 0-60 m.p.h., 12.8 secs.; 0-80 m.p.h., 24.8 secs.

Fuel Consumption: 26 m.p.g.

LONG, LOW appearance of the car and its attractive finish are immediately impressive on taking over the machine.

Even when the hood is up the lines of the M.G. "A" Type are clean and attractive, owing not a little to exhaustive experiments in a high speed aircraft wind tunnel to ensure reduced wind resistance

The M.G.A. Two Seater

WHATEVER may be said one way or another about the suitability of certain types of British cars, for the export market, there can be no doubt about the success of M.G. models, particularly in that economically vital area, the U.S.A. A very high proportion of the Abingdon factory output finds its way across the Atlantic. The American customer has long appreciated the traditional appearance of the "sports two seater," which altered only in detail between the "TC" of 1947, and the "TF" which continued in production until the end of 1955. This perhaps explains the reluctance of the M.G. management to go in for more aerodynamic body lines. But at last the change has come: the new model is quite strikingly handsome and its high maximum speed confirms that elaborate wind tunnel testing has been put to good use. Compared with the T.F., power output is up by a modest 20%, but maximum speed shows an increase of no less than 31%. Weight is hardly changed, what a difference can be made by an efficient body shape!

Rather surprisingly, a tubular chassis has not been chosen for the new model. The new frame is based on that used in the "Goldie" Gardner record breaking car, and is extremely stiff, though not ultra light. The side members are boxed throughout their length, swept up over the rear axle, and swept in at the front of the car, to allow for the necessary wheel movement to provide the excellent 28 ft. turning circle. Apart from the use of cross members, the stiffness of the chassis is increased by considerable bracing at the scuttle structure. The coil spring and double wishbone front suspension is identical to that on the T.F. model. Armstrong piston type dampers are incorporated in the upper wishbone pivots, while similar dampers are used in conjunction with the orthodox semi-elliptic rear springs. Rack and pinion steering is retained, the steering column having one universal joint and carrying a four spoked sprung wheel. The engine is based on the "B" series B.M.C. unit with raised compression and twin S.U. carburetters. The gearbox is also based on the manufacturer's standard component, but is operated by remote control from a very short central gear lever while the clutch operation is hydraulic.

Since the British Motor Corporation officially entered competition motoring, with works sponsored teams, they have obtained a great deal of experience in this field, and some of the results of this experience have been remembered in the design of the production model M.G. "A."

In the 1955 Le Mans 24 hours race, two M.G.s finished in a most reliable manner, covering around 2000 miles each. These cars, designated EX 182, were essentially similar to the car under test, but had higher compression, special cylinder heads, and much higher gear ratios. The engines developed 82.5 b.h.p. at 6000 r.p.m., and with metal tonneau cover and single aero screen, maximum speed was well over 120 m.p.h. If previous history is to be repeated, we shall expect the M.G. Car Company to give, in due course, information on modifying and tuning of the model "A," which will enable private owners to obtain from their cars performance approaching that of the Le Mans cars. There can be little doubt that there is an ample margin of safety in the basic engines, to stand a considerable power increase.

The bodywork proved to be very nicely finished, and comfortable for two people. The seats had a good range of adjustment, held their passengers firmly in position, but might well have given greater support to the thighs. The metal facia panel, with a group of instruments in front of the driver, had provision for the fitting of radio. The instruments, consisting of tachometer, speedometer, oil pressure guage, water temperature gauge, and petrol gauge, were clear and easy to read, and proved nicely accurate. The self cancelling "blinker" switch was well positioned to the driver's right hand, and the central horn button could be worked by driver or passenger, a useful point for rally work. The various switches for the auxiliaries unfortunately appeared to have been scattered over the facia without planning, and it was all too easy to get muddled between them when the car was not familiar. Particularly, the starter and main light switches were in no way individual, and were situated close one above the

Although the traditional radiator has gone, there is little doubt that, from the front, the M.G.A. looks efficient and modern

other. The headlamps were dipped by a foot switch placed in an awkward position high above the clutch pedal.

THE doors carried large pockets, could not be opened from outside, and were equipped with detachable side screens. These latter had spring loaded lower portions to facilitate hand signals, which were rather shallow for the driver with large hands. The hood folded quite quickly and very neatly behind the seats, and when it was erected, a certain amount of luggage could be accommodated in its place. It was commendably draught free and rain proof. The rear luggage boot was largely filled by the spare wheel, and opened by a release behind the passenger's seat, difficult to locate when the hood was folded over it. But the spare wheel, on long trips, could quite easily be mounted on the optional rear luggage rack; then considerable space for luggage, under reasonable security, is made available.

The engine started readily, and aided, in the case of the test car, by a radiator blind, warmed up rapidly. It proved to be outstandingly flexible, right down to about 12 m.p.h. in top gear, but with maximum torque occurring at 3500 r.p.m. the car showed to its best advantage when the gearbox was used to a fair degree. We felt that the overall gear ratio of 4.3:1 was excellently chosen. It provided a genuine maximum speed very close to 100 m.p.h. at about 5750 r.p.m., just over the point of peak power, and the car cruised effortlessly at 75/80 m.p.h., and without protest at much higher speeds. Third also seemed well chosen for road use, giving excellent acceleration between 20 and 65 m.p.h. But 2nd and 1st might well have been higher geared, as it is first is virtually only an emergency gear. But special ratios cost money, and the M.G. "A" is commendably inexpensive.

The synchromesh on the three upper ratios could not quite cope with the very rapid changes of position which the neat gear lever encourages, but was entirely satisfactory for normal driving. Similarly, after a number of vigorous standing starts, some clutch slip was experienced, but only under these conditions. Although the tachometer is redlined at just under 6000 r.p.m., the engine appeared willing to rev to even higher figures without complaint; this might well be useful in driving tests, such as the sports car owner may meet in rallies. He will also be well served by the fine turning circle and excellent driver visibility. But reverse is difficult to engage quickly, largely owing to the fact that being selected by moving the lever fully to the left and back, the driver's hand has to make a back hand movement with which, for anatomical reasons, little pressure could be exerted.

THIS is definitely a car which is in its most attractive state with the hood down. The passengers are well protected by the screen, and even without the side screens there is little buffeting from the wind. Mechanical noise is not obtrusive, nor is that of the exhaust. High cruising speeds are natural, it is a pleasure to drive. With the hood up, the noise level increases a great deal. This is perhaps inevitable with any open car; but it is a fact which we must note. However, the highest maximum speed is obtained with the car in this form; open it will achieve approximately 95 m.p.h.

Fuel consumption will only fall below 30 m.p.g. if the car is driven very hard, and so the 10 gallon fuel tank gives a range of about 300 miles. Engine accessibility is well above average, and the bonnet is released from inside the car. Good tools are provided, though the jack is of the screw type which must be placed under front wishbones or rear springs; this can be a dirty job. Among the available extras are knock off wire wheels, heater, radio, white wall tyes, 4.55:1 axle ratio, twin horns, fog lamps, overall tonneau cover, rim-bellishers, telescopic steering wheel, and radiator blind. The paint and leatherwork are available in a large variety of colours.

It is interesting to make a comparison of data and performance between the new car and the T.F. (1250 c.c.), on which we carried out a test in April, 1954.

	"T.F."	**"A"**
Cub. Cap	1250	1489
Max. Power	57.5	68
At (revs.)	5500	5500
Weight (cwt.)	17¼	17½
Litres/ton mile	2850	3000
Top gear ratio	4.875:1	4.30:1
M.P.H./1000 r.p.m.	15.25	17.0
M.P.H. at 2500 ft./min. piston speed	64.5	72.8
Max. Speed (Mean)	76.5	99.2
0-50 m.p.h.	14.0 secs.	11.8 secs.
0-70 m.p.h.	35.5	22.0
10-30 m.p.h. (Top)	10.1	8.0
30-50 m.p.h. (Top)	14.7	11.3
50-70 m.p.h. (Top)	24.7	14.9
Fuel Consumption:		
Driven Hard	24 m.p.g.	26.5 m.p.g.
Normally	27/29	29/33

The figures speak for themselves: there can be no doubt as to the improvement, and the advantages which can be gained by modern streamlining, and the use of high axle ratios which go with it.

The handling characteristics of the M.G. "A" are essentially modern. They could hardly have been achieved without the post war motor racing experience which has been available to the designers. The rack and pinion steering gives precise control, and it is very light. It is not only light because of mechanical efficiency, but also because no attempt has been made to achieve appreciable under-steer

The capacity of the luggage boot is generous but the fact that the spare wheel is kept there considerably reduces that capacity

Developing 68 b.h.p. at 5500 r.p.m. the 1489 c.c. engine has twin carburetters and drives through a hydraulically operated clutch and four-speed synchromesh gearbox

or strong self-centre-ing action. When a car steers in a virtually neutral manner, a minor and consistent degree of roll oversteer is coupled with eventual gentle tail break away and steering itself is high geared, then, we think, the best handling characteristics are achieved. There is no danger of running wide on a corner and of encroaching on the wrong side of the road. The old fear of oversteer existed when this tendency appeared violently and suddenly, usually due to faulty steering geometry.

The actual cornering capacity of this car is very high, particularly when it is remembered that it has on orthodox rear axle. On very acute bends it is possible to lift one rear wheel and generate wheel spin, this is inevitable with semi-elliptic springs which are soft enough to provide a comfortable ride.

The brakes gave excellent retardation, the response to pedal pressure being smooth and progressive. Braking on corners produced no sign of vice. We were able to produce some brake fade, as evidenced by the necessity to increase pedal pressures, and a reduced degree of evenness in the braking response, together with some smoking and smell from the linings. But this only occurred when a long mountain pass was descended at racing speeds. For all touring purposes the brakes were entirely satisfactory. For those using the "A" in competition the optional wire wheels are available, and they will certainly provide greater brake cooling. The fly-off hand brake was powerful and effective, but perhaps not so handily placed as in the T.F.

TO sum up: we now have at the very low basic price of £640, an open two seater, with 100 m.p.h. performance and handling characteristics which are exceedingly safe, and permit road holding of an order, which, a few years ago, would have only been expected from a far more expensive and elaborately designed car. The bodywork is delightful to the eye, the finish is way above normal for the price range. The occupants are snugly and comfortably accommodated, the all weather equipment is efficient. Luggage space is restricted, but it would be surprising if something had not to be sacrificed.

This is a young man's car, and it will doubtless give great delight to many proud owners. It is an example of value for money in its own sphere, which cannot be equalled by any other nation. There is every sign that this new M.G. is being received in a most enthusiastic manner all over the world. And it must not be forgotten that the excellent M.G. car club, with its immense spread of regional centres, offers social and sporting occasions which bring together enthusiastic motorists, and encourage motor sport. As ever, this latest sports M.G. is the ideal vehicle for entry into the field of competition.

MECHANICAL SPECIFICATION

Engine

Cylinders—4.
Bore—73 mm.
Stroke—89 mm.
Cubic Capacity—1489 c.c.
Valves—Overhead, push rods.
Compression Ratio—8.3:1.
Max. Power—68 b.h.p.
at 550 r.p.m.
Carburetters—2 S.U. Side Draught.

Transmission

Top gear (s/m)—4.30:1
3rd gear (s/m)—5.91:1
2nd gear (s/m)—9.52:1
1st gear 15.65:1
M.P.H. per 1000 r.p.m. in Top Gear—17.0.

Chassis

Brakes—Lockheed hydraulic 2 L.S. at front.
Brake Drum Diameter—10 ins.
Friction Lining area—134 sq. ins.
Suspension—
Front: Independent Coil springs, Wishbones.
Rear: Semi elliptic.
Shock Absorbers—Armstrong Hydraulic.
Tyres—5.60x15, Dunlop.
Wheels—Steel disc, bolt on.

Steering

Steering Gear—Rack and pinion, 2 piece track rod.
Turning Circle—28 ft.
Turns of Steering Wheel from lock to lock—2⅔.

Dimensions

Wheelbase—7 ft. 10 ins.
Track—Front: 3 ft. 11½ ins.
Rear: 4ft. 0¾ ins.
Overall length—13 ft.
width—4 ft. 10 ins.
height—4 ft. 2 ins.
Dry Weight—17½ cwt.

PERFORMANCE FIGURES

Weather: Dry, light wind, temp. approx. 55 deg F.

Fuel: Premium Grade.

Speedometer Correction:

Timed Speed:	20	30	40	50	60	70	80	90	101
Reading -	18	30	41.5	52	63	74	85	94	104

Maximum Speeds:

(Hood and side screens erected)

Gear:	M.P.H. (Normal and Maximum)
Top:	Mean: 99.2 Best: 101.0
3rd:	65/75
2nd:	39/47
1st:	20/30

Acceleration (Time in seconds)

M.P.H.	Top	3rd	2nd	1st
10.30	8.0	5.8	4.0	2.5
20.40	9.8	6.8	4.2	—
30.50	11.3	7.4	—	—
40.60	12.0	8.3	—	—
50.70	14.9	11.3	—	—
60.80	18.8	—	—	—
70.90	24.1	—	—	—

From rest through gears:

0-30	4.5 secs.
0-40	7.3 „
0-50	11.8 „
0-60	16.2 „
0-70	22.0 „
0-80	32.5 „
0-90	47.4 „

Fuel Consumption:

Driven hard—26.5 m.p.g.
Normal—29/33 m.p.g.

Price—Basic: £640. Purchase Tax: £321 7s. 0d. Total: £961 7s. 0d.

(The M.G. car used in our Road Test was kindly placed at our disposal by Messrs. H. Prosser & Son Ltd., 123 Bothwell St., Glasgow, C.2.)

SCI ROAD TEST:

TWIN CAM MGA

Abingdon's most muscular Midget.

Here it is: 1588 cc and 107 hp of racing potential. Widely spaced valve covers, manifolding completely fill MGA engine room.

FOR THE MAN who merely takes a quick look at the products of the MG car company produced since 1936 and who has a smattering of knowledge concerning what went on at Abingdon during the halcyon days prior to that date it is easy to call the marque either stagnant or "commercial" and let things go at that.

From 1929 to 1936 the cars bearing the brown and cream octagon had made things very hard indeed for racing handicappers who had to revise their MG performance estimates upwards with boring regularity only to find that Kimber and company had with equal regularity managed to field something even hotter than before. Then came the Nuffield reorganization and the end of a formal racing and development organization as far as the men of Abingdon themselves were concerned. Help was given as before with open-handed and open-minded generosity to those who wished to race the marque but the factory crew must concern itself with production and the business of building cars for money.

Gone were the days when the production lines found themselves hard put to keep up with the stream of ideas and new designs that poured from the facile minds of H. N. Charles and his design staff. Gone were the taut sports and racing cars with their single overhead cam engines that could twist up a 7000 rpm storm and pump a gutty 120 to 140 horsepower from a miniscule 750 to 1100 cc's. No more J-4's, mighty K-3's or sizzling Q's and R-types were to roll out the doors and onto the tracks. The year 1936 was the year of the rocker-box and the beginning of the bread-and-butter sports car. It was the year of the TA.

Not, mind you, was it the end of the MG Midget. Not at all. It's just that things weren't quite the same.

Yes, to the man who just looked at the surface it was easy to say that the men of Abingdon had gone commercial, that things had changed. But to those who looked beneath the surface it was quite clear that they hadn't changed all that much. The minds in the back room were still as facile as before, the slide rules as well used.

If any proof of this was needed, one has only to look at the MGA. Merged with the mighty BMC combine, John

Thornley's men came up with a new car to fit the new production components and did it in little more than a year. All BMC products must use basic BMC parts and this standardization includes engines, gearboxes, rear ends and the like as well as minor equipment. None of this materiel bore any relation to past practice. Yet, *Voila,* there was the MGA.

To your truly shriven MG owner all of this was horrifying. Nuffield had been heretic enough but this last merger was unspeakable. They reckoned without Messers Thornley, Enever et al. And they also did not notice or refused to see the significance of something else. In 1955 the men of Abingdon showed up at LeMans with three sleek alloy bodied cars labeled EX 182. The summer before they had arrived on the salt at Bonneville with a chunky, brick-like streamliner tagged with the designation EX 179. Both bore the BMC B-type engine which later sat between the rails of the MGA in somewhat more civilized garb. Later, something called an MGA appeared at the Ulster TT Outwardly it was EX 182 but inside it carried an engine with the unmistakable dimensions and covers of a DOHC head. And in the summer of 1956 EX 179 appeared again on the salt with a similar piece of equipment tucked into its chunky insides. And in 1957 came EX 181, a ground missile of the most advanced type and again equipped with that portentious dual cammed engine, this time equipped with a monster 305 cubic-inch-per-revolution Shorrock blower! Output: 290 bhp. Speed? Something in hand over 240 miles an hour.

They had changed at Abingdon, had they? Not much they had! The same men, with a few exceptions, who had bolted together the last R-type, were at the same old stand doing the same old things. And with the same aims in mind — building sports racing cars at competitive prices.

And early this July the news was let out. That double-cammed head for the BMC block was to be a production item —not a conversion piece but equipping an entirely new automobile. Well, not *entirely* new but with enough engineering changes in mounting, gearing and suspension to obviate attempts at shade tree conversion from the standard MGA, which, by the way, continues to form the bulk of the company's output.

In short, after 22 years, the reign of the rockerbox was over at Abingdon. The Marque of the Octagon was once again represented by a production racing sports car. Not that post-Nuffield MG cars have not been raced—they have been and on occasion successfully and well. But, to face facts squarely, they haven't been competitive except on rare occasions with other marques of their own class. The difference is in the point of view—the rockerboxes were street sports cars that could be raced; the early single-stick cars and the new MGA Twin Cam are racing sports cars that can be street-driven.

What hath Abingdon wrought? Basically they have turned out an improved MGA that will go, according to the gear ratios used, some 20-odd miles an hour faster and (again according to the gear ratios used) will do it considerably quicker, especially in the driving ranges of between 40 and 100 miles an hour. Having made the car go that much quicker, they also figured to stop it equally as fast and to this end they have mounted as standard Dunlop disc brakes on all four corners.

Two specific items combine to give the car its speed. First, since nothing beats cubic inches except rectangular money, the basic BMC B-type block has been punched out to a new bore size of 2.969 inches (up from 2.87) for a total displacement of 1588 cc's or 96.906 cubic inches. Then they tossed in the rectangular money with the double overhead cam head. This little item gives the engine 1500 rpm more at the top end.

The head, being the big item, is worth close study. The head itself is of aluminum alloy attached to the block by ten studs. The valves are run in at an included angle of 0 degrees and operated through shimmed cups by two chain-driven camshafts. Clearances are set by changing the shims which are supplied in a large variety of sizes. Each camshaft runs in three renewable white-metal bearings and is driven by a 3/8 inch pitch Duplex roller chain from a half-speed shaft in the left side of the block. This half-speed shaft is driven in turn by a pair of reduction gears from the crankshaft. The tach, distributor and oil pump are also driven by this shaft. Pistons, of course, are special items with three compression rings and one oil ring and are equipped with full floating wrist pins. Compression ratio is given as 9.9 to 1. Hung off the right side of the head is a large log-type manifold bearing two big H6 S.U. carburetors and set up with mounting flanges to take an even larger size. This being an MG and the MG people being the sort of blokes they are new and better things are planned for the engine in the future, hence the big mounting flanges. Makes one wonder what a Stage Four would do considering the effect of such tuning on the pushrod version. As it is, this small bear pumps out 107 bhp at 6500 rpm.

How does this road eater go? Very well indeed, all things considered. SCI's test car was really and truly just that—a moving test bed. One of the first batch to arrive in the U.S., it was bound to have bugs and did. Not bad ones, mind you; just the bugs expected from a fresh production line item.

We picked the car up from Hambro Automotive Corporation in virtually the same shape it had been shipped. It sat in the garage looking, except for the knockoff hubs, just like any MGA. We slid into the seat and about the only immediately noticeable difference was the tach which was orange-lined at 6500 and red-lined at 7000 rpm. Yanking the starter-pull (when *will* they trade that thing off for a proper button?) started the engine into a busy 900 rpm idle and a heady aroma of Castrol "R" arose from underneath. Sliding the butter-soft gearbox into low we eased out the garage doors and into the street, treating the throttle with all the caution rated by a drag machine. It wasn't necessary—the car was as docile as any rocker-head MGA. This applied all

Editor bends the Twin Cam MGA through tight hairpin at Lime Rock during lap-time tests. Added weight of new engine caused considerable lean but the car stuck and handled well, even with "street" tires.

through New York City traffic with the added benefit of being able to stay in a given gear for a longer period of time and over a considerably wider range of speed.

Cruising out into suburbia, we ranged through Third and Fourth gears according to the speed laws on various stretches, keeping the tach wavering between 2500 and 4500. The twin cam engine with its slightly larger size pulled steadily and seemingly equally over this entire range. It was when the 4500 rpm mark was passed that the new engine began to reveal its capabilities, though. If the factory's power curve can be applied to this particular car, the horsepower rating shoots up from 76 to 98 bhp in the space between 4000 and 5000 rpm. This boost can be felt immediately—where the standard pushrod engined car begins to taper off, the twin cam version is just starting to belt out its new-found power. It's not a mad, bellowing slam in the back but a smooth, deceptive rush that can get you from 40 to 70 mph in just over four seconds, using Third gear in the optional close ratio box. Depending on the gearbox used and the rear axle ratio chosen, Third gear is good for anything from 75 to 85 miles an hour, more than fast enough for

we headed off for Lime Rock with the Twin Cam in company with Andy Woods, Hambro service executive. For this trip the car was in standard trim—in fact substandard as facts later proved. It hadn't been touched except for the addition of oil, water and fuel since it had come off the dock. Further it showed only about 600 miles on the meter and the first few hundred of those miles had scarcely been normal break-in driving. Gearing was the standard box and the 4.3 rear axle ratio.

Buckling on crash helmet and stuffing a bag of laundry at left hip to cut side sliding, yours truly began circulating the course, slowly at first and then progressively more quickly until the comfort-discomfort threshold was reached (a somewhat lowered point than normal due to lack of seat belt). The result was six consecutive laps varying between 1:22.5 and 1:23.0. This is representative of fair-to-good time with a rocker-head MGA set up for competition. Not spectacular but indicative of much, much more potential—in other words, fresh off the boat, with nil preparation and with a driver not overly familiar with the car under competition conditions, the "TC" turned in a series of lap times that were competitive

swapped on the site.

At the track the engine fired up with a noticeably sharper, biting rap, denoting valve and ignition timing that was right on the mark. Within three laps we were circulating two full seconds quicker than before and this on a course that was still damp from an early-morning rain. Not bad for a start. Then the rear end gears were swapped for the 4.5's. With the nose-cone all set up we had what was in effect a semi-quick-change rear end and the swap was completed in less than an hour.

Time was short so a lap time was taken with only one standing lap and one flying lap, the flying lap being clocked. Results: another second chopped off the time.

Still using the close ratio box we tried some more standing starts. Bear in mind that the optional box is terrific for racing once under way, but all the gear ratios have been shoved upward toward the high end. Starts with this rig in low are much like using Second gear in the standard box. The time to 30 mph was *still* four seconds flat but just about then the machine really started to charge—it took just eight more seconds to hit 70. Zero to 60 was 9.7 seconds, an improvement of almost four seconds over the time set by the car

Externally the Twin Cam looks little different from the standard version except for the center-lock wheels.

Another tip-off is the tachometer, which is orange-lined at 6500, red-lined at 7000 rpm.

highway passing and, used injudiciously, quick enough to make big black marks on a driver's license. At no point in traffic did the car buck, miss or seem to be lugging except for a slight hesitancy off the mark at traffic lights when too little engine speed was given on clutch engagement. And at no time, even in crawling rush hour crowds did the car tend to overheat as do some other highly tuned machines. In normal street trim with muffler, moderately soft plugs and normal carb needles the temperature stayed at 180° regardless of whether the car was pushed hard in gear or idled down in high.

However, what we were really interested in, as were the service department crew at Hambro, was how the car stacked up on a race course in both normal street and racing trim. Consequently one fine morning

with prepared versions of the standard MGA. Standing starts at first were another matter due to a couple of factors, one being the totally untuned engine, the other being a soft "street" type clutch that wouldn't bite until the engine had lugged down to 2000 rpm. The result was a four-second crawl to 30 mph.

Then we turned the car over to the tender administration of Ed Brown, the man who prepared last year's Austin Healey team cars for Sebring. Ed spent a day setting things to the specs as supplied by the gospel according to Abingdon, adding a straight-through pipe to the tuned exhaust system and stuffing an optional close ratio gearbox under the tunnel. Then back to Lime Rock again with an extra nose-cone for the rear end set up with 4.5 to 1 gears, this last item to be

in untuned street trim.

After these runs, we huddled with Andy, Ed and Frank Harrison, Hambro Service Manager to see what we could sift out of the mass of data. The conclusions were pretty obvious. The car as presently set up with standard gearbox, soft clutch and 4.3 to 1 rear end is ideal for cross country high speed cruising in the Continental fashion and for rallying. For serious racing the set-ups should vary depending on the area involved.

In all cases the competition clutch is almost a necessity—the Twin Cam pumps enough power on engagement to start the normal street clutch slipping after a few racing-type starts. It doesn't slip once under way but it doesn't bite quick enough to slam the car off the mark. Racing tires are a "must" for serious competition work; slightly increased weight and the fiercer thrust of the car peel down a standard road tire, even the excellent ones with which the car is equipped, in one hot practice session.

In the East, where the courses are short and tight, the car should be ordered with the 4.5 rear end and the standard gearbox to allow jackrabbit starts and quick jumps between corners. In the far West where the courses are longer, the 4.5 rear axle and the close ratio box are in order, though the standard transmission will do the job on the twistier, shorter circuits.

As for brakes, don't worry about them. These Dunlop discs are beyond doubt the best production sports car binders in the world, particularly when the dense competition pads are used. They're exactly the same as those used on this reporter's competition Austin-Healey Six-port and will haul that muscular machine down to cornering speed from 115 miles an hour in just a shade over 50 feet hour after hour. They'll do the same for the Twin Cam as well—probably better for that matter due to the lighter weight of the MG. In our regular 10-stop test they showed nil fade and not a fraction of an inch pedal loss. After this we went out and turned an hour's worth of fast laps. Still no fade.

From all we can tell it looks as if inter-marque competition is returning to the small-bore class. The potential in class of the new Twin Cam MGA will be limited only by the potential of the man behind the wheel and of the man who has charge of the horses under the hood.

MGA TWIN CAM ROADSTER

Price at East Coast POE (Basic) . $3345
Price at West Coast POE..... $3345
U.S. Importer: Hambro Automotive Corp.

PERFORMANCE

TOP SPEED:

(Estimated, with 4.3 to 1 axle) 120 mph

ACCELERATION:

From zero to	seconds
30 mph	4.0
40 mph	6.1
50 mph	8.3
60 mph	9.7
70 mph	12.9
Standing ¼ mile	18.8
Speed at end of quarter	85.0

SPEED RANGES IN GEARS:

(Standard gearbox)

I	0-31
II	10-55
III	20-85
IV	25-120 (est.)

SPEEDOMETER CORRECTION:

Indicated Speed	Timed Speed
30	30
40	40
50	50
60	60
70	70.5

FUEL CONSUMPTION:

Hard driving (racing laps)... 12 mpg
Average driving (under 60 mph) .... 23 mpg

BRAKING EFFICIENCY:

(10 successive emergency stops from 60 mph, just short of locking wheels)
Nil fade, Nil pedal loss

SPECIFICATIONS

POWER UNIT:

Type	Four-in-line, water cooled
Valve Arrangement	Double overhead cam
Bore & Stroke	2.97 x 3.5 in (75.4 x 88.9 mm)
Stroke/Bore Ratio	1.2/1
Displacement	96.906 cu in (1588 cc)
Compression Ratio	9.9/1
Carburetion by	Two H6 Su
Max. Power	107 bhp @ 6500 rpm
Idle Speed	800 rpm

DRIVE TRAIN:

Transmission ratios test car		optional ratio
I	3.64	(2.45)
II	2.21	(1.62)
III	1.38	(1.27)
IV	1.00	(1.00)
Final drive ratio (see text)	4.3	(4.55, 4.88, 5.12)
Axle torque taken by	Springs	

CHASSIS:

Frame	Box section
Wheelbase	94 in
Front Suspension	Coil Springs, IFS Unequal length wishbones
Rear Suspension	Semi-Elliptic Leaf Springs
Shock absorbers	Lever and piston
Steering type	Rack and pinion
Steering wheel turns L to L.	2.7
Turning diam., curb to curb	32 feet
Brakes	Dunlop disc, 4-wheel
Tire size	5.90 x 15

GENERAL:

Length	156 in
Width	58 in
Height	50 in
Weight, as tested	2200 lbs
Weight distribution, F/R as tested	51/49
Fuel capacity	12 U.S. gallons

Hubs depart from past practice, using pin drive on disc wheels.

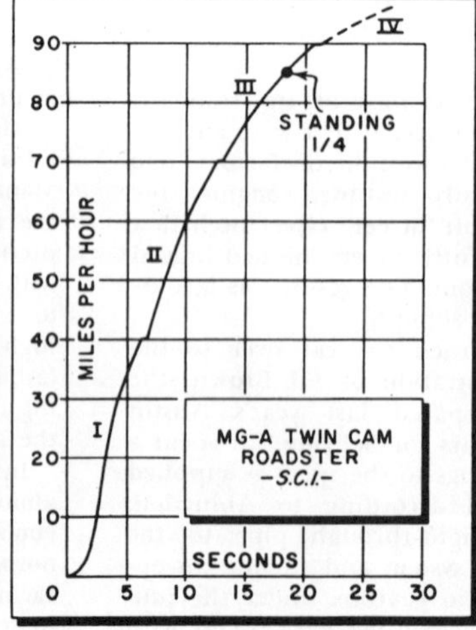

FASTER SAFELY—BY PECO

Outwardly the Peco-M.G. bears no distinguishing evidence of being non-standard apart from the tiny Peco winged transfers on the bonnet, boot and wings. Wire wheels helped to keep the extremely good brakes cool when used repeatedly

IMPRESSIONS OF A SUPERCHARGED M.G.A.

S.C.I. recently sampled the "Peco"-tuned Dauphine, first car to be offered with a full conversion by the Performance Equipment Company of Liverpool. Second conversion to emanate from a Company that came into existence more from enthusiasm for fast motoring and tuning on the part of one of the Directors of the Vernon Farthing Group of Companies, than as a new financial undertaking, it is a supercharger kit for the standard M.G.A. The Group consists mainly of consultant engineers, and amongst the many things they design are silencers and complete exhaust systems for industrial and marine engines, and silencers for jet engines and hydraulic motors. Another member of the Group is Acoustol Oils Ltd., which specializes in importing and blending pure mineral 100 per cent Pennsylvania Oil. The director responsible for the design of the supercharger end-casing and manifolding is Vernon H. Farthing who has a great deal of gas-flow experience and the problems associated with it.

He decided to take the M.G.A. as his next tuning exercise upon the introduction of the high performance Twin-Cam. He reasoned that standard M.G.A. owners would be more than interested in a conversion which would not only outperform the normal unsupercharged Twin-Cam, but which would cost roughly a third of the price increase of the Twin-Cam over that of the standard M.G.A. As Peco make it their policy to market "bolt-on" speed equipment and therefore do not remove or modify the cylinder head, something much more than just new manifolding and carburation had to be used. The obvious answer was to supercharge, but much care had to be exercised in mounting the unit to avoid cutting the bodywork about. Peco sympathize with people who ultimately wish to sell their cars, and who like to transfer any speed equipment they may have to their next vehicle, and they endeavour to design accordingly.

It was found that the Roots-type blower unit made by Sir G. Godfrey could be positioned neatly alongside the engine without modification to the bodywork. Peco-designed castings extend the nose of the blower forward to the fan where it is belt-driven via a divided nose-pulley from the fan belt. The former enables the belt which has a life of about 20,000 miles to be changed without too much bother and without removing the radiator. The kit includes a spare fan belt. Lubrication of the unit (only the gears need oil) is provided by a positive feed from the engine which drains back into the sump via the dipstick hole. The dipstick itself is kept in a rubber sheath alongside the engine. Advantage of this is that the dipstick is always clean when removed from the sheath and taking a reading is achieved simply by removing the flexible pipe feed from the supercharger and inserting the dipstick in the ordinary fashion.

A single 1½ in. S.U. carburetter is fitted, one of the standard instruments but fitted with a special Peco needle; on the model tested this was not fitted with an air silencer and as it is fitted high up, facing rearward and at the back of the engine it should not be necessary in this country. However an air-filter will be available as an extra and will be fitted vertically behind the engine and connected to the carburetter via a flexible pipe. Mixture boosted to a maximum of 5 to 6 lb. per sq. in. passes into the twin ports via a Peco-designed manifold. The manifold design is good judging by the extremely good fuel consumption we achieved.

Apart from the supercharger the Peco-M.G. kit includes a special straight-through exhaust system terminating in a Peco booster. The normal M.G. manifolding is retained with the addition of the aforementioned silencer which has a special built-in resonant chamber in its after end.

The blower fits in snugly alongside the engine with the single S.U. facing aft. No air filter is fitted although one will be offered as an optional extra on production kits. Blower casing is manufactured by Sir G. Godfrey but Peco manufacture manifolding and nose extension for drive

We collected the car in Southport and straight-away drove it back to Buckinghamshire, feeling immediately at home in it in spite of the very much increased power. The handling of the M.G.A. is superb and the additional power proved no embarrassment. The standard drum brakes which were fitted with perfectly standard linings were entirely adequate, in fact the car was completely standard with the exception of the competition clutch which in practice was either "in" or "out".

The engine started readily from cold with little or no use of the choke but would not tick-over until really warm when it idled at 700 r.p.m. with only a slight "whirring" indicating the presence of a blower. To enable warming-up to be accomplished quickly a radiator blind is fitted. We found that generally the car ran very cool at 120 deg. F. and seemed to like it better that way. If caught in a traffic jam for a long period, the temperature would rise to above 160 deg. and the engine refused to tick over cleanly.

The blower has certainly improved the top-gear performance of the car enabling it to be accelerated from 15 m.p.h. to 90 m.p.h. in this gear with ease. Peco advise a rev limit of 5,900 r.p.m. the same as that of the standard car and recommend that only 100-octane petrol should be used. To ensure that one is well aware when this limit is reached a yellow light on the dashboard lights up—the rev limit with a blown engine is more critical than that of the ordinary engine since at all speeds it is obtaining efficient cylinder filling. In a standard engine with standard valves and springs the exhaust gases cannot escape as quickly at high speeds and over-heating results. However even with this limit it was possible to out-accelerate most vehicles on the road. No particular cruising speed suited the car which would go just as fast as the road would allow without any fuss or any sense of being overworked. Compared to the performance of the standard M.G.A. the increase was staggering, we covered 0 to 90 through the gears in 25.1 sec. on a dry road which gave maximum (or almost) wheel grip. This compares with a figure of 50.1 sec. for the standard M.G.A. and 30 sec. for the Twin Cam. This speed came up very quickly indeed even on the shortest stretches of road it was advisable to keep an eye on the speedometer to prevent approaching other traffic too rapidly. During the acceleration tests we took the car through to 30 m.p.h. in first, 50 m.p.h. in second, and just over 73 m.p.h. in third The highest speed recorded during the test period was 104 m.p.h. which is about the lot at the recommended rev-limit. On its return the mileometer recorded just over 6,400 miles and it felt considerably "looser" than on first taking it over. Returning to performance figures, acceleration in the various gears was very impressive: in second gear 20 to 40 m.p.h. took 3 sec., 30 to 50 m.p.h. in third took 4.8 sec., 40 to 60 in 6.1 sec. and 50 to 70 in 7.4 sec. Top gear could be used for overtaking as acceleration was more than sufficient in most cases; 50 to 70 m.p.h. in this gear occupied 8 sec., 60 to 80 m.p.h. 10 sec. and 70 to 90 m.p.h. 11.3 sec. During the test we were unable to take a 0 to 100 reading in view of the weather conditions although we later recorded a maximum.

One of the Peco M.G's most impressive traits was that it could be driven very slowly in top gear, proper cylinder filling obviously being responsible for this. In the wet, wheel spin was quite a problem if the loud pedal was used in excess and was evident even in third gear. When driven quietly the car aroused no interest from other road users since it is indistinguishable from standard form with the exception of tiny Peco transfers on the wings, bonnet and boot. But, if the full performance was used then the blower became evident, the whirring noise low down giving place to a peculiar whistle and then finally a distinct howl as the speed rose. On a light throttle the car ran along with a pleasant warbling of the exhaust.

As to fuel consumption we recorded a figure of a little less than 31 m.p.g. for 331 miles including a return trip to Liverpool from South Buckinghamshire some 200 miles which were covered in 4¼ hours door to door in not too good conditions. At the time of writing a price has yet to be fixed for the M.G.A. Supercharger Kit but Peco have stipulated that it will be less than £100.

In the design stage at Liverpool is a new twin carburetter conversion with a pulse-tuned exhaust system for the Ford Anglia, and Peco have also been carrying out tests on a Mk II Zephyr equipped with a special exhaust system. Readers may remember that they introduced special exhaust conversions for the Ford range, M.G. Magnette, Jaguar range and for the Vauxhall Victor at the 1958 Motor Show. During our visit to Liverpool we were given the opportunity of driving Vernon Farthing's own Jaguar Mk VII equipped with the full exhaust system and terminated by twin exhaust boosters. It gave considerably increased acceleration with little increase in noise and enabled a high cruising speed to be quickly reached and maintained.—D.S. ★

From the rear observant motorists will notice something slightly different. Special Peco exhaust system with straight through silencer is terminated by a booster unit

PERFORMANCE DATA

From rest through gears to:—

	Standard Two-seater	Twin Cam	Peco
30 m.p.h.	4.9 sec.	4.3 sec.	3.6 sec.
40 ,,	—	6.9 ,,	5.4 ,,
50 ,,	11.0 ,,	9.4 ,,	7.4 ,,
60 ,,	15.6 ,,	13.3 ,,	11.2 ,,
70 ,,	21.4 ,,	17.3 ,,	15.0 ,,
80 ,,	32.1 ,,	22.5 ,,	21.4 ,,
90 ,,	50.1 ,,	30.0 ,,	25.1 ,,

Maxima on gears:

First: 30 m.p.h. Second: 50 m.p.h. Third: 73 m.p.h. Top: 104 m.p.h.

Fuel consumption:

30.8 m.p.g. overall for 331 miles (Town and long distance work).

USED CARS on the Road

Apart from minor panel damage below the right side lamp, there is no evidence that the car has been involved in any accident. The chassis and underneath of the MGA are commendably free from corrosion

No. 160 1957 M.G. MGA

PRICE: Secondhand £595; New—basic £663, with tax £996

Acceleration from rest through gears:

to 30 m.p.h.	5·4 *sec*	*to 80 m.p.h.*	38·9 *sec*
to 50 m.p.h.	12·2 *sec*	*20 to 40 m.p.h. (top gear)*	12.2 *sec*
to 60 m.p.h.	18·8 *sec*	*30 to 50 m.p.h. (top gear)*	13·0 *sec*
to 70 m.p.h.	26·0 *sec*	*Standing quarter-mile*	21·2 *sec*

Petrol consumption	23-28 *m.p.g.*
Oil consumption	*negligible*
Mileometer reading	31,065
Date first registered	12 *July* 1957

Provided for test by Eaton Motor Company, Eaton Socon, St. Neots, Huntingdonshire. Telephone: Eaton Socon 236

SURPRISING though it may seem, experience of used cars of all types and ages shows that sports cars, which might generally be expected to be in the hands of enthusiasts, are seldom any better preserved than other less specialized production cars. As a rule, however, they are kept in perfect mechanical condition: service is carried out at the proper times, and repairs are made as required. This impression is endorsed by the MGA which is the subject of this test.

Its body appearance and interior condition are satisfactory but by no means outstanding for a car that is only three years old. It is finished in red, and except in places where the hood and sidescreens have made contact with it (and where there are many scratches), the paintwork is unblemished, but has lost its lustre. Mild corrosion beneath the door sills and the front apron has been treated and brush painted. There are some scratches and rust on the chromium, but the majority of the brightwork on the car still shines well. The hood is in good shape, and its ingenious mechanism makes it easy to raise or lower. When the hood is up, it is rigid and quite reasonably free from squeaks and rattles. Unfortunately, the transparent material of the rear and quarter windows in the hood has yellowed and become very scratched. The same is true of the sidescreens, which now look rather shabby although they are still adequate for their purpose.

Inside the car the black leather seats are well worn, but remain comfortable. Slight sag has occurred, with the result that for drivers of average build the scuttle is unduly high, causing some obstruction to forward vision. Considerable evidence of wear is seen on the interior door trim and on the black carpets, particularly on the left side; and a new rubber surround for the gear lever is needed. Red paintwork of the facia panel is unmarked.

While the appearance of the car may thus be a little disappointing, the mechanical condition is above average for the age and mileage. The only fault not connected with appearance is a severe scuttle shake occurring at between about 60 and 75 m.p.h. In the ordinary way one would expect this to be attributable to unbalanced wheels, but those on the MGA are balanced, and fresh chalk marks on the tyres suggest that it was done too recently for any uneven tyre wear to have put them out of balance again.

Apart from this vibration the car runs very smoothly, and feels pleasantly solid. Without dismantling, it is not possible to pinpoint the cause of the trouble, and while the dampers could be at fault—permitting high-frequency wheel bounce—the tautness of the suspension and freedom from pitching point to some other cause. The rack-and-pinion steering is excellent and remains entirely free from lost movement: the car responds precisely to very small movements of the wheel. Steering wheel kick occurs over rough surfaces, and at the higher speeds this is allied to the scuttle-shake already mentioned.

The car is not lacking in performance, and really high-speed cruising is possible with the MGA. At 70 m.p.h. in top gear there is still a fair turn of acceleration in hand, and the car is capable of more than 90 m.p.h. without too much fuss. For sustained cruising it settles down well at around 80 m.p.h. (corresponding to 4,700 r.p.m.). When the car is accelerating hard, there is an angry snarl from the exhaust, but it is otherwise exceptionally quiet, and there is little engine noise even at high revs. Starting is always immediate, provided the choke is used when the engine is cold; and there is no hesitation during the initial running after a cold start. Normal running temperature is reached quickly.

Second gear is rather too low, but the ratios are otherwise well suited to the engine performance. In the indirect ratios the gears emit a pronounced whine; the synchromesh is effective in the upper three gear positions, and the central remote control lever is admirably precise and light to use.

Reference has been made already to the firm, stable ride provided by the suspension, to which is related the excellent road holding so well known on the MGA. Unimpaired on this three-year-old car the balance on cornering is perfect. Powerful and dependable brakes, with which fade did not occur even with repeated hard use during the test, complete the picture of the car's thoroughly sound mechanical state.

All the tools are complete and in good condition—rare on any used car—and it is also to the credit of the car and its one previous owner that all the electrical and mechanical equipment is in sound working order. With the exception of a well-worn Goodyear on the spare wheel, the tyres are all practically new. They are Michelin SDS on the front wheels, and Dunlop Gold Seal at the rear.

The many accessories on the car comprise a powerful fresh-air heater (which unfortunately will not admit cold air); a socket below the facia for an inspection lamp; radiator blind; two wing mirrors; and a luggage grid on the boot. A point worth consideration is that the car is taxed for the year.

Thoroughly enjoyable to drive, this MGA is sound in all important respects. The engine and all mechanical components have stood up to the mileage covered with commendably little deterioration. In relation to used sports car values current at this time of the year, the price of just under £600 is not low.

The seats fold forward to reveal pockets for the sidescreens, and behind the left seat is a catch—not always easy to find—to open the boot lid. A full length tonneau cover and the toolkit are in the luggage locker

S.C.W. Full Road Test

Routine cornering series for 1600 A-type makes interesting contrast with smaller car's behaviour as recorded in SCW June, '59. Torqueier, stiff-coiled 1600 gets around quicker, stays put better in front (pic one)), but wags more energetically (pic two). Stay-put qualities of front end throw more strain onto tail (pic three) as tester Blain accelerates away from telling test corner area. Tyre row? No.

DOUG BLAIN DRIVES THE

MERITORIOUS

Lessons in making a good car better

BELIEVE it or not, the chalk white MGA 1600 roadster that forms the subject of this test came to us here in Sydney through the kindness of a Sydney citizen with the highly unlikely but purely coincidental name of Gordon Wilkins. Not *the* Gordon Wilkins, we hasten to say, but another one.

It all had plenty to do, as always where M.G.s are involved, with William Street dealers Barclay Motors and our old friend Col James.

"Look," we moaned. "This is terrible. BMC promised months ago to give us some time with the very first 1600 to hit these sacred shores and now it's three days to release date and we still don't have a car. Help!"

And it worked (it always does). Col helped like anything (he always has). He offered us a morning with one of his cars just as soon as he had any, and he promised to book us a full test just as soon as his first customer clocked the right miles. As it happened we didn't take the first offer. We had just missed March's issue, and by the time April's was due we would have had time to put a car through the hoops properly anyway.

That's just how it happened. We rang this fellow Wilkins, congratulated him on the similarity of his name to that of our illustrious European Editor (he already knew, bless him), and at once became firm friends. A week or so later we were waving Gordon goodbye as we headed his snappy A-type out of town towards a threatening horizon and the endless rolling bitumen miles of S.C.W.'s test strip. Actually the weather held for our performance sessions at the strip itself and at Foley's Hill, and rain wasn't actually falling when we recorded the photographic cornering sequence you'll find at the head of this page. The

MGA 1600 PUSHROD

rest of the time the clouds leaked sullenly. The MGA, much to our surprise, didn't.

It's not nearly so hard as you might think to tell a 1600 M.G. from a 1500. Exterior changes are small, but they're well spread about and they catch your eye. The new flat-lens turn indicators at the front are bright orange. The new sliding side curtains have a much bigger clear area than the peek-a-boo abominations they replace. The new tail light clusters are noticeably bigger and uglier than before. About the only outside change you don't notice at first is the little plated scroll that now accompanies the octagon badge at the back and the customary bonnetside air outlets.

Noticeable or not, these are all (apart from the curtains) trivial things. The screens themselves work fine. Sliding perspex panes move in properly lined channels to provide either ventilation or reasonably comfortable signalling room without coming at awkward tricks like blowing out at 90 m.p.h. or sieving water or leaking dust or even rattling.

Far more important are one or two changes that go unnoticed at a glance. Details like disc brakes and an extra 82 cubic centimetres of engine, for some. Stiffer front springs and altered shocker settings, for more.

All these combine almost to make the M.G. a different car.

The bigger engine naturally makes more difference than any other single modified item. About the only thing it doesn't do that's altered is make a different noise. Apart from that, the change is there from the moment you turn the key and tug at the traditional dashboard S-button. The engine takes up with a much harder bite, hauling the M.G. upward through an outstandingly punchy torque curve at a rate that is truly surprising for such an ordinary unit in such a relatively heavy little sports car. This extra torque shows up particularly on the longer, faster kind of main road hill. There's just such a pull on the way to our performance strip — a long, steep grind winding out of a deep valley to reach the high coastal plateau country. It's a punchy sports car indeed that will accelerate up there. Photographer Sandford's faithful 1500 A loses speed noticeably not far from the bottom, is obviously working hard to keep from falling away altogether. Not that it feels incapable of getting up; there's just no loud pedal left, that's all. The 1600 was different. It romped up. No, it wouldn't put *on* any speed after we left the valley, but it held all it had with ease.

Another place the extra kick showed up was on Foley's Hill, a near-Sydney 'climb venue at which we usually put in an hour or so of test time. The smaller-engined MGA, when we tried it there nearly a year ago, had managed rather well in first and second gears (first for starting, second for the rest). Even so, it was obvious to all of us who tried the car then that it could do with a bit more low-down beef to haul it efficiently through the first sharp left-hand bend and around the speed-sapping hairpin Elbow near the top. The 1600's performance proved we were right. At Foley's, more than anywhere else, the bigger-engined M.G. felt a different car. It seemed to love every second we spent there, leaping eagerly off the line with a healthy, prolonged wail from the back tyres, soaring quickly up through the rev range in first gear, hitting second with a real big-car bite and from there soaring on up through the hill's four major bends to peak right out in the short, sharp spurt to the top. It seemed right at home in the Elbow. That corner suits MGAs anyway — their special brand of initial understeer keeps the front wheels tucked right in close while the tail looks after itself — but the 1600's extra beef made things even more satisfactory. We ended up turning in times that were only a second or so outside TR and Twin Cam form!

That makes two ways you feel those bonus centimetres. There's another way, and it's with you all the time. The 1600 actually feels more effort-free, more generally within its capabilities than the car it supersedes. That may sound silly. How can a car that's geared the same feel better just because it gets a bit of extra cubage? But it can, and it does. It's the same kind of difference you feel between the way a car sounds when it's doing, say, 4,000 downhill and when it's turning at the same speed up the other side.

In one circumstance the engine is loafing, in the other it's working hard. Of course the variation in the old and the new A-type is nowhere near as great as that, but it is noticeable in the same way. The 1600 will sit on 80 for hours at a stretch and still sound perfectly within its capabilities and even preferences, whereas the smaller car never would. There was always a feeling of strain, however slight.

The '60 car, because of its unchanged gearing, still has the original A's rather high wear factor (meaning that piston speeds generally thought to be critical cut in rather lower than with most sports cars). Yet it feels so happy in the higher speed range that driving pleasure is up 50 per cent.

Did we find any penalties for this bonus beef? Just one. Clutch slip. After suffering the frustration of having to sit by the side of the road right in the middle of an arduous performance session and wait, not once but five times, for the MGA's

MERITORIOUS MGA 1600 PUSHROD

clutch to cool off, we can only say the present unit is inadequate. Admittedly performance recording is hard on a clutch, but our programme is spaced with that in mind — and anyway, other popular sports cars haven't suffered.

Now about the figures themselves. A glance will show you we failed by a point or so to extract three figures, considered by some enthusiasts to be supernaturally significant, from the 1600 A. You will perhaps be aware also that tests in other magazines overseas have made it clear that the M.G. is in fact capable of 100 m.p.h. — just.

We put our car's reticence down to its relatively low mileage (1700). We usually like to wait a little longer before asking a test car to give of its best, but we've explained all that already. The fact that our acceleration times are a shade down on so-far recorded figures from Britain and the U.S. indicates the same thing, borne out by our own conviction that Gordon Wilkins' car will eventually come to rev just a little more freely. Between now and publication date we hope to have another try at a 1600, this time with 1,000 or so more miles up. We'll let you know what happens.

Speed and no brakes is like whisky and no water. Dangerous. We need only say the 1600's new drum-disc layout works the way you would expect it to. Fade is altogether absent (although one back wheel started locking during our habitual 10-stop workout). Braking effort is even and relentless. To apply the clams from 90 m.p.h. is, as owner Wilkins puts it, like driving into a bed of treacle. For the record then, M.G.s now stop. And what a difference it makes to your peace of mind on a long point-to-point haul! You know at once that the layout is different. Pedal pressures are no higher than before, but the second you do push hard you can feel (and hear) the disc pads bite home. This business of pedal pressures is of course quite a contention point in sports car circles just now. All-drum layouts seldom give rise to high pressures, but they do bring fade worries unless the drums themselves are pretty elaborate. All-disc cars usually need high pressures, but they don't fade. The 1600's system could be the answer for all but the fastest cars.

The other factor that makes almost as much difference is the new-found handling we spoke about. The MGA has always been one of the finest-handling of all sports cars, irrespective of price. The drawback before (and you only get to realise it when you have driven the new one) was that it handled almost too well for its own good. So great was the 1500's ability to dig in and hold its ground in corners that it would run out of power long before it would run out of road. That made for quick, unspectacular progress, but it could become a definite take-it-for-granted virtue after a little experience. We recall having commented after driving the M.G. Twin Cam what an entertaining car it was to drive in comparison with the pushrod A. The reason, we think, was that the T-C had (and still has) enough power to make full use of the roadholding it got from the excellent MGA chassis. A hard tap on the loud pedal would send the tail skipping right out. A mere flick of the wheel would rap it back into line again. The same goes, in a less dramatic way, for the 1600.

It now has just enough oomph to break the back wheels out in the indirects on anything approaching a tight turn. Meanwhile stiffer coils have pinner the front even more securely than before, so the car feels safer than ever. The result? Fun, man. Fun!

The new springing makes quite a difference to the car's ride. It is definitely harder than before, obviously, but careful juggling of the shock absorbers has taken out most of the jarring chop that characterised the 1500, even at the higher-than-normal tyre pressures we used for the speed runs. Probably for the same reason, the 1600 feels a whole lot better to steer at top speed. It's not so ready to dart momentarily from your chosen path on contact with a surface irregularity.

We've told you before about the M.G.A's neat control layout, its steering, its gearshift, its seats. This would make the third time, so let's just skip it for now. Nothing is changed — seats still lousy, steering still wonderful, shift still snicky — and nothing we can say will make any difference.

The important thing is that you get the big message, the one about the things that are exclusively the 1600's. Secure in the hope, well-founded or not, that we've got the word across, we'll leave you to ruminate on a fine little sports car made immeasurably finer. ●

New lights serve little purpose, sliding screens are great. MGA was always pretty.

Technical Details

PERFORMANCE

TOP SPEED:
Two-way average ... 96.0
Fastest one way ... 98.7

ACCELERATION:
test limit ... 6000 rpm

Through gears:
0-30 mph ... 4.0 sec
0-40 mph ... 6.8 sec
0-50 mph ... 9.4 sec
0-60 mph ... 12.9 sec
0-70 mph ... 18.4 sec
0-80 mph ... 26.8 sec
0-90 mph ... NA
0-100 mph ... NA
Standing quarter-mile, two way average, 19.6; best one way, 19.4
Speed at end of quarter ... 75 mph
Best ascent Foley's Hill ... 32.9 sec

MAXIMUM SPEED IN GEARS:
(at 6,000 rpm)
I ... 30 mph indicated
II ... 52 mph indicated
III ... 84 mph indicated

SPEEDOMETER ERROR:
30 mph indicated ... actual 28.6 mph
40 mph indicated ... actual 38.3 mph
50 mph indicated ... actual 47.8 mph
60 mph indicated ... actual 57.4 mph
70 mph indicated ... actual 66.7 mph
80 mph indicated ... actual 76.2 mph
90 mph indicated ... actual 84.1 mph
100 mph indicated ... actual — mph

TAPLEY DATA:
Maximum pull in gears:
I ... 600 lb/ton at 20 mph
II ... 450 lb/ton at 35 mph
III ... 350 lb/ton at 40 mph
IV ... 250 lb/ton at 35 mph
Rolling Resistance:
90 mph ... 100 lb/ton
80 mph ... 85 lb/ton
70 mph ... 75 lb/ton
60 mph ... 55 lb/ton
50 mph ... 45 lb/ton
40 mph ... 20 lb/ton
30 mph ... 10 lb/ton

GO-TO-WHOA:
0 60 0 mph ... 16.5 sec.

BRAKING:
10 successive timed stops from 60 mph:
1st stop ... 2.7 sec. 6th stop ... 2.8 sec.
2nd stop ... 2.8 sec. 7th stop ... 2.7 sec.
3rd stop ... 2.6 sec. 8th stop ... 2.6 sec.
4th stop ... 2.8 sec. 9th stop ... 3.2 sec.
5th stop ... 3.0 sec. 10th stop ... 3.0 sec.
Fade: Negligible (r-h rear brake locked intermittently)

CALCULATED DATA:
Weight as tested (two men) ... $20\frac{1}{2}$ cwt.
Max bhp (nett) ... not stated
(gross) ... 79.5
Max torque (nett) ... not stated
(gross, lb ft) ... 87
Lb/hp (gross) ... 28.9

Mph 1,000 rpm, top gear ... 17.0
Mph at 2,500 ft/min piston speed, top gear ... 72.8
Cub cm/lb ft torque (gross only) ... 18.25
Bhp/litre (gross) ... 50.0
Bhp/ton as tested (gross) ... 77.6
Brake lining area/ton as tested ... not applicable
Piston speed at max bhp rpm ... 2,359

SPECIFICATIONS

ENGINE:
Type: 4-cyl in-line, water cooled
Valves: pushrod overhead
Cubic capacity: 1588 cc
Bore and stroke: 75.4 by 88.9 mm
Piston area: 27.7 sq in
Compression ratio: 8.3 to 1
Carburettor: two SU H4
Fuel Pump: SU electric
Max power: 79.5 bhp (gross) at 5600 rpm
Max torque: 87 lb ft (gross) at 3,800 rpm

CHASSIS:
Type: box section steel, scuttle-braced
Wheelbase: 7 ft 10 in
Track: front, 3 ft $11\frac{1}{2}$ in; rear, 4 ft $\frac{3}{4}$ in
Suspension: front, independent, coils and A-arm wishbones; rear, rigid axle, semi-elliptic leaf springs
Shock absorbers: Armstrong hydraulic
Brakes: type, Lockheed disc front, drum rear; operation, hydraulic,

GEAR RATIOS:
I ... 15.652
II ... 9.52
III ... 5.908
IV ... 4.3

GENERAL:
Length overall: 13 ft 0 in
Width: 4 ft $9\frac{1}{4}$ in
Height (to screentop): 4 ft 2 in
Hood erection time (2 men): $1\frac{1}{2}$ min
Test weather: cool, damp, brisk crosswind
All test runs made on dry, bitumen-bound gravel road with driver and one passenger aboard. High-speed runs made with hood and windows in place. All times averaged from several runs in opposite directions, using where applicable a corrected speedometer.

First Love

By COLIN CARTER

THE M.G. has its disciples, and I am among their number. My first experience of the marque was when several years ago I tried to build a racing 'special' from the remains of an ex-Bobbie Baird K.3. The project didn't come off however. I had gone so far as to shorten the wheel-base by cutting quite a whack out of the chassis, but then one day I got out the jolly old slide rule and started working out complicated arithmetical problems not altogether unconnected with b.h.p., b.m.e.p. wheel dias., axle and gear ratios, frontal area, weight, etc., only to find that its estimated maximum speed was 61 m.p.h. ! (I might have been wrong (in fact I undoubtedly was) but I'm glad now that I didn't proceed with the project, for I would probably still be struggling with it, and it would have cost a fortune.

Undeterred, I later, much later, acquired a very special 'TC.' This had been imported from England and I should really have enquired into its past, for it would have been most interesting I think. The complete body was of aluminium, quite beautifully made, and the rest of it was rather out of the ordinary, too. It boasted 16-in. rear wheels, telescopic shockers, and bicycle type wings. The fascia was just about the most impressive I have seen, covered with knobs and dials—for the life of me I can't remember what they were all for. There were lots of alloy bits on the engine but it hadn't much poke until it had a small fortune spent on it, and there were twin electric S.U. pumps and a subsidiary petrol tank under the bonnet, etc. The brake drums were of beautiful steel, chrome plated, and someone once estimated they cost £40 each. So it was very much "one off."

Anyhow it provided me with a splendid amount of fun, and amongst other things completed the Ulster Trophy at Dundrod at a not disreputable speed, doing 90 down the straight in the process, as well as securing four 4th places at Kirkistown (including the Baird Memorial Trophy). Those were the days of consistent handicapping! But seriously though, an MG.A would have been hard pushed to equal its lap times, although subsequently Bill Patterson's 'TC' and Billy Lacy's 'TD' improved on them quite substantially.

However, the partnership eventually came to an end when during a really arduous snowy winter I could stand the lack of a heater and the highly ineffectual weather protection no longer. The driving position too got me down, for there was nowhere to rest one's left foot, and the bucket seats were exceedingly uncomfortable. The little car, although frequently revved over 6,000, never missed a beat, the only mishap being when a wheel parted company one day after the axle snapped. The crackle of its straight-through exhaust pipe when racing will long linger with me, as also will its prodigious thirst. It was tuned for me by Billy Moore, who looked after Groves' very quick 'TC' so successfully when racing started up again in Ulster after the war. Groves, incidentally, came into the pits after a race at Newtownards airfield one day and within minutes died from a heart attack. It was after this tragedy, I believe, that the R.A.C. insisted that everyone who races must pass a strict medical check each year.

HOWEVER, as usual I am disgressing, for the main topic of this article is supposed to be the MG.A Fixed-Head Coupé I acquired recently. Now the MG.A has of course been on the market for some considerable time, nevertheless the Editor has prevailed upon me to voice my purely personal opinions of it, for what they're worth. So here goes.

The body is aerodynamic, the closed version more so than the open. I think the lines are pleasing, except perhaps for the tail, which is not a howling success. It slopes away to such an extent that there is precious little room in the boot — that's why so many of the models around are fitted with luggage grids. Also the rear number plate sticks up like a sore thumb when it could quite easily have been blended into the body. The car is a strict two-seater and at first glance looks cramped, largely because of the large gearbox mound and the protrusion of half the spare wheel into the space behind the seats. In fact it isn't — once you are in. I say once you are in because it isn't as easy to get into or out of as it might be. Of course it isn't so bad if one adopts the accepted procedure for getting into any sports car (left foot in onto clutch, sit on seat, swing right leg in) vice versa for the passenger, except don't be surprised if you can't find a clutch pedal. My fair lady is inclined to show an interesting expanse of shapely leg, but then that is surely one of the joys of owning a sports car.

Inside there is ample room, not too much and not too little, with the result that the car seems to fit like a glove, and one feels very much a part of it. One sits very low in beautiful leather bucket seats, fully adjustable fore and aft. The first time I sat in one, at the Glasgow Motor Show a couple of years ago, I found that the top of the windscreen was just at eye-level, but this is not the case with the fixed-head coupé. The driving position is distinctly upright, and while this keeps one alert, it does become rather tiresome on long journeys. The protagonists of the straight arm driving stance will not be amused, for even in a car fitted with a telescopic adjustable steering column, it is not possible to practice this method. However, it is no hardship, for the steering is very precise and high geared, so that as soon as one gets acclimatized, one doesn't mind being rather closer to the wheel than is customary.

Visibility through the panoramic laminated glass windscreen is excellent, and there is no distortion. However, on a wet day the lines of the car are such that all the muck flying about deposits itself on the screen, particularly round the sides where the screen wipers won't reach. The side windows are wind-up and the rear window is of the wrap round variety (toughened glass). All round, visibility is first-class. In front of the driver is a most impressive array of instruments and knobs, the positioning of which has obviously been thoughtfully planned.

The horn button however retains its traditional but ridiculous place in the middle of the dash which, incidentally, on the closed version, is covered in p.v.c. material. By the driver's left leg is that excellent M.G. fly-off handbrake, and in just the right place, a diminutive and delightful little gear lever.

Behind the seat is a parcel shelf and on each side of the scuttle is a small but useful cubby hole. Personally, I would prefer pockets in the doors (as in the open version) since this also gives more elbow room.

B.M.C. have a good range of colour schemes. My car was bought off the peg, so to speak and is bright red, with red trim and grey carpets. However, if I'd had a choice, I would have plumped for Old English White with red trim. The finish both inside and out is excellent and surpassed my expectations, as did the quality of the fittings. By contrast to the interior, the paint on the engine has been slapped on regardless. I have somewhat improved its appearance by fitting a finned alloy rocker cover, which also serves the purpose of quietening the tappet noise. The engine compartment is large and accessible, but I swear many loud oaths when trying to get at the points, for the distributor is placed in a ludicrous, inaccessible position.

THE fellow who decided where to put the batteries should be put in a cell (sorry can't help it) because to get at them, one has to remove the tool roll and spare wheel from the boot, and then unscrew two so-called quick release screws holding down a panel behind the seats, whereupon they expose themselves, as does the electric S.U. fuel pump. But it's a decidedly long and awkward operation to top up the batteries and one which garages are inclined to overlook, by-accident-on-purpose of course. The boot itself is not fitted with a carpet, and rain some-

MGA/TR3 POCKET MATCH

PERFORMANCE (Actual)

Accel'n 0—30	5 secs. (3.6)
,, 0—50	10.8 secs. (7.5)
,, 0—60	15.7 secs. (10.8)
,, 10—30	8.1 secs (6.2)
,, 20—40	7.9 secs (5.7)
,, 30—50	8.1 secs. (6)
Standing ¼ Mile	19.8 secs (18.1)
Max. Grad. (Top)	10.7 (8.4)
,, ,, (3rd or Inter)	7.3 (6.2)
Max. Speed (Top)	95 m.p.h. (105)
,, ,, (3rd or Inter)	68 m.p.h. (76)

DIMENSIONS

Overall Length	156″ (151)
,, Height	50″ (46)
,, Width	58″ (55)
Wheel Base	94″ (88)
Track	47″ (45)
Hip Room	46″ (44)
Turning Circle	28′ (35)
Ground Clearance	6″ (6)
Kerb Weight	17.7 cwt. (19)
Tyre Size	5.60 × 15 (5.50 × 15)
Steering (L. to L.)	2⅔ Turns (2⅛)
Weight dist. (2 up)	52%F. (53)

PETROL CONSUMPTION

At steady 30 m.p.h.	44 m.p.g. (43.5)
At steady 40 m.p.h.	47 m.p.g. (41.5)
At steady 50 m.p.h.	43.2 m.p.g. (38)
Tank Capacity	10 galls. (12½)

Irish Basic Price	£945 (895)
English Basic Price	£663 (699)
Annual Tax	£22 (30)
Wire Wheels	£35 (35)
Fixed Head	£75 (75)
Overdrive	No (£75)
Disc Brakes	No (Incl.)
Cubic Capacity	1,489 c.c. (1,991)
Bore	73 m.m. (83)
Stroke	89 m.m. (92)
Comp. Ratio	8.3 (8.5)
Gear Ratios (Top)	4.3 (3.7)
,, ,, (3rd)	5.9 (4.9)
,, ,, (2nd)	9.5 (7.4)
,, ,, (1st)	15.7 (12.5)

Insurance by quotation only

PERFORMANCE (Theory)

Brake H.P.	72 (100)
@ r.p.m.	5,500 (5,000)
Top Gear M.P.H. at 1,000 r.p.m.	17 (20)
Top gear m.p.h. at 1,000 f/m piston speed	29.12 (35)
Piston Area Per Ton (Sq. Ins.)	29.4 (35.3)
B.H.P. per Sq. in. Piston Area	2.77 (2.98)
Lbs. per c.c.	1.33 (1.06)
B.M.E.P. and	130 p.s.i. (145)
Maximum Torque (lbs. ft.)	77.4 (117)
at r.p.m.	3,500 (3,000)
Litres per Ton-Mile	3,070 (3,310)
B.H.P. per Ton	81 (105)
Brake Surface Area (sq. ins.)	220 (370)

how finds its way in whenever its wet. As for the tools, the jack is an abomination, being one of those wind up lever variety, popular in the early part of the century.

The chassis is immensely strong and rigid, which probably accounts for the quite substantial weight of the car. I can't vouch for the rigidity of the open version but my fixed-head model is absolutely free of rattles and scuttle shake.

On the road one's first impression is of how easy the car is to drive. The steering is precise and delightful, the gear lever moves only about two inches, and the brakes are reassuringly powerful. The M.G. gearbox is famous, and that on the MG.A is every bit as good as its predecessors, giving 25 m.p.h. in first, 45 in second, and about 73 in third. Maximum speed is supposed to be about 102, slightly more than the open version because of better streamlining and despite a little extra weight. A surprise was the smooth and flexible top gear.

The roadholding is first-class. Of course the back breaks away if provoked but this is easily corrected. The springs wind up when accelerating hard, and the nose is inclined to dip under braking.

Suspension is firm but not unduly so, and the degree of roll is only moderate.

Tyres, by the way, are Dunlop Gold Seal and not Roadspeeds. The brakes are powerful yet light to operate and after quite a few moderately fast laps at Kirkistown, they showed little tendency to fade. However, on wet days water seems to seep in to the drums and their performance becomes erratic until they have dried out. The headlamps are powerful and quite adequate for fast motoring at night. Heating and demisting is well looked after by the (optional extra) Smith's heater—to get maximum effect though one has to switch on the booster fan which is rather noisy. No ashtray is fitted unless specified when ordering the car.

Although the exhaust is pleasantly quiet, the engine I think can be severely criticized on the grounds of noise. The tappets tap like mad when accelerating hard in the intermediates, and there is also that disconcerting hissing noise which comes from the carburettor intakes, despite the fitting of fair size pancake air filters. All this noise permeates into the interior of the car, even though the bulkhead is lined with half-inch sorbo rubber. The aforementioned alloy rocker cover does something to alleviate tappet noise, but I am seriously considering insulating the underneath of the bonnet lid. Wind noise mercifully is virtually non-existent.

As regards the all-important question of insurance, the MG.A is comparatively easy to insure (mine costs £35 per annum full comprehensive, but with £20 damage excess). I consider this excellent, since with some sports cars I could mention, it is virtually impossible to get anything more than third party cover, less passenger and personal liability, and this costs the heck of a lot!

I wouldn't like anyone to think I don't like the MG.A, for I do, immensely. The 1½ litre B.M.C. engine is noisy, and its acceleration leaves a lot to be desired, as does its fuel consumption. A spokesman for M.G.s has said that even driven flat out, an MG.A should not do less than 28 m.p.g. All I know is that on a run to Dublin I got only 25 m.p.g. and I wasn't driving all that flat out! However, in fairness I should say that it had only 2,600 miles on the clock at the time, and matters will probably improve considerably — they'd better! Also the MG.A fixed-head coupé is by no means a lightweight, and kick-you-in-the-back acceleration cannot really be expected. However, performance is just about adequate, especially bearing in mind the growing congestion on our roads.

What 'sold' the car to me however was not only its excellent finish, and luxurious interior, but its impeccable handling. The MG.A is really a joy to drive, since it handles in the true tradition of the thoroughbred. There are no vices and one feels completely safe at all times.

If you want a bit more 'poke,' M.G. market a range of tuning equipment — special heads with bigger valves, camshafts, etc., or there is the new Twin Cam M.G., costing an extra £180 (£300 altogether in the U.K. with purchase tax) fitted with disc brakes all round.

My personal feeling about the Twin Cam M.G. is that such a high revving highly stressed engine is bound to be noisy and hard on juice. From all accounts, it has not so far been an outstanding success and performance has not come up to expectations. It does seem strange that after quite a few years development, M.G.s have still not perfected the twin overhead camshaft cylinder head.

M.G.s hold several speed records of over 200 m.p.h. with basically B.M.C. 1½ litre engines, and I can't for the life of me understand why they can't make their production cars go quicker. The MG.A engine develops 72 b.h.p. at 5,500 r.p.m., and it seems to me a bit like flogging a dead horse to try and extract substantially more power from it. Consequently I'd like to see M.G.s fitting a bigger engine. If I say more they might send someone over to confiscate my nice little coupé, so I had better make a smart get-away while the going's good. ■

Dudley Colley (R.I.A.C.) presenting the Hewison Trophy to Harry Reardon (Chairman, M.G. Club) on behalf of the winning team (Cecil Vard, Kevin Sherry and Jimmy Millard).

MG-A 1600 MK II

Made in Abingdon on Thames by water sprites

MOST SPORTS CAR enthusiasts have an impression that MG doesn't change models very often. We had the same feeling until the new 1600 Mark II version came along and we began checking back. Actually, this new car is the ninth model in the past 14 years. In case you've forgotten, here is the list:

Year	Model	Remarks	Date tested
1947	TC	1250 cc, 54.4 bhp	Oct. 1956
1950	TD	1250 cc, first i.f.s.	Apr. 1951
1953	TD-Mk II	60 bhp option	Feb. 1953
1954	TF	1250 cc, 60 bhp	March 1954
1954	TF-1500	1466 cc, 65 bhp	Dec. 1954
1955	A	1489 cc, 68/72 bhp	Dec. 1955
1958	A-TC	twin-cam, 1588-cc	Nov. 1958
1959	A-1600	1588 cc, 79.5 bhp	Oct. 1959
1961	A-Mk II	1624 cc, 90 bhp	

Of course, these nine models involve only four bodies, and the new Mark II version uses the same body as when the first A-type was introduced late in 1955. Identification at the front is easy, as the grille bars are now indented or recessed a little over 2 in. at the bottom. At the rear, new taillights provide easy identification.

The principal mechanical changes are a larger and more powerful engine and a drop in axle ratio from 4.30 to 4.10. The cylinder bore has been increased by a thirty-second of an inch, bringing it up to the nice, round figure of 3.00 in. The stroke remains 3.5 in., so the new displacement is 99.086 cu in., or 1624.3 cc. The unit's output is 90 bhp, an increase of 13%, most of which comes from a change in compression ratio; raised from 8.3 to 8.9:1 and requiring premium fuel. The new torque figure was not available to us, but we estimate it to be 100 lb-ft at 3500 rpm.

The drop in axle ratio, though not terribly significant, still means 4.5% fewer revolutions per mile, the exact figures being 3480 on the previous model and 3320 on the Mark II.

Our test car had 4 miles on the odometer when we took it over from well-known MG exponent Gus Ehrman, now manager of Hambro's Los Angeles division. After 1000 miles and a check-up, we took it directly to the test strip for the acceleration tests.

As would be expected, the extra "inches" more than offset the lowered axle ratio; performance figures average about 5% better than we recorded for the MG-A 1600 in October of 1959. Likewise, the Tapley pull readings show a similar improvement, indicative of faster acceleration in each gear as well as improved hill-climbing powers. The drag factor of combined wind and rolling resistance hasn't changed, so the top speed should be well over an honest 100 mph. We did not try a timed high speed run, because we felt that sustained full throttle would be asking too much from an engine with barely 1000 miles of running on it. However, there is no doubt that the extra power and the new gear ratio, which is more favorable than before for best possible top speed, should produce an honest 105 mph at 5700-5800 rpm, depending on tire pressure and the expansion factor. Incidentally, the speedometer error proved to be modest, with the greatest optimism at 60 mph (5%). Higher speeds showed less error; an indicated 90 mph being a true 87.0, for example.

Fuel consumption is about the same as before, despite the increased power and performance. In fact, under certain circumstances it is slightly improved; we averaged 30.8 mpg during the break-in, in which the last 500 miles were run at 65-75 mph much of the time.

During the past 12 years there has always been an MG on the R&T staff, sometimes as many as three. Therefore we feel well qualified to point out that, though the Austin-Healey Sprite is lower priced, the MG remains our choice as the best all-around sports car for the money and one particularly well suited for this market, primarily because both its size and performance are well above the miniature or minimum category.

This Mark II version, though perhaps not as exciting as a completely new model, is a very definite improvement over any previous MG and retains all the well known virtues of the marque.

Among these virtues, good handling and steering rank first. This is not saying that the MG is the best cornering sports car in the world, or that it has perfect steering. But the car has no vices, and a novice or a veteran can get into the MG and put it through its paces without getting into trouble. The steering is very nearly neutral, yet an oversteer-tail-out attitude can be provoked and held with no great worry over "losing" the rear end and spinning out. The steering may feel strange at first because it's so unlike what you're used to. The rack and pinion has a slight frictional effect and, more important, absolutely no play or back-lash. There's no need to move the steering wheel back and forth a few degrees to hold a straight line down the highway. You just set the wheel where you want it and move it occasionally in the direction you want, with no see-sawing. Parking effort is moderate (perhaps a little heavy for the ladies) and the turning circle isn't too good for a 94-in. wheelbase. There is occasional road-shock transmission to the rim but almost no cowl shake, thanks to a very well designed separate frame and body structure.

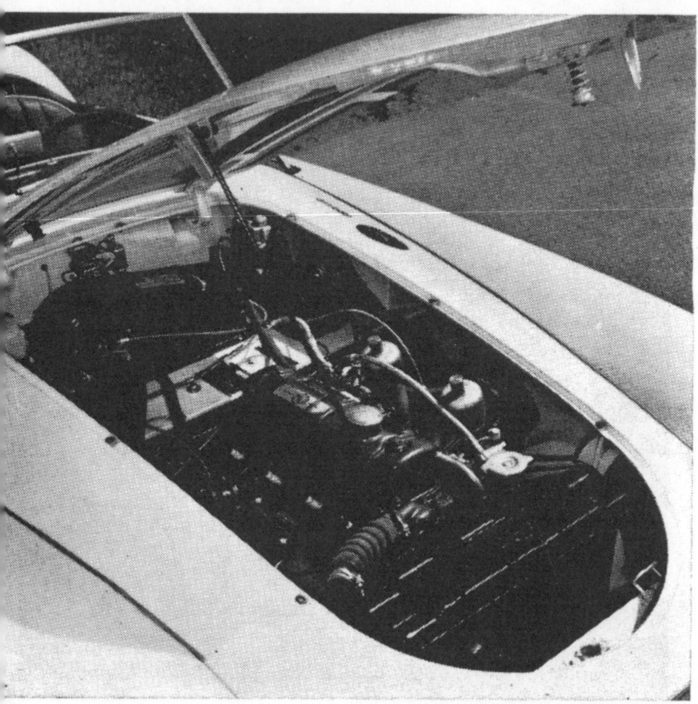

The riding qualities of the MG haven't changed by any noticeable amount since i.f.s. (independent front suspension) was adopted in 1950. Here we feel some criticism is warranted, as most other cars have shown some gradual improvement over the past 11 years. In other words, the MG of 1950 was one of the best riding sports cars on the market; today it ranks among the poorest, excluding the pure competition machines, which are invariably very harsh indeed. A considerable improvement in ride can be had by putting the tires at the rather low recommended pressures (17 to 20 psi), but we much preferred 5 psi more than this for our own driving, as well as for the good of the tires.

Disc brakes in front, drums at the rear were made standard equipment with the previous model and are continued without change. No booster is fitted, nor is one needed. In driving the car no one would notice anything different or unusual about the brakes, and though the disc units are slightly heavier than drums, they certainly do avoid any sign of fade.

In piling up miles on the Mark II, we got an impression that the engine isn't quite as smooth or as quiet as before. Certainly, a higher compression ratio often means rougher running, but we believe most of our impression was caused by a fairly loud exhaust note. The

engine has no noticeable vibration period but, as with any four, there is a trace of rumble when decelerating. At low rpm the engine feels as though it's being abused, yet it actually will lug in 4th gear at 1000 rpm and full throttle gives smooth, reaction-free response. You might say, as a slight exaggeration, that the unit is a small tractor engine in this respect. At the other end of the scale, the tachometer has a yellow zone from 5500 to 6000 rpm, with red to 7000. The unit goes readily to 6000 rpm, but no one in his right mind would ever go beyond this, even momentarily.

The transmission ratios are unchanged and, as with earlier models, the synchromesh on 2nd, 3rd and 4th is very positive and effective. First gear is somewhat noisy, but starts can be effected easily in 2nd if the car is just rolling. We found the shift control extremely stiff and considered installing an extension lever to obviate sore palms during the break-in.

A perennial complaint with the MG is still with us—insufficient room for the feet. A new dimmer switch location is a real improvement, but 10.5 in. between the switch and the accelerator (measured just under the two pedals) are not enough, unless you wear ballet slippers. A pull-type starter switch is also an anachronism that can only lead to broken ignition keys when the car is left in a parking lot.

The revised instrument panel is very businesslike, and the cowl area under the windshield is now covered with black leatherette to avoid reflections. The bucket seats are unchanged, and are still rather upright and a little too close to the steering wheel for most drivers, regardless of their height. Other complaints included no ashtray, no glove box, no ventilation during a rain storm and almost no luggage space.

But, despite these criticisms, the MG remains one of the most desirable sports cars on the market. It is big enough to avoid being called a toy, it is nice looking without being flashy, it steers and handles impeccably, it performs extremely well, and its reputation for durability and stamina is widely acclaimed by many thousands of satisfied owners. In our opinion, this is truly the "universal" sports car

ROAD TEST
MG-A MK II

DIMENSIONS

Wheelbase, in.	94.0
Tread, f and r	47.5/48.8
Over-all length, in	156
width	58
height	50
equivalent vol, cu ft	262
Frontal area, sq ft	16.1
Ground clearance, in	6.0
Steering ratio, o/a	n.a.
turns, lock to lock	2.7
turning circle, ft	31.3
Hip room, front	48
Hip room, rear	n.a.
Pedal to seat back, max	42
Floor to ground	9.0

CALCULATED DATA

Lb/hp (test wt)	27.1
Cu ft/ton mile	81.5
Mph/1000 rpm (4th)	18.1
Engine revs/mile	3320
Piston travel, ft/mile	1935
Rpm @ 2500 ft/min	4290
equivalent mph	77.5
R&T wear index	64.2

SPECIFICATIONS

List price	$2485
Curb weight, lb	2050
Test weight	2340
distribution, %	52/48
Tire size	5.60-15
Brake swept area	350
Engine type	4 cyl, ohv
Bore & stroke	3.0 x 3.5
Displacement, cc	1624
cu in	99.1
Compression ratio	8.90
Bhp @ rpm	90 @ 5500
equivalent mph	99.5
Torque, lb-ft (est)	100 @ 3500
equivalent mph	63.3

GEAR RATIOS

4th (1.00)	4.10
3rd (1.37)	5.63
2nd (2.21)	9.08
1st (3.64)	14.9

SPEEDOMETER ERROR

30 mph	actual, 28.5
60 mph	57.0

PERFORMANCE

Top speed (5800), mph	105
best timed run	n.a.
3rd (6000)	79
2nd (6000)	49
1st (6000)	29

FUEL CONSUMPTION

Normal range, mpg	25/31

ACCELERATION

0-30 mph, sec	4.0
0-40	6.0
0-50	9.3
0-60	12.8
0-70	18.0
0-80	25.4
0-100	
Standing ¼ mile	18.7
speed at end	71

TAPLEY DATA

4th, lb/ton @ mph	200 @ 50
3rd	290 @ 44
2nd	430 @ 35
Total drag at 60 mph, lb	112

ENGINE SPEED IN GEARS

ACCELERATION & COASTING

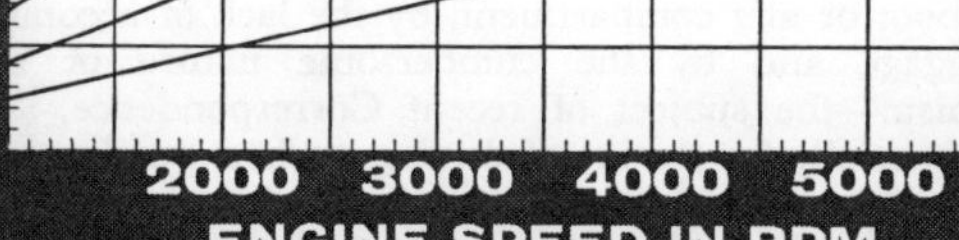

90 80 70 60 50 40 30 20 10

4th
3rd
2nd
1st
R 1 2 3 4
SS¼

5 10 15 20 25 30 35 40 45

ELAPSED TIME IN SECONDS

USED CARS on the Road

No. 196 1960 M.G. MGA 1600

PRICE: Secondhand £625; New—Basic £663, with tax £940

Petrol consumption 26-32 m.p.g. *Date first registered 28 June 1960*
Oil consumption negligible *Mileometer reading 15,942*

ON the numerous occasions when cars offered by dealers in the north have been assessed in this feature they have always seemed to be realistically and fairly priced. With this M.G. MGA, only just over two years old, the same is true again, and the price represents more than £150 depreciation per annum. At the same time, the car is as sound as naturally is to be expected after such a short life, and at the small mileage stated above—guaranteed by the vendors to be genuine.

Slightly better performance is indicated by the acceleration figures, when compared with those of the model when new; indeed, the engine is evidently just in its prime—fully loosened up, yet with insufficient use behind it so far to cause any notable wear. Starting is good, with little need for the choke even for the first start of the day, and the engine pulls smoothly and vigorously throughout its wide rev range. A harsh and somewhat exhilarating snarl of exhaust is heard when wide throttle openings and high revs are used.

Clutch take-up is smooth, and not even full-power gear changes provoke any clutch spin. The gear change is pleasantly rigid and precise in its movement, without being stiff, as was the case when we tested the new car, showing the benefit of use. Fully effective synchromesh remains on the three upper ratios, but the indirect gears are somewhat noisy.

Among the more delightful aspects of the MGA, which encourage one to forgive the model's shortcomings in other directions, are the splendid accuracy of its steering, and certain and predictable handling characteristics. None of these has deteriorated in any detectable way, and the car feels agreeably taut and rigid. The ride is firm without being harsh, and again in this respect the MGA gives the impression of having improved with time and mileage; no doubt these have taken the initial stiffness out of the suspension.

On the mechanical side, only the brakes show signs of deterioration. There is some roughness, in hard braking just before the car comes to rest, and pedal travel is rather more than is normally associated with front disc brakes. Fully adequate braking is still available, however, without need for heavy pedal pressure and the fly-off handbrake holds the car securely on a steep gradient.

Rather more deterioration is evident in the appearance of the car, and although Portland Autos appear to have made a good job of preparing the MGA for sale, there is no doubt at all that the car has been well used. Marking of the hood material and discoloration of the rear and quarter windows in the hood detract from the appearance when the car is closed, but in the open condition, the MGA retains its original smartness. The exterior is finished in bright red, and the paintwork is free from chips and scratches. The chromium is fair.

Inside the car, there is some wear on the carpets, and considerable creasing of both bucket seats suggests that a lot of the mileage has been covered "two-up." The seats remain comfortable and give good support, but the cushion of the passenger seat tends to slip out of its mounting. The interior painted metal facia and p.v.c. door trim are sound. Quite a good seal is made by the sidescreens, which on this later model of the MGA have sliding windows.

An H.M.V. radio, with large speaker concealed behind the facia grille, has been added to this used MGA. The other accessories are the standard fresh-air heater, which admits some hot air even when turned off, wheel trims, a parking light, and a luggage grid whose chrome has rusted

All the electrical equipment, including the comprehensive array of instruments, is in sound working condition. Nearly new Michelin X tyres are on the fitted wheels; and the spare has one of the original Dunlop tyres, about a third worn. Vibration above 70 m.p.h. indicates the need for the wheels to be balanced. Portland Autos state that this is to be done before the car is sold. The owner's replacement of the tyres apparently was from choice, and not because the old covers were worn out. Stowed at the back of the luggage locker, whose release catch is concealed behind the passenger seat, is the toolkit. Still practically complete, it includes a screw jack and a wheelbrace.

In many ways, the MGA is a particularly impracticable car by design, with such shortcomings as the inability to lock the doors, boot or any compartment, by the lack of accommodation for luggage and by the cumbersome nature of the hood mechanism—the subject of recent Correspondence. In other ways, especially for the joy of driving it when weather conditions allow it to be open, and for its safe handling characteristics, it is very attractive. Particularly remembered is the ease with which it was held to a dead straight course at speed, on a day when many other cars were wallowing about in a strong wind.

PERFORMANCE CHECK

(Figures in brackets are those of the model when tested new, 9 October 1959)

0 to 30 m.p.h	4·4 sec	(4·6)	0 to 90 m.p.h.	32·8 sec (36·4)
0 to 50 m.p.h.	9·2 sec	(10·3)		
0 to 60 m.p h.	12·8 sec	(14·2)	Standing quarter-mile	19·1 sec (19·3)
0 to 70 m.p.h.	16·4 sec	(18·5)	20 to 40 m.p.h. (top gear)	9·2 sec (11·0)
0 to 80 m.p.h.	23·7 sec	(26·6)	30 to 50 m.p.h. (top gear)	8·5 sec (10·9)

Car being sold by Portland Autos (Sheffield) Ltd., 64-84 West Bar, Sheffield, 3. Telephone: Sheffield 21186-7.

Road Research Report: MGA 1600 Mark II

► The MG engineering division of the British Motor Corporation received a directive last year that the MGA was to be improved once again. Top speed was to be raised "comfortably clear of 100 mph," cruising speed was to be raised appreciably and these two performance aims were to be met with no major change in engine design or body sheet metal. The result is the MGA 1600 Mark II – mission accomplished!

The Mark II scores heavily in providing the wanted power and speed without extensive changes in a basically excellent design. The top speed of the roadster in street trim is about 105 mph and a 90-mph cruising speed is accomplished without undue effort. Despite the performance gains, the result of using a 1622 cc, 90-bhp engine and a 4.1 to one rear axle ratio, the price of the Mark II is only $5 more than that of the 1600 which it replaces. Without a doubt it's the best MG yet; as one enthusiast commented, ". . . it's the most fun I've had driving an MG since my TC." After more than 3000 miles of Road Researching the car we can only say we agree emphatically.

Looking only slightly different from its predecessors, the Mark II features a "pre-bashed" grille in which the applique grille-surround is retained in outside shape and size but with curved inner bars which are more nearly vertical. The resulting platform should be a likely place for mounting driving lights. The rear fender line is denuded of the bulky 1600 taillights and horizontal units are mounted inboard below the trunk lid. The dashboard now has the leatherette covering and bright metal edging of the coupes and an anti-reflective leatherette cowl covering. On former models the dash was painted and with some body colors, notably white, there appeared to be a "mirage" floating at eye level as the cowl reflected in the windshield.

One thing that fortunately has not changed is the almost impeccable roadholding and handling of the MGA. With added useful power, the car's maximum in a given corner is up-rated yet the steering, suspension and brakes are still more than adequate to cope with the toughest situations.

THE FIRST OF THE MGAS

While it would be interesting and enlightening to trace the development of the make from the first MG (a hopped-up Morris Cowley) built in 1923 by the late Cecil Kimber of Morris Garages (from which the name was taken), it would fill volumes . . . and already has. More to the point is the story of the MGA series cars. These represented a completed break with past MG traditions in design if not concept. Perhaps that's why the "A" suffix was chosen, although some claim it's because the engine used is directly related to Austin power units. MG fell heir to this bit of machinery after the British Motor Corporation was formed in 1952 through the merger of Morris Motors and Austin of England.

The first of the MGAs was the 1500, built between 1955 and 1958. The earliest of these (recognizable by the single rear window) arrived toward the end of 1955. Altogether 58,750 of these cars were built. With its 68-bhp engine the MGA opened new experiences in speed, acceleration and roadholding to MG veterans and novices alike. However, it was realized the product could be improved and minor but significant changes were made, beginning with the mid-1957 cars. These included a change in engine type at car number 61504 when the 15GB engine was replaced by the 15GD.

The horsepower had already been upped to 72 when, earlier, the compression rings, the oil rings and the valve guides were changed to reduce oil consumption, a full-flow oil filter was specified and a revised distributor (Lucas DM2 "pre-tilt") was installed. This latter item featured easier point adjustment. In addition, the front spring coils were made of heavier-diameter wire for better control and the shock absorber valving was stiffened. Heavier clutch pressure plate springs were introduced at engine number 16225 and the starter and generator were changed at car number 487, the latter being the "windowless yoke" type which helped keep dirt and moisture out, but which required almost complete disassembly for checking the brushes about every 12,000 miles. The improved MGA 1500 was recognizable externally by the three-piece rear window which afforded better top-up vision, and by better-marked instruments.

ENTER THE 1600

The major step was the MGA 1600, the first of 31,086 built in 1959-1960. Externally the only differences from the 1500s were larger flat-lensed sidelights and revamped taillights in which the turn signal was placed above the taillight/brake unit. A bit of script was added to the sides of the hood and trunk lid stating the car was a 1600, and the disc wheels were changed to accommodate the new disc brakes used on the front wheels.

The only cockpit changes were the adoption of sliding plastic side curtains in lieu of the lift-the-flap type of the 1500, the addition of a third top hold-down at the center of the windshield, added weatherproofing under the windshield, and the use of a flap to fasten the top's side curtain openings to the top framework. The simpler-fastening tonneau cover (with its reduced number of fasteners) was retained from the latest 1500s.

The 3.5-inch stroke was unchanged, but the bore was increased from 2.875 to 2.968 inches. The engine type designation was now 16GA as the displacement was boosted from 1489 cc (90.88 cubic inches) to 1588 cc (96.9 cubic inches). The power was increased from 72 bhp at 5500 rpm to 78 at 5500 and torque figures went from 77.4 pound-feet at 3500 rpm to 87 at 3800. The 8.3 to one compression ratio was unchanged but the connecting rod bearings were narrowed slightly as the crankshaft web was stiffened for the greater power. Valve lift was decreased slightly and the length of the exhaust valve guide was increased while its widened inside diameter was kept from late 1500 cc cars when the valve stem clearance specification was changed. The crankshaft, piston, valve spring and camshaft specs were unchanged. The oil pump was modified as to specification but not design with the result that the minimum and maximum hot oil pressure figures were reduced from 30-80 pounds per square inch to 15-50. Needles in the H4 1½-inch SU carburetors were changed from GS to No. 6. Ignition timing was changed from 7° BTDC to 6° BTDC.

The ten-inch-diameter front drum brakes were scrapped in favor of 11-inch discs, still using a Lockheed system. The brake/clutch master cylinder was changed for easier filling and greater capacity and the specified brake lining was changed from Ferodo DM12 to DON24. Oil capacity of the rear axle was cut from 3.25 U.S. pints to 2.4 pints and the modified rear axle outer seal of late 1500 cars was kept to reduce chances of leakage.

The factory-listed curb weight increased from 1988 pounds to 2016 and the turning circle increased from 28 feet to 30.6 feet, to the chagrin of gymkhana drivers.

STEADY DEVELOPMENT

Other miscellaneous running changes were incorporated in 1500 and 1600 MGAs at various times. These included a timing chain tensioner starting with engine 259. At engine 3289 the transmission mounting plate was machined differently to keep any engine oil, escaping through the rear bearing seal, from entering the clutch. Tappets and pushrods, having increased spherical diameter on the ball end of the pushrods and the seats of the tappets, were introduced at engine 5504. At engine 5682 a chrome top ring was introduced for longer life and less oil consumption. Other changes included a modified crankshaft oil return thread starting with engine 15GB/6615, modified pistons and stronger wrist pins starting at engine 15GB/U/H38484. These are interchangeable with older types but only as complete sets.

In line with this recommendation from MG, it might be well to clarify the difference between the 15GB and 15GD (1500) engines from which the 16GA (1600) engine was derived. The change to the 15GD engine was at car number 61504 although some earlier ones had this engine. It differs in the placement of the starter higher on the transmission mounting plate as BMC standardized starter location. Modifications were also made to the transmission itself, the right-hand toeboard, the transmission cover and the drive shaft. As a result, if you have an earlier 1500 MGA (15GB block) and would like to install a later type (15GD) or a 1600 power plant (16GA), the factory advises against it, although by using a suitable adaptor plate it can be done. The main gearbox change, internally, was the switch to a different third motion shaft and drive shaft so that the forward universal joint comes in front of the sliding splines which formerly were in the transmission extension itself. This arrangement is in line with common BMC practice.

There were changes in the water pump to use a one-piece bearing and starting with car No. 24954 an additional accelerator return spring was introduced. Later 1500 cc cars used a modified clutch release lever and an early change was the use of left-hand thread on the left-hand rear axle hub nuts with right-hand threads on the other side.

Although this recital of specifications may be pedantic, it's done with good reason: to underscore the MG policy of *constant* improvement, to demonstrate that while the various MGAs may appear only slightly different they are in fact quite changed from former cars, and to assure readers that the Mark II is new, but not *that* new.

IMPROVING THE BREED

What's been done in producing the Mark II parallels what was accomplished with the 1500 when the 1600 was devised. The car as such will make current MG drivers feel right at home, yet they will enjoy the results of engineering refinements. While the original change to the 1600 did not increase top speed appreciably compared to the 1500, it did improve acceleration. The time to 70 mph was cut from 19.3 to 17.8 seconds. With the Mark II acceleration is even guttier, cruising speed is raised significantly and top speed is well within the cited goals. All this is accomplished with engine changes, the only other mechanical change being the switch to the 4.1 to one rear end ratio from the 4.3 cogs in the 1500 and 1600s. This coupled with the ten percent displacement increase and the 19 percent power boost gives the new MGA a true deep-breathing, seven-league-boots *Continued on page* 142

Checking the level of the two six-volt batteries behind the seats is a tedious but essential job, requiring removal of the parcel platform.

The Mark II's tool kit contains fewer wrenches and such than former models but features a ratchet jack, improved lug wrench and hub cap puller.

The Mark II's grille retains a family resemblance to earlier models by using the traditional octagon and shape but has a more integral look.

The leatherette facing gives the dashboard a more finished appearance while the cowl covering eliminates eye-level ghosts in the windshield.

A fleet, ready-to-go stance is enhanced with the new rear-end treatment. The effect makes Mk. IIs look longer and lower than 1500 and 1600s.

An improvement over the 1600's taillights, the horizontal units on the Mk. II still don't have the built-in look of those on other BMC autos.

Road Research Report: MGA 1600 Mark II

Importer:	**Hambro Automotive Corp.** **27 West 57th Street** **New York 19, N.Y.**
Number of U.S. dealers:	**650 in 50 states**
Planned annual production:	**15,000**
Dollar value of spare parts in U.S.:	**$5,000,000**

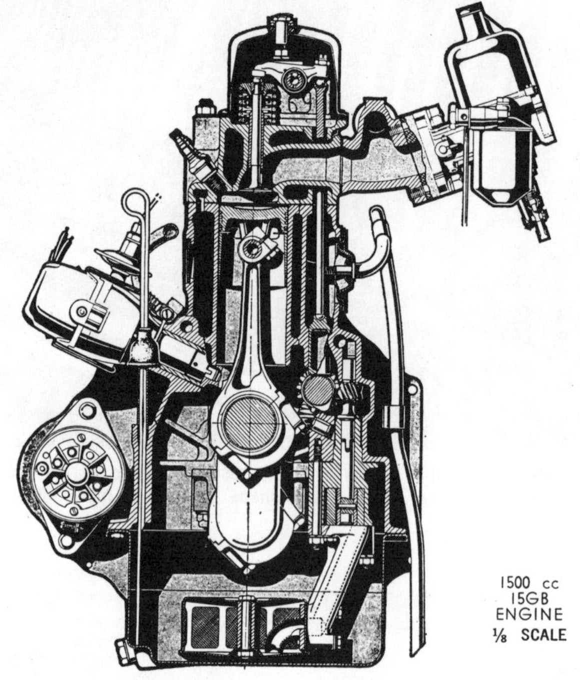

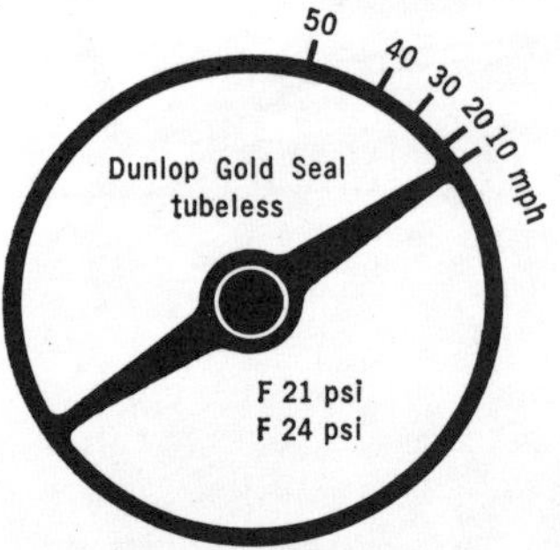

Steering Behavior
Wheel position to maintain 400-foot circle at speeds indicated.

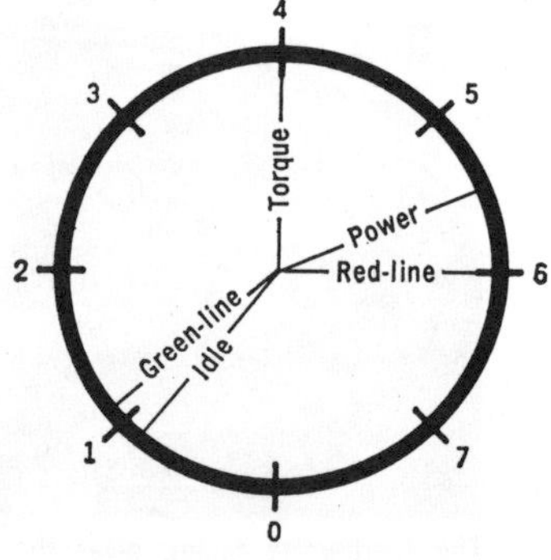

Engine Flexibility
RPM in thousands

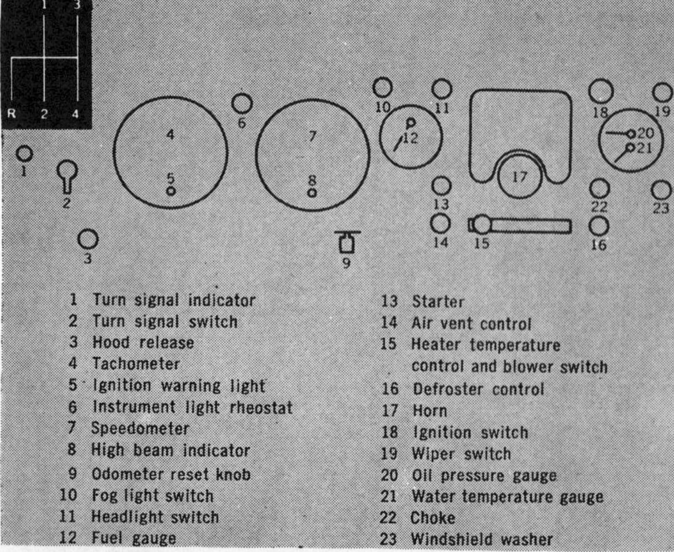

1 Turn signal indicator
2 Turn signal switch
3 Hood release
4 Tachometer
5 Ignition warning light
6 Instrument light rheostat
7 Speedometer
8 High beam indicator
9 Odometer reset knob
10 Fog light switch
11 Headlight switch
12 Fuel gauge
13 Starter
14 Air vent control
15 Heater temperature control and blower switch
16 Defroster control
17 Horn
18 Ignition switch
19 Wiper switch
20 Oil pressure gauge
21 Water temperature gauge
22 Choke
23 Windshield washer

PRICES:

Basic price, POE East and Gulf coasts:	
Roadster with disc wheels	$2449
Coupe with disc wheels	2685
Options fitted on most cars imported:	
Heater/Defroster	65
Windshield washer	15
Tonneau cover	35
Total price of car as tested (at New York)	2564
Other regular production options:	
Whitewall tires	35
Wire wheels	100
Detachable hard top	275
5.90 x 15 Dunlop Roadspeed tires	45
Four-wheel disc brakes, knock-off disc wheels and Roadspeed tires	250
4.55 to one rear axle ratio	50
Other options available through local dealer:	
Thermostat bypass (11G176)	1
SU H6 1¾-inch carburetor (AUC780)	113
Intake manifold for two of above (AEH200)	23
Set heavy-duty valve springs (1H1111 & 1H1112)	11
Oil cooler kit, complete (8G2282)	94
8-inch competition clutch assembly (AHH5457)	121
Parts for close-ratio gearbox conversion:	
First motion shaft (1H3297)	30
Laygear (1H3298)	35
Second speed gear (1H3299)	18
Third speed gear (1H3300)	17
3.90 ring and pinion set (ATB7236)	68
4.30 ring and pinion set (ATB7156)	37
4.30 complete assembly (ATB7283)	84
4.55 ring and pinion set (ATB7146)	34
4.55 complete assembly (ATB7280)	84
16½-inch wood rim, light alloy steering wheel (AHH5800)	50
Andrex front shock absorbers (AHH5609 & AHH5610)	48
60-spoke wire wheel, light alloy rim (AHH8000)	119
60-spoke wire wheel, steel rim (AHH8001)	38
25-gallon fuel tank (AHH5990) with accessories	104
18-gallon fuel tank (AHH5863) with accessories	163
Quick-action filler cap (AHH5498)	20
Hood strap (AHH5518)	5
Competition windshield assembly (AFH2591)	89
Parts needed to install front anti-roll bar	60
Shop manual, 1600 (AKD600B) and Mk II supplement (AKD1982)	11
Tuning manual, 1600 (AKD819A)	1

OPERATING SCHEDULE:

Fuel recommended	Premium
Mileage	21-28 mpg
Range on 12-gallon tank	260-335 miles
Oil recommended	SAE 10W/30
Crankcase capacity	3.9 quarts (4.5 with filter change)
Change at intervals of	3000 miles
Number of grease fittings	10
Lubrication interval	1000 miles

ENGINE: (BMC "B" series)

Displacement	99 cu in, 1622 cc
Dimensions	Four cyl, 3.00 in bore, 3.50 in stroke
Valve gear:	Pushrod-operated vertical overhead valves, stamped rockers.
Compression ratio	8.9 to one
Power (SAE)	90 bhp @ 5500 rpm
Torque	97 lb-ft @ 4000 rpm
Usable range of engine speeds	1100-6000 rpm
Corrected piston speed at 5500 rpm	2970 fpm

CHASSIS:

Wheelbase	94.0 in
Tread	F 47.5, R 48.8 in
Length	156.0 in
Ground clearance	5.5 in
Suspension:	F, ind., coil spring, wishbones; R, rigid axle, semi-elliptic springs
Turns, lock to lock	2.7
Turning circle diameter between curbs	31 ft
Tire and rim size	5.60 x 15, 15 x 4J
Pressures recommended:	Normal, F 21, R 24 psi; Fast driving, F 23, R 26 psi
Brakes: type, swept area	F 11 in disc, R 10 in drum; 350 sq in
Curb weight (full tank)	2044 lbs
Percentage on driving wheels	48%

DRIVE TRAIN: (BMC "B" series)

Gear	Synchro?	Ratio	Step	Overall	Mph per 1000 rpm
Rev	No	4.76		19.52	—3.8
1st	No	3.64	—	14.95	4.9
			64%		
2nd	Yes	2.22		9.08	8.2
			62%		
3rd	Yes	1.37		5.62	13.0
			37%		
4th	Yes	1.00		4.10	17.9

Optional close-ratio gearbox:

Gear	Synchro?	Ratio	Step	Overall	Mph per 1000 rpm
Rev	No	3.20		13.13	—5.6
1st	No	2.44	—	10.00	7.3
			51%		
2nd	Yes	1.62		6.64	11.0
			28%		
3rd	Yes	1.27		5.20	14.2
			27%		
4th	Yes	1.00		4.10	17.9

Final drive ratios: 4.10 to one standard; 4.55, 4.30 and 3.90 optional.

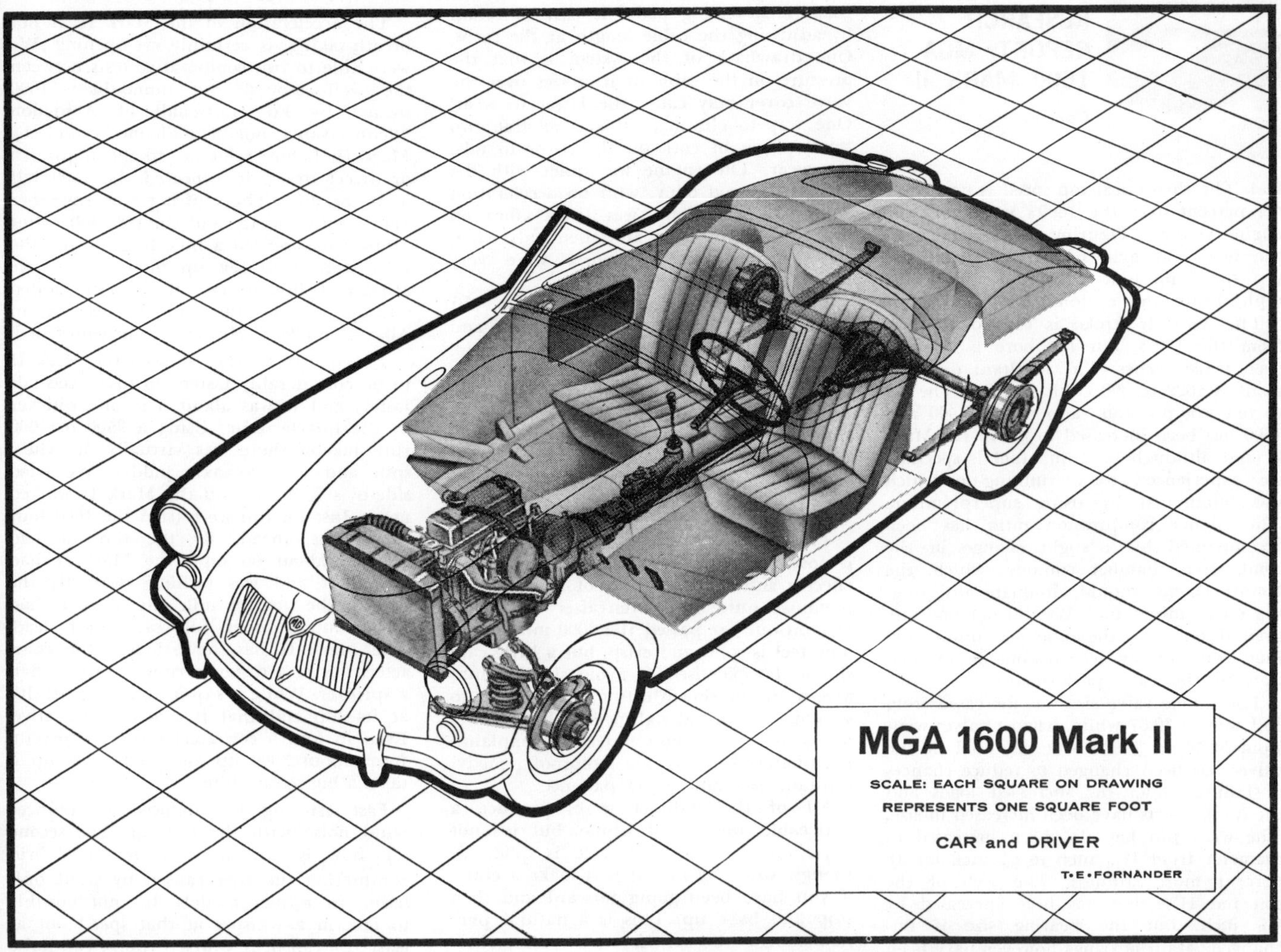

MGA 1600 Mark II
SCALE: EACH SQUARE ON DRAWING REPRESENTS ONE SQUARE FOOT
CAR and DRIVER
T·E·FORNANDER

Top Speed: 105 mph (estimated)
Standing ¼-mile
MGA 1600 Mark II
Temperature 75° F
Wind velocity 5 mph
Altitude above sea level 800 ft
Curve is average of 6 runs
Test weight 2310 lbs
TRUE SPEED MILES PER HOUR
INDICATED MPH
1234
SPEED RANGES
ACCELERATION TIME — SECONDS
0 2 4 6 8 10 12 14 16 18 20 22 24 26 28 30
0 20 40 60 80 100
30 40 50 60 70 80

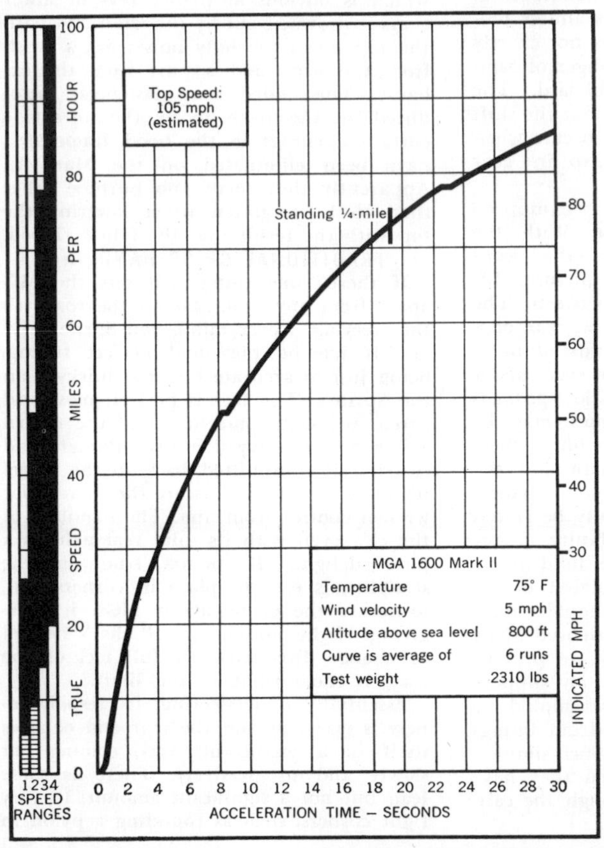

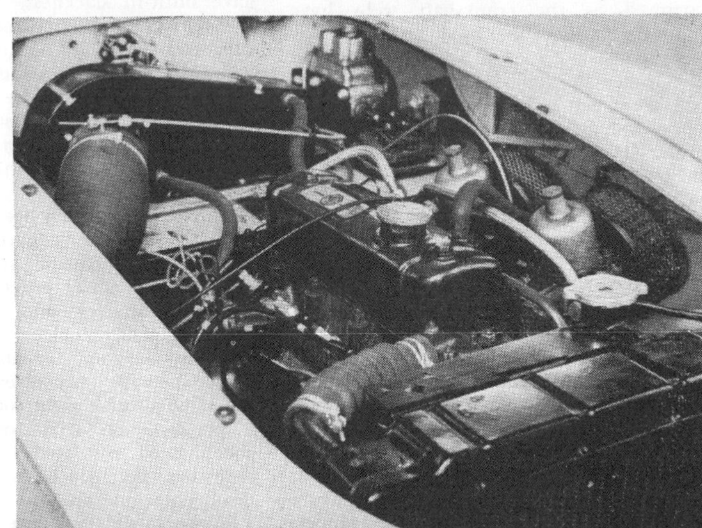

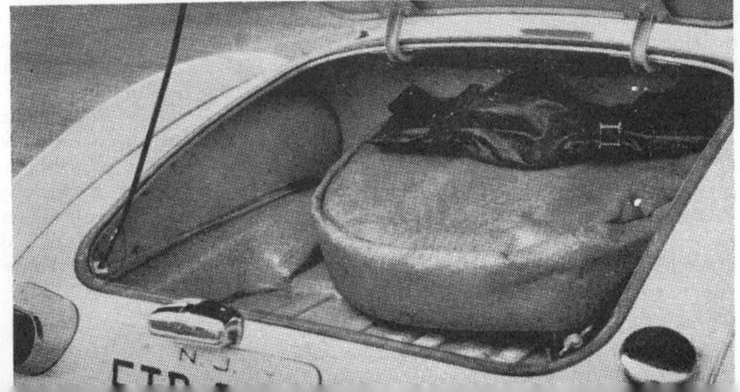

ROAD RESEARCH REPORT: MGA 1600 MARK II

Continued

feel. The theoretical top speed is now some six percent over the 1600's with *only* the engine changes. Figuring the usefulness of the new rear axle ratio, MG places the top speed up nine percent, i.e. over 107 mph, using the optional hardtop.

The 3.5-inch stroke is carried through from the 1500s, but the bore is now an even three inches. The resultant displacement is 1622 cc (99 cubic inches). The 8.3 to one compression ratio of the 1500 and 1600 has been increased to 8.9 in the Mark II and although premium fuel is specified we experienced some running-on which was eliminated by using superpremium. The higher compression ratio has been accompanied by a slight change in the combustion chamber contours which, the factory claims, should eliminate any pinging on premium fuel. We did not find any preignition — just the annoying running-on. Fuel consumption was reasonable in relation to the car's performance.

The intake valve size was increased from 35.1 mm to 39.67 while exhaust valves went from 32.54 to 34.13. Material used in the valves has been changed to reduce chances of failure under the increased loads and the intake ports have been increased in size. The wrist pin has also been increased in diameter from 11/16 inch to 3/4 inch for 18 percent more stiffness. The web of the con rod H-section has been increased by 1/16 inch, but the bearing size is unchanged. Main bearings however have been narrowed as the crankshaft webs have again been thickened by 1/8 inch. A further change in specifications is a new form of cylinder head gasket consisting of 0.15 inch of asbestos faced with a 0.066-inch copper sheet turned over to seal the water joints. It is based on a 0.009-inch steel sheet which is turned over to make a fire wall around the periphery between the bore and head.

RAPID RESPONSE

Our test car, a light blue (one of six colors available) roadster with disc wheels, lived up to the MGA tradition of fast starting. We have found with MGAs, 1500, 1600 and now the Mark II, that the choke need be used only in the coldest weather. Ours idled a bit faster than the usual 900 rpm and ran roughly when temperatures got into the 90s in traffic. Nevertheless it never overheated, the highest temperature being about 190° with running temperature about 160-165°. Warmup was rapid and for winter use a 185° thermostat is available either from Smiths or one of the American firms. An option, incidentally, is a radiator blind that may be controlled from the cockpit.

The responsiveness was excellent, even with the Rube Goldberg accelerator linkage which starts, naturally, on a left-hand-drive car, on the left side of the transmission tunnel, uses a bar to cross the tunnel and then connects to a Bowden cable which recrosses to the left side of the engine where the carbs are mounted. A good, crisp-feeling pedal is easy to retain by adjusting the cable length at the carbs. One drawback of the system is that the pressure on the cable as it crosses over the valve cover may cause the latter to wear. One way to eliminate this is to glue two small pieces of cork on the cover to take the wear. The engine was quiet with the typical pushrod o.h.v. whir on acceleration and cruising. There was little vibration except at lowest rpm and then only when the underhood temperatures were very high.

The clutch was free from stiffness, but took hold a bit high. It was positive and even under violent use showed no slip. There have been owners' reports of what sounds like a slipping clutch at high-rpm shifts but these may usually be traced to clutch slave cylinders that are sticking slightly. The flywheel on the Mark II is eight pounds lighter than before.

COGS AND STOPPING

The traditional H-pattern shift linkage is positive, requiring only small motions to effect a shift. The amount of force needed remained quite high even after the odometer on our car passed the 3000 mile mark. The feel is solid and crisp, but a little care should be exercised to avoid shifting into reverse when downshifting from third to second. The initial tightness of BMC boxes seems to be an almost universal complaint. Fortunately there is one foolproof remedy: constant use and great patience.

All of the indirect gears produce a noticeable amount of whine, but it's not objectionable. The rear axle is quiet although you may find it will make a clunk if you have been going forward and then stop and back up. This is a natural phenomenon as the splines on the drive shaft have built-in slackness. The handiness of the gearshift is so natural it's almost possible to overlook. The knob is not exactly hand-filling, but there's no danger of ramming your fist into the dashboard. The only annoying characteristic about the shift is the balking that sometimes occurs when trying to engage the non-synchro first gear when stopped.

The MG has always been "over-equipped" in the stopping department. With the Lockheed disc/drum system, the word "fade" just doesn't enter the picture. Adjustments are few and far between. The discs adjust themselves and the rear ones seem to be good for thousands of miles before needing any attention even under the most abusive right foot. A low pedal is phenomenon that sometimes may be encountered, but according to our experience the potency is still there and the dead-center stoppability doesn't change. This low-pedal feel may usually be traced to air in the system or a faulty master cylinder which permits some fluid blow-by. The unit should be replaced or rebuilt. The disc units seem to shoulder most of the braking load and experienced MGA drivers advise a bit of caution to prevent locking up the front wheels on slippery surfaces. Pad life for the discs should be equal to that of the riveted drum linings and of course replacement is much simpler. Pads should be replaced when they have worn to 1/16 inch, visible through the caliper units.

IT REALLY DOES PERFORM

The acceleration of the Mark II, if not breath-taking, is certainly eye-opening. We were able to run comparative tests between the well-seasoned, but unmodified, 1600 owned by Ed Gottschall of Abingdon (Pennsylvania, not "On-Thames") and the Mark II. Before referring to the stopwatch or direct drags, it *appeared* the 1600 felt more nimble. The shifting was smoother (more miles on it) and the ride felt softer (things had settled a bit). In addition, the 1600 seemed to rev up more freely (we attributed this to two things: the added mileage on the car and the use of an Abarth muffler). However, our senses lied.

Timed 0 to 60 runs showed the Mark II to be considerably faster, up to 3.4 seconds faster, and it was about a second quicker in the quarter-mile. Using a 3500 to 4000 rpm takeoff there was virtually no wheel spin and no rear axle judder. We tried side-by-side starts and the Mark II walked away. Just for fun we started the 1600 four car-lengths ahead. By the time it had reached about 60 mph the Mark II had caught it and was pulling away. By the end of the quarter mile the Mark II had picked up another full car length lead. The Mark II has, nevertheless, the characteristics of a distance runner rather than a sprinter. While it's quick off the mark it's at its top end that it really comes alive. Even in fourth cog acceleration is forceful from about 3000 up and from 4000 up it takes a big second bite.

Fast cruising is enhanced by reduced wind noise with the top up. The second top bow is now attached to the fabric, eliminating the roar caused by wind buffeting in former models. It's not possible to talk in a whisper at that speed but at least you can hear yourself think. Fan noise which is obvious at higher revs in lower gears is drowned out by the wind and with the top down the only noises are a swish from the wind and a purr from the exhaust. The added snap fasteners, introduced on the 1600s to fix the top's side curtain openings to the hood framework, have been eliminated on the Mark II. Apparently they served no purpose other than to be forgotten when lowering the top with the result that the fabric ripped.

TRADITIONAL CRISP HANDLING

If there's one thing that sets the MG apart from any other car on the road it's the steering. Never mind, you Sprite drivers! It has no play and perfect timing, being just as accurate but less finicky than the Sprite's. The feel is perfect, most will agree, although some may find the return action on the heavy side. Even though road reaction is transmitted back to the wheel it's done in a way to assure the driver, not wrench control from him. The handling of the car, even with its solid rear axle, is a pure delight. It points true on the straights, is easy to place in corners and, to re-use the cliche about MGs, it's forgiving. Slight motions are all that's needed to change directions, yet full feel of the road is there right to the limit.

Essentially understeering, its responsiveness is excellent and the rear end behaves itself in a predictable way, coming out slowly and progressively. There is some lean but not a significant amount. In very tight corners, such as rounding a pylon in a fast gymkhana, the inside rear wheel will lift, but that's an indication you weren't taking the fastest way around in the first place. With the Mark II's added power, it becomes even easier to turn around within the car's 94-inch wheelbase when you want to. The Dunlop Gold Seal tubeless tires ran quietly, gave a good feel and adequate bite but we found higher than recommended pressures an improvement. The stiff suspension transmitted all the bumps to the seat of the pants but reduced their intensity. The result is the feeling of knowing at all times what the car is doing in relation to the road.

There are still no outside door handles on the MGA, entry being gained by tugging a cable in the door pocket. Entry and exit are typical sports car fashion; either you adapt to it or it's inconvenient. The seats themselves are leather faced over sponge rubber and have seat cushions that are quite soft and comfortable for long periods. There is only a hint of real bucket shape, but the center arm-rest helps keep the driver in his place. Seat belts are better yet and we understand that later Mark IIs will feature built-in seat belt mountings as does the new MG Midget. Leg room is good and there is room to squirm. The seat position itself is low and the placement of the rear view mirror on the cowl adds to obstruction of the right front fender, which is why some gymkhana drivers remove them in events. One enterprising owner added wooden blocks to the bottom of the seat to raise himself a bit (without jamming his thighs against the steering wheel) and relocated the mirror at the top edge of the windshield, hanging downward below the top clip.

REFINING A FINE INTERIOR

The controls and gauges rate acclaim for their positiveness. Although they are scattered in an "artistic" way all over the dash they are easy to read and reach. The near vertical 16½-inch steering wheel is placed slightly high, but this allows leg clearance. A smaller-diameter wood-rimmed wheel would be a nice replacement and would retain the adjustable-reach feature of the standard wheel. The flat-X design of the spokes, incidentally, may be traced directly to the MG EX 179 record breaker.

The pendant brake, clutch and accelerator pedals are well placed for competition use. Although we know one large-footed driver who put an extension on the gas pedal to facilitate heel and toeing, most people wouldn't need it. To eliminate the clanking when the pedals are released, wrap tape on the small tubular stop. The dip switch location was lowered on the toe board with the 1600 and is kept there on the Mark II; it's more convenient than the 1500's. Missing on the left-hand-drive models is a left-foot rest that is found on RHD 1600s and Mark IIs; it's still in the car, but the passenger doesn't need it. Speaking of pedals, one accessory we'd urge all new owners to make or buy immediately is a scuff plate for alongside the gas pedal. The bare carpeting will wear out very quickly. As a general recommendation we'd urge getting rubber carpeting to protect the floor mats too and advise against resting the left foot on the convenient diagonal side member. That's a potential wear point also.

The fly-off hand brake, even in left-hand-drive cars, stays on the right side of the transmission tunnel. Its location is excellent; there's no need for it on the driver's side. Placing it there frees the between-the-seats area for an occasional third passenger and allows easy exit, unlike cars which have the brake left of the driver's seat. Its action is such that release is a quick, positive movement and accidental release is very unlikely. Incidentally, the amount of travel needed to set the hand brake gives a good indication of the rear lining adjustment. If more than a couple of inches is needed, adjust your rear brakes and the hand brake is set automatically.

DASH AND DIAL DETAILS

As can be seen from the instrument panel diagram all the necessary gauges come installed. We've seen MGAs in which owners moved the water temp/oil pressure gauge to the slot occupied by the gas gauge. It's a good Saturday project. Others we've seen have removed the radio speaker grille, replaced it with a plate of aluminum and installed an ammeter to supplement the ignition warning light. The direction signal switch is a pneumatic unit and its flashing cycle may be adjusted by turning a screw on the back. A pre-wired fog light circuit is built in. To install either a fog or driving light all that need be done is run a wire from the lamp to the red and yellow lead located behind the grille on the right side, and plug in. The body of the lamp acts as the ground. If both fog and driving lights are used, the fog light may be wired as described and the driving light hooked up to the high beams with an over-ride switch installed either on the dash or under it.

All the instruments are legibly marked and there is a resettable trip odometer that's useful for rally work. If you are very sharp-eyed it's possible to read the tenths of miles column down to hundredths and it's possible to advance the odometer to corrected mileage figures. Do not, however, attempt to zero or advance the odometer when the car is moving; the instrument will break. The map light on the far right of the dash is useful, but experienced rallyists will usually install a cigarette lighter and plug into that or wire their clipboard light into the dash fixture. Incidentally, there is still no ash tray in the MG although one is available as an accessory through dealers (Part number AHH 5539, $8.10) or accessory shops. A bean-bag type works well but may tend to be self-emptying on hard corners or at speed when the ashes fly out, so we'd urge one that's attached and has a lid, or else slip empty soup cans into the door pockets.

The heater/defroster is up to its job in all but sub-zero temperatures when most of the warmth escapes through the top. Wind sealing was very good but our test car leaked rain in the annoying places: from the top of the windshield, under the cowl and the edge of the doors. This was in contrast to a 1500 owned by a staff member which scarcely leaked at all. Ventilation with the top up is adequate though the driver's legs get warm. Most of the fresh air through the heater outlet dumps onto the transmission tunnel. A last comment about the top and side curtains: in new cars they are very stiff; use graphite or dripless oil on the top joints and a silicone spray on the window tracks; watch out for scratching the plastic rear windows and side curtains by keeping them free from grit.

The two door pockets are a useful size but there is no lockable glove compartment. Perhaps MG should snitch the Sunbeam Alpine's arm rest/glove box. There are no locks on the doors and none on the trunk either, although accessory shops sell one for the latter. We'd advise new car buyers to remove the spare key from its hiding spot under the hood (it's screwed to the heater) and also would recommend installing a trunk lock and a battery cut-off switch. The MGA, like almost all British convertibles, is disturbingly easy to start without the key. One owner uses his fog light switch in the ignition circuit so that the key must be turned and the fog light switch pulled out to start the engine.

INSPIRES HOME MAINTENANCE

Owning an MGA of any vintage is not only enjoyable, it's an education. It's the kind of car that encourages (but doesn't require) backyard tinkering. Unfortunately the Mark II's tool roll, stored in the trunk, is equipped with many fewer tools than former models but if you have American wrenches they will fit most of the nuts and bolts on the car. If you are so inclined, plug changes, valve adjustments, carburetor tuning, timing, changing the points, etc., are easily accomplished. About the only truly difficult routine task for the backyard Alf Francis is changing the oil filter, which is most easily accomplished with the aid of a second person. We know of one "clique" of MG owners who used to meet regularly and aid each other in working on their cars. It's the kind of car that inspires that sort of camaraderie.

A funnel and length of small-diameter rubber tubing facilitates filling the transmission. The front shock absorbers can be topped up in the same way, while an accomplice moves the car up and down (the rear shocks must be removed for topping up) so shock absorber fluid can be added. The "grease gun" in the tool kit of former cars would be good to get. It is never used by most owners or it is tried once and discarded because it "doesn't work." The reason for its nonoperation is simply that it's not a grease gun but an oil gun and is perfect for lubricating the steering rack and pinion with hypoid oil. The location of the two six-volt batteries out-of-sight-out-of-mind behind the seats renders them subject to neglect, dirt and water. Lucas sells a handy battery filler that prevents overfilling them when topping up. One of the few modern cars with a crank, it is useful for dead-battery starts or for turning the engine when adjusting the valves or installing points.

We've found the lifespan of the standard fan belt to be unpredictable. On our test car it lasted 2100 miles; on the 1600 we referred to it lasted a little longer and it lasted about 12,000 miles on the 1500 we mentioned. American companies make a replacement; if you can't find MGA listed, check under Metropolitan, Austin A-55, certain Ford six-cylinder trucks and, surprise, Volkswagen through at least 1960. There are, no doubt, others that will fit.

ART OF STORING LUGGAGE

With the basic body shell now in its seventh year of production, one can only guess at the number of luggage racks that have been sold to supplement the negligible trunk space. Most of the wide shallow capacity is occupied by the spare tire. MG offers its own rack (part number AHH 5495, $58.21) and there are several others available from accessory shops. If you travel with a passenger or much more than a toothbrush and a change of clothes, you'll find one useful. One owner we know installed a rack, decided which pieces of luggage he would carry on it and had a canvas cover made to fit. This presents a neat appearance and keeps the luggage dry, probably drier than the test car's trunk which leaked. Lift-the-dot fasteners hold the cover to the trunk lid. The screw-type jack of earlier MGAs has been replaced with a ratchet type and the wheel lug wrench has been improved. The bumpers of the car are more decorative than functional and a grille guard may be considered a wise investment if you park on the street much. Parking too close to other cars may result in numerous little dents in the aluminum doors too if you aren't careful. The trunk lid and hood, incidentally, are also aluminum.

As will be noted in the specifications list, options enable the Mark II owner to tailor his car to his own requirements. One of the new packages this year results from the death of the MGA Twin Cam, a promising machine that just never got off the ground. Production has ceased on this model and only 2111 were made between 1958 and 1960. However for $250 over the basic price it's possible to get four-wheel disc brakes, knock-off disc wheels and Roadspeed 5.90 x 15 tires, all of which were standard on the Twin Cam. We were surprised to find when checking our research on MGAs that the performance of the Mark II is comparable to the Twin Cam in street form. Zero to 60 time for the off-the-dealer's-floor Twin Cam was about 13 seconds and its time for the quarter mile was around 18½ seconds. Considering that the Twin Cam carried a substantially higher price than the Mark II and that its power was well over 100 bhp, the comparison puts the Mark II in a very favorable light indeed.

As this Road Research Report went to press, full competition equipment and specifications for the Mark II had not been compiled by BMC. The items listed were produced for the 1600; all are suitable on the Mark II. Pending the issuance of a Mark II tuning manual, the one for the 1600 should give valuable information including part numbers for all the bits and pieces that make up the various kits and recommended stages of tune.

RENEWING AND REVOLUTIONIZING

For those who find, after thousands of miles of good and faithful service, that the original engine is beginning to get tired, BMC has a sound plan for refurbishing the power. It sells what is called a "half engine," consisting of the block, pistons, rods, crank, camshaft, front mounting plate, etc., fully assembled. You provide from your original engine the head assembly, front timing chain cover, oil pan and some other parts. The cost of the unit is $280 for a 1600 engine. Two part numbers are listed, 48G158 or 48G186. A similar half engine will eventually be offered for the Mark II. There is no exchange on your old engine; you buy the replacement half engine outright. The availability of such components should enable owners of 1500 cc cars to boost their power in the simplest way.

Regardless of the adequate stock performance and the enticing possibilities offered through tuning procedures, some owners may eventually want to swap engines. The weight of the stock unit is 370 pounds, a figure heavier than Buick's more powerful aluminum V8. One reader has sent us pictures of his MGA with a Falcon six (see C/D, Sept. 1961) which he says gives added power and reduced weight too. Another popular swap is to the Chevy V8. Like they say in the old song, "There ain't no substitute for cubic inches."

Nevertheless the MGA, particularly in its latest Mark II version, represents full value received for money expended. Tracing its heritage directly to special Le Mans cars and Bonneville record breakers, it is the latest and most eloquent expression of the company's Safety Fast slogan. It's a solid car that gives satisfying performance through a skillful blending of many stock components, reflecting the shrewdness MG engineers have exhibited right from the start. While it may be something less than *avant garde* with a separate body and chassis and a solid rear axle, these features don't affect the car's performance adversely. In fact, they have benefits in the form of truly predictable handling and low cost of maintenance and replacement. If you overdo it and crinkle a fender there's no need to buy half a car—just bolt on the new one.

The Mark II should extend the reputation MGs have won for reliability, performance, finish and fun in all corners of the world. Like the former types they are perfectly adaptable to use by boulevard sportscarteers or grimy-finger-nailed hard-driving enthusiasts. Even the chic coupe possesses the "I-can-take-it" quality the make is known for. For current owners of MGs we have a prescription: the Mark II is just what the doctor ordered. —*C/D*

100,000 MGAs!

More than one hundred thousand 'MGA's have now been built since 1955 — a world record for the production of one basic type of sports car

On 31 December, 1930, an unsupercharged M.G. Midget established the first International Class Records ever achieved by the Abingdon marque, at speeds up to 87.3 m.p.h. In September 1959, during the last attempt at the Bonneville Salt Flats, Utah, the latest M.G. record-breaker broke half-a-dozen International Class Records at speeds up to 254.91 m.p.h. For 30 years the M.G. Car Company has upheld a reputation for record-breaking that has been unequalled by any other car manufacturer.

In March this year, however, the Company established a record of a different sort when a handsome gold and ivory 'MGA' rolled off the end of the assembly line. This was the 100,000th car of this type to be built since full-scale production of the model commenced in August 1955. In less than seven years the Company had established a production record which is believed

Our heading picture shows the 100,000th 'MGA', a 1622cc Mark II finished in gold and ivory, posed with 'Old Number One', which dates back to 1925 and is still in running order. The 'MGA' chassis frame had its first taste of really high speed in EX 179, the M.G. record-breaker of 1953 (left). Also in the picture are George Eyston, Syd Enever (M.G. Chief Designer) and John Thornley

to be unique. To the best of our knowledge no sports car manufacturer in the world has ever reached such an output with a single type of car.

The M.G. Car Company was faced with a difficult problem in 1954, when the decision was made to replace the well-loved if angular 'T' range by a completely new and much faster car. As John Thornley explains in his book, *Maintaining the Breed:*—'The T types, all of them, had earned for M.G. an enviable reputation for rugged reliability. They were not machines which had to be coddled; they were built to go anywhere, to keep going and to put up with more than the average measure of abuse. The new car had to be in no way inferior in these respects. For years, M.G.s had been built under the slogan "Safety Fast" and this, at Abingdon, was regarded as no empty phrase but rather a challenge. A car could easily be built which was too fast for its own inherent stability, as certain examples in the world-wide race for higher and higher speeds were tending to prove. The new car would have a maximum speed of the order of 100 m.p.h., and some of them would be bought, as M.G.s had been bought down the years, by tyro drivers. Above all, therefore, the new car had to be stable, to keep "its feet on the ground", to have stopping power commensurate with its performance and to be entirely free from any of those vicious unpredictable tricks which can so easily arise—and, unfortunately, not infrequently do—from careless or incompetent design.

'The designers' brief, therefore, was to make a car which was, first and foremost, "safe" as defined above; which, secondly, was at least as rugged, as well-appointed and well-finished as its predecessors; and, thirdly, was to sell as nearly as possible at the price of the 'TF'. Only then were speed and acceleration to be considered and they should, of course, be as good as could be contrived. The above sequence is important. It underlie the confidence in the future success of the car, and of its continued acceptance by a discriminating public. It is *not*, be it admitted, a prescription which wins races—the more is the pity—but for every owner who wishes to go racing, there are a hundred and more who do not. And they are entitled to—indeed, must be given—their motoring and their fun in the safest possible form.'

That was the recipe for the new model, which eventually became known as the 'MGA'. How it came into being is also an interesting story. The chassis frame was a close copy—modified only for convenience in production—of that used in EX.179, the M.G. record-breaker which was built in 1953/4 as a successor to Lt. Col. Goldie Gardner's famous car. And this frame, in

The 'MGA' ancestry goes back to 1951 and this special-bodied 'TD', designed by Enever, which George Phillips drove at Le Mans that year

The development project car, EX 175, resembles the production model much more closely. However, it was still powered by the rather tall XPEG 'TF' 1500 engine, which neccessitated a bulge in the bonnet top

The production prototypes, under the development code EX 182, were given a thorough test at Le Mans in 1955 and performed impressively . . .

. . . paving the way for the production cars which began rolling off the lines at Abingdon in August 1955. This is one of the early production 'MGA' 1500s being put through its paces

The 'hot' version of the 'MGA' was the 1588cc Twin Cam model, which appeared in 1958 and was hailed with delight by competition enthusiasts, performing outstandingly well in the hands of many of them, including winning its class at Le Mans in 1960. However, the high-efficiency twin-overhead-camshaft power unit tended to be temperamental when neglected or ill-treated by less knowledgeable drivers and only a relatively small number were built. Dunlop disc brakes all round were fitted as standard together with distinctive centre-lock disc wheels, both items now being optionally available on the 'MGA' 1600 Mark II

turn, was identical to one which Sydney Enever had designed some time before for EX.175—not a record-breaker, this, but an experimental chassis which was fitted with a body similar to that designed by Enever for the 'TD' that George Phillips drove at Le Mans in 1951. The family connection between the Phillips car, UMG.400, the development project car EX.175 (registered number, HMO.6), and the production version of the 'MGA' is quite clear from their appearance.

The chassis and bodywork had already been subjected to extensive testing, and only the question of the engine remained. At this stage another difficult decision had to be made. The evergreen 1250 c.c. engine of the TB/TC/TD/TF range had already been enlarged to 1500 c.c. and had virtually reached the end of its potential development. So it was decided to use the B.M.C. 'B'-type power unit, which was already proving immensely successful in the 'ZA' Magnette. A new development project number was allotted—EX.182—and under this label a batch of prototypes was built for further testing, which included the Le Mans and Tourist Trophy races of 1955.

Thus was born the 'MGA', which went into full production in August 1955. Although four different versions have appeared since then, the basic chassis, engine and bodywork have been retained, and each version has offered the same three ingredients—safety, rugged strength and reasonable price. The recipe seems to have been a successful one.

F.W.McC.

The 'MGA' 1600, seen here beside the Thames at Abingdon, was introduced in 1959 and apart from the increase in engine size from 1489cc to 1588cc, it featured Lockheed disc front brakes with drums at the rear and minor styling changes

ROAD TEST/13-62

MG-A Mk. II Competition

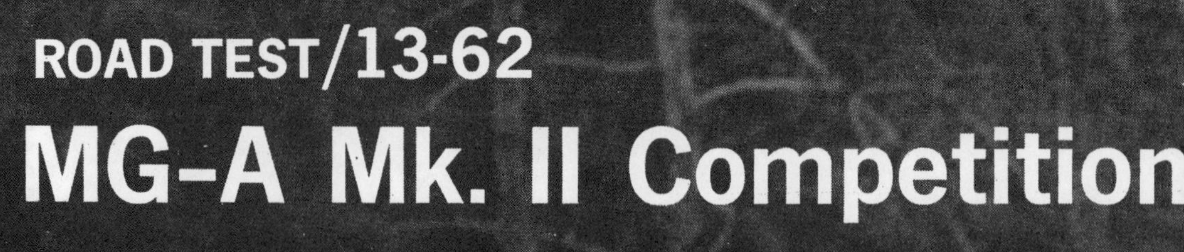

For the competition-minded, BMC continues to improve the breed.

OVER THE PAST FEW YEARS we have often heard the complaint that though many sports car manufacturers list a mass of options with which one can make a raceable car out of a production street machine, such a car can't be purchased so equipped. In other words, to take advantage of these good things one must strip down the standard vehicle and add the options oneself, or pay someone else to do it.

Actually, though there is cause for the complaint in the average case, most cars can be purchased fully equipped if one is persistent enough and willing to wait while a special order is processed. The main reason for the difficulty is that quotas for U.S. delivery are fixed far in advance and special orders tend to throw a very large Whitworth monkey wrench into the well-planned works. Too, local distributors are reluctant to stock such cars on the gamble that the order will come through.

While one answer to the problem has been to convert these cars on the dealer or distributor level, MG has come up with another. This one gives the customer a partially prepared car, with a fully raceworthy chassis, coupled with a stock MG-A Mk II engine, which the customer can prepare to suit the rules that govern racing in his own area or, perhaps, leave showroom stock for rallying or just plain enjoyable ironpants motoring in the *pur sang* manner.

Designated the MG-A Mk II Competition, the car is basically the standard Mk II with all of the competition chassis modifications completed and charged for, but with credit given for the stock items and no labor bill. The result is a legally "prodified" chassis at far less net cost than the do-it-yourself job on a standard version, with the added factor of knowing that the job was done according to and by the precepts of the men of Abingdon. The tab is less than $500 over the list price of an absolutely standard, non-deluxe MG-A, instead of the $800-and-up that would be charged by the local speed wizard who may or may not know what he's doing.

Outwardly the car looks like the late-lamented Twin Cam, with its pin-drive knock-off disc wheels and unpretenious demeanor. In fact, we have a strong suspicion that there may have been some Twin Cam chassis laying about when they discontinued the DOHC engine production. Quite obviously the car has the stiffer front springs used in the Twin Cam and the big, meaty anti-sway bar as well. The four-wheel disc brakes, with hard competition type pads, are also in outward evidence. The rear end is equipped with the stiffer competition springs and both ends have the racing shock absorbers, with the result that jumping up and down on either front or rear end produces a reluctance of movement that borders on the obdurate. Such seeming stiffness would normally lead one to believe that the ride might be somewhat like that of a plank dragged through a stone quarry, but such is not the case. The ride is definitely on the firm side but is anything but harsh. Bounce and rebound rates have been well-chosen and balanced to give good control without producing the roughness that too often goes with competition type suspension systems.

Not apparent to the casual glance or to the casual passenger are several other items aimed at making the car raceworthy. Most important is the close ratio gearbox that eliminates the wide spread between Second and Third gears. In fact, all the intermediate gears are of higher ratios than in the standard box. We fail to see why First gear should be as high as it is, since it isn't synchronized and so cannot be used at any decent rate of speed. Its high ratio makes it just a little bit ticklish to get the car off the line without bogging down, but the other two intermediate gears are very nicely spaced and help avoid those situations wherein one finds oneself trying to figure out whether to over-rev in Second or lug the engine in Third. Aiding the getaway problem posed by the high First is the competition 4.55 to 1 rear-end gearing which, while it cuts down the absolute top speed, gives the car all sorts of acceleration in the gears. With the engine brought up to whatever stage of prodification the local club rules allow, the combination of low rear-end gearing and close ratio transmission makes the car a pretty fearsome machine in its class.

(continued)

Pointing its inside "toe" a tad at the turn apex, the option-equipped Mark II scurries through a serpentine route in the hills "sticking like paint" to the choppy asphalt surface.

Showing a reluctance of suspension movement that borders on the obdurate, the Competition Mk II is not a race car per se, *but the basis for a sizzling "prodified" for* pur sang *use.*

Slicing through a dirt-covered downhill, the car depends on its big, meaty anti-sway bar and RS-5 tires for stability.

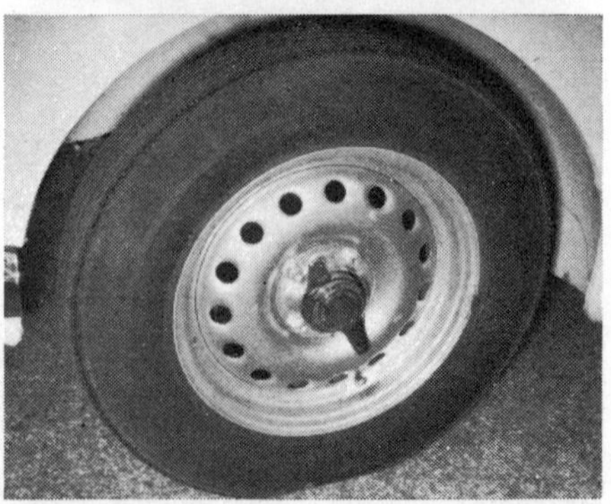

With the exception of the knock-off disc wheels—of Twin-Cam derivation—these above views are like the normal Mk II. Instrumentation is complete and there is luggage space for weekend touring. Performance options are yet to be included, but everything needed for maximum roadability has been installed.

Hidden between the grille and radiator is a small Smith oil cooler. The engine compartment is otherwise like stock MG.

PHOTOS: RANDY HOLT

Dunlop caliper-type brakes and 9½-inch discs are mounted both front and rear, provide the car with superb stopping.

MGA MK II

Our test car was picked up from Hollywood Sport Cars with zero mileage on the clock and was stiff as starch when we started out. This soon loosened up and things got easier to do as each day went by. Shifts, at first an effort, got to the point where the lever seemed to be almost automatically pulled into the proper gate if any effort was made to match engine and gear speeds, especially on down shifts. Lever movement on the close ratio box is similar to that on the normal box with, if anything, shorter throws and the total H-pattern covers little more than the span of a large man's palm. Steering is, as on virtually all MGs, direct and with a strong return action which is all right for street use but just a bit stiff on the track. Reducing the caster angle of the front wheels cuts down this return considerably and this minor change in setting is S.O.P. in track preparation. Strong return or not, it is possessed of as nearly pinpoint accuracy as can be found on a production car, with little or no kickback from the road.

During the course of our test, we were fortunate or unfortunate enough to have some of the foulest weather to hit Southern California in a decade. While the hard top left something to be desired in terms of sealing over the top of the windshield (a nickel-and-dime repair item at worst), the rest of the car was adequately weather-tight even in strong gusts and 80 mph speeds. Even when splashing through deep puddles and flooded intersections there was no sign of leakage up through the floor or around the pedals. More impressive than the weather-tightness, however, was the rock-solid stability in both wet and wind. Part of this was undoubtedly due to the Dunlop RS-5 tires, which are a far cry indeed from the Roadspeeds of yesteryear. They clung to road like paint and, with the wide-based competition rims, were completely stable and totally predictable. How much of the stability was due to the tires and how much to the solid suspension is hard to determine. However, the combination provided near perfect road holding and predictability, even under the most abominable conditions of wind and rain. Side gusts, a bugaboo for most small cars, were no problem with the MG-A Competition; in fact, they were hardly noticeable even when other small cars, both sports cars and sedans, were having visible trouble staying on a straight line.

Thanks to the stock engine and the high First gear, the 4.5 rear-end gearing did not make itself felt in taking acceleration times. The close ratio box and low ratio rear-end balanced each other out, and the result was that the times were virtually identical to those shown by the standard machine tested before. However, even with a dead stock engine, lap times around a road circuit should be considerably better, due to the combination of gearing and suspension that would permit higher cornering speeds and to the superb braking that allows diving far deeper into turns than is possible with the standard set-up.

What the MG people have here, then, is a car that a novice can use in stock form for drivers' schools and practice sessions in complete safety, and still have a car that is perfectly suitable for the street. For the man with a competition license, it is a car on which all the heavy conversion work has already been done, leaving only super-tuning or allowable engine modifications to be done. In short, the MG Competition is a race car basis rather than a race car *per se*. While more expensive than the standard version, it provides a means by which the purchaser can end up with a competitive car at considerably less cost than that of converting the standard MG-A and bringing it up to a similar state of preparation. For those interested in Class F Production competition, this latest offering from Abingdon is well worth the price of admission. —

— *John Christy*

TEST DATA

VEHICLE ....MG-A
PRICE (as tested) ..$3190 POE L.A.
MODEL ....Mk II Competition
OPTIONS ....See text

ENGINE:

Type: ....BMC Type B — 4-cyl. 4 cycle water-cooled
Head ....Removable, cast-iron
Valves ....Overhead, pushrod/rocker actuated
Max. bhp ....90 @ 5500 rpm
Max. Torque ....97 lbs. ft. @ 4000 rpm
Bore ....3.0 in. 76.2 mm.
Stroke ....3.5 in. 88.9 mm.
Displacement ....99 cu. in. 1622 cc.
Compression Ratio ....8.9 to 1
Induction System: ....Twin SU carburetors
Exhaust System ....Cast manifold, to single pipe & muffler
Electrical System: ....12V Lucas distributor ignition

CLUTCH:

Borg & Beck
Diameter ....8 in.
Actuation ....Hydraulic

STEERING:

Rack & Pinion
Turns Lock to Lock 2.5
Turn Circle: ....30½ ft.

TRANSMISSION:

Ratios: 1st ....2.45 to 1
2nd ....1.62 to 1
3rd ....1.27 to 1
4th ....1.0 to 1

BRAKES:

Discs, front and rear, 11 inch dia.
Swept Area ....569 sq. in.

DIFFERENTIAL: Hypoid

Ratio ....4.55 to 1
Drive Axles (type): Enclosed, semi-floating

CHASSIS:

Frame: ....Steel, conventional box-section
Body: ....Bolt-on steel assemblies
Front Suspension: .....Unequal "A" with arm shock forming uppers, coil spring
Rear Suspension: ....Live axle, semi-elliptic leaf springs, arm shocks
Tire Size & Type: ....5.90 x 15 Dunlop RS-5

WEIGHTS AND MEASURES:

Wheelbase: ....94 in.
Front Track: ....47.5 in.
Rear Track ....48.75 in.
Overall Height ....50 in.
Overall Width ....58 in.
Overall Length ....156 in.
Ground Clearance ....7 in.
Curb Weight ....2013 lbs.
Test Weight ....2338 lbs.
Crankcase ....4 qts.
Cooling System ....10 qts.
Gas Tank ....12 gals.

PERFORMANCE

0-30 ....3.9 sec.
0-40 ....6.4 sec.
0-50 ....8.7 sec.
0-60 ....12.4 sec.
0-70 ....16.5 sec.
0-80 ....20.3 sec.
0-90 ....29.1 sec.
0-100 ....— sec.
Standing ¼ mile ....20.4 sec. @ 74 mph
Top Speed (av. two-way run) ....104 mph

Speed Error	30	40	50	60	70	80	90
Actual	29	39	48	57	67	76	86

Fuel Consumption:
Test ....23 mpg
Average ....28 mpg
Recommended Shift Points:
Max. 1st ....44 mph
Max. 2nd ....64 mph
Max. 3rd ....82 mph

RPM Red-line ....6,000 rpm
Speed Ranges in gears:
1st ....0 to 44 mph
2nd ....25 to 64 mph
3rd ....35 to 82 mph
4th ....40 to 104 mph

Brake Test: 76 Average % G, over 10 stops.
No Fade encountered

REFERENCE FACTORS:

Bhp. per Cubic Inch 0.99
Lbs. per bhp. 22.3
Piston Speed @ Peak rpm ....3220 ft./min.
Swept Brake area per Lb. ....0.276 Sq. In.

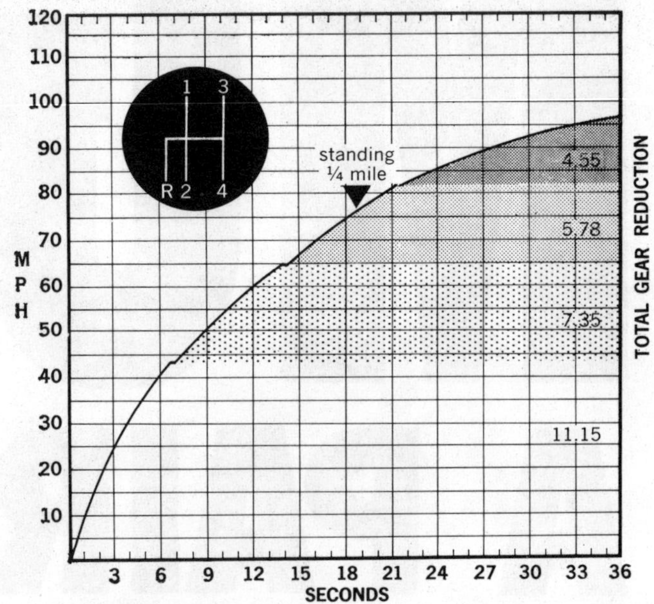

MT Road Test

MG's A PAIR

Testing two forms of the pioneer sports car—the 1600 Mk II and compact Midget

by Jim Wright, Technical Editor

IN THE YEARS prior to the second war to end all wars, sports car activity in this country was limited mainly to a small group of East Coast well-to-do's. The day of the mass-produced high-performance automobile hadn't arrived, and one had to have plenty of dollars to afford the high initial cost of what was then available (Alfa, Bentley, Bugatti, Mercedes, etc.), and the equally high cost of importing the parts to keep them running.

But the big war and the years immediately following it put an end to all of that. American G.I.'s who were stationed in England and on the Continent, and therefore away from wives, sweethearts, mothers, Detroit advertising and other sedentary influences, found out that a car could be something more than a means of getting from here to there or something that looked real good sitting in the driveway.

They discovered what the English and the Europeans had known all along — *real* driving is an art form and, besides that, it is also a lot of fun. When it came time to return Stateside many of the boys didn't want to leave these new-found thrills behind, so they looked around for something they could afford to bring back with them. Not being the millionaires our foreign cousins imagined them to be, most of them found the answer to their needs in a small, inexpensive, open two-seater that had been introduced shortly after VE Day by a small English firm at Abingdon-on-Thames. This, of course, was the now-classic MG-TC, the car that is generally credited with kindling the fires of the sports car movement in this country.

In the years since those first few TC's reached these shores back in 1947, the marque has undergone six model changes (not including the Midget, which was introduced last year), while over 150,000 units have been purchased by presumably happy Americans.

The current 1600 Mk II and Midget models are a far cry from the old TC with its solid front axle, clamshell fenders and monstrous 19-inch wire wheels. Both offer greater performance and handling, more economy, are more comfortable and have a bit more room and luggage space. But if we said the newer versions are more fun to drive, we'd be lying. Easier maybe, but there was just something about driving a TC that made it a thrill all by itself. Discounting this bit of nostalgia, the two present-day MG's are greatly improved in all departments and can be viewed as excellent examples of the development of a breed.

The MOTOR TREND test cars are both fairly standard models. The Mk II came equipped with optional wire wheels, heater/defroster, and an engine oil cooler. The Midget's only options were whitewall tires and deluxe wheel covers.

The TC offered a 76-cubic-inch engine that managed to produce 54 hp at 5200 rpm, or .71 hp per cubic inch. The Mk II puts out a healthy .90 hp per cubic inch from 99 inches (90 at 5500 rpm). The Midget draws 49.4 hp out of its smaller 57.9-cubic-inch engine, which breaks down to .85 hp per cubic inch.

We searched our files for some acceleration figures for the TC and found a 0-to-60-mph time of 23.5 seconds. The Mk II, with two aboard plus instrumentation, produced 0-to-30, 0-to-45 and 0-to-60-mph times of 4.4, 8.1 and 13.8 seconds, respectively. A top speed of 73 mph was clocked at the end of a standing quarter-mile, with an elapsed time of 20.5 seconds. Although it is generally conceded that the Mk II can top 100 mph, the best we could get out of it down the long Riverside Raceway backstretch was 92 mph. The old TC used to take all day to get up to a maximum of just under 80 mph.

The Midget, while not as quick as the Mk II, still offers some very lively performance for its size. Our 0-to-30, 0-to-45 and 0-to-60-mph times in this mighty mite averaged out at 5.8, 11.0 and 20.0 seconds. The quarter-mile e.t. was 23.2 seconds, with a speed of 64 mph. On the top end we clocked a maximum of 78 mph, but with more room we think the 85-mph advertised top speed would have been possible.

Both cars have a 6000-rpm red line, and this is the figure we used for our shift points. The Mk II could be wound to 6500 rpm, but not without protest. We took the Midget to 7000 rpm and it felt very smooth at this point. In fact, it is downright amazing how smooth the Midget engine is over the entire rpm range. This is in direct contrast to the Mk II engine, which feels rough all the way up.

The Midget engine is complemented by a gearbox that is equally smooth. Quick shifts, either up or down, were no problem in this car. The ratios, while not exactly close, were closer

BACK IN EARLY DAYS THE MG-TC WAS A REAL TIGER ON THE TRACK AND NEVER FAILED TO DRAW ATTENTION OF THE MAN ON THE STREET.

than those in the Mk II, especially between second and third gears. The Mk II also had the added disadvantage of being hard to shift in any gear. This has always been a bad point in MG transmission. The test car had over 8000 miles on it, so it wasn't stiff because it was new. Every time we drive one of the big MG's we always end up with a sore hand from attempting quick second-to-third-gear changes.

The smaller transmission has quite a step between first and second gears, at 3.2 down to 1.918, but the step to third at 1.375 is just about right for street use. In contrast the Mk II box has big jumps between first and second, and second and third (3.637, 2.215, 1.373). The step between first and second is tolerable, but there is just too much between second and third. It causes a noticeable flat spot in acceleration on the way up and renders second gear almost useless as a braking force on the way down.

There were no fuel consumption figures in our files for the TC, but a check with several owners of restored models showed that they were getting around 25 mpg in city driving and as high as 32 mpg on the road. The MT Mk II had an overall average of 23.8 mpg. This included a high of 26.9 mpg on one tank where a lot of open-road cruising at 65 to 75 mph was the order, and a low of 20.3 mpg where most of the miles were racked up charging around town.

The Midget, of course, was much more economical. Highway driving in the 60-to-70-mph range brought us a high of 36.4 mpg. Mixed freeway and city gave 34.6 mpg, and hard city driving produced a low of 27.3 mpg. Our overall average was 32.7 mpg, which makes this one a real economy champ in the high-performance car field.

The brake setup on the Mk II is just about the best in its class. Big, 11-inch Lockheed discs are used at the front, with 10-inch drums at the rear. We used them very hard during our acceleration and top-speed runs, and the hotter they got the better they worked. When the factory says that brake fade has been eliminated, we can believe them. We never encountered a trace. All our stops were straight-line, and the brakes never showed any tendency to lock up or grab. The Mk II's stopping distances from 30 and 60 mph at 36 and 136 feet, respectively, are the shortest we've ever seen for a car this size.

The brakes on the Midget are good — for drums — but can't compare to the Mk II's. They have to be punished before fade sets in, but it does set in, and then they have to be cooled. The deluxe wheel covers are louvered to promote better cooling, but

BOTH MODELS HANDLE VERY WELL IN CORNERS AND WITH RIGHT PREPARATION CAN BE MADE TO STAY WITH THE BEST IN THEIR CLASSES.

MG's a Pair

the cool-down period would be shorter with conventional covers. All stops were straight-line and there was only a slight trace of fade apparent at the end of our third crash stop from 60 mph. Stopping distances from 30 and 60 mph were just about average at 42 and 152 feet.

Both cars have a very comfortable ride for production sports cars. That the factory has been able to manage this at no apparent sacrifice in handling qualities can be counted as quite an achievement. The Mk II's suspension layout is fairly conventional. An independent coil spring/wishbone setup is used at the front. The lower wishbone is a welded stamping, while the upper is a forging and is connected directly to the Armstrong lever shock. Semi-elliptic springs are used at the rear with Armstrong lever shocks.

Due to its firm suspension the Mk II will corner completely flat even without the optional anti-roll bar installed. Ride is not too choppy on rough surfaces.

Tonneau, spare tire and tool kit are stowed in the trunk but there is still enough room left over for a couple of soft-type overnighters for short weekend trips.

Correct jacking point is at the center of the car but uneven ground dictated this location to remove front wheel. Big, 11-inch Lockheed discs work the greatest.

The top can be put up by one man if he's not in too much of a hurry but it's much simpler with two. When not in use the top is stowed out of sight behind the seats.

Aluminum framed, sliding plexi-glass windows are a big improvement over early celluloid and fabric curtains. They are stowed behind the seats in a protective cover.

The Midget is a much easier car to throw around than is the Mk II mainly because of its forgiving nature.

MG's a Pair *continued*

The Midget's front suspension is basically the same as its larger brother's. At the rear it is completely different. While it also uses a rigid axle, its method of locating and attachment takes a different form. At each side there is a quarter-elliptic spring with 15 leaves having the bottom and master leaf attached to a bracket below the axle tube. To control brake and driving forces, there is a parallel radius arm mounted on the same bracket but above the axle. The two rods, therefore, act as trailing arms to locate the axle end-wise and to restrain it from rotating. The springs act to locate the assembly against side forces. One of the big advantages with this arrangement is that the springs are relieved of torque so wheel hop and accompanying wheelspin are reduced to a minimum when accelerating from a rest or when covering rough stretches of road.

Neither car was equipped with the factory-optional front anti-roll bar, but both behaved admirably under all types of cornering conditions. Both cars corner almost dead flat. The Mk II is a bit easier to get out of shape with, but with the right gear there is enough reserve power and the steering is quick enough to keep all but the most inexperienced driver out of trouble. We thought that the Midget had the edge in all-out cornering power. Both are basic understeerers and both exhibit final oversteer. The neutral steer range in the Midget is broader than in the Mk II and this, plus the excellent rear suspension, is the reason that the Midget is more forgiving than its big brother. One has to make some pretty disastrous mistakes to get into trouble with this one.

The highway ride is very good in both cars, despite the stiff suspension and short wheelbases. At flat-out speeds they are extremely stable and all but the most severe cross-winds have little effect on them. Both use fast, light, rack-and-pinion steering systems (2⅔ turns lock-to-lock in the Mk II, 2⅓ in the Midget). Rough roads will cause a certain amount of pitching in both cars at lower speeds but both are sure-footed enough to take this type of road at speed.

The Mk II offers enough head-, hip-, and leg-room for people up to six feet and of average build. The bucket seats (leather covered) are well contoured, well padded and very comfortable. An almost full complement of instruments (no ammeter) is provided, and all are easy to find and read from the driver's seat.

Seating in the Midget is not so good. Our near-six-foot frame was decidedly cramped. With the top up there was no headroom, and with it down our eyes were above the top of the windshield. This can be blamed on entirely too much padding in the otherwise well-shaped bucket seats. The Austin-Healey Sprite, of which the Midget is a direct descendant, fit us very well and the only difference we could find between the two was in the amount of seat padding. As in the Mk II, all the instruments except an ammeter are provided, and all are conveniently placed for the driver's perusal.

Top bows are stored in a fitted case in the trunk when not in use and must be assembled and installed before top can be put in place. Rear cushion is an option.

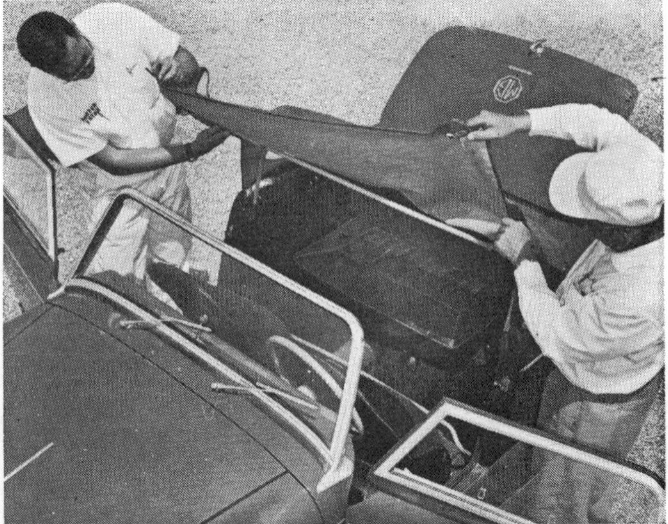

With the bows in place it is a simple matter to fit the top. A rubber seal on the top's leading edge slips into a groove on the windshield to effect a tight seal.

Brake and clutch master cylinders share the same casting and are fed by the same fluid reservoir.

MG's a Pair

The tops for both cars are manually operated and not too much of a job for one man — unless he's in a hurry. In the Mk II the top swings down behind the seats. In the Midget it is stowed, along with its bows, in the trunk.

Exterior and interior finish and detailing are of excellent quality, which is an MG tradition that stretches back even further than the TC. Both have functional trunks that should support the needs of two for weekends. The engine compartments aren't too crowded, so servicing and tuning won't be any problem.

After spending quite a bit of time in both cars we personally prefer the Midget. While it isn't as fast as the Mk II, we feel that pound for pound and inch for inch it offers a shade more performance and a whale of a lot more fun. For another thing, it is quite a bit cheaper, initially, and much, much more economical to operate. Besides that, it comes closest to having that certain indefinable something that made the TC the car that it was. /MT

MG-A 1600 MK II

2-passenger convertible

OPTIONS ON CAR TESTED: Heater/defroster, wire wheels, oil cooler
BASIC PRICE: $2599
PRICE AS TESTED: $2804 (plus tax and license)
ODOMETER READING AT START OF TEST: 8081 miles
RECOMMENDED ENGINE RED LINE: 6000 rpm

PERFORMANCE

ACCELERATION (2 aboard)
0-30 mph .... 4.4 secs.
0-45 mph 8.1
0-60 mph 13.8

Standing start ¼-mile 20.5 secs. and 73 mph

Speeds in gears @ 6000 rpm
1st .... 30 mph
2nd 50
3rd 78
4th . 92 mph max. @ 5100 rpm

Speedometer Error on Test Car

Car's speedometer reading	30	45	52	62	74	84
Western electric speedometer	30	45	50	60	70	80

Observed miles per hour per 1000 rpm in top gear .... 18 mph
Stopping Distances — from 30 mph, 36 ft.; from 60 mph, 136 ft.

SPECIFICATIONS FROM MANUFACTURER

Engine
Ohv in-line 4-cylinder
Bore: 3.0 ins.
Stroke: 3.5 ins.
Displacement: 99 cubic inches
Compression ratio: 8.9:1
Horsepower: 90 @ 5500 rpm
Torque: 97 lbs.-ft. @ 4000 rpm
Horsepower per cubic inch: 0.90
Ignition: 12-volt coil

Gearbox
4-speed manual, synchro on top 3 gears; floor shift

Driveshaft
One-piece; open tube

Differential
Hypoid
Standard ratio: 4.1:1

Suspension
Front: Independent; coil and wishbones with Armstrong lever shocks
Rear: Rigid axle, with 6-leaf semi-elliptic springs and Armstrong lever shocks

Steering
Rack and pinion
Turning diameter: 30.6 ft.
Turns: 2⅔ lock-to-lock

Wheels and Tires
Wire — knock-on
5.60 x 15 Dunlop 6-ply tubeless tires

Brakes
Lockheed hydraulic; disc front, drum rear. Front: 11-in. dia. cast-iron disc
Rear: 10-in. dia. x 1¾ in-wide cast-iron drums
Swept braking area: 350 sq. ins.

Body and Frame
Conventional steel box section frame with bolt-on body
Wheelbase: 94.0 ins.
Track: front, 47.5 ins.; rear, 48.75 ins.
Overall length: 156.0 ins.
Curb weight: 2072 lbs.
Curb weight on front wheels: 53%

MG MIDGET

2-passenger convertible

OPTIONS ON CAR TESTED: Whitewall tires
BASIC PRICE: $1995
PRICE AS TESTED: $2150 (plus tax and license)
ODOMETER READING AT START OF TEST: 1384 miles
RECOMMENDED ENGINE RED LINE: 6000 rpm

PERFORMANCE

ACCELERATION (2 aboard)
0-30 mph .... 5.8 secs.
0-45 mph 11.0
0-60 mph 20.0

Standing start ¼-mile 23.2 secs. and 64 mph

Speeds in gears @ 6000 rpm
1st .... 29 mph
2nd 50
3rd 72
4th . . 78 mph max. @ 4750 rpm

Speedometer Error on Test Car

Car's speedometer reading	30	45	50	60	70	80
Weston electric speedometer	30	45	50	60	70	80

Observed miles per hour per 1000 rpm in top gear .... 16 mph
Stopping Distances — from 30 mph, 42 ft.; from 60 mph, 152 ft.

SPECIFICATIONS FROM MANUFACTURER

Engine
Ohv in-line 4-cylinder
Bore: 2.478 ins.
Stroke: 3.00 ins.
Displacement: 57.9 cubic inches
Compression ratio: 9.0:1
Horsepower: 49.4 @ 5500 rpm
Torque: 52.5 lbs.-ft. @ 4000 rpm
Horsepower per cubic inch: 0.853
Ignition: 12-volt coil

Gearbox
4-speed manual, synchro on top 3 gears; floor shift

Driveshaft
One-piece; open tube

Differential
Hypoid
Standard ratio: 4.27:1

Brakes
Lockheed hydraulic drums
Front and rear: 7-in. dia. x 1¾-in. wide cast-iron drums
Swept braking area: 110 sq. ins.

Steering
Rack and pinion
Turning diameter: 32 ft.
Turns: 2⅓ lock-to-lock

Suspension
Front: Independent; coil and wishbone with Armstrong lever shocks
Rear: Rigid axle with ¼-elliptic, 15-leaf springs, control links and Armstrong lever shocks

Wheels and Tires
Steel disc — 4-lug bolt-on
5.20 x 13 Dunlop 6-ply tubeless tires

Body and Frame
Integral welded frame and body
Wheelbase: 80.0 ins.
Track: front, 45.75 ins.; rear, 44.75 ins.
Overall length: 136.0 ins.
Curb weight: 1525 lbs.
Curb weight on front wheels: 54%

African Journey

DRIES OOSTERVEEN, a Dutch member of the M.G. Car Club, last year tackled the 12,000-mile journey home, from Nyasaland to Holland, overland alone in his 'MGA' 1600. Here is the story of this African marathon, as he told it to Wilson McComb

AFRICA today is, for the European, a strange place to live in—as you may have noticed if you read your newspapers. Most of the continent is in a state of constant upheaval as the inhabitants try to adapt themselves to changing values which are, in many cases, completely foreign to them. Inevitably, the unrest that results from this situation affects everyone, from farm labourer to prominent politician.

Still, I like the life. I have been working in Nyasaland for nine years—I hitched-hiked there from Holland in 1953—and I intend to go on living in Africa. Home leave is pleasant, of course, and the long journey to Europe need not be boring if you resist the temptation to step aboard an aeroplane. In 1957, for instance, I bought a 500 c.c. A.J.S. and rode home overland via the West Coast to Tangiers. The trip took four months, and it was certainly not without interest.

In 1959 I was again due for home leave, but the political situation put that idea out of the question because I was a reserve police officer. I had to stay where I was, so I consoled myself by buying an 'MGA' 1600—the first in Nyasaland—in which I enjoyed some 25,000 miles of pleasant motoring. Eventually, last September, I was free to take my home leave. My time was my own, I had a car that had proved its reliability under rugged conditions, and I had not yet travelled through the eastern part of the continent. The decision was inevitable; I would drive home in my M.G.

Preparation for the journey fell into two categories: gathering together the necessary documents, and preparing the car. The first task proved vastly more difficult than the second, and it seemed that there was endless paperwork to be dône in search of visas and permits of every conceivable kind. As for the car, I fitted it with a sump guard, a guard for the fuel tank, an extra leaf in each rear spring, and a home-brewed luggage carrier which was not a success (it fell apart quite soon). Spares included an ignition coil and contact-breaker, sparking plugs, carburetter float, gaskets, oil-filter element, spare valves, radiator hoses, two fan-belts, brake hoses and a master cylinder reconditioning kit. Most of this was unused. On 18 September I started my long journey to the north—by travelling south! This was not as crazy as it sounds; I had to go first to Salisbury to collect some visas. It also provided an opportunity to visit Geoff Stevens of the M.G.C.C. Southern Rhodesia Centre. I am an Unattached Overseas Member myself, but Geoff promised me a mammoth party if I completed the journey successfully. I must pay him another visit soon . . . . .

On the way to Salisbury, I was amused by the notices warning motorists to beware of elephants crossing the road. No elephants have been seen in these parts for the past 20 years. One local wag has modified a notice near Fort Johnston so that it now reads 'Beware of *pink* elephants'. Another notice that is seen from time to time is

Motorway—African style! Dries Oosterveen encountered appalling road conditions on many parts of his route, such as this stretch of mountain road beside Lake Tanganyika. He carried drinking water bags on the front bumper—the recognised way of keeping the water relatively cool

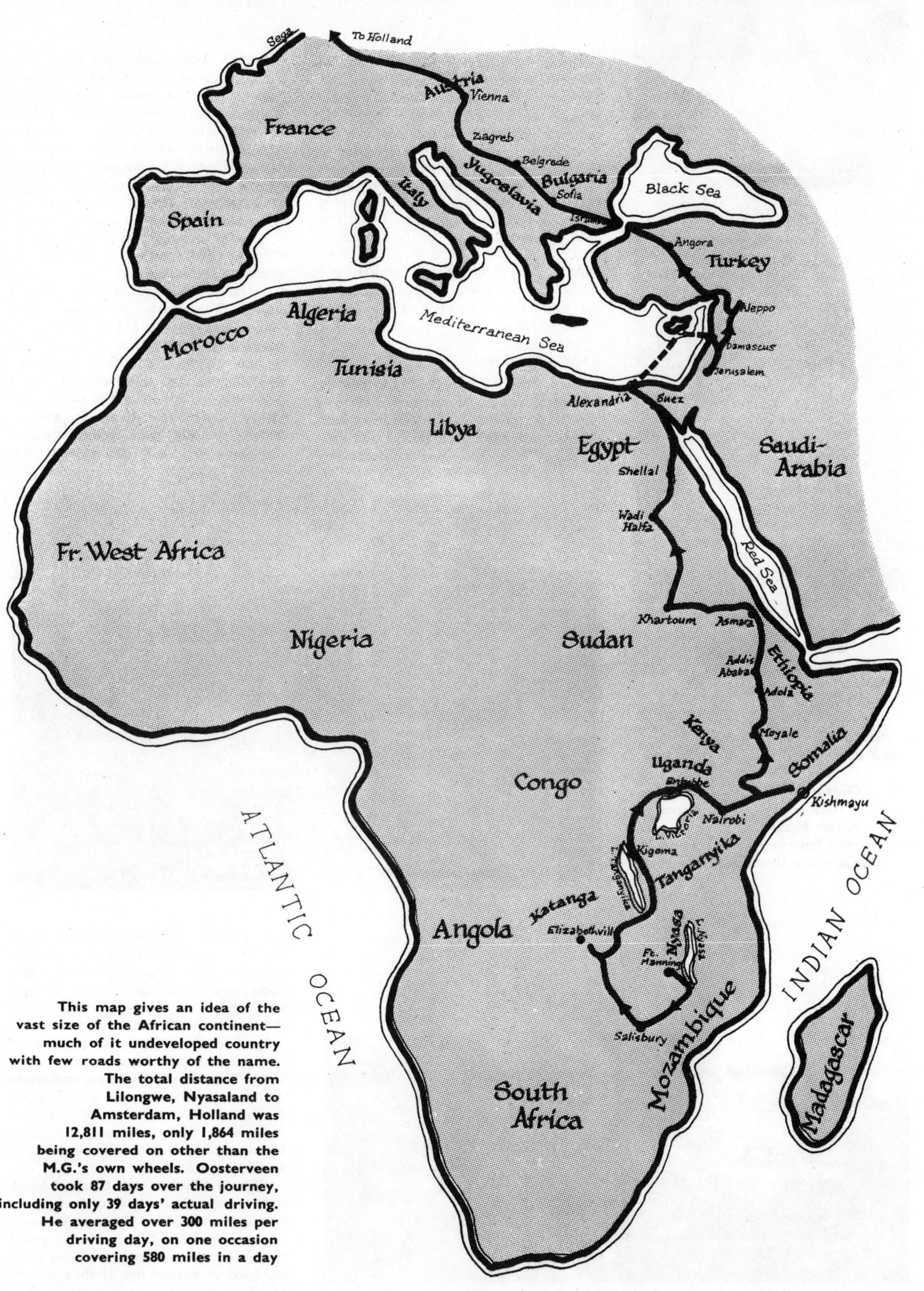

This map gives an idea of the vast size of the African continent—much of it undeveloped country with few roads worthy of the name. The total distance from Lilongwe, Nyasaland to Amsterdam, Holland was 12,811 miles, only 1,864 miles being covered on other than the M.G.'s own wheels. Oosterveen took 87 days over the journey, including only 39 days' actual driving. He averaged over 300 miles per driving day, on one occasion covering 580 miles in a day

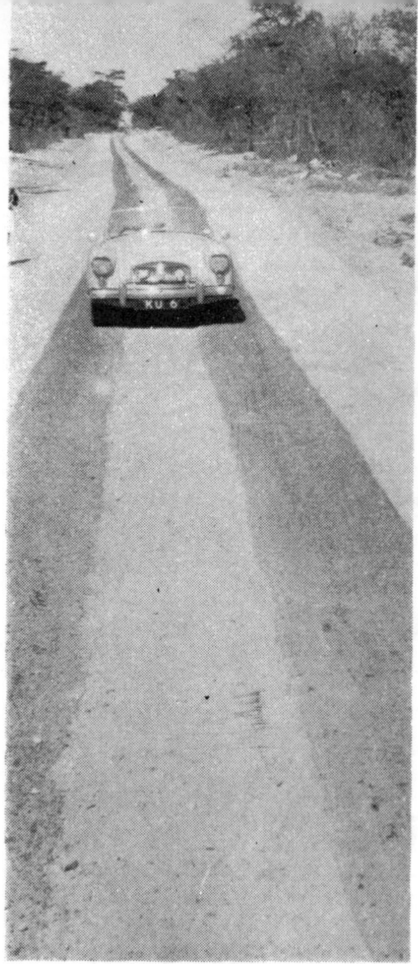

'Danger—Africans Crossing'. This is not intended as a gratuitous insult to the Africans, but is a very necessary precaution because one so often encounters drunken villagers on the road. Without care, the motorist may easily run into one, and this is a situation to be avoided at all costs. A motor accident involving an African usually results in a riot, and quite often a lynching thrown in for good measure. I had not gone very far myself before the windscreen of the M.G. was cracked by large stones, flung at the car by African children as I passed through a small village. But I did not stop—I have lived long enough in Africa to know better.

A VISIT TO KATANGA

From Salisbury I turned north, passing through Northern Rhodesia and heading towards Katanga. It was noticeable how little traffic there was to be seen about here. Stoning and burning of houses and cars, especially those belonging to Europeans, had been commonplace for some time. Only a few weeks before, two Britishers in a Land Rover, attempting to drive home from South Africa, were stoned by Africans and their vehicle wrecked, so that they had no alternative but to return to South Africa. However, I experienced no difficulties and had the roads to myself. I also spent a day in Katanga, where I saw a lot of soldiers and police, but was not molested. I was warned not to travel alone, but as there were no other vehicles going in my direction I had little choice.

For the next 600 miles or so I was driving through Tanganyika on lonely, sandy roads—for two days I saw nothing but thorn trees! Here it was a big event to meet another car; both drivers would stop, get out, and have a conversation before continuing on their way. The sandy roads were a curse—about 40 m.p.h. was the highest possible speed, and averages of 20 m.p.h. were good going. On one occasion I stopped to take a photograph,

'Strip roads' are common in many parts of Africa (above). Two strips of tarmac are all there is to drive upon and if another vehicle is met, one or other has to ease off into the soft sand and dust at the side. Bridges, too, can be very primitive and Oosterveen prudently inspects one (right) before crossing. A less hazardous crossing was of the Equator (below) which is just a white line across the road

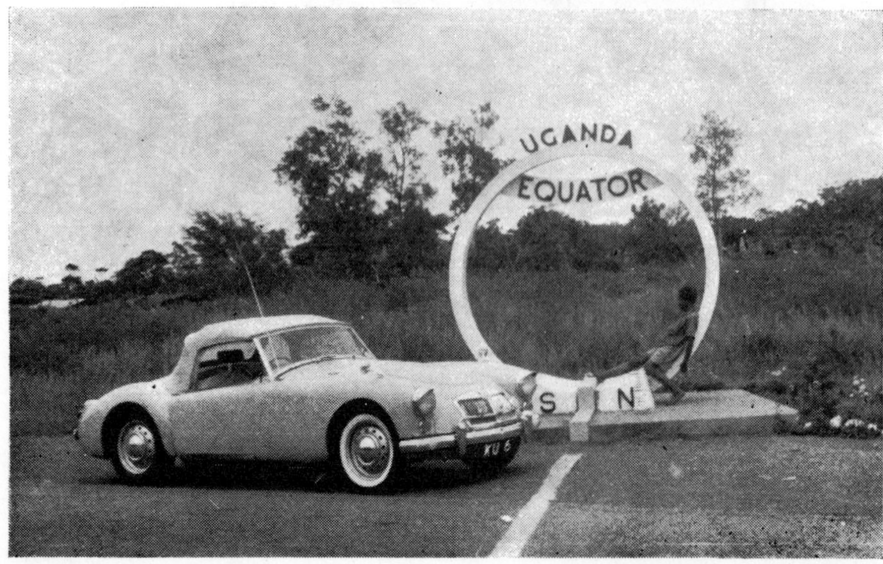

and found the M.G. stuck in the sand when I tried to restart. For two and a half solid hours I worked, digging with bare hands, filling the holes with grit, letting the tyres down, and so on. Thereafter I picked my photographic spots with more care.

At Kigoma, on the eastern shore of Lake Tanganyika, I rested for two days in a local hotel before driving on to Ruanda Urundi—where, by the way, one drives on the right, as in several parts of Africa. It could be a little confusing, but many African roads are such that one drives in the middle anyhow.

When I reached Ruanda Urundi I found this formerly Belgian-owned territory in the midst of elections. The giant Watutsis, once the rulers of the land, had been deposed by their erstwhile serfs and were now being murdered or burned out of their houses.

Tribesmen inspect the 'MGA' in Somalia. In other parts of Africa the natives were less friendly towards Europeans and the windscreen was cracked by a rock flung at the car as it passed through one village

Thousands fled to Uganda, where special camps were set up to receive them. The new Prime Minister moved into office and, three days later, was shot in the stomach. That meant more rioting, and more refugees fleeing to Uganda.

Skirting the northern shores of Lake Victoria, I drove through Kenya towards Somalia. Here, in the Northern Frontier district, one must have the local District Commissioners' permission to pass through, for there is always the chance of encountering Somali tribesmen, who cross the borders as they please and are not always on their best behaviour. A few miles outside Kishmayu I had to turn back, however, because of tremendous floods which made driving impossible. Because of this unexpected and lengthy detour, I ran out of petrol near Garisso. I was able to beg four gallons from a soldier in charge of a mobile generator, and eventually reached Moyale, a small outpost on the Kenya/Ethiopia border, where I was well received by the Ethopian District Governor.

BY LORRY TO ADOLA

For 12 days I waited in hopes of a break in the rains, but none came and everything was still under water. So I started to look for a lorry. Only one was available, and it was owned by a Somali. How much would it cost to hire for the 330 miles to Adola? The Somali suggested 500 Ethopian dollars (about £75). I suggested that this was on the high side. He disagreed; it was, after all, the *only* available lorry. With the help of the Governor's weighty influence we reduced the price by rather more than 50 per cent. (to £30, in fact) and the M.G. was loaded up.

Nowhere—in Europe or in Africa—have I seen such a road as this. It had not been repaired for 30 years, and some of the mud was three feet deep. Ditches, gulleys and rock outcrops, sometimes three or even four feet high, were as common as a fly on a camel, and it took us a full day to cover 80 miles. Even in the dry season it would have been quite impossible to drive the M.G. over this road, and in the rains it was indescribable. The ancient lorry crashed and bounded in all directions, while my unfortunate car was smashed and ground against its sides. Indeed, more damage was done to the bodywork by this ride than by the whole of the rest of the journey.

Back on my own four wheels again, I found that the engine had begun to consume alarming quantities of oil. I called a halt at a small camping site in Addis Ababa, and took a look inside. What I saw explained everything only too well: the entire engine was filled with fine, fine sand—rather like face-powder—which had penetrated every imaginable corner of the car, and lay in the oil-filter like a horrid, gritty sludge. I spent a restful four days removing the engine, with many stops for beer or lemonade, and fitting Opel piston rings (the only type available) which were filed down to suit. Then I put the engine back and hoped for the best. I expected that the oil consumption would be reduced, but would rise again after a few thousand miles. And that is just what it did!

On 8 November I left Addis Ababa and drove over the Mussolini Pass, where the misty rain was so thick that eventually I had to stop because I could not see a thing. Fortunately a slow-moving tanker appeared, lit up like a Christmas tree, and by following this I was able to continue on my way to Asmara. Here, in the Rift Valley area, the differences in altitude were so great and so sudden that a headache soon resulted. By comparison with Ethiopian passes, those of the Alps are mere billiard tables. At Asmara I was almost within sight of the

In Jordan one drives up from the Dead Sea to find this sign at the top of a long rise, for the famous salt lake is some distance below true sea level

After his long journey, Dries Oosterveen came to see us at the Abingdon factory and brought his 'MGA' with him, neither being the worse for their arduous journey. Dries also brought a collection of press cuttings (below) from several parts of the African continent

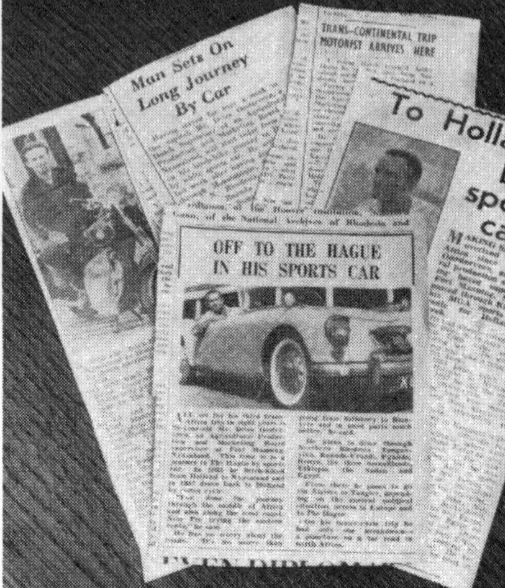

Red Sea, and felt justified in considering this a milestone on the journey. Europe now seemed definitely within reach.

At this stage, perhaps I should mention that I always tried to avoid seeming over-confident about the journey—which was, after all, more than 12,500 miles in length. I refused to make boasts about how long it would take, or even that I was sure of completing it. When people questioned me, I just said that I'd see how far I would get.

Again in Asmara I was warned not to drive alone, as local political agitators had an uncomfortable habit of taking pot-shots at passing motorists to while away the tedium of life. But there wasn't very much I could do about it, so I turned westwards to Khartoum. I crossed the Ethiopian/Sudanese border at Tessenei, and was immediately aware of being in an Arab country. The houses and the people themselves were a different shape and a different colour.

One crosses the Atbara River by driving over the railway bridge. No notice is given of approaching trains, so the drill is to stop, listen carefully, and then make a dash for it. Sometimes a train appears from the opposite direction while one is on the bridge, which is rather a long one. It is then advisable to reverse, for the average train is larger than an 'MGA'.

INTO THE DESERT

There could hardly have been a greater contrast than between the mountains of Ethiopia and the desert country where I now found myself. On many occasions I would encounter dry, sandy stretches where it was best to accelerate. If this failed, a quick change down to third or second would make the tyres bite through to hard ground, and usually sufficed to pull me through. On the way to Khartoum, I came across a lorry lying on its side in the middle of the desert, with no clue as to how the accident had occurred. Beside it lay three natives. They had been there for three days, so they were very dead, and there didn't seem to be anything I could do to help. I drove on to Khartoum.

The authorities do not allow one to drive alone across the Sudan, so I had to wait seven days before getting a passage for the M.G. on the train to Wadi Halfa, on the Nile. However, Khartoum was in the midst of preparing for Revolution Day, so I spent most of my time photographing the preparations and celebrations. This occupation was not as boring as it may sound, for one was strictly forbidden to take photographs.

It took 36 dusty hours to cover the 584 miles by train to Wadi Halfa, where I had to board the Nile steamer. Here I ran into difficulties at first. They could not help me, I was told. The M.G. would not fit into the ordinary steamer. When I made it clear that I was not English, but Dutch, a special barge appeared as if by magic. For the next two days and nights I sailed down the Nile in company with two Danish hitch-hikers whom I had already met in Uganda, Kenya and the Sudan. I saw several early Egyptian temples and graves already partly covered by the rising waters of the Nile.

Two hundred miles later I disembarked at Shellal, just south of the Aswan Dam, and immediately became involved in a verbal skirmish with minor Egyptian officials. Their ingenious procedure is to present Europeans with a variety of forms

The road to Khartoum takes in the edge of the Sudanese desert—just flat, featureless sand and the sun blazing from a cloudless sky—not a good place for a breakdown. In fact the authorities will not allow a traveller to cross the main desert alone and Dries had reluctantly to put the car on a train

which must be filled in. The forms are printed in Arabic—but a translation may be had for £5. Needless to say, I was not prepared to play—or to pay, either—but the experience was typical of what happens nowadays in Egypt. I skirted the Red Sea northwards to Suez, with a detour to admire the Sphinx and the Pyramids, and in 200 miles saw only four other cars. My disgust at Egyptian behaviour increased as I made my way through Suez to Alexandria. Being yelled at, shoved, spat upon and cursed by mere youths for failure to produce baksheesh on demand is something I do *not* appreciate.

At Addis Ababa the African sand had worked its way into the engine and necessitated the fitting of new piston rings. The job was done in leisurely fashion under far from ideal conditions, but fortunately the beer was good! In Somalia, in the lower picture, Dries is seen bedding down for the night beside the car. He assured us that in that part of Africa, the natives, wild animals and insects permit this practice

DETOUR TO JERUSALEM

At Alexandria I was lucky enough to secure, inside two days, a passage to Beirut. The ship sailed first to Limassol, where we made only a short stop before going on to the Lebanon. I decided to make another detour at this point, driving southwards through Damascus to Jordan and visiting Jericho, Jerusalem, Amman and the Dead Sea. As on many previous occasions, I slept in the car that night. The experience was worth having, but I disliked the way the Jordanian side of Jerusalem had been commercialised as a tourist attraction. Then I turned north again through Aleppo to Killis, on the Syrian/Turkish border, where I found the customs post closed and had to drive the 120 miles back to Aleppo. It was somewhere near here that I hit a deep rut at 80 m.p.h. The M.G. shot into the air and landed with a crunch. The bonnet, boot-lid and both doors flew open with the shock of the impact. This, I thought, is the end of my trip; certainly the end of my suspension. But when I pulled myself together and inspected the car, I found not one spring-leaf broken or any other damage done.

When I finally entered Turkey, I was most impressed by all that I saw. The roads were well planned, the people were friendly, and everything seemed inexpensive. I made my longest one-day trip of the journey (from Adana to Istanbul, a distance of 580 miles), for I was beginning to smell home. Behind me lay the Red Sea and the Dead Sea; ahead was the Black Sea and Europe just beyond.

BEHIND THE IRON CURTAIN

After crossing the Bosporus and entering Europe at last, I came rapidly aware that I was in a freedom-loving country. An innocent conversation with some Bulgarian girls, who asked me to send a picture postcard from Africa, led to a stern interview with the security police. The girls' names and addresses, which I had noted down, had to be returned. In Sofia, too, the amount of anti-Nato propaganda to be seen in the streets was most noticeable. When I reached the Bulgarian/Jugoslavian border, I tried to change my Bulgarian money into some other currency. That could not be done, I was told. All right, I said, I would take it with me. No, that was not allowed either. Very well, could I have the amount credited with my own bank? No, that could not be arranged. My patience completely exhausted, I started to tear up the bank-notes—and was promptly charged with 'damaging Government property'. You can have the Balkans, as far as I'm concerned.

Through Belgrade, Zagreb and Vienna I made good time to Germany, where I visited some friends. Next morning I found the radiator water frozen solid. Somehow, the use of anti-freeze solution was one precaution that had not occurred to me when preparing the car in Nyasaland . . . .

It was not long before I found myself in Holland, telling the tale of my experiences to Pim van der Veer of the M.G.C.C. Dutch Centre. Then I reached home, late one January night.

Half-an-hour later, my 'MGA' had disappeared. The police found it next day in Amsterdam: the clock and speedometer were ruined, the rear hood panel and side-screens were torn to pieces, and the radio had gone. As Pim remarked afterwards, one sometimes wonders where the jungl begins.

A cliché perhaps, but no-one could drive through Egypt without photographing his car beside the famous pyramids, and Dries is no exception. This was almost his last view of Africa, before crossing to Europe

Buying an MGA

An MGA in this sort of condition is now sought after and prices have shown a steady rise in recent years. There were no significant changes to the body during the model life from 1955-1962. The car was a dramatic change from the traditional MG sportscars with their separate wings, cutaway doors and exposed slab fuel tank, but they were still based on a chassis.

MGA owner, Michael Brisby, tells you what to expect and what to look for when buying this classic sportscar.

There are no legends surrounding the MGA. It is not — and never was — a ferocious, fire-breathing projectile and people who want that sort of motoring should look elsewhere. Like most production MGs the MGA looks pretty ordinary on paper and never had any strong claims to be other than a very attractive choice for those who like a sports car to be reliable, reasonably economical, tough and, above everything else, fun to drive.

The MGA is not without its faults and shortcomings, but, in 1980 — twenty-five years after the model's announcement — the MGA has lost none of the attractions which led to it selling in larger numbers than any previous MG. The passage of time allows most of us to overlook many of the MGA's irritations and accept it as one of the better classic sports cars.

A surprising number of people have never forgiven the MGA for not having running boards, a fold-flat windscreen and a slab fuel tank like its predecessors. The critics choose to overlook the contemporary opinion that the TD and TF MGs were unjustifiably quaint (a view particularly strongly expressed by the American market) and ignore the fact that the MGA grew out of the TD.

The body shape of the MGA was the responsibility of Syd Enever and was designed to cut the wind resistance of the MG TD raced at Le Mans by the photographer George Phillips in 1951. Despite the fact that the driver poked out into the air-stream like a lighthouse at the end of a pier the more arodynamic body markedly improved the TD's top speed although the car retired with an engine failure.

Enever wasted no time in designing or

instigating a new chassis which featured side rails which swept out wide in the cockpit area to permit a low driving position. A few minor alterations were made to the "LeMans" body and the MGA proper was ready to go into production in around 1953; however, BMC senior management, who were not very sports car orientated, hesitated and the car did not appear until 1955.

The Fixed-Head-Coupe took the radical break with MG traditions a stage further with wind-up windows and saloon car comfort if one ignored the high noise levels. This car is wearing the optional wire wheels. Coupes now fetch almost as much as the comparable Roadster and both cars offer reliable everyday transport with reasonable economy and performance. The MGA's road-behaviour was very good for the period.

PARTS SUPPLIERS

Some of the better known parts specialists include:

Westwood Portway Group (Peter Wood), Westwood, Twyford, Buckinghamshire.

Motobuild Ltd., 128 High Street, Hounslow, Middlesex.

Terry Hird Spares Centre, 7 Rosemont Road, Hampstead, London NW3 (parts and mechanical)

NTG Motor Services Ltd., 21 St. Margaret's Green, Ipswich, Suffolk.

Simon J. Robinson, MGA Centre, Cleveland Street, Darlington.

M.C. Griffiths, Preston Candover, Basingstoke, Hampshire (Parts)

Mike Allison, Cubbington Road Garage, Cubbington, Leamington Spa (Body and mechanical)

Good Ideas, North Place, Highbridge Street, Waltham Abbey, Essex (Trim)

Toulmin Motors Ltd., 103 Windmill Road, Brentford, Middlesex. (Parts)

Howe Exhausts and Cams, Rear of Hollyville Cafe, A20 West Kingsdown, Nr. Sevenoaks, Kent (Performance parts)

Vic Ellis, Sports Cars, 234 Trussley Road, London W6. (Tuning & Service)

Andreason Racing and Tuning Ltd., Derby Road, Eastleigh, Hants.

The chassis is strong but not massive and should not be considered everlasting. A fore and aft braced hoop across the front of the front bulkhead lends considerable stiffness to the chassis, but the side rails must be checked carefully — easier said than done with the body in place. A body-off restoration is quite feasible and enables the chassis to be properly inspected and repaired — few chassis have escaped some rust damage.

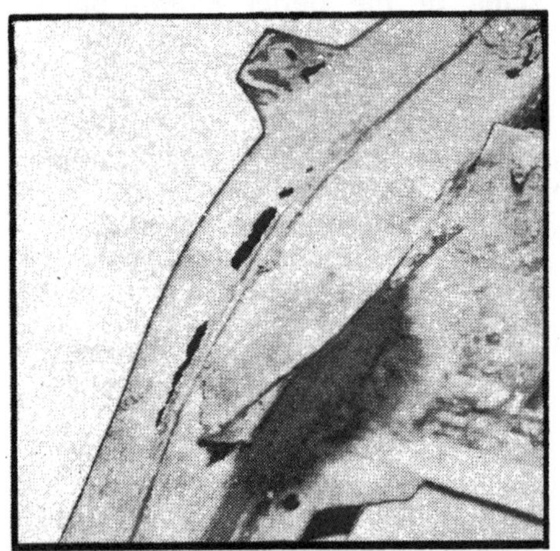

The sill structure lies close to the chassis as can be seen here. This ideal trap for mud and water can create problems — the inner face of the sill may well be missing on some cars. So look and probe thoroughly.

This is the area of the chassis adjacent to the rear door post where rot can occur. Top centre is the body mounting bracket, and the bracket and side face of the chassis rails sometimes rust there as well.

It is not uncommon for the chassis to rust badly near the body mounts just ahead of the forward door post — a situation made worse by the presence of a wad of felt **within** the chassis rail in this area which retains water.

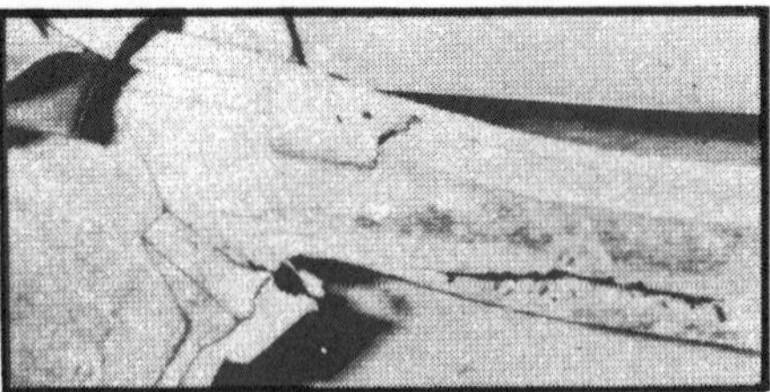

Where the floors butt against the inner face of the chassis rails corrosion can set in quite badly — not easy to spot with the floors in place, but repairable.

The condition of the inner sill and door post structures can often be judged by looking at the front and rear wings. The bottom of this wing is badly rotted and the rust is extending up the door post area — a good indicator of problems in the internal body structure.

The fingers point to where rust occurs on the rear wings of both Fixed Head Coupe and Roadsters. Reproduction wings cost about £500 (per set) and some specialists do sell repair sections. If the sill and door post structure seems sound try gently rocking the car by holding the top or the rear door-post and pulling gently; apply the same test to the base of the sills.

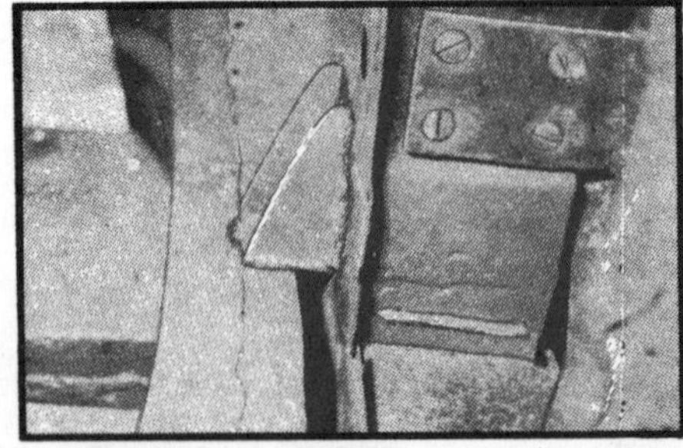

On a car that has had any restoration work done you are likely to find signs of repairs in the area of the forward door post and around the body mounting bracket at the base of the inner panel — or signs that a new door post has been fitted. Fixed Head Coupe doors are much heavier than those of the Roadster but they share the same post design.

Buying a

ROAD TEST

Having given the car a thorough examination the prospective MGA buyer should try the car if that can be done legally. Newcomers may not find the gear ratios ideal with quite a gap between second and third gear, but the change should be quite pleasant and there should be only moderate transmission noise. Acceleration is not outstanding on any but the Twin Cam MGA. Steering should be excellent with plenty of feel, no lost movement and only moderate kick-back through the steering wheel. Handling should be very predictable — if it is not something is wrong and the front suspension is often the culprit. If the car rolls a lot when cornering, plunges under braking and floats over undulating surfaces the front dampers are definitely worn out. If these complaints are accompanied by noises and steering kick back or jarring then the front suspension is almost certain to require overhaul. Braking performance and stability should be well up to the performance of the car.

MGA FACTS

Introduced in late 1955 the MGA was the last chassis-based MG and while the mechanical components were borrowed from the BMC range the body and chassis were definitely not. Weighing around 18 cwt and with only 68 b.h.p. in 1500 form the MGA was not notably fast in a straight line, but its very responsive and predictable handling outshone a number of its contemporary rivals. A very high proportion of early MGA production was exported to the U.S.A. and of the total build of 101,081

MGA

(Continued)

cars about 60% were exported. Sales fell towards the late fifties and by the 1960s the lack of comfort and luggage space, added to the car's modest performance caused sales to fall away rapidly until production ceased in 1962 to make way for the MGB.

WHAT TO PAY

After a spell when the MGA was notably under-valued prices have risen steadily to the point where non-running candidates for complete restoration often fetch over £300. The Twin Cam in the same condition might easily be twice the price of a push-rod car. There is no price advantage in looking for a Fixed-Head-Coupe rather than a Roadster at the lower end of the market and it will fetch only very slightly less than the equivalent Roadster at the top end of the market. Spares and reproduction parts supplies are now good and restoration standards are improving rapidly. Good examples change hands for between £2,500 - £4,000 and price is very dependent upon condition, originality and standard of any restoration work done or required. Cars with fibreglass wings are about £600 less than comparable examples with new or very good steel wings.

PARTS SUPPLIERS

The parts situation is now so good that very few MGAs are being broken up.

The nose of the MGA is not visible from the driving seat and prone to attack from high mounted bumpers. Replacement bumpers and grilles are available from specialists, but damage to the front lower corners of the front shroud is more difficult to rectify.

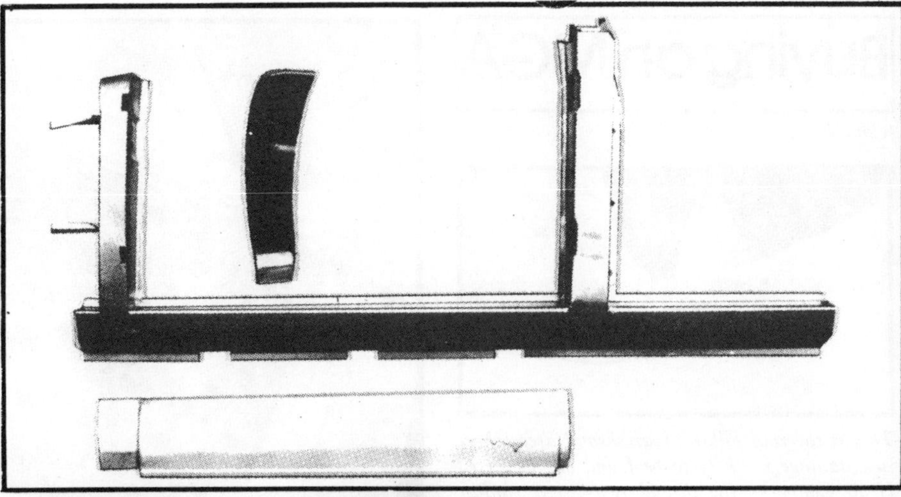

The inner sill and door post structure are often badly rusted — this is a replacement section with the non-structural outer sill in the foreground. (Panels by Motobuild).

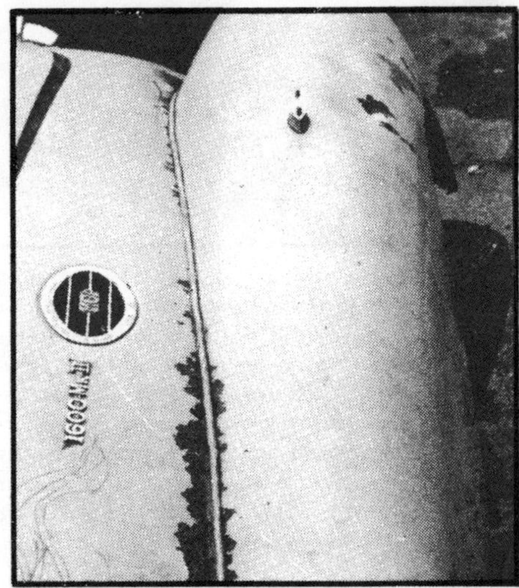

The point where the bolt-on wings and the shroud edges meet, front and rear, is a good indicator of general body condition. It is not uncommon to find the wing beading partially embedded or submerged in plastic filler — wings are expensive and repairs to the edges of the shrouds require skill. Reproduction front and rear shrouds are very expensive.

Production Figures
1955-1959 MGA 1500 (1489 c.c.) 58750
1958-1960 MGA Twin Cam (1588 c.c.) 2,III
1959-1961 MGA 1600 (1588 c.c.) 31,501
1961-1962 MGA 1600 MK2 (1622 c.c.) 8,719

Distinguishing Features.

MGA1500 — Announced at the 1955 Motor Show in Roadster form, wire wheels optional. Fixed Head Coupe version available in late 1956 slightly faster due to better aerodynamics. Early cars with 68 b.h.p. — later raised to 72 b.h.p. High proportion of the first year's production (13,000 cars) were exported.

MGA Twin Cam — Recognition features were the peg-drive knock on wheels and Dunlop disc brakes front and rear. The 108 b.h.p. engine added at least 15 m.p.h. to top speed at the price of greater fuel consumption, a reputed thirst for oil and temperament. Ignition timing and fuel mixture are critical, accessibility to the engine poor and this high performance version has always been haunted by a reputation for mechanical fragility. Not for the unskilled or unsympathetic mechanic.

MGA 1600 — A bore increase gave the same capacity as the Twin Cam and disc brakes at the front improved braking. Detail lighting changes.

MGA 1600 Mk II — Revised engine and increase in capacity to 1622 c.c. gave more power and the final drive ratio was dropped from 4.3 to 4.1:1 More detail changes to lighting arrangements and a revised grille.

MGA 1600 Mk II — de Luxe This car is essentially a Twin Cam fitted with a push-rod engine to absorb the parts left over when the Twin Cam was discontinued after an unexpectedly low production run. Not many made — shares the wheels and brakes of the Twin Cam.

General — Detail changes were made to the interior trim and lighting arrangements but the body was not altered during the MGA model life. The sidescreens and hood design also received attention.

Buying an MGA

(Continued)

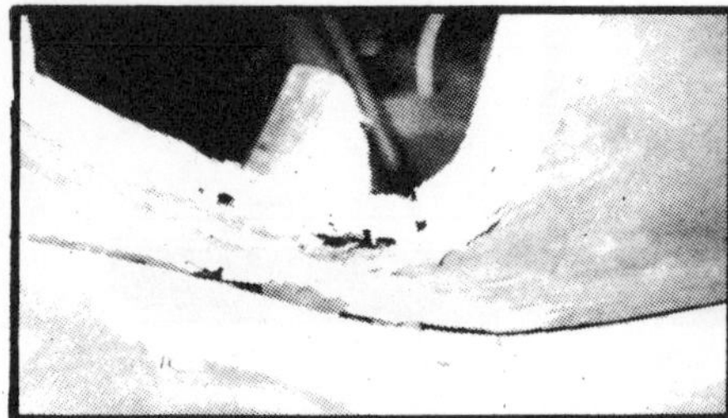

This is the roof pillar / rear shroud area where rust damage is likely to be found on the Fixed Head Coupe — the shroud rusts at a similar point above the forward part of the rear wings on the Roadster.

This severely corroded boot area shows what ***can*** *happen! Check the boot floor and wheel arch sides carefully and also look at the lower edge of the boot aperture gutter which was not provided with drainage and may well have allowed rust to eat into the rear shroud below the boot lid. While in this area glance below at the condition of the fuel tank — many are now due for replacement.*

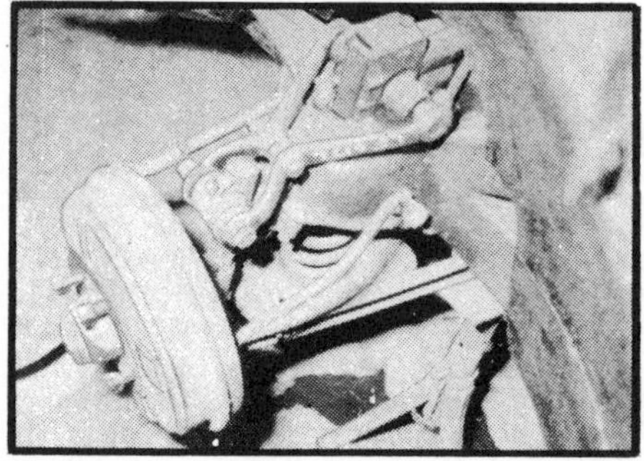

It is well worth taking a close look at the front suspension. The inner lower wishbone bushes sometimes perish and the holes in the bottom wishbones for the bolt passing through the lower trunion elongate if not greased.

If the assembly has not been greased regularly wear is likely to be found in all the moving parts. Road behaviour is very dependent on the condition of the front shock-absorbers. Early MGAs had all drum brakes sometimes alleged to fade; later cars had discs at the front. The Twin Cam and de Luxe versions had discs all round. Spares for the drum braked cars are easier to find. The steering rack lasts well if kept lubricated and the gaiters are sound. The cost of parts to overhaul the front running gear soon mounts up.

An MGA engine bay is not a model of tidiness and oil filter changes are fiddly. Performance from the B-series engines is not dramatic, but they last well. Valve train noise is often noticeable and oil leaks are not uncommon. Spares are not a great problem and the cars are generally reliable. The absence of the ducting from the heater to forward of the radiator will encourage fumes to enter the interior of this example.

The fascia is fairly simple, note the central horn push. Provision was made for a radio, but interior noise levels are not the lowest. A steering column adjustable for reach was an option, but newcomers find the wheel close to the chest even when it is as far forward as it will go. The wheel rim cracks at the spokes, particularly on Roadsters, but the steering is excellent. The leather faced seats did not have adjustable backrests and many people consider the seating to be poor. Trim is relatively simple to restore. The Roadster's sidescreens flap badly if they are not in good condition and the hood does not stow easily. The Fixed Head Coupe is not noted for low noise levels, but the trim lasts better.

MGA

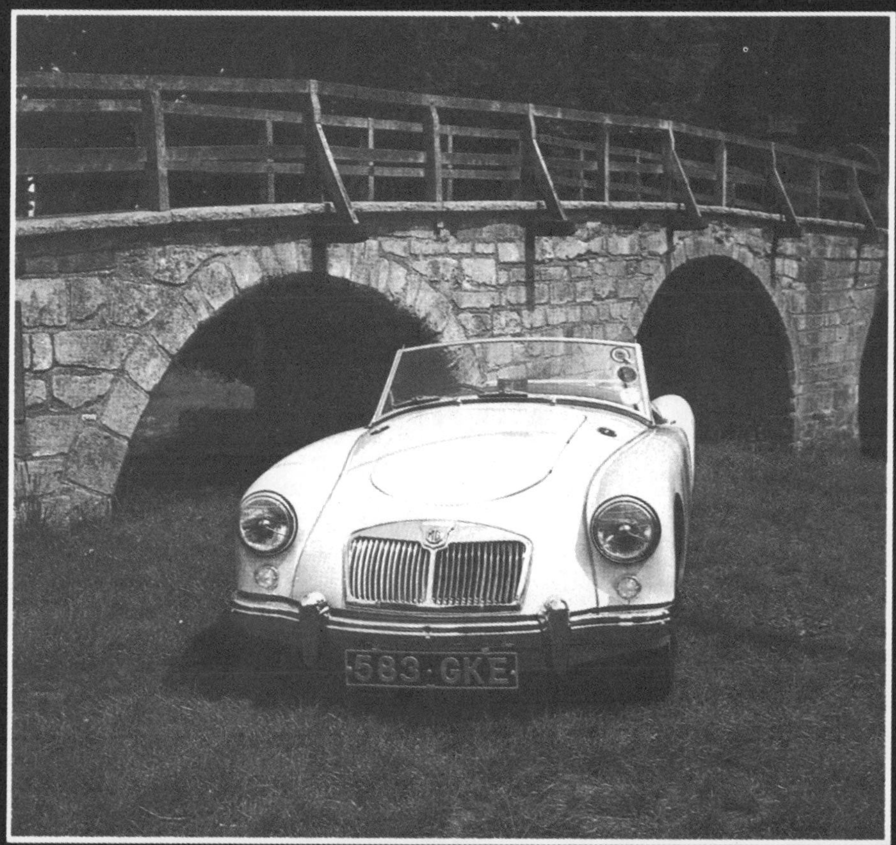

The introduction of the MGA 1500 was a long awaited event by both the motoring public and the press. The new car before introduction was code named EX 182 and was a direct replacement for the MG TF Midget although it was developed from the earlier TD. The car had been finished some two years before it was introduced and was at that time purely as a design exercise. Three prototypes were built with the code name EX 182 and were officially competition cars, destined to appear at the Le Mans 24 hour race in June 1955. It was originally intended to announce the all new MG to the public at the beginning of June and then enter three of them at Le Mans, however a delay in the supply of bodies meant that the prototypes had to race rather than production versions. The Le Mans outing proved successful, with a developed version of the new BMC 'B' series engine as introduced on the ZA Magnette saloon with a capacity of 1489cc. The team met with reasonable results with two cars coming fifth and sixth, the third car driven by Dick Jacobs however crashed in the aftermath of a disaster which killed over eighty people, when a Mercedes left the track ploughing into spectators. Three cars later entered the Ulster TT race, two of which were utilising experimental twin cam engines. Again the results were encouraging, proving the new MGs high speed reliability, just what was needed for a successful launch to the new car.

The success of the MGA was quite staggering, in the first full year of production in 1956, more than 13,000 cars were built, which far exceeded the entire production achieved over a four year period with the TC. It was evident that MG had come up with the right car at the right time, with an extremely attractive body, its flowing lines were to become one of today's most desirable classic cars. The 'B' series engine was fitted in standard tune and initially gave 68bhp at 5500 rpm and later being raised to 72bhp at the same engine speed. The independent coil spring and wishbone front suspension system was directly related to that of the MG TF, whilst the half elliptic sprung rear axle was that fitted to the ZA Magnette. It is worth mentioning that several traditional MG features were incorporated from previous models which included lever arm dampers that formed part of the front suspension wishbone layout and twin six volt batteries wired in series mounted either side of the prop shaft behind the seats. The weather equipment was also adopted from previous models being of basic self assembly with separate side screens incorporating flaps to allow hand signalling. The MGA did however have flashing direction indicators like its predecessor, the TF.

The dashboard too was a welcome return to traditional styling with a pronounced absence of octagonal instrumentation. The MGA had sensible circular dials, with the rev counter and speedometer placed in direct sight of the driver behind the steering wheel on each side of the column. The fly-off handbrake was mounted on the side of the transmission tunnel, which was effective and ideally placed, likewise the gear change was precise and located in the optimum position for speed of operation. Optional extras included a radio and a fresh air heater, also the car could be ordered with standard steel disc wheels or centre lock wire wheels. Other desirable extras included a 4.55:1 axle ratio, telescopic steering column and a tonneau cover. A works hardtop was not available immediately but followed a year after the car was introduced.

As indicated before, the MGA was an immediate success, with just over 1000 cars being built before the end of 1955 and in 1956 they were streaming through the factory gates at Abingdon at the rate of 300 a week, in total no less than 58,750 examples were sold with a large percentage finding their way into the American market. This was obviously due to the fact that the car broke new ground in terms of styling, performance and safety, being more civilised and smoother than the TF. After only a year in production, the roadster was joined by a closed-in version, the MGA Coupe. This car was totally different in concept to the open topped car with many refinements found on saloons of the day. Wind-up windows, a wrap-around front windscreen and similar rear screen. Lockable door handles were fitted making the car secure. A total of 100lbs was the difference between the roadster and the coupe, which meant the car was somewhat slower than the open top version. The coupe was to remain in production throughout the range of ensuing models and was available with all the models including the 1600, Twin Cam and the extremely rare 1600 De Luxe model.

By 1959, time and progress was telling on the MGA. Competitors such as Triumph had introduced disc braking and they also had a weight advantage over the MGA. This no doubt brought about the introduction of the 1600 version with increased power and disc brakes, making 100mph both possible and safe. The MGA remained in production in various forms right through until 1962 when the MGB was introduced, over 100,000 models had been produced and the factory was proud of the fact that sales had outstripped the Triumph TR series which had proved more successful in previous years.

MGA

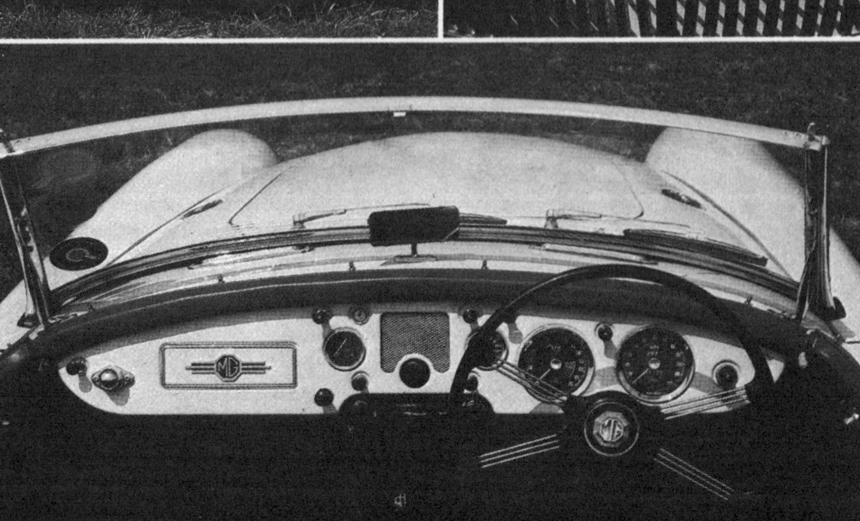

Specification
Engine:
Type: In line water cooled
No of cylinders: 4
Bore/stroke: 73.025 x 88.9mm
Capacity: 1489cc
Compression Ratio: 8.3:1
Valve operation: pushrod overhead valve.
Carburation: Twin semi-downdraught SU.
Power output: Early cars: 68bhp @ 5500rpm
Late cars: 72bhp @ 5500rpm
Maximum torque: 77lb ft @ 3500rpm.
Clutch & Gearbox: Dry clutch, part synchromesh 4 speed manual.
Brakes: Lockheed hydraulic, 10″ drums all round.
Tyres: 5.50-15″ on 4″ rims with steel disc or centre lock wire wheels.
Suspension: Front; coil springs, wishbones and lever arm dampers. Rear; live rear axle, half elliptic leaf springs and lever arm dampers.
Wheelbase: 7′10″
Track: front; 3′0″
Width: 4′9.25″
Price on introduction in 1955: £595
Number built: 58,750
Performance
Maximum speed: 98mph
Acceleration: 0-60: 15.6 secs.
Fuel consumption: approx 27mpg.

MGA

The MGA 1500 featured, belongs to Malcolm Badger of Market Harborough. Malcolm is well known to Members participating in MGOC concours and Condition Award competitions at National Events. He is the person with the thankless task of arranging and co-ordinating these shows and as a result is rarely able to enter his concours MGA at major events. The car has won numerous awards however at shows where Malcolm is not officiating. Malcolm is also a founder Member of the South Leicestershire MG Owners' Club who along with Dick Gardiner formed the Club in 1976, although they are both still actively involved with the area, they have channelled their efforts into starting a business specialising in MGs. The company, known as Malick Cars operates from Bridewell Lane in Kettering and they are both encouraged by the way the business has taken off and the good reputation they have earned in a relatively short space of time.

Malcolm purchased the car as a total wreck in December 1980 for £175. It was advertised as an unfinished project, the previous owner having stripped the car down to the chassis and then giving up, possibly thinking he had taken on more than he could handle. Malcolm trailered the car home to his small single garage in a dismantled state with numerous bits and pieces in loads of different boxes. He carried out all the work himself completed the car in just under two years. As can be seen from the photographs, the MGA has been restored to a very high standard with great attention to detail and I was very pleased that Malcolm gave me the opportunity to drive his prized possession around the beautiful Leicestershire countryside. On sliding into the driving seat, the first thing that strikes you is the very comfortable driving position, with your hands falling into the virtually upright large diameter steering wheel. Straight arm driving is not possible however, due to the close proximity of the wheel, although there is some adjustment on the telescopic column which allows more freedom. Although you do feel very low down compared to the driving position for example on an MGB, you soon get used to peering down the long bonnet knowing that the front of the car ends somewhere beyond where you can see!

The pedals do at first seem quite close together, although after a few miles and one or two gear changes your feet soon find the correct pedal! The gear lever is short and ideally placed, allowing quick and precise gear changes, the absence of synchromesh needing some adept double-declutching. Our drive was carried out naturally with the hood down and I was quite surprised how remarkably quiet the car was with minimal wind buffetting, enabling normal conversation in the cockpit at speeds in excess of 60mph. All the controls are within easy reach and the speedometer and rev counter are very well placed in direct vision through the steering wheel. The car handled very well on a variety of road surfaces giving complete confidence at all times. At slow speeds the ride is somewhat stiff over bumpy road surfaces but as speed increases, the ride begins to smooth out. Steering is quite light yet positive with a lock to lock of 2.75 turns you would expect it to be less positive. Acceleration although not of the 'kick in the back' type is certainly quite brisk for the size of engine related to the weight of the car. Braking is quite adequate although when slowing from speed you feel as if you need to stand on the pedal to bring the car to a halt, this is due totally to the fact that there are drum brakes all round with no servo assistance, as with anything strange it is alright once you get used to it. All shortcomings considered it is still a car that I would not mind owning myself . . . one day perhaps?

Article and photographs by Richard Monk.

STOP THIEF

Most people know, I think, that one cannot stop an expert car thief, if he is really determined. But we can through various devices make it so difficult, and most important, time consuming to overcome, that he must consider the risk of being discovered too great. So it was during the fitting of the alarm, that I tried thinking like a would be thief.

On the subject of the alarm system, I'll simply say that a little thought when installing any electrical anti-thief system, can improve its effectiveness even further. The point of this article, is not of alarms, but of handbrake locks. I was going to install the handbrake lock as a last line of defence. A handbrake-lock when fitted to MGB's or Midgets can be released quickly and easily with one or two very simple tools, that can be carried in the pocket. Without touching the lock release can be achieved either by depressing the push rod (exposed in the h/brake stem) or slitting the tunnel carpet and tripping the pawl direct. Either operation takes only seconds to do. The more I thought about the problem, the more I became absorbed with finding a solution. I was determined to find an answer, because I realised that with a trembler alarm on the car, plus a handbrake well locked on, a thief would have quite a job. Should he decide to tackle the handbrake, by going for the cable underneath he had to move or raise the car. In so doing, hopefully he'd set off the alarm. Should the thief tackle the alarm first it will sound long enough to attract attention. Assuming he gets inside unchallenged, he then finds a well guarded handbrake. Naturally then the answer was to make the release mechanism of the handbrake, less vunerable. In doing all this, we hopefully have raised that risk factor that might deter the thief. For those who haven't already realised it, I have a GT. those of you who have roadsters the handbrake lock is even more important. The idea of making up the shrouds to enclose the working parts of the handbrake absorbed my time for quite a few months. The finished item was quite neat and now meant that the ratchet and panel could be greased without contamination of the carpet. Grit couldn't get in the teeth, thus avoiding accidental release of the handbrake! So the 'Pawlguard', now named and patented, is available to Club members in limited numbers. Most are for MGBs/Cs and some for Midgets.

For MGBs, its necessary to know if you have a long or short handbrake. This is identified by looking at the elbow or bend below the grip. Short handbrakes have the tubular grip welded right on the elbow. Long handbrakes the grip tube starts a good inch up from the elbow. Remember though, for the benefits of anti-theft, its recommended to fit it in conjunction with a combination lock, as available through Club Special Offers. Persons interested, can contact me on 0702-202806 (Hockley) or write for details to 'Pawlguard', 90 Greensward Lane, Hockley, Essex SS5 5HF.

G D SUTTON

MGA
Ex works Coupé

The original green log book of 151 ABL displays the first owner as The MG Car Company Ltd, Abingdon and the date of first registration as the 26th October 1961. The log book is one of many indications that this car is an historic MG but a cursory glance at the MGA gives the impression of a fairly standard MGA Deluxe Coupé. This could not be further from the truth for when you start examining the car in detail there are plenty of clues to its glorious past.

151 ABL was built up by the Abingdon Competitions Department on an MGA 1600 Mk2 Deluxe chassis and was one of only 35 cars that were constructed as Coupés (12 were 1600s and 23 were 1600 Mk 2s); 6 other Coupés joined the ranks as works competition cars, three of which were built up to compete in the 1962 Sebring race. The MGA Deluxe was the term applied to MGAs that were fitted with Dunlop centre-lock pressed steel wheels and four wheel disc brakes as an option. This was to be a considerable modification and involved no less than 190 different part changes from standard Mk2 specification. These cars were constructed on the now defunct MGA Twin Cam chassis and it is generally felt that this was an easy way to dispose of the surplus chassis left over from the discontinued Twin Cam production. The early cars also used what was left of the stock of Twin Cam body shells, these were detectable by the removable front wheel arch panels, later cars used standard MGA body shells. Other items used from the Twin Cam were the steering rack, brake master cylinder and starter solenoid, externally the cars carried standard MGA badging and it was only the centre-lock disc wheels that gave the indication that it was a Deluxe model. The Deluxe was never listed by the factory as an individual model and was only referred to as an option available on the standard MGA 1600, in all 395 Deluxes were produced, 290 of which were Roadsters. 242 of the Roadsters were built up for the North American export market.

In 1962 a new manager was appointed to the Abingdon Competitions Department and this was to prove a significant year for the BMC's renowned rally team. Stuart Turner was keen to utilise the potential of BMC's more successful cars and to engage the best drivers and navigators. A thoroughly dedicated squad of Abingdon mechanics was to back up what was to become the most successful team ever assembled which helped Turner achieve as many Class wins as possible. 151 ABL was really the last of the MGA based works rally cars to compete successfully before the introduction of the long awaited MGB. The car was effectively a Twin Cam Coupé as previously described, but had a 1,622cc pushrod overhead valve engine fitted and every available piece of competition equipment including a twin choke Weber carburettor. Its first outing was in the hands of twin brothers, Eric and Don Morley, in the 1962 Monte Carlo Rally. The Morleys' started off from Oslo with surprisingly good conditions and was not until they reached the south of France that conditions deteriorated with heavy ice and snow. A fine performance by the two brothers landed them a win in the two litre Class and second overall in the Grand Touring category behind the 'big' Healey 3000 and a creditable 28th overall. Following on to the Tulip Rally in May, the Morley brothers were to change their allegiance to the Healey camp, although still with BMC. ABL 151 was on this occasion to be driven by Ruano Aaltonen with Gunnar Palm as co-driver, Aaltonen having recovered from a horrific crash on the earlier Monte Carlo Rally. Similar to the Monte, the Tulip Rally was run on a handicap basis and again ABL won the two litre Class against strong opposition from a team of three works TR4s which ran full 2 litre engines. Aaltonen's test times showed him to be the 6th fastest car in the event but owing to a very complicated 'class improvement' handicap system he ended up 15th overall despite finishing ahead of the Morley twins in the 3 litre Healey which was the fastest car on the Rally! Notably Aaltonens ascent of the Col de Turini was the fastest beating every other car in the entire field including Porsche and Works Mercedes and he was a clear 13 seconds ahead on this stage of the Healey and an E type Jaguar!

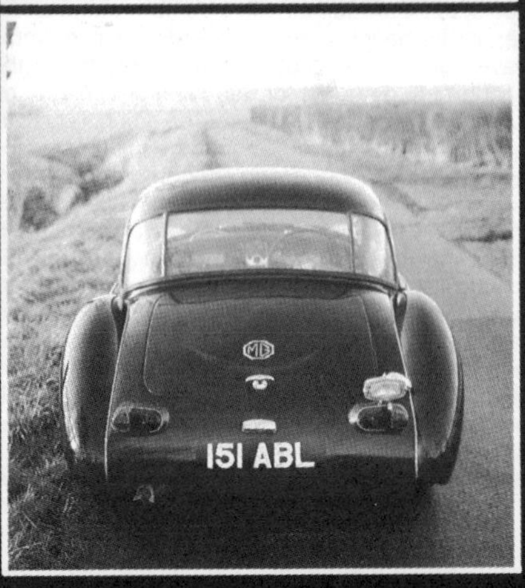

The third and final outing for the car was in the hands of John Gott and Bill Shepherd on the 1962 Leige-Sofia-Leige where unfortunately it was forced to retire. This rally was deemed the toughest in the world with the drivers pitting their skills against endless dust, rocks and impossible time schedules. They were not alone as most of the field were forced to retire, ABL suffered two ruptures on two separate occasions to the underside of the petrol tank by flying rocks.

It is by good fortune that 151 ABL survives today having been in the hands of many different enthusiasts throughout the years. Currently the car is owned by Cambridge businessman and MGOC Member Peter Clark who recently purchased the car at auction in order to compete with it in historic rallying. Peter has over the years been very active in National and International rallying but has decided that a more sedate and enjoyable pastime would be to enter such rallies as the Classic Marathon, Coppa d'Italia, Coppa delle Alpi and the Historic Monte Carlo. He felt that as the sport was becoming more and more popular the only way to secure entries on such events was to have the 'real thing' and this he certainly has in 151 ABL. Peter is fortunate that one previous owner, Gordon Ogilvie, painstakingly researched and documented the history of the car and was keen to return the car as near as possible to its original rally specification and as can be seen the car looks the part. Original features include a tuned 1622cc engine with raised compression, high lift camshaft, oil cooler, close ratio gearbox and free flow exhaust. Other clues to its past are the Monte Carlo and Liege transfers on the rear screen, navigator milometer, auxilliary lighting, spare wheel bulge in the boot lid and twin boot well-mounted petrol pumps. Peter also proudly owns another Ex-Works MGA, MRX 42 and it is his intention to restore both cars to as near perfect condition as possible and to use them as they should be used on the historic rally circuits in Europe.

MGA
Ex works Coupé

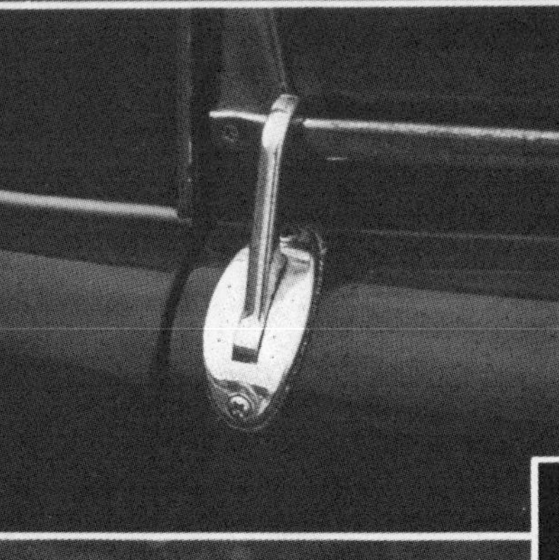

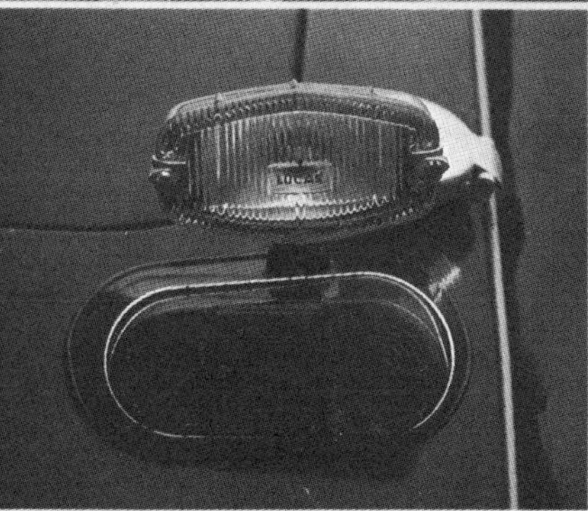

SPECIFICATION:
Engine: 4 cylinder in line
Capacity: 1,622cc
Valve operation: Pushrod overhead
Bore and Stroke: 76.2mm × 89.9mm
Power Output: Approx 110 @ 5,500rpm
Carburation: Twin 1¼″ SUs
Gearbox: 4 speed, part synchromesh
Clutch: Dry plate
Suspension: Front: Coil and wishbone. Rear: Half elliptic
Wheels: Centre lock pressed steel
Brakes: Dunlop disc front and rear
Wheelbase: 7′ 10″
Track: 3′11½″ front; 4′0¾″
Number built: 325 (in 1600 Mk2 Deluxe form)

Discovered after being buried for 10 years, this MGA yielded valuable parts for the rebuild

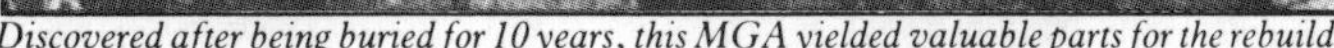

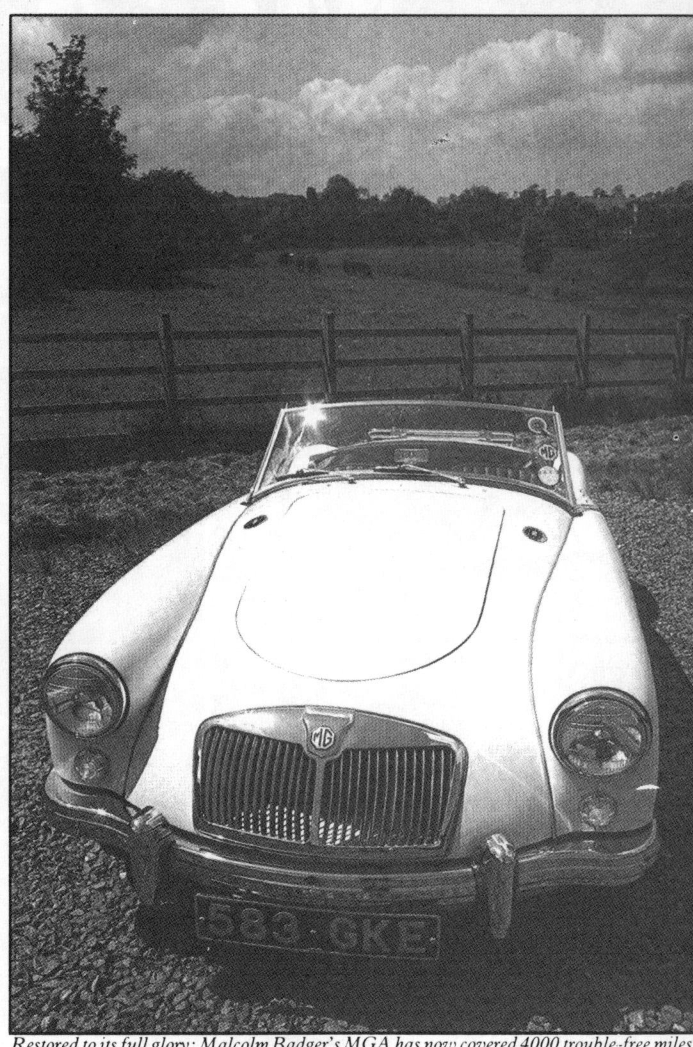

Restored to its full glory: Malcolm Badger's MGA has now covered 4000 trouble-free miles

'A' REINCARNATION

Starting with a buried wreck, Malcolm Badger restored an MGA Roadster from virtually nothing! Lance Fisher-Skinner tells his story

For Malcolm Badger, eventual ownership of a MGA Roadster was the result of a 25 year enthusias for sports cars, with MG at the top of his list. H enthusiasm blossomed when he was a 16 year ol trainee mechanic in the late fifties. Encouraged by a employer who had links with the motor racin fraternity, this early introduction to the 'sportin life' progressed through constant contact with th exciting cars which frequented the garage an through always being within earshot of his mentor race track reminiscences. It was inevitable that on day he would own a sports car himself.

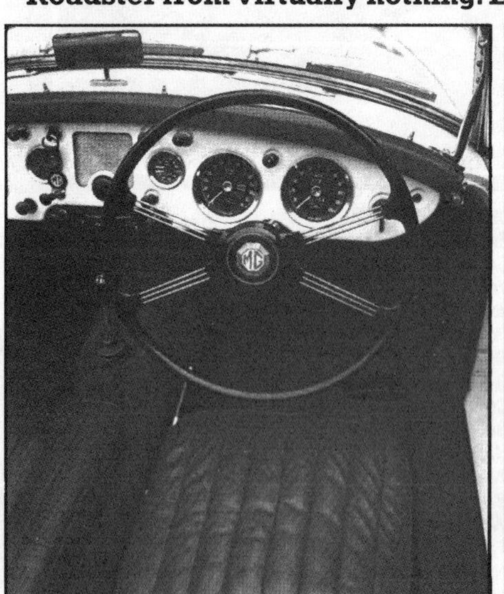

Interior has naturally received complete re-trim in red

'Twenty years ago it would have been taken to the scrapyard as junk ... sometimes I would wonder if it was worth it'

Years later, lady luck intervened, presenting a ring of related coincidences along the way which ad a surprise around the corner.

He had owned an exceptional example of a TA, in 'hite and red, way back in 1964, and this had ventually moved him to become a founder member f the South Leicestershire MG Owners Club. The 'A was eventually replaced, but he still yearned for n MGA.

During a chance conversation, he discovered that n acquaintance possessed an MGA which he had ntended to restore, but which various commitments ad prevented him from tackling. Malcolm's esponse was immediate: when could he see it? This 'as met with the revelation that in fact there wasn't nuch to see, compounded by the fact that Malcolm 'ould have to wait a further two weeks for the nveiling. He was not deterred, the fortnight passed uickly, and a 20 mile journey found him staring umbfounded at something that might well have een used as a sea anchor.

"What a terrible shame!" is Malcolm's euphemism or that now distant recollection, for the 'A' had been ying in state for some 10 years, stripped down ready or the intended rebuild. After removing the seats nd other assorted oddments resting on the bonnet, nd rubbing his hand along the wheel arch, Malcolm's despondency was confirmed when he discovered that what had appeared to be just plain muck vas in fact a thick slimy brown rust sediment. He ecalls that at that moment he was forced to concede hat the 'A' was indeed a complete and total wreck.

His disillusionment, however, was short-lived. It ranspired that the 'A' was registered in 1959, the 'ery same year that, as a young lad, he had formed a irm attachment for them. His mind was definitely nade up when he realised that the chassis number ndicated that this car was only 72 short of the end of he 1500 model. That clinched it, and he was letermined to take this opportunity to turn a lifelong lream into a reality. He asked the owner if he was prepared to sell, and his offer of £175 was accepted, ot a bad buy considering that now, some four years ater, MGAs in need of restoration regularly fetch over £1000, although that sum would secure an nfinitely better proposition than Malcolm's total vrite-off.

Bodywork: major hurdle

A week later saw him make two trips in a Ford Transit loaded to the roof with all the bits and pieces which had previously been removed from the car, nd a further trip with the bodyshell carried on a borrowed transporter. After a few days spent in appraisal, he realised that rebuilding the body would be the major hurdle, and that the engine would be the east of his headaches. After sorting out the jigsaw of parts, he set about preparing a shopping list for replacements and non-existent items. The task proved to be a long and exacting process as he was determined to rebuild the 'A', part for part, just as it would have been when it originally left the factory gates. The following two week hunt for many of what transpired to be elusive items took in London and most of the Home Counties.

It was during this seek and find exercise that Malcolm stumbled on another startling revelation that occurred as a result of a visit to a motor factor to secure a handbrake cable. While there he was asked by a fellow customer what he required the cable for, and when he explained that he was rebuilding an 'A' this chance acquaintance said that he had once *buried* one, sometime, somewhere! Malcolm could not let this comment go by without further investigation ...

Extensive enquiries established the approximate location, in the middle of a nut wood on a local farm a few miles away. With the farmer's permission he started digging, and after a few days of back-breaking spade work the old 'A' was unearthed. To Malcolm it was like 'One Step Beyond', more like fiction than fact. What they discovered was a 1957 MGA Roadster that had originally been dressed in Old English White with red interior, most of which had disappeared. The car had been laid to rest 10 years previously – indeed, only two months separated the date of the incarceration of the two MGAs.

Compare totally rotten cockpit area panelwork ...

... with fabricated repair sections now in place

That tricky straight edge where wing line meets shroud

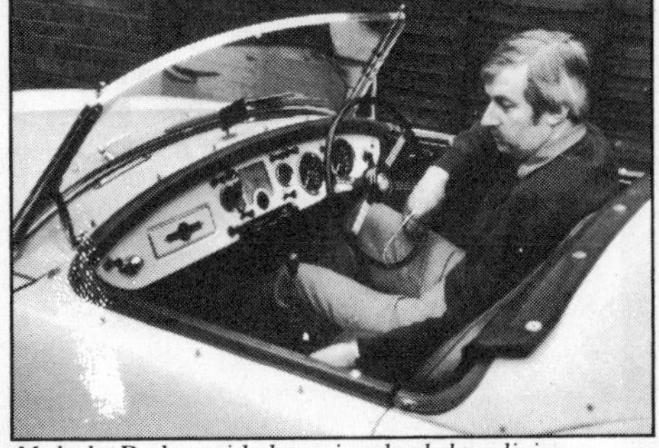

Malcolm Badger with the project that led to a living

Despite the appetite of Mother Earth, Malcolm was able to salvage two wheels and numerous odds and ends attached to the engine which were still in a restorable state. To top it all, he also found the remainder of the handbrake cable for which he had been searching! The remarkable state of preservation of many of the parts can be illustrated by the fact that one of the tyres was still inflated to a pressure of 19lbs!

Back at the garage during that first winter, Malcolm realised that his major problem was going to be the body. It caused many 'down' days which were only rescued by returning from burning the midnight oil in the garage to pore over countless reference books to try to visualise the end product. The major bodywork headache was the front section, where the left-hand section of the shroud between the wings meets the wing line at a right angle. This was eventually accomplished by taking a piece of cardboard, taping it to the still intact opposite wing and then drawing around it to shape. It was then cut out and taped into position on the damaged side to mate with a plumb line which had been stretched from the front of the shroud to the first door post. This procedure indicated that everything would be level. Malcolm was then able to manufacture the necessary steel sections using the cardboard cut-out as a template. Then came relatively easier times, and he went on to manufacture all the floor support panels and the inside panels for the front door posts.

Five top coats

Finally, when the body resembled an 'A' and was glass smooth, he applied two preserving coats, an acid edge primer and a standard cellulose primer, complemented by no fewer than five top coats of Old English White. After manufacturing the floorboards of marine ply and treating them with yacht varnish, and joining the body and the chassis together, Malcolm displayed the shell at the Town and Country Festival at Stoneleigh the following summer.

This was first fruit of what would eventually total 16 months of labour. The long overhaul of the engine, the replacement of all electrics and all rubbers was smoothly accomplished. The seat covers, the trim and the carpets were eventually secured and Malcolm fitted them himself. He was always careful to ensure that every item related to the original pattern. From welding to wiring, through a full overhaul of all things mechanical to the body restoration and the very last coat of paint, it was all a one-man operation, with assistance only when heavy lifting was involved.

When the 'A' was finally ready for the road, its first showing was a feature appearance in the local press, complemented by Malcolm's compilation of an extensive photographic record, a stage by stage visual tale of the rebuild and a reminder of the problems encountered. By this time he also had a new occupation, restoring and selling classic cars and also carrying a large stock of those parts which he discovered were so necessary but often so difficult to obtain.

"I was so involved in the building of the 'A' that I now run a business restoring and selling them." Reflecting on his 'ups and downs' Malcolm strongly recommends that if anyone is intent upon buying an MGA for restoration they should seek the advice of someone who has already gone through the mill. He was at pains to stress, "... if the 'F' sections have gone on the front and rear door posts ... fit these before the body is removed from the car to ensure that the body line is correct!"

The MGA has now completed approximately 4000 miles since the restoration without a murmur, except for the dynamo which short-circuited on the second time out. Looking back on an interest that was to become an occupation Malcolm reflected with pride, "20 years ago it would have been taken to the scrapyard as junk as it really was past redemption ... and sometimes I would stand in the garage on a Sunday afternoon when it was boiling hot outside and I would think, 'Is it really worth it?' But when I drove it to the garage for its MoT, the full realisation of my efforts flooded back to me and I knew that it really was worth it!"

MGA Twin Cam

The MGA Twin Cam was announced in 1958 and was the product of a lengthy and involved development but disappointingly returned one of the shortest production runs that Abingdon had seen. This certainly makes the car somewhat a rarity with only 2111 cars being produced between early 1958 and early 1960. The twin cam was to utilise an engine that was never fitted to any other car and was developed from the B series unit, prior to this the PB was the last MG to use an overhead cam engine in 1936. For ease of production, economy and reliability the standard pushrod type of engines were used by MG from then on, but it was evident that performance suffered as a result and it was when the Abingdon engineers became frustrated at trying to extract more than 60 bhp from the B series Austin derived engine that was powering the MGA and Magnette cars that attentions were turned to the production of an overhead cam unit. The Company was also keen to get the name of MG back into serious competition, particularly racing, as this had been shelved some years previously during the Nuffield rationalisation.

It was Gerald Palmer who was a design engineer at the Cowley plant who originally set the wheels in motion for a twin cam conversion of the B series engine. In his plans he set the two lines of valves at 90 degrees symetrically opposed and it was intended that as many of the existing B series engine components as possible should be utilised. The basic designs were then handed over during 1954 to the Morris Engines Division at Coventry to be developed further. It was not until the summer of 1958 that any production units were available for fitting into the MGA and therefore the development work was quite a protracted affair. There was however a prototype twin cam engine which appeared in an MGA that competed in the Dundrod Tourist Trophy Race in Northern Ireland as early as September 1955. At that time there was also another prototype twin cam engine that was under development by the Austin engineers at Longbridge and this too was scheduled to power an MGA in the same race, but due to rev limitations and carburation problems the car never appeared. The Austin unit was a totally new design and not based on any other existing engine with the valves inclined at an angle of 66 degrees it proved to be a very smooth engine that also fitted well into the MGA engine bay. This particular engine however was very short lived and apart from running EX 182 at Le Mans it was never to be seen again. The Morris twin cam was not to achieve any success in Northern Ireland due to mechanical problems although it was considered promising enough to form the basis of a new production car and development was started more or less immediately.

Further development engines appeared in EX 179 and EX 181 record cars during 1956 and 1957 before the final production version was ready in the summer of 1958. These units were, as Gerald Palmer had intended, based on the B series block, albeit with many changes. The unit was bored out from 73.025 mm to 75.4 mm giving a capacity of 1588 cc, this was to take advantage of certain competition regulations, the bores being siamised. The crankshaft had narrowed main bearings and an extended nose to carry the timing chains, whilst the con rods were considerably strengthened. Heavily domed pistons were fitted to these con rods to allow a very high compression ratio of 9.9:1 which meant that the engine had to run on high octane 5 star fuel in order to get the best performance. A special light alloy cross flow cylinder head carried twin overhead camshafts with valve operation via Coventry Climax style inverted bucket-type tappets. Hemispherical combustion chambers had two valves per cylinder operating at an included angle of 80 degrees. The front of the engine displayed a very complex looking alloy casing which housed the drive gear and duplex chains for the camshafts and distributor. Two smart looking alloy cam covers adorned the top of the cylinder head whilst a large finned aluminium sump helped to keep the lubricating oil cool. The carburation was by 1¾" twin SUs with flexibly mounted float chambers and they appeared on the left hand side of the engine as opposed to the right hand side on the standard pushrod engine. New manifolding was produced with separate downpipes for each cylinder making the engine unit look very business like.

At the end of the day the impressive results achieved from all this lengthy development on what was basically a B series block made the exercise worthwhile. A very healthy 108 bhp at 6700 rpm together with a maximum torque figure of 104 lb ft at 4500 rpm meant that the new MGA Twin Cam was to be no slouch!

There were other obvious changes that were made to the MGA in producing the Twin Cam. The Chassis did differ slightly to that of the 1500 MGA and there were important changes to the brakes and wheels. In view of the 113 mph performance attainable, Dunlop 10 ¾" disc brakes were fitted both front and rear together with Dunlop centre lock disc wheels carrying Dunlop Road Speed tyres. Wire wheels were not available as an option. The brakes were different to any other type of system used on MGs previously and due to the large braking surface area of the discs they were most efficient and did not require servo assistance. One drawback of the system however was the relative inefficiency of the handbrake which worked on the rear discs by means of a separate caliper with small pads and a pivot system that readily seized up without regular maintenance. Externally there were virtually no visible differences in the body compared to that of the MGA 1500 with both a roadster and a closed coupe being available. It was really only the wheels and the discreet Twin Cam badges that were fixed to the top bonnet surround adjacent to the air intake grille and on the boot lid below the MG Octagon that betrayed its identity. The instrument layout was almost the same as the MGA 1500 but with a tachometer that read 7500 rpm and a speedometer that took account of the top speed of 113 mph. The instrument fascia panel was given a face lift, being tastefully covered in leather, whilst leather was also employed on redesigned, better padded seats of the bucket type. These seats however were only fitted to the roadster as the coupe had a slightly different design that gave more support and were known as 'De Luxe seats'.

Problems with reliability very early on in its production life affected the sales of the Twin Cam quite markedly and despite its sparkling performance the car was regarded as a commercial failure due to its cost, reliability and stiff competition from Triumph in the form of the TR3A and Austin Healey with their 100/6. Both these cars offered better performance and the Triumph was significantly cheaper by some £144. Abingdon's biggest problem was the poor reliability which in the main was caused by the very high compression ratio necessitating perfect ignition timing and the use of top grade fuel. With either not at their optimum, holes could very easily be burnt in the pistons. This coupled with the engine's large appetite for oil caused by chromed rings and chromed bores soon earnt the Twin Cam a bad reputation. These problems were attended to by Abingdon but only shortly before production ceased in mid 1959. In the short production life of two years only 2,111 examples were produced, 1,801 of which were roadsters. There is no doubt at the time, the Twin Cam was a car that Abingdon was not particularly proud of, but today the car quite rightly has its niche in the MG history book and is a much desired classic.

The proud owners of the concours MGA Twin Cam featured this month are Derek Baker and Richard Hutton who will be very well known to MG Owners in the Southampton area. They are partners in the well established MG Owners' Club recommended company, BHB Engineering situated in Onslow Road. Both Derek and Richard embarked upon the restoration of YLJ 455 approximately 13 years ago when it was purchased as a running vehicle but in need of a total strip down and rebuild. The car was put into store for about a year before serious work commenced and it was then regarded as a spare time project. However as both Derek and Richard were busy running their specialist workshop and also engaged in entering MGAs successfully in both MGOC and MGCC race championships, spare time was at a premium and the restoration became rather protracted. The vast majority of the work was carried out by the two of them with only trimming and paintwork entrusted to other specialists. Bearing chassis number 2332 the car is a 1958 model and has some refinements that were originally available as optional extras. A fresh air heater is one and a rather rare useful accessory is the remote controlled radiator blind which is activated from the cockpit by pulling a ring situated to the left of the steering column. The Twin Cam was finally finished in May of last year and promptly collected the first prize in the MGCC concours at Silverstone. Since then the car has won several other awards although Derek says they are not actively seeking them, they simply like taking the car to shows for enthusiasts to enjoy and if they pick up some awards into the bargain then it is a nice return for their efforts. He says that the main pleasure is driving this classic MG and after our photographic session in the New Forest, Derek put the Twin Cam to test through the twisting Hampshire country lanes and whilst trying to follow him in my V8, I understand exactly what he means!

MGA Twin Cam

SPECIFICATION
Engine: Four cylinder, in line, cast iron block, alloy head.
Capacity: 1588cc
Bore & Stroke: 75.39mm x 88.9mm
Main bearings: 3
Compression Ratio: 9.9:1 initially, then 8.3:1
Valve gear: Twin overhead camshafts with shim adjusted bucket tappets.
Carburation: Twin semi-downdraught 1¾″ SUs
Power output: 108 bhp @ 6,700 rpm
Maximum Torque: 104 lbft @ 4,500 rpm
Transmission: Four speed manual gearbox with synchromesh on 2nd, 3rd and top.
Clutch: Borg and Beck dry plate.
Suspension: Front – independent by coil springs, wishbones and Armstrong lever arm dampers. Rear – Live rear axle, half elliptic leaf springs. Armstrong lever arm dampers.
Steering: Rack and pinion.
Wheels and tyres: Dunlop pressed steel centre lock disc with 5.90-15 Dunlop cross ply tyres.
Brakes: Dunlop disc brakes front and rear 10.75″ diameter discs.
Length: 13′0″
Width: 4′9.25″
Height: 4′2″
Wheelbase: 7′10″
Performance: 0-60 mph; 9.1 secs
Maximum speed: 113 mph
Number built: 2,111 between 1958 and 1960
Price new: Roadster; £843. Coupe; £904

Chris Longridge had a mammoth struggle to establish his car's right to keep its original registration number. He uncovered some fascinating MG history in the process

Seven years of driving sensible modern hatchbacks is a long time and my memories of carefree motoring in my MGB were fading fast. A visit to the MG Car Club event at the National Motor Museum in August 1984 was the final straw. It was time, I declared, to get another MG — and this time my heart was set on an MGA.

Several months of diligent searching later and I ran down a likely looking MGA at a local dealership. It was showing the effects of a couple of years disuse and needed some restoration but was just about roadworthy so I purchased it and set about bringing it out of retirement. The first step was to get its licence renewed, a simple enough task, or so I thought. A quick visit to our local post office shattered any such hope. I was told that it was likely that the car's original registration number would be lost altogether as the previous owner had neglected to re-register its green log book with the DVLC.

I telephoned the DVLC who confirmed that at present the car's number, KMO 326, was void. The clerk at the end of the line was sympathetic but, as the regulations stated, they would only consider reallocating the original number if we could prove that the car had a special historical significance. Otherwise I would have to register the car with a new number with no relevance to the car. But did the car have any historical significance? Remembering what the dealer had said to me when I bought the car, this seemed a distinct possibility. It was time for Sherlock Holmes to go to work!

The dealer had mentioned that the car was once owned by Roger Enever, the son of MG Chief Engineer Sydney Enever, and at an early stage in its life had been used for MGB prototype development work. At the time the name Enever meant nothing to me, but as I researched into the background of MG in an effort to establish my car's history I realised that Sydney Enever was just the person I needed to get in touch with. My first move was to contact the MG Car Club. They were most helpful, telling me that yes, there was a Mr S Enever on their list, a long-established club member. Was this the Sydney Enever of MG Works fame?

Another phone call established that it was indeed. I spoke to Sydney Enever's wife, who kindly passed me on to their son, Roger, who she thought could help me. With great excitement I listened to Roger recall his days with KMO 326, but he had more information than I could take in over one telephone conversation so we agreed to meet. Frustratingly, he was just about to embark on a lengthy business trip abroad, so the earliest date we could set for this meeting was several months hence.

In the meantime the MG Car Club advised me to write to Anders Clausager of the British Motor Industry Heritage Trust. This I did, giving full details of the car and quoting its chassis number. Imagine my surpise when I was told that officially my car didn't exist! The last recorded chassis number was 109070 and mine was 109071.

Eventually I was able to meet Roger Enever for an interesting discussion about the car. He confirmed that the car was a prototype, possibly the first of the experimental department's MGAs and recalled that surprisingly it had started life as a two-seater, being later converted for experimental work during the development of the coupé derivative. He also clearly remembered his father having to remove the original chassis number plate so as to give the car a normal chassis number when he bought it for him from the works early in 1964. Armed with this information I wrote back to the DVLC.

Their response was encouraging but posed me a difficult task: they would be happy to consider my application for the reissuing of the original number if I could supply documentary evidence from the manufacturer confirming the car's historical significance. Fair enough, but the leads were drying up; Roger Enever had mentioned that his father, now in his eighties, was not in the best of health and could supply no more information than we already had, while neither the MG Car Club or the BMIHT had any documentation of the car's existence. The one avenue open was to contact the sole name on the green log book, Peter Cornwell, who owned the car before it was passed to the dealer who sold it to me.

After making inquiries I managed to contact Peter Cornwell who, it emerged, had enjoyed rallying the car during his 18 years of ownership and shared with me his happy memories of it. Unfortunately, he had no knowledge of the car's life before he owned it. He did, however, mention that he'd bought it through Parade Motors of Mitcham in Surrey, and his stepson recalled that while they were on a sailing holiday in Cornwall they'd met a sailing

Above, KMO 326, looking slightly tatty round the edges while awaiting restoration but with original registration number intact

Left, although it looks quite standard the car has several unusual features dating from its development days, including MGB front disc brakes

Photographs: Maurice Rowe

nstructor who turned out to be an ·x-MG employee who had been nvolved with the car at Abingdon. They couldn't remember his name, but hey could remember where they had stayed — the Lugger Inn at Fowey. Sherlock Holmes now had two clear eads — Parade Motors and the sailing nstructor in Cornwall.

Andrew Smith of Parade Motors confirmed that Sydney Enever had asked him to sell KMO 326 on his behalf. The car was bought by K R Clark of Chipstead in Surrey on May 8 1965, and he in turn asked Parade Motors to re-sell it a year later, when it was bought

MGA EXPERIMENTAL

by Peter Cornwell. This completed the chain of ownership from the MG Works to the present day, but I still hadn't established the car's early history.

Contacting the Lugger Inn in Cornwall was the next move. A telephone call revealed that the sailing instructor in question still lived in the area. He turned out to be John Sharpe, who had joined the MG Car Company in August 1959 as Technical Assistant to the Development Department. Discussions with John proved fruitful. He revealed that he had actually driven KMO 326 on his first day with the company, to a meeting in Swindon with Pressed Steel. Later he drove the car for many miles of development work, which included carrying out cooling tests and exhaust system assessment. In due course the car was converted to MkII 1600 mechanical specification.

John recalled that, accompanied by test driver Tom Haig and foreman fitter Cliff Bray, he had taken the car, along with a black fixedhead MGA 1600, to Germany for maximum speed durability testing: "The aim was to maintain maximum speed over 25,000 miles", he told me. "We used the *Autobahn* between Munich and Hof, at the East German border. This was the old Munich-Berlin highway, little used after the war as the road had been destroyed at the border.

"Dividing our mileage by our elapsed running time gave us an average speed of about 100mph — not bad a quarter of a century ago, when you compare it with our present day overcrowded roads and speed limits! We had trouble with one engine which was caused by pulling valve crash in top gear. In fact both cars were used for the test.

"One of the last tests I recall using a fixedhead MGA for was to assess MGA versus MGB maximum speed capability with the same engine and using optimal final drive ratios and tyre sizes. The MGA proved to be 4mph faster than its replacement, the MGB!"

John suggested that to fill in the car's very early history I should contact Henry Stone, pointing out that "At Abingdon our budget was not large — our staff consisted of Syd Enever, Chief Engineer; the Chief Development Engineer and myself; Chief Chassis Draughtsman, Chief Body Draughtsman, approximately 10 Draughtsmen and 10 Fitters; unfortunately no archive keepers."

I met Henry Stone at the 1986 MG Regency Run. He recalled that my car was originally the first prototype MGA development tourer, painted in Tyrolite Green, and believed that the chassis from this tourer was later used to produce the first prototype coupé, subsequently given the registration mark KMO 326.

Shortly after meeting Henry, I had a real stroke of luck. Former MG Chief Engineer, Don Hayter, had seen KMO 326 mentioned in an MGA Register newsletter and sent in a letter which to my delight verified Henry Stone's

"The MGA proved to be 4mph faster than its replacement, the MGB"

memories. He confirmed that "this was indeed one of our development cars, specially ordered from the bodies branch as the first representative production standard-build car. It did many miles using development parts and comparative alternatives supplied by manufacturers, and was at that time painted gold and brown.

"However, the registration number wasn't on this car originally, but on a Tyrolite Green MGA Tourer — also an earlier development car, one I used myself on almost daily journeys to Coventry and MIRA. I also used it when I got married so it has strong personal associations for me."

All the information I needed to confirm that the car had played an important part in MG history was now verbally complete but I still had to produce documentary evidence for the DVLC. After discussing the matter with Don Hayter he kindly offered to take on the task of obtaining this vital proof.

At the next year's Regency Run he was able to hand me copies taken from the Roneos kept by Cliff Bray, and originally signed by Alec Hounslow — the Chief Development Engineer then responsible for the complete MGA programme. These confirmed the Experimental number and the Autobahn test carried out in September 1961, and identified KMO 326 as a development shop car in August 1963. Don Hayter also found that before it was bought by Syd Enever the car had been used for detailed development of the 1,622cc engine and suspension and brakes later to be fitted to the MGB. Now I understood why the dealer who sold me the car had told me that MGB front discs were fitted and that the car had been used for MGB development work.

Finally, 2½ years after I first tried to re-register KMO 326, I was able to write to the DVLC giving full details of the car's history and documentary evidence of its significance in the development of the MGA and MGB. A week or so later the DVLC's reply arrived. In trepidation I opened it to read, to my elation, that "in view of the historical significance of your particular vehicle it has, exceptionally, been decided to allow registration under the number KMO 326."

And with this matter brought to a successful conclusion all that remains is the straightforward — by comparison — task of restoring this fascinating and unique MG.

Above, previous owner Peter Cornwell on his way to a class win in the Lands End Trials

Left, pictured in September 1961, KMO 326 takes a brief pause from high-speed endurance testing on the Munich to Hof Autobahn